The Monkey's Wedding

by

"Fundisi"

**One hundred years
of love, hate, bloodshed,
betrayal and miracles.**

ISBN 978-1-4092-8740-7

The Monkey's Wedding

By
Fundisi

Mother and her older sister with her parents in their pole and grass home,
Rhodesia - 1918
I dedicate this book to them and the many friends who showed me kindness.

The Monkey's Wedding

Contents

Johnny and me, off on our adventures in Africa.

Preface - What is a Monkey's Wedding?

In Africa there is a saying that describes the paradox of sun shining through rain and the most superb effects it causes especially when rainbows form. It is called a "Monkey's Wedding". Mother used to say the monkeys were crying because there was no pot of gold at the rainbow's end. I don't think she had a happy life. The saying conveys the joy of a wedding and the inevitable testing and sorrow in life, a mixture of sadness and joy. It seems to go further and convey the meaning of having to endure something that is both bitter and sweet. Anyone who has seen African rain with sun shining through will be aware of the strong colours and shadows created by such phenomena and the brilliant rainbows that form as sunlight catches millions of tiny droplets. Because the clouds are high the rainbows seem to span the entire sky with sometimes double rainbows, rare beauty in the midst of storm. The contrast of dark clouds and brilliant sunshine is one of the most beautiful sights one can see. Behind the sunshine, in the dark centre of gigantic clouds where great bolts of electrical power are generated, thunder rolls and lightning flashes and everything shakes as if two worlds clash, one of sunshine and one of darkness. When we were children we would exclaim with glee "look mummy, a monkey is getting married" and the thunder would crash all around us and vibrate right through our bodies. Then as the heavens opened we could smell the rain as it fell on African dust.

This narrative is like a "Monkey's Wedding". It is true, or as true as I can recall. It covers a hundred years in Africa and is about people who lived through the clash of the British and Boers, the birth of the British colony of Rhodesia, two World Wars, the rise of Black Nationalism, the Rhodesian Declaration of Independence, the Liberation Struggle that brought Independence to Zimbabwe followed by a cruel regime and land grab with subsequent mayhem and destruction of a once beautiful land. It covers the transition from colonialism to "freedom", civil war and genocide of people, millions of refugees, death and starvation. From ox-wagon to space travel, these were tumultuous times.

This account is not an historical record but an insight into the lives of people who lived, loved, fought and died to bring what they believed was progress to a turbulent country. It is set in Zimbabwe. Before Independence it was called Rhodesia, known as the *"The Jewel of Africa."* To find out about Rhodesia one has to read dated accounts of British colonial Africa or speak to an old timer who can still recall those times. The early white settlers are gone and their descendants are scattered around the world. Some can remember the stories their grandparents told about Rhodesia but recent publications about British endeavour in Africa don't seem to mention it much. Little credit is given for Rhodesia's contribution to the development of Africa or loyalty to Britain of both black and white Rhodesians through two world wars. Rhodesia seems to have never existed, its history swept under a carpet. In its wake came a state named Zimbabwe. It was supposed to have been democratic but it sank into appalling mismanagement. This book is to honour Zimbabweans in the land and in exile, whether African, European or Asian, many of whom endured great adversity.

I cannot expect those who have not lived in Africa to understand or agree with things expressed in these pages, absurd and bizarre as some of them are. However, the contents will help to give insight into the way of thinking of a people who were moulded by their British background and the rough ways of Africa. It is a glimpse of what happened behind the news headlines and faces of politicians, behind the intrigue and stereotypes of world opinion. It is an insight into Rhodesians and their troublesome times and after them Zimbabweans with their difficulties. I must tell you from the start that I was born of British parents but Africa is my motherland and her people my people. Africa was good to me and the wonderful, gentle people of Zimbabwe treated me kindly. But in the end I was lucky to get out with my life for I endured the Liberation War and after that survived a vicious militia who had no compulsion about killing anyone that got in their way. You may disagree with some of my perceptions but I reiterate that the experiences recorded are true or as true as I understand them to be. There are always two sides to every tale and two sides to every face. Born of British parents I can only give one side but I try to show glimpses of the other for I associated closely with African people for nearly forty years.

There are two sides to Africa, one is beautiful and full of gentle folk and one is cruel and very sad. One is the "official" side told by news media and politicians, the other is the "unofficial" side experienced by people. One side is tainted by political, tribal and racial intolerance and the other is the human side of courage and bravery. In this account I attempt to show both sides and the stories behind many faces, scarred but brave. A renowned African custodian of oral history said of the ruined city of Great Zimbabwe that it was a story that must be remembered and yet forgotten at the same time.* Its namesake, the nation of Zimbabwe, has a chequered history and when you have read this account you may understand how bitter-sweet it is. The events that led Rhodesia to make its "Unilateral Declaration of Independence" and then go into a war it could not win are complex and resulted in great tragedy. The results of the Zimbabwe "State of Terror" are worse. The question one can ask about Rhodesia is "Why did it happen?" and of Zimbabwe "Was this democracy?" This book traces historical events within the lives of people of those times.

The African word *"Fundisi"* (pronounced *fundeesy* with a soft *u*) means "gentle teacher" and was used of me by African colleagues during more than three decades of mission work. My name is not important, it's the story that matters and in order to preserve the privacy of people names have been changed or not given in full. This is also to ensure their safety. However, all incidents, events and people are as real as real can be. I have used colonial names and colloquial terms relevant to the historic context and those names that changed after Independence are only used in this account subsequent to that time. I have tried to record my experiences and those of others in a way that would convey our perceptions of them at that time whether as children, youths or adults and in the context of the changing historical values in which they occurred. No offence is intended. This is not really my story for if you lived there it could be yours too for in many ways similar things were shared a thousand times. I hope it will refresh your memory of past joys and triumphs in a land that was truly grand and if you never lived in Africa may it give you insight into what it was like. However, it is mostly a sad tale. In fact it is a tale of terror unleashed upon kind, gentle and hospitable people in a wonderful land.

Africa is a magical land of mixed emotions, of tragedy and triumph, sunshine and storm, and sorrow in the midst of joy. Those who have lived there will have evocative memories that stir deep within their souls. Many people in Africa have searched for adventure, romance and wealth, and many have ended up looking like monkeys. When I was a kid I had a friend who was a monkey. He came as an orphan and clung to me, his tiny hands grasping me with a grip of steel. When I tried to pry him off he screamed pitifully so dad had pity on him and said I could keep him. He gave us so much fun as he grew and learnt many tricks. He smacked his lips together all the time making little noises as if he really could talk and even though he stole our food and broke things we grew to love him. He would stuff his mouth with food until his cheeks bulged. Sometimes he would grab more food than his mouth could hold and run off clutching as much as he could and once he had hold of something he never let go. As he grew bigger his canine teeth also grew, hidden from sight behind those smacking lips and one day the inevitable happened, he bit me and blood and tears were everywhere. Then our friendship was over, he was dangerous and had to go. I still love monkeys and never tire of their antics but behind their playful games lurks danger. Mother used to say, "see no evil, speak no evil, hear no evil" and she had three little monkey ornaments, one covered its eyes, one covered its mouth and one covered its ears. As a child I had no grasp of evil, it seemed far from our peaceful world but like monkeys we were blind to what was coming, deaf to the warnings, heedless of the signs.

How does one catch a monkey? African hunters tell a story of how it can be done. First one must get a calabash and cut a small hole in one end. Then place some tasty morsels of food inside and leave the calabash tied with strong string to a firm stay. When the monkey comes along and sees the food inside the calabash it extends its hand in and grasps the food but then finds it cannot get its hand out without first letting go of the food. As it will not let go of the food it can in this manner be easily caught or killed. It's just a story but the moral is not to hold onto something that will ultimately cause ones own demise. There comes a time when one must let go. Another old African saying is, "If you have drunk sweet water you will return and drink again." Yet another is similar; "The hunter who waits by the waterhole will not be disappointed." Animals always return to the place where the water is pure. But when the waterhole is muddy or dry the animals move on. I have seen a whole herd of buffalo pass a muddy pool and walk miles further until they found fresh water. There was a time in the land of my childhood when the spirit in the land was pure but something bad happened.

When I was a minister I spoke in many places to people from different backgrounds. Once in London I was invited to speak at a church whose members were all of African stock. At the beginning of my talk I asked a simple question;

"All those born in Africa please raise your hands."

To my surprise very few did and so I triumphantly lifted mine and said, *"I was born in Africa."* The impact of what I said was not lost on such an audience. There was thunderous and happy applause for they considered it no mean event to have been born in the land of their roots. Their ancestors had left Africa long before, mine had gone there from foreign shores. Through the years many people in Africa lost everything but we can never completely lose our heritage for we are Africans not only because we were born there but somehow Africa is also born in us. I was born in Africa and grew up there; born out of place, a colonial child in an African land.

You may or may not have been born in Africa, but will you come with me to visit that great land? Can we stroll together through its silent places, the haunting hills and plains that hold within them so many memories and conjure up so many dreams? As we visit these places may they yield their fragrance, like wisps of wind, and brushes of colour and so paint vivid scenes upon the canvas of our minds. Anyone who has walked the wild paths of Africa will know how they twist and turn, divide and then come together again, only to part once more until eventually they lead to their destination. As one walks these wild paths great vistas unveil, strange people appear and all manner of animals are seen. This is like the story that unfolds through these pages, like a torturous path twisting through the paradox of life in Africa, sometimes glad, sometimes sad, and always exciting. I am not a professional writer and because this account is true it does not follow a nicely laid out pattern as a novel might do. I ask you to overlook any mistakes it may contain and I invite you to step along the winding pathways that end at lonely graves where the brave lie forgotten and where only the soft breath of Africa kisses their neglected rest beds, where in the hot dry day the hard clay holds them fast and at night the stars dance in the African sky.

Fundisi

9

Book 1

Born in Africa – Good Years

Sometimes I am asked, "What was it like to grow up in Africa?"

"The Place of Slaughter"

My romance with Africa started when I was very young. Africa was my backyard where I played as a child. What an exciting yard it was. My birth was the result of the happy celebration held by my parents at the end of the Second World War when dad came back from fighting in North Africa and was reunited with mother. It was the end of 1945 and on that happy Christmas I was conceived and came forth nine months later in September of 46. Born in Bulawayo my first gasp of air was African. Bulawayo was my place of birth but it means *"Place of Slaughter"*, perhaps not the best place to be born in. Let me give you a glimpse of the history of my hometown, capital of the old Matabele kingdom where King Lobengula the last of the great African kings ruled his warrior people. As one can gather from such a name as "Place of Slaughter" old King "Loben" was at times a bit heavy handed with his subjects. He ruled as any despot would, at times kindly and generously, at other times ruthlessly and without mercy. All this ended in 1893 when he fled from white invaders who attacked Bulawayo. These whites were volunteers in the private army of Cecil John Rhodes and under the command not of a general but a doctor. His name was Dr Jameson. On the 4th November 1893 he and his men entered the scorched remains of the royal kraal to the sound of bagpipes played by an ex-pipe major of the Royal Scots Guards who had written a special composition for the occasion called "March to Bulawayo."

Pursued by white soldiers Lobengula fled north in the vain hope that he could make a new home across the Zambezi River but he was sick both in heart and body and his wagons made slow progress. The whites were anxious to capture Lobengula now that he was on the run. Some of them had fought in the Anglo-Zulu war and a few had been scouts in the Indian campaigns of the "Wild West." Perhaps this made them think they were invincible for the arrogant whites pursued the fleeing king like jackals nipping at the ankles of a wounded lion thinking they could taunt and insult him. However, although he was old and sick he was still a lion and old lions still could kill. Fate intervened when a flash flood caused the Shangani River to rise and cut off a group of soldiers who were then surrounded by warriors. Led by a Scotsman called Alan Wilson they made a "last stand". On the banks of the swollen river Lobengula's warriors dipped their spears in blood and thirty-four white soldiers perished. Even though they were not soldiers of the Queen it is said that before they succumbed they stood together and sang "God Save the Queen." This is just mythology but it illustrates the popular sentiments of the time and loyalty held for Britain. The Matabele usually disembowelled their enemies in the tradition of their Zulu forefathers so as to release the spirits of the dead but whether they did so on this occasion no one knows for only whitened bones were found much later. However, the warriors respected their fallen foes by saying afterwards "they fought like lions." In Rhodesian history it is called "Alan Wilson's last stand" and he and his men became heroes. The remainder of the white soldiers retreated in tight formation pursued by warriors who savaged their flanks until, after many days and thoroughly exhausted, they eventually staggered back to Bulawayo now occupied by settlers. By then old, sick "Loben" was tired of living and he and his faithful *"induna"* (chief) drank poison and died lonely deaths in the bush. They were buried in a small cave. It is said that a vast fortune in gold and diamonds was also buried somewhere out in the veld. He was the last of the great African kings of central Africa and had ruled his tribe with absolute authority but he was outmanoeuvred and many of his warriors slaughtered by the settler army. With loss of king and finest men Matabele society was devastated.

The white soldiers who perished might have been awarded the VC had they been soldiers of the Queen but they were not. Rhodesia was not colonised by a British force but seized by a private "army" in the pay of the British South African Company. However, the British government had unofficially given its director, Cecil John Rhodes, the green light to take the land that was to be called after him. The new nation had been birthed three years before in September 1890. It was called directly after the mining magnate and "colossus" of the south, Rhodes, whose money had made it all possible. His "Pioneers" had raised the Union Jack at a place they named Salisbury in honour of England's premier, Lord Salisbury. Other names such as Fort Victoria and Victoria Falls, named after Queen Victoria, all reflected aspects of British Empire and the whole of southern *Zambesia* was declared to be "exclusively within the British sphere of influence" and Britain was quick to claim the new territory as part of the Empire. Having first settled in Mashonaland it did not take long before the white settlers raised the Union Jack over the charred remains of Bulawayo in Matabeleland and rebuild it as their own.

Soon after Jameson captured Bulawayo Rhodes gave a pugnacious speech and congratulated his private troops for their "destruction of ruthless barbarism south of the Zambezi" and promised rewards of land and loot. However, not everyone back in England was happy with his heavy handed tactics so he added that if the "mother country attempted any interference it should take care lest his Pioneers follow the example of the American colonists." and his Cape Times newspaper published this threat with the comment "the British Government might find itself faced with the necessity of crushing a new Republic, which would cause more blood than the whole Matabele nation is worth." Nevertheless, his speech seems to have had a prophetic ring to it for one day Rhodesia would indeed declare independence and even become a republic.

The Zulu Kings

King Lobengula observed the traditions of his Zulu forefathers before him. He had called his kraal "Gubulawayo" after Shaka's capital in Zululand. Lobengula was the son of King Mzilikazi, a renegade who fled from the wrath of Shaka the great Zulu King whose reign brought fear to friend and foe alike. According to some historians he was ruthless with his enemies and sometimes with his friends. His capital was called the *"House of Slaughter."* Records of his brutality describe how his armies pillaged tribes, killed those who resisted and stole their livestock. This thirst for power threw the Southern African region into chaos in what was called the *"mfecane",* or "time of trouble". All the loot went of course to Shaka and the people of southern Africa became refugees in their own land. Shaka's brutality is now played down and denied. Recently a handbook was published which teaches leadership skills from Shaka's example. Fortunately it does not mention techniques of execution.

Mzilikazi was one of Shaka's best generals until he made a serious error. After a particularly successful raid Mzilikazi decided to keep the substantial booty for himself. When Shaka heard of it he was furious and sent an *impi* to kill Mzilikazi who in 1822 fled with a small army into the interior of southern Africa. Mzilikazi's name was appropriate for it means *"Great Road"* and a missionary who got to know him in later years called him the *"Black Napoleon"*. His army, small as it was, swept across the South African veld and after a few years he established his own kingdom in the region of modern-day Pretoria. He started a new nation and controlled an "empire" of over 30,000 square miles, a supreme achievement. However, it was not long before Boers from the Cape trekked into this area to get away from the British and he found himself fighting again, this time with whites. He did not like whites coming into his domain and decided to withstand them and 6000 warriors threw themselves against a small band of Boers. The handful of Boers repulsed them and the warriors were forced to retreat, spears could not stand against guns. Mzilikazi then gathered his people and trekked north, crossed the Limpopo River, and after many adventures the main group settled on a well-watered plateau far away from the whites. Here they became known as the "Amandabele".

Determined to rebuild his kingdom he embarked on new campaigns and after overwhelming the local Shona people and enforcing his own rule upon them the "Matabele" settled down to a life of peace and quiet Matabele style which meant regular raiding jaunts into Mashonaland and wild parties celebrating the booty. An account by a missionary tells what he saw when he entered a Shona village after a typical raid by the Matabele. He described how bodies of men and women had been pegged down and left to the heat of the scorching sun and the cold dew of night. They had been fastened to the ground in a row and left to pestering flies and ravenous beasts. To add to their agonies a huge fire had been lit at their feet and the ashes were still warm.[1] One wonders if these were exaggerated reports.

Mzilikazi wanted to get as far away from the whites as possible but it was not long before they were again at his doorstep this time asking permission to hunt and do other things that white people did. It seemed his newly claimed domain was not going to have much peace after all. When he died in 1868 his successor Lobengula built a new kraal and called it "Bulawayo." Lobengula was an enlightened man but this did not stop him ruling in the old tradition or from raiding tribes. The Matabele warriors pillaged to the north and east and came back with fat bullocks and young maidens with fat buttocks. The Shona never forgot.

It is no longer politically correct to say there was tribal friction at that time and it is claimed that conditions were exaggerated by the invading whites to justify their occupation. It is also said that Lobengula spread the myth of his control over the Shona to serve his purposes in claiming to be sole ruler of the region. This may be true but there was resentment between the tribes and this was to bear consequences in later years. The seeds of slaughter were sown long ago.

Rhodes of Kimberley

When Mzilikazi died Lobengula emerged as king but his monarchy was doomed from the start for whites came seeking concessions of all kinds. From the diamond fields in the south the exceedingly wealthy mining magnate Cecil Rhodes saw his opportunity and planned to extend British influence into Africa and at the same time make another fortune. In a period when European nations were grabbing huge tracts of Africa he was frustrated with the inactivity of the British. His aim was to take control of as much "unclaimed" land as possible and his dream was to build a railway from Cape to Cairo, all on British soil of course. This was to bring "civilisation" to Africa which was his justification for his vision.

Rhodes made a huge fortune from diamonds at Kimberley in the Northern Cape. It all started with the discovery of what was called the "Star of Africa" and soon people rushed there from America, Australia and Britain and from all around South Africa. He started work on his brother's claim, bought other claims and ended up having a syndicate that controlled the entire place, DeBeers Consolidated Mines. Men laboured and died to make his millions. There were several open shafts in the vicinity of the town. Just one, the "Big Hole", eventually produced 14 million carats in diamonds. To yield this the diggers moved over two and a half million tons of earth. It is said that a day did not pass without at least one person dying in the Big Hole from accident, sickness, murder or suicide. Kimberley was a rip-roaring town and in its rough and tumble people made and lost fortunes in a day. By the age of twenty-eight Rhodes was a millionaire and a Member of the Cape Parliament and eventually became Prime Minister of the Cape Colony. Educated in Oxford he was deeply influenced by the popular sentiments of the day, namely that the English were a supreme breed who were to establish colonies that would make England the supreme world power. A leading figure of the day put it this way, "This is what England must do or perish: she must found colonies as fast and as far as she is able, formed of her most energetic and worthiest of men: seizing every piece of fruitful waste ground she can set her foot on and there teaching these her colonies that their chief virtue is fidelity to their country, and their first aim is to advance the power of England by land and sea."[2] Rhodes was to become an important force in the process of British expansion into Central Africa and he and his close associates poured vast amounts of money into the development of central Africa. They built railways, bridges and roads and gave funds for education and building. He was a ruthless man who was either loved or hated and his eyes were set on the fabled wealth of Ophir.

The Land of Ophir

Rhodesia lay between the Zambezi and Limpopo Rivers and was interspersed by huge granite outcrops with a central watershed and rich mineral deposits. The land is well wooded with beautiful Msasa trees on the central plateau and Mopani forests in the low hot areas, with stands of evergreen jungle in the steaming valleys and patches of temperate forest on the cool mountain slopes of the Eastern Highlands. The climate is hot in summer but with mild winters when the grass turns golden brown and a cool breeze from the south sweeps across the land. In the first flush of a September spring the hills become clad in beauty as Msasa trees burst into shades of pink, maroon and rust with tender fresh leaves. Then the days get hotter and hotter until the first big clouds appear, forming huge castles in the sky. The skies blacken and the rumble of thunder and flash of lightning signals the start of the rainy season. The hot days of Christmas are punctuated by singing cicada beetles and a welcome storm or two relieves the heat. After three or four months the rains dwindle and by the month of May autumn sets in with cool days and clear skies.

In antiquity this land was called "The Land of Gold" and was identified as the ancient land of Ophir. In about AD 947 El Mas'udi described this land in glowing terms; "Meadows of gold and mines of gems" and wrote of the land of Sofala "which produces gold in abundance and other marvels". The name Sofala has links with India and in Sanskrit, the ancient language of the Hindus, it means *"beautiful shore"*. There are thousands of ancient mines and gold diggings scattered through Zimbabwe. Old Portuguese maps named the Limpopo River "Rio De Spiritu Santo" - "The Holy Spirit River" for this was the land of promise. Rhodes promised his pioneers first pickings of these fabled riches in the land which he claimed his own. In ancient times this area had been famous not only for its gold but also for its iron and other minerals. Indians, Arabs, Phoenicians and the ancient Egyptians sent expeditions to this land seeking its riches. Ships sent from Dhofar on the Arabian peninsular took three years to return. Where did they go? Yemen was the place from where the expeditions set out and their destination was the East Coast of Africa. A place called Sofala just south of Beira is the most southerly point that ships could reach on the trade winds. The name is significant. In the Septuagint, the ancient Greek translation of the Old Testament (written about150BC), the name Ophir is translated as Sophara (Sofala) which shows how far back the name goes. Eventually the East Coast of central Mozambique and the interior became known as the Land of Sofala or Ophir and traders came seeking its riches.

It was these deposits that Rhodes had his heart set on but Lobengula considered the whole place belonged to him. However, Lobengula was himself an invader. He was born near Pretoria in SA and came as an infant to Zimbabwe when his father Mzilikazi migrated there. Lobengula may have been uneducated but he was not stupid. With the influx of whites into his domain he knew his time was up. He once likened himself to a fly being stalked by a chameleon. Just as a chameleon slowly stalks a fly until it is within reach and then suddenly with lightning speed sticks out its long, sticky tongue and – zap, it is all over, so in the same way Lobengula saw his own eventual fate at the hand of the whites. The king's court was set in the dust, flies, dung and heat of the royal cattle kraal. It was here that whites came seeking from him endless concessions and treaties to hunt and prospect. Numerous concessions were given and many were the arguments that resulted as concessions contradicted one another. Adventurers, missionaries and mining magnates all grabbed for spoils in the scramble for Africa.

1890 – the "Pioneers"

Rhodes sent representatives to Lobengula and wrangled from him a concession that granted permission to dig for minerals throughout the whole region. He virtually "bought" the whole land with a promise to pay Lobengula a hundred pounds a month and to supply him with one thousand rifles and one hundred thousand rounds of ammunition. The Matabele had suffered devastating casualties from Boer guns and Lobengula knew the importance of having his own guns and the bait was too much for him. Rhodes formed the "British South African Company" and supported by Westminster and the great white Queen he planned for settlers to move into central Africa and claim it for the Empire. He needed strong young men to possess his new country. In 1890 a number of "pioneers" struck out from Kimberley and headed north with the aim of opening the interior to European settlement. The "Pioneer Corp" was a hastily put together band of unlikely entrepreneurs not even numbering a thousand. Each was promised fifteen mining claims and a farm of three thousand acres as part of the pickings. The actual "pioneers" were only about 200 and were accompanied by about 500 "police", about 150 African workers and a string of ox-wagons.

Rhodesia

The column of wagons was guided by a hunter called Frederick Courtney Selous. He was familiar with the land for he had spent time there as a young man hunting elephant. He shot many of them as well as other animals and got to know the country very well. Fortunately Selous had a change of heart and became a renowned naturalist and his illustrious bust stands in the British Museum of Natural History.

After a long trek the pioneers raised the Union Jack at Fort Salisbury which soon became a frontier settlement for prospectors, hunters and traders. Jameson the doctor who had practised in Kimberley, hand picked and close friend of Rhodes, became the administrator. He had done much to secure a concession from Lobengula. For weeks he had endured the sticky, dirty dung and flies of the royal court all the while nursing the king's gout and sore eyes. It was largely due to his efforts that the king finally ratified an agreement. Lobengula even made him into an honorary *Induna*, a ceremony that entailed Jameson stripping off his clothes and dressed in skins and ostrich plumes taking the salute from a ragged march-past of royal warriors.

When Jameson and his Pioneers settled in Mashonaland the days of Lobengula were numbered. It was less than three years later and on trumped up fictitious charges that the settlers clashed with him. In July of 1893 Matabele warriors raided villages in the vicinity of the white settlement of Fort Victoria. They did no harm to Europeans but had an altercation with some Shona. This is just what Jameson needed as an excuse and he put aside his honorary Matabele chieftainship and with the approval of Rhodes prepared to make his march on Bulawayo. He took to his new career of frontier fighting with zest and it was the beginning of this wild and fateful campaign that resulted in the defeat of the last King of the Matabele and the conquest of the last remnant of the mighty Zulu nation. Jameson raised a force from local whites that numbered 652 settlers with a similar number of Africans who acted as wagon drivers and workers. It was hardly an army, more like a bunch of prospectors with guns. Amongst them, however, was the royal cousin to Lobengula, Kumalo, who hated Lobengula for having murdered his entire family in one of his royal purges.

On the march to Bulawayo the column fought two battles with the Matabele. At the first, the Battle of Shangani, they beat off an attack. Then just twenty miles from Bulawayo they fought the Battle of Bembezi. The Matabele had set an ambush but fortunately Kumalo being versed in the ways of his people warned Jameson who avoided the trap and instead formed a *laager* (defensive square) and prepared for battle. This probably saved the whites from annihilation. Two of the best fighting regiments, the Imbesu and Ingubo, broke cover at just 400 yards in a full frontal charge. The swiftness and sheer shock of it caught the white settlers off guard. A number of men were stationed as pickets some way from the laager. As the bugle sounded an alarm they scrambled for their horses but two men had difficulty catching their mounts. Trooper Thompson failed to catch his and was unable to escape the advancing horde and stabbed to death. Trooper White managed to mount his horse but promptly fell off and the horse bolted without him. White was a marathon runner but immediately became a sprinter and outran the swiftest Matabele warriors. In later years when that piece of land became a farm the title deed was called "White's Run".

The full frontal assault of 1400 warriors was halted less than a hundred yards from the laager. The new British maxim guns had opened up and stopped them. The bravery of the warriors was no match against their withering fire and they fell dead and wounded like hewn trees. In the next hour several more attempts were made to charge the laager. All failed. A newspaper correspondent with the column wrote of what he saw and described the bravery of the warriors as they faced the maxim guns at a distance of a hundred and ten yards as one of the most magnificent displays of physical courage that Africa has ever seen. At least 500 of the best warriors died. Their bodies lay heaped in the grass.

The Matabele called the Maxim gun "scockacocka" from the sound it made as it fired 500 rounds a minute. As a new British invention the first time it was ever used in action was against the Matabele. It became greatly feared among them for they could not stand against it no matter how brave they were. Many were slaughtered and it opened the way to the "Place of Slaughter".

As mentioned, Jameson sent his troops on a furious pursuit of the fleeing king and it gave the Matabele a chance for vengeance. The white soldiers killed on the banks of the Shangani River were part of the same column that had inflicted such heavy casualties at Bembezi but this time they had no maxim gun to stop the warriors. However, the capture of Bulawayo and the death of Lobengula led to a temporary defeat of the Matabele nation. The whites now ruled over two different tribes, the Shona and the Matabele but peace would only be brief before hostilities broke out again in 1896.

New Year 1896

Three years after capturing Bulawayo Jameson, alias Dr. Jim the administrator whom Rhodes had appointed, decided to once more change his career and become a General. He rounded up five hundred white settlers in Rhodesia and in December of 1895 rode south to liberate Johannesburg from the Boers. The whole thing was contrived by Rhodes as a means to annex the gold mines of the Transvaal Boer Republic. It was done with the knowledge of the British Colonial Secretary Joseph Chamberlain who covertly supported it.

Trouble had been brewing between the white tribes of South Africa for a long time. In 1886 gold was discovered in South Africa in the Transvaal, a Boer Republic. Yet it was English miners who rushed to the goldfields and worked the claims and this created tension with the Boer administration. The wealth of the new mines was not missed by Rhodes who soon opened his Consolidated Mines Company in the new gold fields and set out to make a second fortune. Although Rhodes had sent his pioneers to occupy the "Land of Gold" no great gold deposits had yet been found there. However, the gold mines in Transvaal were making fortunes and it had become the most valuable piece of real estate in the world. He had to find a way to annex the entire wealth of the mines. The tension between the English miners and the Boer government was the excuse for him to get involved.

It seems Jameson's time in the remote colony of Rhodesia had caused him to lose his mind. His subjugation of the Matabele must have gone to his head for he decided he could conquer the Boers in the same way, with a handful of poorly equipped men and a lot of bravado. Late in December of 1895 he set out to invade the Transvaal on a trumped up excuse to rescue the *"uitlanders"* from Boer oppression (*uitlanders* meant "foreigners" a Boer term for English miners). Jameson's attempt to become a world famous British General failed and he and his entire force were captured near Johannesburg on January 2nd 1896. It was not a good start to the New Year; they had suffered over sixty casualties, sixteen of whom were dead. Jameson was sent for trial in England and it caused the downfall of Rhodes as Cape Premier. The Boers never forgave Rhodes and this event contributed largely to the circumstances of ill feeling that led to the Anglo Boer War. It achieved nothing except to consolidate Afrikaans people and after this fiasco it was inevitable that conflict between the two white tribes should take place. Things simmered until war broke out in 1899. Rhodes never lived to see final British victory in this disastrous war for he died at Cape Town in March of 1902. His body was laid in a railway carriage and carried north to "his" beloved land of Rhodesia where it was taken to Matobo Hills and laid to rest in the lonely grandeur of the great granite monoliths and mighty *dwalas* (hills). Rhodes died just two months after Queen Victoria died. It was the end of an era, that of the great Victorian Empire.

Not only did Rhodes help start two wars, the first being the subjugation of the Matabele and the second being the Boer War, he was also in a way responsible for a third, the outbreak of rebellion in Rhodesia. Jameson's ill-conceived attempt to "save" British miners from the Boers was doomed from the start but it also depleted the administration in Rhodesia of the vital presence of men needed for the protection of settlers. Jameson had formed most of his private army from local whites and when they left for Johannesburg there were only a handful of armed men left in the whole country. The subsequent rout of Jameson caused the Matabele to realise that whites were not invincible and news that Jameson was under lock and key was their key to freedom. Somewhat upset by the loss of their old ways and urged on by their spirit mediums they decided this was the moment to rebel.

1896 – The "Rebellion"

The Matabele were thoroughly disenchanted by the way the BSA Company had ruled them since 1893. The Company had taken away almost all their grazing lands and instead awarded them remote "reserves" in dry and waterless areas. Those who were not trans-located remained as squatters on land now apparently owned by white settlers. Understandably, this upset them. Large numbers of their cattle were also "acquired" by settlers some of whom were allocated huge tracts of land. Then a disease called Rinderpest broke out among cattle and the spirit mediums blamed the disease on the whites. In order to contain the disease the whites shot healthy cattle as well as sick and the Matabele could not understand why. Out of an estimated 300,000 cattle they were left with about 40,000. With the departure of so many whites to fight in the goldfields of the Transvaal the country was left indefensible and the people did not need a lot of persuasion to believe the eradication of the whites was the solution so they took up arms. Similar discontent was felt among the Shona who also rebelled.

It was a brutal conflict. Within the first few days 140 white men, women and children were killed. Notable clashes took place with small groups of white soldiers facing mass charges that carried Matabele warriors within meters of overwhelming them. The whites lost numerous men as they ran the gauntlet of thousands of ruthless warriors. It was clear the Matabele had not lost any of the fighting skills of their Zulu forefathers.

In Mashonaland similar events were taking place. The rebellion was called in Shona "*Chimurenga*". Within days 130 white men, women and children were massacred. A group of civilians was cut off at an isolated fort in the Mazoe Valley about twenty miles north of Salisbury. Several whites were killed and a handful of men were sent to rescue them. They too were surrounded and so a second group set out from Salisbury to help them. They got to the beleaguered community but they too were attacked. Holding the warriors at bay they put three women into a cart and made a heroic dash back to Salisbury. For 16 miles they fought off thousands of Shona fighters. Several horses were shot from under them and several men killed but they made it back under cover of darkness. One man said it was like riding through the "Valley of Death." The leader was eventually awarded the VC.

Much later in the 1950s construction work in the vicinity of the old Mazoe Fort unearthed the skeletons of a man and a little dog. They were the remains of a white prospector who had tried to get to the Fort during that time of upheaval. At the outbreak of the Rebellion he had been in the far north and walked many miles through hostile territory and under cover of darkness approached the Fort. The story goes that he was within shouting distance and called for directions when he was suddenly attacked and killed. The settlers at the Fort heard the barking of his faithful little dog until it became silent. Their bones were found lying side by side. Even in death the little dog had not left his master's side. What happened out there in the lonely African night? Were they killed together or did the little dog keep vigil at his master's body and die of hunger and exhaustion?

Eventually over a tenth of the white population were slaughtered and their rotting corpses lay scattered through the land. Women and children were massacred and the survivors were understandably upset by the way their families were killed. They reacted with anger and seeds of bitterness on both sides were sown.

Reinforced by British soldiers and after several months of fighting and at the awful cost of over eight thousand Africans and hundreds of whites the uprising was eventually quelled and the country at last opened for permanent white settlement. Several acts of bravery by British soldiers earned medals that included a couple of Victoria Crosses. The white population of Bulawayo was then only a few thousand men and less than 100 women. Shortly after the end of the rebellion there was a general exodus to the south as whites scrambled to get out of the colony. Then in October 1896 a soldier let off his rifle at a hawk sitting on one of the buildings and hit an arms magazine instead. Eighty tons of dynamite exploded killing ten men and wounding another thirty. It was about the only event of significance until the South African Anglo-Boer War broke out. The South African War started in 1898 and 1,700 white soldiers from Rhodesia enlisted to fight. This was a higher proportion than any other British colony an achievement to be repeated in two World Wars. There was no lack of loyalty to Britain. Only at the end of the war did people once again begin to make their way north to seek opportunities in the new colony. Gold mines were opened and a continuous stream of settlers came looking for new lives.

And so, this was how Lobengula's royal kraal became my place of birth. It became Rhodes' town for he ordered that the streets should be wide enough to allow an ox wagon to turn with a full team of sixteen oxen in yoke. Can you imagine how wide the streets had to be for that? They are the widest streets I've ever seen. It was laid out with beautiful parks and paved roads and the statue of Rhodes placed in its broad street from where it surveyed activity and growth. A "scockacocka" was also placed on a plinth in the middle of the street as a permanent reminder of white supremacy and black subjugation. The Place of Killing was finally tamed, or was it?

The Early 1900s
Among those who made their way north was a young Scotsman from Aberdeen, Walter, who had fought with a Scottish regiment in the South African

War. That war was a brutal affair and he saw all the horrors of the conflict. His experience so traumatised him that at the end of the war he decided he would not stay in South Africa where there was so much ill feeling between Boer and Brit nor was he going back to his cold "home country" so he absconded, changed his name, and soon after the end of the war in 1902 disappeared into the new colony of Rhodesia. He wanted to get away from the brutal scenes he had witnessed and to get lost in the lonely bush of the north where the wide open spaces were washed with sun and where men could forget the horrors they had experienced. Perhaps there were other compelling reasons for his leaving. Perhaps he had violated army code or maybe he was running from the law. What ever reasons compelled him to travel north are now lost forever.

When the pioneers occupied the territory they dispersed to claim their winnings. Mines were pegged and strong young men were now needed to work them. Walter found lots of opportunity to do just that. It was tough work to say the least. If he had wanted to get away from things he could not have chosen a more suitable place for soon he was working at a mine with an appropriate name, Lonely Mine, away in the bush 50 miles north of Bulawayo. It became one of the wealthiest gold mines in Rhodesia and was at one time the deepest mine on a quartz reef in the whole of Africa.

In those early days women were in short supply but Walter was fortunate to meet Anne just out from the Scottish Borders. She had sailed on a boat from Southampton to Cape Town as nanny to the McKenzie family but why she endured the tough trek north to rough, dangerous Rhodesia I cannot say. Why she left home is a mystery; perhaps she had a broken love affair or some other setback. Maybe she sought adventure. Whatever her motives to embark on the long journey from Southampton to Cape Town and on to Bulawayo certainly required courage. The Zeederberg Coach was the means of transport used by the wealthy but all lesser mortals came on transport wagons enduring the slow pace of the oxen and sometimes walking beside the wagons or sometimes riding on the bone-breaking vehicle. When the railway was opened travel became easier but it was still a long, difficult trip. Walter must have used all his charm to win Anne for they were married in the frontier town of Bulawayo at the start of an arduous and perilous life together. Anne must rank among those intrepid women who helped open the great frontiers of the world. In the early 1900s the white population of Bulawayo and the whole district was less than 6000 whites mostly men. When the Great War broke out in 1914 Walter volunteered once again for duty but was told that because of his mining skills he was considered strategic manpower and was required to keep the home fires burning. And so it was that two people, one having changed his name and left the army and the other having mysteriously left home and family, found each other in the wilds of Africa. It was men and women such as Walter and Anne who helped build this new nation.

In due course Walter and Anne had two daughters, Dorothy and Sheila. The colony was a rough place for two small girls. They grew up on isolated mines in true pioneer fashion. Their home was rough pole-and-dagga thatched huts. Their school was the bush and their only friends were little *umfaans* (children). They faced a sometimes brutal life in the wilds of Africa with no luxuries. By the time they were in their teens the family had moved to Connemara Mine near a small town, Que Que. In those days lions and leopards and other big game roamed the country.

A Young English Rookie in the 1930s

Sheila, their youngest daughter, eventually went to Bulawayo to train as a teacher. After her graduation she started teaching at a little school in Plumtree situated near the border with the British Protectorate of Bechuanaland and became acquainted with a young policeman just out from England. Ted was posted to the lonely outpost of Fort Rixon where the Matabele rebellion had first broken out. The Fort was established in 1896 to protect white settlers and was built by a contingent of police. It was made of stones heaped together with sturdy logs. A small cemetery below the fort contains the graves of settlers who died during the uprising for it was here that the first deaths of settlers in Matabeleland took place. Among them was a young, newly married bride and groom who were visiting their newly acquired farm for the first time. It was not a good honeymoon. They were ambushed on route and the groom was killed but the bride managed to escape into the bush. She hid in a *"donga"* (gully) for several days but was discovered and killed by the Matabele. One can hardly imagine the terror she experienced during those fearful days alone in the bush.

The upkeep of the cemetery at Fort Rixon was a police duty and once a year one of the policemen posted there, it being a two-man station, had to visit the graves and renovate them. It was a lonely spot for any young man to serve at but Ted was doing his duty for king and empire. He was recruited in London in the 1930s to join the British South African Police and together with a small group of fellow recruits was soon on a ship to Africa. The haunting sound of ship horns and the sight of a lone piper standing on the quay at Southampton was Ted's last impression of home for he never set foot again on English soil.

Every day at the sound of the bugle the Union Jack was raised and fluttered bravely over his little outpost in the middle of nowhere. Apart from the chirping of crickets there was not much nightlife. The nearest bit of civilisation was at Insiza, twenty-three miles away where the White family of the marathon runner ran a small "hotel". This hotel had a reputation for hospitality and was the nearest thing to city night-lights. It stood alone near a small one-hut railway station and passengers could disembark and have refreshments. The old road from Bulawayo to Gwelo went right past the front door and travellers could pause for a rest and exchange news.

For Ted there was one saving grace at Fort Rixon. In those days the police patrolled on horseback and every station had a couple of horses. Ted loved horses. Since childhood he had grown up with them. When forced to work as a youngster because of financial shortages during the depression in England he got a job as a stable hand. When old enough he joined the Metropolitan Mounted Police in London. There was not much he did not know about horses. Police horses were a mixed bag and there were some pretty mean beasts among them. One at Fort Rixon was a notorious animal feared by everyone because of his malicious streak. His name was Satan. No wonder he was disliked! When it came to horses, however, Ted loved a challenge and he took the beast on. Without breaking the spirit of the horse he drummed a bit of discipline into him, won his confidence and made him into a new creature. After that he was fine to ride, high spirited and full of character, game for anything. Ted trained him to stand stock still when he fired his rifle from the saddle. Renamed Kit, he was always ready for a bit of fun. He would pick up his feet, cock his ears and show interest in everything around him, prancing along, dodging shadows and shying away from movements. He was quite a handful, the kind of horse Ted enjoyed. Riding a spirited horse in the wilds of Africa was a huge change from patrolling the grey crowded streets of London.

World War 11 - 1939

At this time world events caught up with Ted even though he was stuck away at the end of the Empire. War was brewing in Europe and nerves were jittery. When it boiled over Southern Rhodesian contributed many fighting men to the Allied cause and among them was a contingent of police who were sent to Ethiopia to establish British administration after the Italians were ousted. It was a sad day for the young men as they parted with loved ones. Ted had no family in Rhodesia but he was very much in love with Sheila the girl from Plumtree and as he journeyed north he was particularly lonesome. He spent about a year in the war zone and then managed to get approval to marry his sweetheart. How he did this is a mystery as no policeman could do so without permission from the police hierarchy. There was little prospect of approval when on active duty but Ted was obviously an ingenious young man and very much in love for he and Sheila were not only married in Ethiopia but she was also granted approval to live there and they had there first child, Johnny. After some years in Ethiopia it was decided that Sheila should take Johnny back to Rhodesia, Ethiopia not being a suitable place to bring up a young child.

After the war Ted returned and reunited with Sheila I was born in Bulawayo, in that far flung corner of the British Empire. Fort Street, where mother gave birth to me, was where the old fort stood during the heady days of rebellion when settlers came under attack by Matabele warriors who kept them holed up like rabbits that could do little but venture out during the day and run back at night. Born of British parents and a second-generation colonial through Sheila I grew up in a colony that was trapped in the last days of a dying Empire. Unlike

Bechuanaland and Swaziland which were Protectorates administered for indigenous people Rhodesia had been granted self-government, whatever that meant. It gave the local whites the idea that the country was their permanent home and that as part of the British Empire they were secure. I learnt at school that much of Africa was in the Empire and coloured red but in truth I was a white child in an African land.

The 1940s and 50s

My memories of growing up in Africa are supremely grand for it was a continent full of grandeur. My childhood was filled with sunny days and amazing discoveries. The year 1946 in the post war period was a time of new hope during which Southern Rhodesia had an influx of immigrants escaping the depredation of war ravaged Britain. The young colony offered vast tracts of uninhabited, undeveloped land and many ex-service men came to farm. Other British people came from India when Britain granted the nation independence in 1947. Many of them came with only a suitcase and the clothes they stood in having lost everything in the upheaval. Britain encouraged people to come to Rhodesia for Britain was recovering from war and desperately needed food and raw materials, things Rhodesia could provide. So many immigrants came that a housing shortage resulted that compelled the Rhodesian government to build cheap houses with thatched roofs and mud bricks baked in the sun. Africa's warm, sunny climate made up for hardships and most immigrants were willing to work hard. It was a time of rapid progress. Then in 1953 the Federation of Southern and Northern Rhodesia and Nyasaland took place. It was considered a great success and it looked as though there would be glorious years ahead but the experimental partnership was to turn foul and a time of madness was coming. The good days were going to turn bad.

My early years could not foresee the coming drama and were made of grand stuff. The colony was still young enough to be wild with abundance of wild animals and wild people. Britain and her allies had just won the Second World War and there was a certain colonial flavour mixed with British tradition and whites had an attitude of confidence and optimism. It was an era when people stood together and helped one another. We were British and very proud of it but indigenous people were mostly considered secondary and largely inconsequential.

Rabson versus Rabson

One of my earliest recollections was the night our cook had an argument with our gardener. Rabson was our cook. That is not to say he knew much about cooking but it was his title and he wore a starched white uniform and worked in the house. Mostly he did the washing up and swept the house but mother taught him basic cooking and he graduated to preparing Sunday roasts. As children we had two treats. One of them was our Sunday lunch. Weekday meals were pretty basic; porridge in the morning, bread and some home grown fruit for lunch and a simple meal at night. Sundays were special. We had an old wood stove that once one got the hang of cooked beautifully. It was the family tradition on Sundays to have a roast, often rolled beef. We made a feast of it with dumplings and radish and hot English mustard. Sometimes we had a fat farm chicken. First though it had to be caught and then Rabson would lop off its head with the kitchen knife. I would watch the execution with keen interest. He placed its neck on a wooden block used just for this purpose. Down came the knife with a thud. Rabson seemed to enjoy it. If he let go of the chicken too soon its headless body would dash off spouting blood everywhere while all the time it looked up at us out of one eye from its severed head lying at our feet. I think Rabson did this on purpose as part of the fun. I found it all quite educational.

Sunday lunch was served in grand style laid out on a starched white embroidered tablecloth with napkins and silver cutlery. There was a bell on the table and when we sat down mother would ring it sharply and Rabson would enter in a dignified manner dressed in his starched white tunic and carrying the roast, which dad would carve with a hunting knife he carried with him wherever he went.

Our gardener was also called Rabson and there was some rivalry between the two. Rabson gardener was not allowed indoors and did not wear a white tunic. Neither did he get such a grand wage as the princely some of two pounds ten shillings a month. However, both of them lived in the compound at the rear of the homestead and on Sunday evenings once the week's work was finished there were two things they both loved to indulge in more than anything else so as to break the monotony of life. They loved to drink "*kachausu*", a highly potent mix of pure alcohol carefully distilled in a secret bush camp and smuggled into the compound under cover of darkness. It was also called "*skokiaan*" and very illegal. They also loved to gamble not with cards but in a game using little round pebbles placed in a series of small holes dug in the dusty floor of the kraal. This particular Sunday the game had gone well for Rabson gardener who had been on a winning run. As the night progressed into the early hours of the morning Rabson gardener succeeded in relieving Rabson cook of his wages, most of his clothes and his youngest wife as well. He had two as was the custom with men who earned a better wage and could afford to pay the "*lobola*" bride price. With spirits high and emotions charged the situation was too much for Rabson the cook who decided to end the game permanently, pulled out his kitchen knife and stabbed his victor in the chest and belly.

We awoke in the dead of night to the drunken wail of Rabson gardener as he stumbled around our house trying to find the way in. Eventually he found the front door and rapped upon it repeatedly all the time crying out in a raucous voice that he was dying. By now both Johnny and I were wide awake with excitement and dread as we watched dad pull out his 45 colt revolver, his old war issue, throw open the door and demand to know what the noise was about. Rabson was spilling blood from his wounds. Unperturbed dad went to the compound and dragged Rabson cook out of his hut where he had collapsed in a drunken stupor unable to make a quick get away. Rabson gardener was lifted into the back of our old Chevy truck where he passed out and Rabson cook was thrown into the front where he also passed out. Dad delivered them to the relevant authorities, one to hospital and the other to police cells. He saved two lives that night for fortunately Rabson gardener survived due to the expertise of the doctors and after some months made a full recovery and even returned to work. Because Rabson gardener survived, Rabson cook escaped a possible murder charge that could have meant the death penalty and instead was given six months for assault, which he served. One day he pitched up at home and asked for his old job back but by then mother had found someone else and begun all over again the arduous task of instructing the new cook in the marvels of house work. The two Rabsons greeted one another as long lost friends with gleeful laughter and fond handshakes as they asked after one another's health as is the custom of Africans. All was forgiven.

What intrigued me about the incident was seeing dad's formidable revolver which he kept locked away so this was the first time I had seen it "in action." When he took it out he somehow became different, another person who I did not known and later when we asked him he told us it was his old war weapon. When the inevitable question came as to whether he had ever shot any one with it he replied he had but was not proud of it. It stuck in my mind as a funny kind of answer.

Ethiopia and Somalia

As mentioned, during the Second World War dad was part of the contingent of British South Africa Police (BSAP) sent from Southern Rhodesia to Ethiopia and Eritrea. He served with the rank of captain and after various escapades on the frontier was based in Addis Ababa. Mother travelled overland through Africa and joined him in Ethiopia for a war-time wedding. In those days this was a daunting journey for a woman to undertake especially in war. She left Bulawayo and travelled by train over the famous Victoria Falls bridge, through Northern Rhodesia into the Belgian Congo and up to Lake Tanganyika, by ferry over the Lake into Tanganyika and on to Lake Victoria which she crossed on another ferry to Kenya, through the Rift valley by truck, down through the Kenyan highlands to Nairobi and then overland through Kenya into Somalia to Mogadishu. From there she flew north in a military plane to the northern tip of Somalia to link with the highway that eventually took her the last six hundred miles by military convoy into Ethiopia. She must have been in love! She was soon married, a war time wedding with no luxuries. It was the first of many epic trips she would make through her life. In Ethiopia she found that the Emperor required her services as a teacher and she was employed to tutor his young daughter, the Royal Princess, as well as other members of the Royal family. Mother got to go for tea at the royal palace and became quite friendly with the Princess. My parents rented a suitable residence in the main quarter of Addis Ababa and opened a school for pupils approved by the Imperial Secretary. I think the need for a school with a qualified teacher to cater for the Emperor's children was the trump card dad played when he persuaded his commanding officer to approve his marriage. Certainly very few men on active duty had the privilege of taking along their wives. For years afterwards mother corresponded with the Royal Princess who attended her school. Unfortunately the fortunes of the royal family eventually ran out when the Emperor, the "Lion of the Tribe of Judah", was overthrown in 1974. He was old and soon died, smothered with a pillow by the upstart Mengistu, or so it was said.

Once in British controlled Ethiopia and married it was not too long before mother was pregnant and Johnny was born. Dad became British Public Prosecutor and spent his time keeping order, rounding up criminals and fighting various skirmishes with rebels. One night a gang attacked the staff quarters in which he and a couple of others were sleeping. Undeterred he pulled out not one but two revolvers and with one in each hand let off a volley of rounds in true cowboy style. The attackers melted into the darkness and he and his friends went back to sleep. After that he got a reputation as a cool character. The Rhodesian police appropriated some armoured cars brought up by the South African Corp and dad saw more action in Eritrea and was awarded the Star of Africa and other medals for his efforts. He never wore them but I knew it was all true. In our house there were some outstanding memorabilia and trinkets to prove it all; brass and silverware from North Africa, an Ethiopian sword and a knife with a handle made of Rhino horn, beautifully woven baskets as well as a vast *"kaross"* made from black and white Colobus Monkey skins that adorned the lounge. It was an exotic room and made me dream of Africa. And then there was the family photograph album. There were photos of dead rebels and huge snakes, of elephants and lions, of dead crocodiles with human limbs protruding from open stomachs and of far off, strange unfamiliar places and even stranger people. The tales I heard of Africa with its savage ways did not unsettle me, however, for I knew it was now safe, dad was a policeman and controlled everything. Africa was the place for me.

Police Work

With the war over dad was posted to Figtree Police Station and demoted to sergeant because his commission was only for the duration of the war. He became a member of the Memorial Order of Tin Hats (Moths) as did other veterans who fought for the British. Every Armistice Day on November the 11th the old warriors would gather at a Service of Remembrance for those who had paid the supreme price for king and country. The Last Post would sound and someone called out Binyon's immortal lines *"They shall not grow old, as we that are left grow old: age shall not weary them, nor the years condemn. At the going down of the sun and in the morning we will remember them."* Those gatherings left a profound impression upon me, the pride of being British and belonging to the

British Empire. When the National Anthem was played dad stood as straight and as still as a lamp post and I copied him and stood as straight and still as I could.

As children of a policeman Johnny and I spent our early infancy at remote depots in the bush. Johnny was christened in Plumtree school chapel in the small village near the border with Bechuanaland Protectorate. The village claim to fame was the boarding school that became renowned as one of the "better" schools especially among farmers who sent their children there. I was christened in the tiny chapel at Figtree which at that time was very remote and where dad served in a two man police post that administered a vast district in Matabeleland. It owed its fame to a large fig tree that grew in the vicinity and under which visitors in the late 19th century camped while waiting for permission from King Lobengula to journey into his domain.

I can vaguely remember the routine of police camp life especially the prisoners in their white prison tunics with little arrows painted all over them. The arrows, I was told, were to help the prison guards line their gun sights to shoot them if they ran away. Bands of prisoners, attended by African Prison Guards armed with Second World War 303 Lee Enfield rifles, swept, weeded, cleaned and did all the maintenance work required around the police camp as well as schools and other government buildings. Actually, no prisoners were ever shot. They were a very content lot and few ever made a break for freedom. In fact they seemed to roam freely with the guards herding them like sheep. They were a mixed bag of petty thieves and a few dangerous murderers but they all seemed pretty harmless to me. When our paths crossed I talked with them and they greeted me politely. An African nanny looked after Johnny and me during the daytime and Africans were good to us for we were the master's children. When I got tired nanny would heave me onto her sizable hip wrap a towel around me and then bounce me onto her broad back, tie the towel ends above her large bosom and there I would have a good sleep. But she had to be careful as mother disapproved of it. Dad was in charge of police affairs throughout the district and often went on patrol. He was gone for weeks. In the early days before the war he went on a horse but later he rode a motorbike and the *askaris* were promoted from foot to bicycles. The land was wild and things still quite raw. His district was about the size of a British county for which there were two European policemen. Dad was accompanied by a couple of constables and mules carried supplies. They camped on the open veld and sometimes he shot a buck for fresh roast or pot stew. Dad told stories about those early days. One day he was patrolling on his horse when a man confronted him with a musket. There were many hundreds of old Tower Muskets in the country from the old days before the rebellion when they were sold to the Matabele. Obsolete weapons from the Napoleonic wars were dumped on unsophisticated markets around the world and the "Brown Bess" flint-lock musket was widespread in southern Africa. They were formidable weapons when loaded with chunks of metal and charged with powder. Sometimes the strength and quantity of the powder was too strong and blew the gun to pieces right in the face of the owner, sometimes killing them and sometimes disfiguring them. This man lifted his musket and being very close aimed straight at dad's chest. Next thing, to his surprise, dad found that he was about twenty feet up in the air looking down on the whole scene below. He saw himself seated on his horse about to be blasted away and never could explain how he left his body. Fortunately the shot missed but the story stuck in my mind. When dad came back to earth he arrested the man and disarmed him and the musket was hung above the mantle in our living room right under a curved "Royal Artillery" sword which belonged to dad's grandfather and had his initials engraved on it. I often wondered how many people it had cut to pieces. Dad's family had been active in the Empire in diverse ways for many years and his Uncle George had gone to Sudan in the late 1800s as part of the British Administration but got "lost" and never heard of again. When dad left for Rhodesia he also lost touch with most of his relatives. It seemed the colonies did this to people.

The Matobo Hills

Figtree nestled in the foothills of the rugged Matobo Hills and dad would take us there for picnics. These hills are now a World Heritage Site and are renowned for their historical importance and wildlife. It was in these hills that the Matabele regiments kept the white settlers running around like rabbits during the rebellion of 1896. The hills are a vast jumble of granite outcrops, the most extensive in the world, with a labyrinth of caves just like rabbit warrens. In fact a substantial population of "Rock Rabbits" or Hyraxes live in the hills and have impregnable dens among the thousands of caves. One of the largest populations of raptors live there, as well as many antelope, rhino, giraffe, leopards, baboons and a host of other creatures. Long before Africans came to the region Bushmen lived in these hills and they decorated the caves with extraordinary art. It was in the Matobo Hills while chasing the Matabele warriors during the Rebellion of 1896 that Baden-Powell birthed his vision for the Boy Scout movement that grew to become the international movement of today. He served with British South African Company Scouts and it was from this most unlikely birth that the Boy Scouts grew. At that time the Matabele warriors had retreated into the tangled *kloofs* and granite caves where they ran merry circles around the British soldiers. It was like chasing rabbits in a warren and perhaps they would still be fighting if Rhodes had not come along and made peace.

Baden-Powell was a ruthless soldier. At the Siege of Mafeking during the Anglo Boer War he stamped his own brand of leadership upon the town. His rule was harsh but he pulled the inhabitants through seven months of horror but not without great cost mostly to the local Africans who had little food and harsh conditions. He held court and on at least one occasion had a man guilty of breaching his laws summarily executed. He had done the same during the Matabele uprising when the father-in-law of one of the spiritual leaders was captured and shot. Fortunately his principles of how to deal with one's enemies were not taught to Boy Scouts.

It was in the Matobo Hills that Cecil Rhodes stamped his charisma upon the warring warriors. Much is said about Rhodes that degrades him but there was a time when he stood tall. The Matabele admired courage in any man and did not miss his stature as a leader. After rebellion had broken out in Rhodesia Rhodes travelled to Matobo to join the fight against the Matabele. At times he charged after the warriors on his horse with nothing but his shooting stick. The Matabele were quick to note his daring. However, after one particularly bad battle in which eighteen white soldiers were killed and others wounded Rhodes became pensive. He knew there was little prospect of British troops being able to defeat the warriors who were entrenched in the hills. Although he was not in charge of the British military he nevertheless announced that he was going to make peace with the rebels. The British officers were taken aback at his intention but he sent word to the warriors through an intermediary and arranged for an *"Indaba"* or peace conference. Then with a handful of companions he rode into the hills and although outnumbered and surrounded by hundreds of sullen warriors armed to the teeth with spears and knobkerries he simply dismounted and unarmed walked right into their ranks. The power of his bearing compelled them to lay down their weapons and sit down and talk. The Matabele had a list of grievances and went on to tell Rhodes that they were not in their words "prepared to become his dogs". Several *"indabas"* followed and Rhodes' methods worked, the Matabele made peace and many lives were saved as hostilities ended and they came in from the hills. It served Rhodes' purposes for now he could get on with developing "his" new land. The Matabele honoured the peace and for years there was amicable respect for whites but in Mashonaland the war dragged on a bit longer and many died.

While in the hills Rhodes was overwhelmed by their majesty and he requested to be buried there at a lonely spot overlooking an immense panorama of mile upon mile of tumbled granite kopjes, one of the truly majestic places in southern Africa. Rhodes was so moved by the place that he said, *"The peacefulness of it all, the chaotic grandeur of it; it creates a feeling of awe and brings home to one how very small we all are."* Rhodes is buried not far from King Mzilikazi, on the summit of a huge round granite outcrop called "Malindidzimu", "The Dwelling Place of Spirits". The entire area is a vast monument to nature and totally eclipses man. To capture the grandeur of the spot one has to quietly contemplate the immense and brooding power that pervades the place and the enormous energy required for its formation.

The vast financial empire Rhodes established influenced Southern Africa for many years. Sadly, despite the great advances achieved during his career what Rhodes left was a legacy of ill feeling between Boer and Brit and between whites and Africans. Two of the most influential men in Southern African history lie in the Matobo Hills, Mzilikazi the "Black Napoleon" and Rhodes the "White Imperialist" an unlikely pair brought together by the events of the time. They lie almost within sight of each other in this vast monument of grandeur. A leading *induna* commented after attending the funeral of Rhodes, that it was curious that both Mzilikazi and Rhodes were buried close together on the tops of mountains in Matobo. He said the Matabele had thought much about it and believed that the spirit of Mzilikazi had always been with Rhodes. The Matabele respected Rhodes and called him "The separator of bulls" the bulls being the British and Matabele. Rhodes still lies there despite a wish by Zimbabwe to exhume him and send him back to England and these majestic hills still hold a sense of great wonder.

Dad loved the hills and took us to them. They are a rugged paradise filled with huge outcrops of granite and massive, jumbled boulders interspersed by beautiful glades of trees and grass. Baboons were common. Their barks echoed around the rocks and Johnny and I, always inquisitive, fearlessly ran after them crying "Boon, boon." Great fun was had by all. Birds, reptiles and wild animals were everywhere. In about 1936 a film was made set in the hills. About thirty or so British South African Police played the part of the pioneers and hundreds of Matabele, probably some of the original combatants amongst them, once more donned their fighting regalia and went through all the motions of the epic struggle albeit this time with rubber spears. It must have been a sad day for the old warriors to know how far they had fallen from their former glory. What capped it all was when an irate "pioneer", frustrated with the ineptitude of the "warriors" to co-operate with the finer points of what was required on set and wielding a *"shambok"* (whip) drove an *"impi"* (battalion) through the veld like a flock of cackling chickens - their final degradation. But the Matabele always walked with dignity despite the loss of their status. If they respected a white official they would give their greeting by standing stiffly, raising an arm and giving a deep, resonating "Nkosi." It was similar to the way they honoured Rhodes when at his funeral the gathered remnants of the fighting impis stood shoulder to shoulder and shouted their royal salute, *"Bayete Nkosi"*, raising and beating their shields with their knobkerries, a deafening sound that had in the past put great fear into their enemies.

As already mentioned Baden-Powell became famous for his formation of the Boy Scouts. Dad was a Scoutmaster and took scouts on outings. Johnny was a scout-cub and I though small traipsed along and learnt how to tie knots and make fires. Dad taught me bush skills. He taught me how to call up little Duiker buck. By placing a broad-leafed grass blade between one's fingers and blowing in a certain manner a kind of bleating sound is made. Dad could sit quietly in the bush and softly repeat the call until an inquisitive Duiker tiptoed into view. He learnt how to do that from an old Bushman. The Bushmen or San were the original people of the country who once roamed freely but were displaced by blacks who came from the North. They were Stone Age people, skilled hunters and gatherers who lived in small family clans at peace with one another and were no match for the iron-age invaders. They were the artists of Africa and the caves in Matobo Hills are filled with thousands of graceful paintings depicting them hunting, running and dancing and all manner of beautiful wild animals.

Picnics

Picnics were exciting occasions for a child and had all the potential of an African Safari. There were all manner of interesting and dangerous creatures all around us and sooner or later we stumbled on them or them on us. No sooner had mother spread out the picnic cloth than ants, big ones, and small ones, ones that nipped and ones that stung, invaded us. Then the flies would swarm in. There were small ones and big ones. The most feared were the blood sucking "horse flies." They had a long, sharp proboscis that could penetrate the thickest skin and clothing. Without any warning a stabbing pain would indicate that one's blood was rapidly being stolen. They were invariably too quick to kill and sure enough soon another piercing cry would indicate who had sustained the next piercing. Then there were the little Mopani Bees, a minute species of sting-less bush bee. They could not hurt but were infuriating for they would descend upon one in search of moisture and would hover around ones eyes, ears and nostrils, invading them and crawling into them. If mother opened anything sweet the real bees would arrive. The African bee is a vicious little creature and can be dangerous. When provoked they sting painfully and can kill animals and people. Other creeping creatures crawled up to join the picnic; large centipedes scurried through fallen leaves, spiders fell out of trees and blister beetles popped up. They could inflict serious harm by spitting lethal venom that caused terrible blisters wherever it contacted skin as I discovered when my chest took a frontal dose. Sometimes a friendly lizard would creep up and munch the ants eating our crumbs. There were also the inevitable snakes. Africa was full of them although the majority were harmless but seldom did a picnic pass without a good snake scare. All kinds were encountered, most slithering away as fast as they could. The excitement was all part of the fun and great times were had by all. At the end of the day we would wearily return bearing the battle scars of our outing, stings, cuts and sunburn. On returning home one had to carefully examine one's anatomy for ticks. They would latch onto one's most private of parts and could cause nasty sores not to mention tick fever. So much for the pleasures of Africa! More people in Africa have died from insects than from lions. The real dangers lie with the little creatures rather than the "big five."

Ranching in the African Bush

After some years dad lost interest in trying to make the police his career and went ranching. Although the British South African Police had a good reputation the salary of thirteen pounds a month was not enough to meet the demands of a growing family. Dad was a policeman through and through but family life changed all that so he threw in his uniform and became a ranch manager. We went to live on a ranch half way between Antelope Mine and West Nicholson far in the remote bush. Antelope Mine was one of many mines in the district. Others were Lazy Owl Mine, Leopard Mine, Tiger Reef Mine, Python Mine, Bush Tick; the names were fascinating and conjured up vivid pictures of life in the wilderness. In those days there were large cattle ranches in Matabeleland and there were lots of wild animals on them as well. Dad had to look after several thousand cattle and about twenty thousand acres of bush. It was genuine cowboy stuff, African style. Sometimes dad also had to do vermin control. "Vermin" was anything that got a taste for beef and killed the cattle; lions, leopards, hyenas etc. They had to be shot. It was a lonely life but dad enjoyed it. He loved the bush, horses and all wild animals.

Dad was born in England and left school at an early age due to the death of his father and the difficulties his mother had during the years of recession. Later he joined the London Metropolitan Mounted Police. He was in that force for some years and during that time learnt the ways of the military. His training never left him and all his life he carried himself with the air of a military man, well disciplined, straight and tall. He never slouched in a chair, never dressed too casually. When he rode a horse he sat so straight you would have thought he was on the Queen's Parade. While serving in London a recruitment drive to get young men to join the BSA Police in Rhodesia caught his attention.

"Join the BSAP. Young men who can shoot and ride required for service in Southern Rhodesia."

Dad signed up and soon found himself sailing out of Southampton on a Union Castle mail ship bound for Africa. After a period of training and familiarisation with the land and customs of the people he was patrolling the bush in a vast district. What a change from the wet streets of London.

Dad's dad was an engineer who worked for Marconi the man who developed the wireless. Marconi's company was registered in London in 1899 and under Marconi's leadership three cardinal principles were adhered to; that only the best engineering skills would suffice, that quality should never be sacrificed for cost and that a vigorous experimental policy should be pursued. Grandfather was associated with the company all his life but during the First World War he was with British Intelligence and active in the art of cryptography, the breaking of coded messages. After the war he continued with Marconi but died while still fairly young. The family was quite well-to-do but in the depression dad found work as a stable boy. It was here that he developed his amazing empathy with horses. However, he seldom volunteered any information about his family and spoke of his youth in terms that conveyed hardship. When he left Britain he never returned. To me it reflected a very negative impression of the "home country" as most of the older generation called Britain. As I grew up I never knew whether I was British or Rhodesian. I was African and Africa was the "Promised Land" filled with all manner of interesting things. Johnny and I had an insatiable interest in everything that moved and this got us into all kinds of predicaments. One day we wandered off, he on his small bike and me on my tricycle. We made it down to the river where we were busy paddling, crocodiles and all, when fortunately someone missed us and sent out a search party. Another time I decided to go and look at the nice cow in the paddock only to be rescued in the nick of time from a dangerous bull.

Bush life and Night Creatures

At night mother would light the paraffin lamps. They worked off pressure and she would pump until the lamps shone brightly and gave off a hissing sound. The hiss of lamps and smell of paraffin linger with me even now. African nights were dark with long shadows thrown by the lamps and strange sounds all around from crickets, frogs and owls. The creepy crawlies flocked in; beetles, moths, and what we called "dive bombers" a harmless kind of large flying ant but very intimidating, all winged in and crashed around us. Some of the beetles were four inches long and armed with formidable pincers and also emitted a hissing sound. The hissing of lamps with the hissing of insects, flapping of wings and thumping of bodies all added to the general mayhem and we found ourselves ducking and diving to dodge the aerial bombardment. With the abundance of nocturnal insects Geckos soon became permanent residents in our home. They have pads on their toes that enable them to walk up walls and even upside down on the ceiling. They would dart in and grab huge moths with their powerful jaws. No matter how much the moth flapped once caught it could not get free and after a while disappeared down the Gecko's throat and the discarded wings would float down to the floor. Geckos have a powerful grip as I found out when I grabbed one that promptly bit me and held on as I flapped my hand around like a moth trying to shake free. On the ground hunting spiders, hairy, large and swift, armed with formidable pincers abounded. Six-inch centipedes scurried in as well as the inevitable scorpions. Big bullfrogs also came to the light at the back door for a feast. They would grab an insect in their mouths and with a big gulp swallow at the same time close their eyes and push down. The insect would disappear. Then their eyes would reopen with a look of profound astonishment and satisfaction. We were taught from an early age not to walk around the house bare foot, to shake our shoes before putting them on and to turn down our sheets and check the bed before climbing in.

There was always great excitement when a snake paid a house call. It would slither in oblivious to the shrieks and panic it caused. All kinds of snakes came, small and large, harmless and dangerous. Dad handled the dangerous ones with ruthless skill. Some were killed with a stick and the really big ones shot with his shotgun. I remember a huge snake that got into the bedroom and another in the kitchen and another under the bath and another…too many to recount. One day dad shot a Black Mamba that got into one of the huts in the compound. It measured nearly twelve feet although they can get up to fourteen. We often had Egyptian Cobras, widespread throughout the whole of Africa, and Spitting Cobras that could spit a stream of venom into one's eyes from ten feet. One day dad stabbed a giant Puff Adder with the point of his umbrella and carried it away in triumph. Once as a child when I went for a stroll in long grass I looked down and saw to my horror a huge Black Mamba lying on top of the grass level with my thighs. Adrenaline took over and my reaction was so fast that I cleared the snake and the grass and was twelve feet away in a fraction of a second. Pythons came at night and raided the chicken coop. They found a way in through the wire mesh but after swallowing several chickens were too bloated to get out and were found in the morning. Sometimes the chickens gave us warning when we heard their hysterical cackling and then someone had to rush to their rescue. Pythons even took dogs. Our friends had a python slither in one day and it swallowed their Dachshund. The evidence was unmistakable, the huge snake with a large bulge in its middle curled up in the dog basket. In our paddock there were mulberry trees that we liked to climb. The fruit attracted birds and in turn these attracted snakes. Very often we shared the trees with several snakes at one time. It was in this way that I learnt how to discover snakes by listening to the chattering alarm cries of the wild birds and to observe them dive bomb the snakes. It was great fun. We had more snakes than we had visitors so I soon lost any real sense of fear of them; they were just another of the many interesting and dangerous things that were quite normal in Africa.

There were numerous other creatures. Large wall spiders abounded in every house. We called them "flatys." The big ones were about three inches across and very flat so could slip into the smallest crack. They could run up walls and even upside down across the ceilings but they sometimes fell on top of us. If they bit then a nasty swelling developed which could develop into a serious infection. Then there were the "putsy" flies. The favourite place for them to lay their eggs was in our underwear hanging on the clothesline. When the clothes were worn the eggs came into contact with warm skin and hatched and the little larva quickly embedded themselves deep in one's flesh where they grew fat feeding on one. As they grew bigger the swelling became painful. One had to be careful not to crush the maggots. They had to be left until large and then they could be coaxed out by placing some petroleum jelly on the breather hole. With air cut off the maggots would stick their heads out to breathe and then they could be gently squeezed out leaving a gaping hole in one's flesh and a nice fat maggot in the hand. One could have several at one time eating away at one's body as I found out and bear the scars to this day. The joys of Africa!

The Little PK House

In those days every house had a little shed at the back of the garden. This was the "little house", PK for short, also known as the "long drop". It was a lavatory constructed over a deep pit. A wooden seat with a hole cut in it was placed over the pit and one sat upon this to relieve oneself. It took some mental discipline to force one's bare bum over the dark interior of the bottomless pit and sit as it were hanging in space. The most interesting part about these little sheds was the assortment of creepy crawlies that made it their dwelling place, everything from big fat transparent Geckos to spiders, wasps, rats and snakes. Sometimes a snake would actually get into the interior of the seat and poke its ugly head out just as one was about to plonk oneself down for one's private business. Very often fast evasive action had to be taken to escape the swift descent of angry hornets for they were avid builders and often constructed a nest in the rafters above the seat of honour. Just when one had stripped to a suitable level and made oneself comfortable on the seat one would notice the nest hanging precariously above with a dozen twitching rear ends armed with long painful stings ready to dart out and deliver a painful jab. This called for one of two choices; either a careful and painstakingly slow withdrawal in order not to arouse their wrath or if the situation demanded, a rapid explosion off the seat and out. It was not unheard of for people to erupt from the shed with shrieks and screams in various stages of undress. One learnt very soon to have a good look around before compromising oneself. Once seated over the dark abyss one could be entranced for hours by the activity of the different creatures that called it home. Spiders in particular were interesting to watch as they spun their webs. Both Black Widow Spiders and Button Spiders made nests in the PK.

It became very much an adventure to walk the long path down to the PK every day and sometimes even at night. In the dark one would imagine all the dangers of Africa lurked nearby. Every shadow, every rustle held potential hazards. Clutching a paraffin lamp one would bravely face the terrors and hurry back as soon as possible. Long shadows danced around one, moths, beetles and other night flyers dive-bombed the light and creepy crawlies slithered along the path. Sometimes the PK seemed an endless distance from the back door and the long walk was an experience no one else could walk for you, you had to walk it by yourself.

The Rhodesian way of Life

Another feature of country homes was the Rhodesian boiler. This consisted of a forty-four gallon drum supported by a brick structure over a furnace. Firewood was collected and stacked ready for burning and every afternoon the furnace was lit to heat the water for the evening baths. The water would emerge from the tap at a slow trickle because of poor pressure but steaming hot. The vicinity of the boiler was favoured by the staff as the place to discuss important issues of the day and the fire was often used to boil a kettle or bake some "spuds". The workers quite often trapped an animal such as a wild cat that had taken fowls and it was at the boiler that I learnt how to skin and salt the pelt in order to preserve it. I began to learn about some amazing creatures.

Homesteads in Africa faced a particular danger, white ants or termites. They could literally eat one out of house and home. Under cover of darkness and with the stealth of an invading army they would invade the home quietly eating away the timber until only a thin veneer was left with nothing inside. The floors, walls, ceilings and roof, even the furniture could be rapidly consumed without one even knowing. The first sign of danger was when one fell through the floor, or the ceiling collapsed, or one's finger went right through a door. One had to be constantly vigilant and defend one's home by spraying poison. Then there were countless other ants of all sizes and colours. The sugar ants were large handsome ants that emerged at night and raided the kitchen. Anything sweet like a bowl of sugar or open jam jar was soon covered in ants with the result that it was impossible to completely remove them and one would have ants in the tea or on the bread. They were professional thieves working under cover of darkness and if the light was switched on would scamper away like naughty children caught in the act of raiding the kitchen. There were also delicate little black ants that industrially worked day and night scurrying along their trails, fetching food or carrying soft white eggs to warmer places for incubation. One night we woke to find our beds invaded by millions of them seeking warmth. Then there were huge Army ants, heavy-duty black jobs over an inch long with long sharp pincers that could nip with a vengeance and rear ends that pumped in poison that stung like the devil. They gave off a strong scent of formic acid, part of their formidable arsenal. They were as fierce as an army of warriors and marched across the terrain hissing like a battalion of Matabele on the warpath. The most spectacular ants were large flying ants up to two inches long and so fat and juicy that when they emerged from their borrows after a storm they attracted every living thing in the vicinity to feed on them from lordly eagles to humble lizards. We called them "thunder ants" because they came out when it thundered. They spiralled upwards in clouds of thousands and drew hundreds of birds; swallows, doves, bulbuls, kestrels and many more. Mongooses, wild cats, honey badgers, monkeys and baboons also fed on them - nothing was too aloof to eat the humble flying ant. As children we would dare one another and into our mouths they would go after we had pulled off the wings.

Old colonial houses had large pantries. These were sealed with a tight fitting gauze door so as to keep ants, cockroaches, weevils and mice out of the food. The verandas were also screened with gauze. Not that this always worked. Snakes came into the house in search of mice and it was impossible to keep weevils and other insects out. We often had extra protein with our flour or porridge. One night we sat down to a meal with guests. First course was noodle soup and it tasted delicious. The guests commented on it and had seconds. However, due to the inevitable extras I found dished up in farm cooking I had developed a habit of examining food very closely and to my shock discovered that most of the noodles were in fact nicely cooked large fat maggots. I dared not breathe a word for fear of bringing the whole house down so closed my eyes and gulped my serving and then sat back and watched in silence as the others relished their helpings. They even had seconds! It was bettered on one other occasion but this time with clear soup. Cook had dished up some tasty soup and comments had been favourable. He was pleased and with a big smile volunteered the technique used. He had strained the soup through dad's socks, but not to worry, he hastily added, "They were dirty socks."

Perishables were kept in a home-made cooler constructed from a double layer of wire netting between which were placed pieces of charcoal. Water was periodically thrown onto the charcoal and with the help of a breeze it cooled by evaporation and the contents kept chilled. Mother eventually managed to purchase a paraffin fridge. She had a regular weekly routine for house chores but had a servant to help. On Monday the laundry was done, a laborious affair bent over a hot tub thumping and squeezing, wringing out the clothes and then pegging them on a long wire in the back yard. Everything smelt of Lifebouy soap, clean and fresh. Tuesday was ironing day, done with an iron full of hot coals. Wednesday was when the floor and furniture was polished using a brand of polish called Cobra Polish which was a fitting name seeing how many snakes called in. And so it went on. Every room had a special day when it was cleaned and dusted from top to bottom. This was necessary because the dust in Africa accumulates at a frightening speed. We children were also given our tasks to do, to make our beds, clean our rooms, polish our shoes, wash the dishes, clean the bath, and other daily chores. Mother did not believe in letting us off lightly. The day that sticks most in my mind was the day when the silver and brass were cleaned. Our house was full of stuff from Ethiopia and North Africa. The "cook" would carry it out to the veranda and put it on newspaper. Out came rags and everything was polished until it gleamed with a rich glow. All the while loud exclamations of encouragement mixed with the latest news and punctuated by jovial outbursts of laughter were exchanged by cook and gardener and anyone else who was within ear shot. Rural Africans were great talkers, shouters is a better description, for their conversations are invariably conducted in the loudest possible decibels irrespective of how close the participants happen to be. This is because it was considered rude to talk in whispers that cannot be heard by everyone for this would mean one was spreading tales. At the end of the morning the silver and brass were proudly carried back and placed where they could be best admired and everyone felt much better for having cleaned them. Polishing days were happy days.

Life on the Ranch
Life on the ranch was primitive and lonely but at times idyllic in simple isolation. Once a month we took a long drive into Bulawayo to stock up on all necessary supplies for the home. There were rations for the labourers; meal, sugar, salt and soap. Members of staff were also given meat when dad shot a buck. Dad never dismounted but shot from the saddle for he had trained his horses to stand still when he fired. This made shooting for rations fairly simple as wild animals

allowed him to approach very near when mounted on horseback. He had learnt how to do this when he was on patrol as a policeman. Dad had a strong and sometimes vocal disdain for anyone who boasted of their hunting abilities, especially anyone who claimed to have shot an elephant. He said he could see no merit in shooting such a magnificent beast so large one could hardly miss. His outspoken comments quickly dampened any hunting tales. I think he had a great admiration for all things wild and he shot only when necessary for the pot. He was a good marksman and seldom needed a second shot to bring down a buck. He always went for the bucks and never the mothers that might have young. He shot Kudu bulls but I know he admired their grace and majesty and hated to hunt them. Nevertheless the labourers had to have a regular provision of meat as well as other vital supplies and he also made some fine *"biltong"* ; strips of salted, dried meat.

At month's end the staff lined up outside dad's office and entered one at a time to receive their wage and rations. They stood as straight as they could and saluted with a loud *"Nkosi."* Then they signed the book beside their name, which usually meant placing a simple cross laboriously made with a shaking hand and much concentration for none of them could write. Then there was the matter of credit or what they called, *"squellet"*. A register was kept of loans and these were deducted from their wage. But more difficult to control was the credit system they conducted between themselves. It was the custom for the men to pool their money month by month and give it all to an individual, the others going without cash in hand and simply living on their rations. In this way every few months one of them received a substantial sum of money with which he could really launch out and buy something desirable like a new jacket, shoes, or some other item of importance. The others would gather around with much jesting and loud exclamations of appreciation as they admired the new purchase and of course it brought great esteem to the purchaser. The greatest prize was a pair of dark glasses. This made the others go wild. Unfortunately too often the valued item was soon lost, stolen or broken but it was good while it lasted.

Dad was also the local dentist, mother the unofficial district nurse. If toothache was severe dad would sit the patient down, firmly grasp the offending tooth with his pliers and working it back and forth with the skill of an expert pull it out. The workers called mother *"Nkosikas"* and she dispensed medicine to them, their wives, their children and their babies. Sometimes they came with appalling injuries. Children fell in cooking fires and sustained deep burns. Sometimes they were scolded with boiling water. Sometimes snakes bit them. They would walk for miles to be attended for ailments of all kinds. There were occasions when a birth had complications and their midwives couldn't cope and dad had to rush the woman to hospital. When they were sick the psychological effects of having a pill often worked wonders. Real "powerful medicine" was an injection and the more painful the better. The workers considered themselves part of our extended family. If anything went wrong they would simply appeal to dad with the words *"Baba Nkosi*, you are our father."

After shopping we would wend our way to Haddon & Sly tea room and there enjoy a treat with smiling waiters in starched tunics bearing down upon us carrying trays loaded with all things nice, cold beers and iced cool drinks, milk shakes and ice creams. If there was time mother would take us off to the old Museum where rows of stuffed animals looked out of glass cases with glassy stares. They enthralled me, the buck, monkeys, and birds. There was so much to see and find out. In Bulawayo I saw my first lion, a sleepy, smelly old beast locked behind huge bars in a brick cage. Then after a full day well spent with all of us thoroughly exhausted we would drive back in the dark getting home late. The return trips were the best part because there were so many animals to see on the road. At every turn there were the bright eyes of Africa caught in the reflection of the car headlamps. The bush was alive. There were buck and wild cats, jackals, owls, hares, bush babies, porcupines and aardvarks and all the other creatures never seen during daylight. Driving at night could be dangerous as large antelope especially Kudu and Impala would sometimes leap in front of a car and even crash down on the bonnet or windscreen causing serious accidents. One of the scariest sights was when a Pennant Wing Nightjar rose like a phantom out of the darkness and fluttered silently in the headlights looking like an apparition. They have a pair of long primary wing feathers that appear very ghostlike. Dad always tried hard to miss any of the nocturnal animals even the smallest. He would stop to let a column of ants cross the road. That impressed me. On these drives Johnny and I would fall asleep to the drone of the old Chevy truck and dream of Africa. The long rank grass over six feet high grew right up to the road verge and crowded in on us. A flash of lightning on the horizon momentarily lit the night sky and the cool cleansing rain in the night air and the sound of crickets chirping above the noise of the engine are impressions that will stay with me for ever. What a place to grow up!

Mother was a teacher and from an early age taught us at home. A room was converted into a classroom and posters stuck on the wall. She got us into reading about Winnie the Pooh and Christopher Robin and Piglet, Eeyore and Owl. I read how Christopher Robin *"spent the morning indoors going to Africa"* but all I had to do to was step outdoors and Africa was all about me. Christopher Robin could only dream of Africa, I was there and instead of a 100 acres of English woods there were 20,000 acres of wild ranch with real African animals. I loved owls but eagles were a close second. At the back of the house in a large tree a pair of Bateleur Eagles had built a nest and had a big white chick. They are beautiful birds with bright crimson faces. I would sneak out to see them and was interested to find what their latest meal had been for at the bottom of the tree lay the skulls and bones of their prey; squirrels, mongooses, snakes and rats. Sometimes I worried if the eagles would catch my special speckled hen. I did not know then that Bateleur eagles do not prey on poultry. She was a beautiful bird and I spent hours in her pen talking to her which she appreciated for she laid lovely big eggs. I told her many times that I would never eat her but one day she was missing. When Sunday lunch came a great roast chicken was dished up and I ate her for she had fallen to Rabson's knife. Such is life! I continued to speak to animals and still do with some success for I am sure they understand much more than we think. As a kid I had many enjoyable conversations with baboons, birds, buck and other creatures.

As children we also listened to conversations on our telephone "party line". Our only means of communication with the outside world was a big black telephone that hung in the hall. It had a handle a bit like a fishing reel which when yanked produced the desired call. About a dozen or more subscribers shared the same line and there was a simple system of rings that enabled callers to indicate which subscriber they were calling. By cranking the handle one could ring the required code in a series of long and short rings. Our code was three shorts and a long but we learnt the rings for other people and when we heard them ringing Johnny and I picked up the receiver to listen to their conversations. We heard a lot of interesting things that way, stuff that children should not hear.

Near Death and a new Start

Those early years became disruptive in painful ways. Our parents found they were not as compatible as they had hoped and began to pull apart. Dad loved the life of freedom on the ranch but with a young family, low income and the isolation, mother began to feel lonely and discontent. It was about this time I caught a bad dose of measles with severe complications and without medical attention nearly died. Johnny too had been seriously ill. All this began to tell so dad moved from the ranch back into town where mother could get a teaching job and we had our first taste of real school.

Dad joined the Native Labour Department that governed African labour regulations and disputes. He started at Gwelo but was soon posted to Selukwe, a small village about twenty miles away nestling in the hills of the Great Dyke. The Dyke is a band of mineral-rich rock which dissects the entire country and is over 300 miles long, the longest linear mass of rocks in the world and clearly visible from outer space. The main industry of Selukwe was the chrome mine with several gold mines in the vicinity and a farming community in the surrounding district. The sound of mine sirens sounding in the dark early hours of the morning was imprinted upon my young mind. The mine had a network of narrow gauge railway lines on which several small steam engines ran. As a special treat we were allowed to ride on them travelling in the engine cab with the fiery furnace radiating heat as the stoker furiously kept up the steam and we whizzed around the steep gradients and sharp curves. One of my most vivid memories of Selukwe was Ferny Creek a popular picnic place with a trickling stream overgrown with ferns and cool undergrowth. There were monkeys and snakes and other exciting things to discover. Once on a picnic when clambering around on the steep banks I grabbed a root only to find it turned into a snake. Screams and excitement followed. Picnics were a regular feature over the weekends and we often went out to wild places where we saw baboons, monkeys and almost invariably, snakes. I became even more interested in everything that moved and the more dangerous the better.

Our Aardvark Den

My interest in creepy crawlies started with those that came into the home but as I grew a little older I ventured forth to seek them outside. Near our home was a large field of scrub to which I resorted to look for beetles, bird nests and lizards. I was astonished at the diversity of life in the incredible world around me. There were *"jongololos"*, a type of large African millipede, *"tok tok"* beetles that derived their name from their habit of thumping the ground with their abdomen, brilliant coloured *"horkor-monikies"* a type of large agama and much more. At the end of the field an Aardvark had dug a tunnel into an anthill. Johnny and his friend decided to enlarge the tunnel and make it into their den. The entrance was about twenty four inches across and went into the anthill for about ten feet where it opened into a small chamber where they kept a candle and box of matches to give light. About half way down they "reinforced" the tunnel with some old planks from a fruit box. I was allowed into the den and had to worm my way down the tunnel crawling on my belly and at the end could sit awkwardly in the chamber. We also used to crawl down the storm drain pipes. They were quite wide and went for hundreds of yards. At the time we thought we were very clever.

Life was idyllic until my first encounter with hospital. I had a hernia so I was admitted to the tiny government hospital. Came the day of the op and I was wheeled into the theatre and held down on the table by two strong nurses and a pad clamped firmly over my face that forced me to breath in chloroform. I struggled. Nightmarish patterns whirled around my brain and rushing sounds filled my head until I ceased kicking and woke up later with a horrible headache and painful groin.

The Royal Tour

Selukwe was a small community and everyone knew everyone else. One family was the Smiths. They had a butchery and bakery. They were well liked by all and their son Ian just back from the war was in politics. Everyone was loyal to King and country and the national anthem was sung at every function and school assembly. Then the King died and overnight the young princess was thrust into the limelight. She was on a visit to Kenya watching elephants at the time and it was there in the heart of the African bush that she got the sad news of her father's death. When Queen Elizabeth was crowned the euphoria of being British grew. I also noticed that mother could have been the Queen's older sister for she looked so much like her with similar mannerisms.

Southern African links with the British crown went to the very crown itself for in the crown placed upon the head of the young princess was a large diamond cut from a huge stone found in 1905 in the Premier Mine of the Transvaal. This diamond weighed 3106 carats and in 1907 was given to King Edward V11 for his 66th birthday present. It was cut into nine large gems and more than one hundred small ones. The largest was set in the British royal sceptre. The size of a hen's egg it weighed 530 carats. The next largest weighed 317 carats and was set into the Royal Crown that was placed on the head of Queen Elizabeth at her coronation. They were the crowning jewels from her loyal subjects in Africa and seemed to symbolise the close links we had with her. It was inconceivable that one day all this would end.

The Rhodesians set their affections on the young queen and at her coronation the whole country was a-buzz with excitement. Then the Queen Mother and Princess Margaret paid Rhodesia an official visit in 1953. The Queen Mother was immensely popular and large crowds gathered wherever the Royal party toured; the local whites cheered and Africans took off their hats in respect. We all went into Gwelo and stood by the side of the road and waved our little Union Jacks as the official entourage drove by. It was not the first time she had come to see us. She had accompanied King George in 1947 when she brought both her daughters, Princess Elizabeth and Princess Margaret. Special cups and other memorabilia were issued to commemorate the visits and we all felt so proud to be British.

Federation of Central Africa - 1953

1953 was the year of the inauguration of the Federation of Rhodesia and Nyasaland a federation of three countries, Northern Rhodesia, Southern Rhodesia and Nyasaland. Each country had its own government and there was a central Federal Government as well which related to the British government. Five governments to administer it! After her coronation one of the first things the Queen did was to sign it into being. A British spokesman said of it that it was *"the only practicable means by which the three Central African territories can achieve security for the future and ensure the well-being of all their peoples."* The prospects seemed infinitely good and it had the potential to *"become a state as great as Canada as well as a bulwark against the rising menace of communism in Africa."* Its constitution was so strong that in the opinion of the British Secretary of State the Federation *"could only be liquidated by the unanimous consent of all four governments plus the British government."* Other colonies in Africa also formed a federation; Kenya, Tanganyika and Uganda.

The Federation depended largely on the wealth of Northern Rhodesia's copper mines. The other member of the Federation, Nyasaland, bordered a huge inland lake rich in fish, part of the Rift Valley system. It was also a good farming region for tea and tobacco and developed a strong agriculture industry. Southern Rhodesia was the main manufacturing partner and had an extensive mining industry with gold, asbestos, nickel and other important minerals as well as many productive farms. The Federation promised great potential and recruitment in Britain was started. White settlers were encouraged to come and many came to settle permanently.

Everything looked hopeful, everyone was patriotic: *"We're part of the British Empire, God Save the Queen, Britannia rules the Waves"* and *"The sun never sets on the British Empire"* were popular catch phrases. However, behind the scenes there were mixed motives in forming the Federation. After the Second World War Britain decided to liquidate the Empire and embarked on a fast track policy of ridding itself of its colonies and dependencies. Yet in the midst of this Britain set up the Federation. Against all the trends of the time Britain approved such a venture. Why? Behind the decision were disturbing factors. The South African election of 1948 had put white Boer nationalists in power. The Central African Federation was formed as a liberal counterpoise to the Afrikaner bastion in the south and a buffer against communist interests to the north. It would also block whites in Southern Rhodesia attempting to join South Africa something Britain feared. Britain also needed raw materials to develop its own industry and Western based Companies established financial empires and reaped big dividends. A majority hand-over would be delayed but this delay ultimately led to conditions that would give rise to Rhodesia's Unilateral Declaration of Independence, UDI.

Rhodesia Loyal to Britain

Generally Rhodesians were loyal to the crown. During WW1 large numbers volunteered and over sixty percent of the white male population were on active duty. This commitment to the home country was not new for during the Anglo-Boer War many men fought for Britain. When the Second World War broke out many young men enlisted; some served as pilots and others fought in various army corps. Rhodesia gave a higher number of fighting men in proportion to her overall white population than any other British colony. Africans also served in various African corps. During the war Rhodesian farmers served the British cause by growing food. In Britain's darkest hour many Rhodesians heard the call and responded. Among them was young Ian Smith who joined the Airforce Training Wing which operated at Guineafowl just outside Gwelo. Southern Rhodesia became home for the Air Training Group which contained 14 separate units, 10 of them flying schools where pilots from all over the Commonwealth trained for the British war effort.

Smith saw service in the Middle East and North Africa and was shot down over Italy and spent several months behind enemy lines fighting with the local resistance movement. He escaped and resumed active service. He later became Prime Minister and was to declare independence from Britain. I doubt whether a PM born in Britain would have done so. However, it was a sad day when British citizens who gave so much for Britain and served her loyally felt compelled to break links with their motherland. The question is, "What made them do it?" Something went terribly wrong as we shall see.

Amongst all the jubilation of the Royal visit mother needed a break from dad and got a job at Guineafowl which had been converted into a school and here we got our first taste of boarding in the old barrack rooms. Mother had a room in the staff quarters but Johnny and I were in the barracks and had to fend for ourselves. I think I was the youngest. I can still remember the lonely nights when I needed mother and would cry for her. Then the others would tease me as a "cry baby". It was a lonely time. Sometimes mother came to the barracks to see how we were. This was worse because then I was teased as "mother's baby". Children will be children and fights were inevitable. I recall one night a fellow traveller picked on me and went too far in name-calling. A full-scale brawl broke out with Johnny yelling encouragement and the whole barracks in a frenzy. The fight seemed to last for ages as our bodies went over and under beds from one end of the barracks to the other in the style of a Wild West brawl until I emerged the victor only just.

When dad and mother reunited we moved to a small town called Gatooma the centre of farming and mining. Mother went on teaching and became deputy head at the local school and dad went on solving labour disputes. Gatooma was the centre of a cotton growing area and had a large cotton mill. There were disputes among the workers but dad had a way with people and his sense of fair play and justice won him respect from both workers and management and he was successful in solving problems.

These were our "good days" in Africa, the government was secure and life was stable, most people had sufficient food and many had access to clinics, hospitals and even schools as education made huge progress. However, many African people felt oppressed. The first rumblings of concern came from the north. People began talking about killings and uprisings sweeping through the continent. The rise of African Nationalism became a regular subject for debate among whites during evening sun-downers, a custom in many homes. The Saturday sun-downer was our second great treat as children for on Saturdays we could join in and have a soft drink. After the heat of the day as the sun went down the grown-ups poured themselves a stiff toddy, the kids would have a Hubbly Bubbly or some other cool drink and all would relax on the *"stoep"* (veranda) or lawn discussing the latest news which revolved around subjects such as whether there would be good rains that season, how the latest cattle sale had gone, the man who had been gored by a buffalo or the woman taken by a crocodile while drawing water. A new subject became popular, the Mau Mau killings in Kenya. We listened with bated breath to snatches of conversation about people being hacked to death, secret blood rites and cattle being mutilated. Early impressions on my young mind at that time were that Africa was a savage place but very exciting.

Trouble in Kenya – The Mau Mau - 1952

After supper every night dad turned on the radio to listen to the BBC World Service. It was a religious routine. World News followed the chimes of Big Ben and then no one dared speak a word as dad listened intently to the state of world affairs. Crises were everywhere and of course there was "cold war" and deteriorating events in Eastern Europe. What dad mostly wanted to hear was the "State of Emergency" in Kenya declared in 1952. Whites were murdered in their homes and Africans violently killed in secret rituals. Cattle were hamstrung. The country was in high tension. "Mau Mau" meaning "Hidden Ones" was a group of nationalists who used secret rites to initiate members into killing anyone who stood in the way of attaining Independence. The British administration did not negotiate but brought in reinforcements and together with colonial forces they hunted the Mau Mau. It took several years of harsh conflict before it was concluded. What my parents found disturbing were the tales about faithful employees collaborating in these gruesome murders. It seemed no one was safe for even after years of service some workers would turn on their white employers and slit their throats. It was enough to put the jitters in you but Kenya was far away and everyone said it could never happen to us and life went on.

Sputnik

On the 4th October 1957 Russia launched "Sputnik" into orbit. It caused great excitement and much discussion in the evenings about what man would achieve next. People sat glued to their radios to hear about it. Old timers who had trekked into the country with an ox wagon shook their heads in wonder. Who would have thought man could put a satellite into space. As more satellites were launched it became a favourite game for us at Saturday sun-downers to sit on the lawn and view them as they passed overhead. African nights are crystal clear and one can see forever it seemed. Right across the sky stretches the vast expanse of Milky Way with countless stars and we would have competitions to see who could find Orion, the Dipper, Leo and of course the Southern Cross. Dad would bring out his old telescope and when the moon was full we would try and count the craters. The idea that one day someone would walk upon it was quite preposterous. For us the rest of the world was a long way off and life undisturbed except for the latest raid by lions on nearby ranches.

The Circus Lions

There were no lions in the immediate vicinity of where we now lived and my first contact with them was at a circus. When Boswell Circus came to town we all went to see it. Karl Fisher the lion trainer had a great act. The climax of his show came when he grabbed his favourite lion by the jaws, prized wide its mouth and thrust his head between its gaping fangs. Everyone held their breath and no doubt he did too for the smell must have been awful. With the crash of cymbals and the sound of a fanfare the act ended with a flourish as Fisher emerged unhurt from the lion's mouth. However, during one act there was a mistake and the lion closed his mouth too soon and Fischer squirmed around in the ring trying to get his head out before the lion acquired a taste for his blood. Eventually he managed to prize the mouth open and get out dripping blood. It was nearly the end of his career but the people loved it.

There were many stories about the early days in Rhodesia and one went somewhat along the lines of Karl Fischer's act. Apparently a couple of old timers in Wankie who were out of money decided to start their own circus with an old semi-tame toothless lion in captivity. They attempted to train the animal and put on a similar act for the locals with one of them getting into the cage. Fortunately he managed to get in and out without getting eaten and it went down well with the locals. It reminds one of a statement the President of Zambia once made of Britain many years later when he called it a "toothless bulldog."

Childhood Impressions of African Culture
Growing up in the 1950s my impression of African culture was shaped by my limited childhood perceptions. I saw dad show respect to Africans and he had a certain admiration for their unfamiliar customs but he got exasperated when things went wrong which often happened. This was due to the language barrier and a general lack of training and expertise among the people. In the 1950s there was fairly good rapport between the races and dad was a master at diplomacy and they respected him for this. I never heard mother be impolite to anyone and she always championed the under dog. So we were not brought up with a deliberate bias but somehow things deteriorated. I think horrendous killings elsewhere in Africa began to affect whites. As children we eavesdropped on conversations and picked up crucial points that established our values and I heard whites being disrespectful and rude. Some settlers described Africans in a derogative manner as "cutters of wood and carriers of water." This seemed a fair description of their main activity and function; the men were forever cutting trees and the women balanced large water pots expertly on their heads as they made their way in single file along meandering bush paths. The men would carry nothing and walked ahead of the women who came along behind at a discreet distance and carried the suitcases, the wood, the water pots, the babies and everything else too. However, their culture and way of life was different and some whites did not seem to appreciate that Africans did not have electrical power or running water; they had to fetch wood from the bush and water from the river.

I remember the great frustrations mother had when trying to keep food from being pilfered. Cook had a voracious appetite for all things sweet such as sugar, jam and honey and these had to be kept under lock and key. Copper pennies had to be hidden away. The big Rhodesian pennies had a hole in the middle so that they could be strung and made into a necklace which was the way Africans carried them. Yet we would often go out leaving the whole house unlocked and return to find nothing disturbed. They were a paradoxical people testing ones patience to breaking point and then suddenly coming out with a disarming smile and unexpected generosity. They were loveable and hospitable and the average white fitted easily into the patronising role of surrogate parent.

Their value system was very different from the whites. African people were more community minded in their culture. The chief owned everything on behalf of the people. There were private possessions like cattle but the elders and chief had a large say. Land was communal but allocated to individuals within the community. All this bred the concept that everyone shared everything. Therefore the master's property was there for everyone and they had no hesitation about sharing it. After all, whites were their "fathers and mothers" and having some benefits was in their opinion acceptable. It was a losing battle to keep things safe from their quick fingers. Some of them made sharing an art and could crack any system. For example if there were six packets of rice in the pantry all would go well until one came to the final packet. On opening it one would discover it full of sand. From the outside it looked good. Of course no one had any idea as to how the sand got there.

Generally, African people were happy, helpful and polite. They loved to please and spoke with this in mind irrespective of how true it was. When travelling in rural areas dad would stop to ask how far our destination was. Invariably the answer was *"maningi duzi"*, very close. This was because we were travelling in a car but the answer may have been different if we were walking, then it was *"maningi katchana"*, very far. Many miles further on when he asked again the same answer would be given. This was their philosophy, to always please and any other answer simply would not do. They were easy-going and laid-back, stoical in nature accepting things as they came. Maybe they had learnt this from the harshness of Africa which is far too big to fight. They were masters of procrastination having developed it to a fine art. The whites would rush around, shout and rave and get things done but get worn out in the process whereas Africans would plod along at their own pace and conserve their energy knowing that tomorrow would come soon enough. Their philosophy was not to worry about anything except their immediate needs. This was most frustrating for whites but whites had heart attacks whereas they did not. The African way was to let things work at their own pace and time.

They were a people held in a religion that strengthened this concept. Whatever happened was the will of the ancestors, there was little one could do to avoid it. When adversity came they accepted it and faced pain with little emotion. Some people did not seem to show sensitivity to the sufferings of others whether animal or human and I saw incidents of cruelty but noticed if asked that the perpetrators would look genuinely nonplussed and unable to comprehend what the fuss was about. When I grew older I came to the conclusion that two things contributed towards this mind set, the general harsh conditions most had grown up in and the religion under which they lived which gave them inner strength but sometimes robbed them of emotion and held them in bondage. Most showed great love for their children and families, and sacrificed their own well being for them. They were the most loyal and passionate of friends.

African superstitions kept them bound in fear. Chameleons were held in dread. They would not touch one for fear of death. Just the sight of us handling a chameleon gained instant attention. Chameleons are not venomous and rely on tactics of intimidation and can change colour from a lovely placid green to a terrible shade of black, puff out their throat and hiss in a fearful manner. Normally, however, they are quite benign creatures. A chameleon can look in different directions at the same time. Its eyes work independently and one can look in front and one behind simultaneously. They would slowly stalk their prey, usually a fly, their little eyes revolving in all directions and as Lobengula had said suddenly out came their long sticky tongue with a lightning *zap* and the fly was gone in a flash. The sight of us children carrying chameleons made local people recoil in horror and when we realised this we could not resist the urge to chase them holding the chameleon extended at arm's length and yelling at the top of our lungs. The poor people would scatter with screams of terror that mingled with our screams of glee. Africans were superstitious of other creatures. Owls were a cause of foreboding and if one alighted on a house or hut and hooted there would soon be a death they said. Hyenas were the most dreaded of all creatures for they were ridden by "witchdoctors" who in the dead of night conducted "house calls" to villages. Any sign of a hyena was considered a terrible thing. This is understandable when one listens to the hideous laughter of a gang of hyenas in feeding frenzy.

Africans gave names to their children that vividly illustrated their disposition and philosophy to life. Babies were often named according to the circumstances of their birth. Names such as Happiness, Beauty, and Precious spoke volumes. Lovemore, Honesty and Proud reflected the pride of the parents. Other names such as Sugar and Sweetness reflected their love of sweet things. Sometimes things went wrong and names such as Sadness and Loveless told the story. Other names were Sixpence, Shilling, Ticky and Salt-full. Many had Biblical names learnt from the missions such as Elias, Philemon and Isaac - they loved the prophets.

As white children we mixed freely with African children of our own age. Children are not aware of inequalities as adults are. We all played bare foot in the dust of Africa. We ran along the twisting bush paths, swam bare-bummed in the rivers, climbed the trees and shared *"sadza"*, the staple diet of Africa which was a stiff porridge made from maize meal. It was eaten by rolling portions in the hands and then dipping the balls into a central bowl of relish or meat. We all sat around the fire and dipped together into the same pot.

Two great killers in Africa are malaria and bilharzia (Schistosomiasis). The Rhodesian government did much to curb them but it was impossible to grow up in Africa and not catch bilharzia. Every river and dam was infested with it and as we often swam catching it was unavoidable. Not that we had permission to swim, in fact our parents forbade it but we often paddled in the *"spruit"* and when older sneaked out of the house at night to the local dam where we had "midnight swims." The warm nights of Africa made these swims very enjoyable and the hot days of summer made the *spruits* and rivers irresistible. Of course there were greater dangers lurking in the rivers. Crocodiless were there too but we missed them or they missed us. The treatment for bilharzia was in itself punishment enough for our disobedience. A long course of injections followed every infection. Malaria was more serious and we took quinine every week. Fortunately neither of us got it but mosquitoes were abundant during the wet months and we slept under nets which also kept out spiders and bugs.

"I am about to kill you"

It was a great time to be alive. Everything was deceptively peaceful but underneath was a volcano about to explode. Even in those days there was a rising tide of dissent bordering on hatred. One day I had an experience that brought the fragility of life unmistakably to my notice and stamped it indelibly upon my mind. A young man currently employed in the garden took a dislike to me. I may have said something disrespectful but one day when I was alone at our isolated farm surrounded by bush he decided to get me. He approached me and grabbed me with his long powerful fingers in a vice like grip around my throat.

"I am about to kill you" he said with a deadpan face and a demonic gleam in his dull eyes as his fingers twisted like steel cords around my neck. I was helpless in his iron grip.

I was only a young child and there was nothing I could do. I tried my best to keep composure and looked him straight in his eyes. He glared back at me and after an eternity he changed his mind, let go and swaggered off, leaving me relieved but in shock. The incident had a profound and enduring influence on me. I was badly shaken and like so many children felt that I was to blame and was guilty of something terrible. I was too afraid to tell my parents because I believed then he really would kill me. It had a permanent effect on me. I clamped up and never said a word to anyone and could not forget. From that day I watched my back. As a child I had trusted people. That was now over for I lost my innocence about human nature and was introduced to the dark ways of humanity that lurked beneath the veneer of law and order.

Colonial Administration

At that time whites were in control of all aspects of administration. There were less than a hundred thousand whites in the whole country but they controlled the entire infrastructure, government, police, justice, industry, commerce and agriculture. They also had most of the benefits. However, Africans were not entirely neglected. At the time of Federation in 1953 they numbered about three million in Southern Rhodesia. When the Pioneers first trekked into the country there were an estimated three hundred and fifty thousand people scattered throughout it. White settlement brought stability. Conflicts between the tribes ended and improved health facilities and better food production contributed to a rapid explosion of population. Mission and government hospitals were built and vaccination and immunisation programs were set up. At the time of the Federation indigenous people benefited as income became available for their development. African primary schools were built as well as rural clinics and hospitals. But advancement was slow compared to the whites who were less in number. The land needed roads, bridges, electricity, water systems and much more. In pre-colonial days proper farms did not exist. The local people simply threw in a few seeds of sorghum and maize and herded their goats and cattle. They had a slash, burn and move on method of agriculture. When a field became unproductive they simply made another field somewhere else. The people mostly chose to cultivate sandy soils as these were easier to till with hand hoes and many Shona people lived in or near granite hills where they took refuge from Matabele raids. The white settlers chose clay soils but it is nevertheless true that the administration claimed good areas and allocated Africans marginal or fringe areas less suited to intensive farming. It must be remembered, however, that no Africans were farming extensively. Lions still roamed the country which was by no means cultivated. When the infamous Land Tenure Act was passed thousands of people were moved from "white areas" to "African areas" and this caused much hardship. At this time white settlers awarded themselves vast tracts of land. The Land Apportionment Act of 1931 declared millions of acres open to whites as well as the millions awarded in 1925. The result of this policy was that poorer sandy land began to support greater numbers of African people while white farmers grew a greater harvest that could support a far larger population than the old methods of slash and burn. However, most people still grew food for themselves and archives show that although poor and conditions harsh they were often healthy and the population began to rapidly increase.

African Ways

African people love to talk and will do so for hours periodically bursting into laughter for they can find humorous anecdotes in the most common events. When we travelled on the dusty roads they would lift their hats and wave in cheerful acknowledgement as we passed in our vehicles unfortunately leaving them covered in a cloud of dust and spluttering for air. The *"umfaans"* ran from their huts and shouted greetings and waved to us from the roadside and we responded with smiles and waves. Africans were hospitable and if one visited their huts they would emerge with a gift no matter how poor they were. Sometimes it was a pumpkin, or a chicken, or a tin mug of sweet milky tea, and if it was beer brewing season then a mug of thick, grainy *"chibuku,"* the African home brew beer made from sorghum and other grain. Africans worked miracles of their own for their income was not high yet most people had basic necessities. Workers and their families were supplemented with rations; meat, fuel, uniforms and accommodation. They kept vegetable gardens behind their huts and had a field for maize. They also caught flying ants and locusts and Mopani caterpillars which were tasty and eaten with relish. At times trees would be covered in them, large, hairy bright yellow and orange caterpillars. To prepare them to eat one simply held one end and squeezed and out popped the unpalatable insides leaving the flesh to be sun-dried after the hairs had been scorched off. Africans loved a party and sometimes they would sing beautiful harmony but most weekends the drums would beat out the monotonous, monotone sounds of Africa all through Saturday night waxing and waning as the beer drinking and dancing fluctuated until they were in a drunken stupor by Sunday morning.

Funerals were treated with demonstrations of emotional grief with mourners wailing and ululating, women collapsing and the mourning going on all day. They certainly knew how to hold a wake. Large amounts of beer were consumed and a cow killed and eaten. Then possessions left by the deceased had to be divided among relatives, some claiming more than others, so tension was high. Seldom did a widow get anything. When it came to funerals every employee had about six mothers, countless brothers, sisters, aunts, uncles and endless other relatives whose funerals they had to attend and every funeral required several days off work. The annoying thing was that people died at the most awkward times especially over Christmas holidays.

Africans very quickly summed up a European's character with his or her strengths or weakness often giving them a name that pointed to their prominent characteristic. So employers got names like *"Ngulube"* (warthog) if he had a big handlebar moustache that reminded them of the upturned tusks of a warthog, or if he had a particularly handsome beard *"Mandevu"* (bearded one) or *"Nyati"* (buffalo) if he was grumpy, and so on. They were very observant but invariably polite, respectful and diplomatic. It was rude to come directly to a point in conversation or ask a question. This had to be done in a round about manner after a long excursion touching on everything else under the sun. I learnt some of these things from *"Madala"* (elder) who lived in the little hut behind our house and who always welcomed me when I called on him. He was ancient and mysterious. I heard it said of him and I certainly believed him to be a Matabele *induna*, perhaps one who had fought Alan Wilson. He had only one eye which had a cataract over it. The other eye was gone completely and all that remained was an empty red socket. This never ceased to catch my attention for he seemed to gaze at me from the empty hole but he never told me how he lost it. Perhaps it was when he fought the whites I decided. He had lots of stories to tell. He had known the great white chief "Lodes," he said with a dull twinkle in his one eye and his face wrinkled in a thousand crevasses as the memory brought a smile. "Yes, Lodes was indeed a great chief." He could not pronounce the 'r' of Rhodes. "Lodes had saved the Matabele people from perpetual war and brought "peace and prosperity," he told me. I believed him. Then there was the matter of his secret gold mines and a vast treasure of diamonds. He knew where there was so much gold that a whole regiment of soldiers could not carry it away but this was a secret he could tell no one. "You must hurry and grow up quickly so that we can go together to collect the treasure," he said to me. Yes, he would take me there but I must tell nobody. Was it King Lobengula's treasure I wondered? Rumours were that the king had fled with his gold and diamonds and they were buried in a secret cave in the bush and no one but his closest *indunas* knew where. So I was determined that when older we would go together and fetch the treasure and become rich but I took too long and he died. He also told me that one day the whites would leave. I said "no" but he chuckled with a dull glimmer in his cataract eye.

Changing Times

As I grew older the country changed. The 1946 census, the year when I was born, gave the number of whites in the country as 82,382 and Africans as 1,607,000. All men had to carry *"situpas"*, identification papers, on which was all necessary information about the bearer; where they were born, their birthday often unknown, and their signature usually a mark such as a cross. Africans were divided into two main groups; the Shona had been there for over a thousand years but the Matabele arrived in the 19th century. The Shona then suffered some persecution. Evidence for this was still visible. Early settlers found bones of victims lying scattered in the bush where they fell when fleeing the Matabele. White children whose families settled in these areas played with skulls and leg bones and built little dens with them. Under British administration infant mortality dropped and adults lived longer. When I was at school I learnt that the population was now three million and increasing. From a few hundred thousand in 1890 they had increased to several millions. At the time of early white settlement there had been vast tracts of empty land. A witness at the raising of the Union Jack wrote: *"On September the 12th 1890, we held a grand parade and in the name of the Queen formally took possession of all the un-possessed land in South Central Africa."* The settlers considered the locals not to have possessed all the land for much of it was still empty.

Many early settlers gave up the hardships in this untamed land and returned from whence they came. Those who remained battled on against the odds; many perished, killed in uprisings or dying of disease or through accidents and wild animals. A few succeeded and made a pathway for others to follow. Their indomitable courage built a land out of a wilderness and despite the difficulties the settlers dragged a people caught in a time warp into the twentieth century. Central Africa never experienced the numbers of settlers that America had and where great numbers of indigenous people died of sickness and other causes.

Rather, it was the coming of settlers that caused a population explosion. When settlers first arrived a non-racial society was impossible, the cultures were just too far removed. When missionaries set up hospitals the people were afraid of them for they had their own *"ngangas"* (doctors) and *"muti"* (herbal remedies) and they looked on hospitals as places where people died. It took years of work and education to bring change. As the country progressed the world did too, faster than the country. I found myself in a time warp without even knowing it. We were brought up under the values our elders had given us, values of white supremacy, but these values were rapidly changing and the British Empire was collapsing. What had been considered noble a few years before was fast becoming expendable and despised. Europeans in Africa were beginning to feel a trifle insecure trapped in their own time warp and a rapidly changing situation.

The state of affairs in the country became more and more a topic for discussion. Dad discussed it for hours but he never really let anyone know who he supported politically. He was of the old school and truly believed that his vote should be kept secret and as a civil servant he should not be active in politics. One day on the way home we stopped by the house of Bill Harper and he and dad spoke at length, Harper leaning over the garden gate. He was the leader of the Dominion Party, the forerunner of the Rhodesian Front. He evidently presented many things to dad for he waved his arms, shook his head and shrugged his shoulders. I didn't understand any of it but stormy days lay ahead. I can truthfully say that I never heard or saw my parents abusing people, either verbally or physically. Dad showed all people dignity mixed with quiet humour. There was a rapport between the races although some whites were harsh. Mother had grown up with Africans and she had a heart for them. She would not stand by and see anyone mistreated in any way and was known to speak her mind. Dad was firm but fair. He told me that people should treat one another as if they were totally alone in the bush. "Imagine" he said "that you were miles away in the bush walking along a path and someone came walking along the same path towards you. How would you treat them?" I knew what he meant for as a child I would wander alone in the bush and was not afraid until I met someone then I would hide. The way of people in Africa as they approached one another was to greet one other from a distance. A loud conversation would follow during which the intentions of the other party were established. If friendly they would then approach closer and become more intimate. There would be no arrogant superiority or rudeness by either person but each would be polite and win the friendship of the other for life itself might depend upon it.

The Great Treks South

It was the custom in those days for families to embark on a *"great trek"* to the sunny beaches of the Union of South Africa. It was a three day journey in dad's old 1947 Chevy truck and all manner of hazards had to be negotiated. Dad was very proud of his old Chevy. It was khaki in colour, had a divided windscreen, stylish front mudguards on which were mounted head lamps and a high radiator grill on the front of the bonnet. He referred to the truck as her but called her the *"Iron Duke"* the question of genders not being important and he made some benches in the back for us kids to sit on. Roads were narrow strips of tar built during the depression years of the twenties and later by Italian prisoners rounded up by dad in the war years. In order for vehicles to pass they had to get off the narrow strips onto the dirt and billows of dust and stones flew up. Because holidays were usually at Christmas which was the wet season there was added danger of flooding of low-level bridges. Rivers were often raging torrents from bank to bank with travellers stranded on either side and I recall times when we sat on the banks waiting for the water to subside sufficiently to cross. At such times little camps mushroomed with people waiting patiently often days at a time. Fires with kettles boiling, people chatting exchanging news and views, dripping wet, mud and water, these are the images in my mind. Slowly the river dropped and someone would roll up their trousers and venture onto the bridge to test the depth. When it was low enough braver drivers would inch across guided by someone wading ahead. Some vehicles were swept away. Once, as we inched across a swollen river, I felt the big truck sway in the powerful current but dad revved the engine and the tyres gripped again. At last we got to the border between Rhodesia and South Africa at the Limpopo River. It was a fascinating river and Kipling wrote about it in his "Just So Stories", for it was here at the *"Great, grey, green, greasy Limpopo all set about with Fever trees that Elephant got his trunk, best beloved."* In his story it was a crocodile that pulled the elephant's trunk to its present length. When we got to the river there were still crocodiles in it and they lay basking on the sand banks. All along the narrow, winding roadside mighty baobab trees stood like statues and the rugged hills crowded in around us. This was the stuff of Africa.

During my childhood we embarked on several trips south. They were our equivalent of the *"great treks"* that the Boers undertook when they trekked from the Cape away from the British. They were brave people who loaded their wagons, in-spanned their oxen and faced great obstacles in order to make a new life in the heart of Africa. Our treks were in the opposite direction and by the time we got to the sea dad and mother were worn out and needed the holiday more than ever. Dad was a steady driver seldom going over forty-five miles an hour and we slowly progressed towards our destination. I spent the time counting raptors perched on telephone posts. Raptors were so common that almost every second post, tree and fence had one on it. The cables were laden with thousands of Swallows, Swifts, Rollers and other birds. The numbers and variety were truly amazing. Secretary birds, Korhaans, Bustards and other birds strolled across the grasslands filled with fluttering Whydahs all in a flurry because it was nesting time. There were millions of birds! When we arrived in Durban we drove north on a track through thick jungle to a Catholic boarding home near Umhlanga Rocks. Those days were warm and sunny and the beach littered with shells with rock pools full of marine life. When we went to town we went for rides in the rickshaws and big Zulu men pulled them dressed in traditional finery complete with massive bull horns on their heads. They would leap in the air and prance down the road like royal warriors. Oh how the mighty had fallen, a Zulu warrior pulling tourists like an ox!

Those were the days when Union Castle ships ferried people to Africa. There was the *Rhodesia Castle* and the *Kenya Castle,* the *Balmoral Castle* and the *Arundel Castle* among others, and they carried young hopefuls to a new life in Africa. We went to the harbour and saw the big ships come in and went on board some of them. Dad loved the sea and enjoyed the ships. There was also Durban Snake Park where we could lean over the walls and gaze mesmerised at snakes. We recognised them for they were our neighbours back home. What glorious days all too soon over and then came the long haul home. Johnny and I would sleep in the back and dad slowly drove the miles away.

Mother once more left dad and got a job at a farm school near Norton where the first massacres took place at the outbreak of the Shona rebellion in 1896. An isolated family of white farmers at Porta Farm were massacred and their home burnt down. However, the district was now peaceful and the school was situated among huge gum trees in an idyllic setting. I went with mother and stayed in the dorm at school. It was a good and a bad time. I had to fend for myself. Once again I cried my eyes out every night and felt totally abandoned. However, I found lots of little creatures to keep me content. I found two abandoned baby bats and nursed them with an eyedropper. They were cute, grew strong and eventually flew off. It was the wet season and after thunder storms all the children would romp around in the puddles. A wealth of wild life could be found in them; water beetles that could give a nasty bite, water scorpions that were harmless, big vivid green and yellow Goliath Bull Frogs weighing up to 1kg and other strange creatures. Flying ants emerged in their droves and everything looked and felt so much fresher and hopeful after drenching rains had cooled the land after the long hot summer months. October was called *"suicide month"* because of its intense heat and humidity and everyone's nerves were stretched to breaking point. Once the rains broke, however, tempers cooled and life became bearable again. Then the flying ants came out in their millions, big, fat and fresh and many were eaten, either raw or fried. When fried they tasted like bacon. Other delicacies were green crickets that gathered at night around the streetlights. They tasted like peanut butter. Then there was the boarding school menu with Bread and Butter Pudding a speciality; to this day I cannot eat it.

A Lonely Childhood

When mother got back with dad we moved to a small house on a ranch outside Gatooma. Things began to look up. This is where I really got into bush life. There were no neighbours and I had no friends but we had an aviary with birds and tortoises and all kinds of waifs and orphaned creatures.

There was the loveable little baby monkey that was a total reprobate, completely untrustworthy and able to inflict a nasty bite. There was little *"Pembwe"* the baby duiker. She was delightful with big soft eyes and the wettest of noses. We nursed her and she grew strong eating out of our hand the lush alfalfa grown for the horses. The day came when dad insisted she should go free but she hung around the homestead for months and eventually had a baby of her own. One evening she came back with it and although we could not touch it we felt especially happy that she brought it back to show us. There was a Long Tailed Shrike, a little terror that grew up on grasshoppers and never failed to dominate all who came in contact with him. We pulled the legs off the grasshoppers before giving them to him but when he was big he just ate them legs and all after bashing them senseless on his perch. These were the days when children could still be children and there was time to do lots of things. I liked to get away and spent hours alone in the bush. Sometimes I would take a frying pan and some eggs and after a long walk make a fire and cook what I considered a slap up meal. The doves I sometimes caught tasted especially nice freshly plucked and roasted on a stick over an open fire. I learnt what wild fruits were edible and I plucked figs and wild plums for pudding. I learnt how to recognise tracks of wild animals, little mongooses and wildcats, springhares, buck and many others. It was very exciting. As a child I had psychological problems but being young was not able to deal with them. This caused isolation from family and friends. To add to my difficulties my parents were Victorian in outlook and behaviour. There was little outward expression of affection, no cuddles or hugs and not a lot of laughter. I remember once dad gave me a short embrace after I fell off my pony at a gallop. I lay on the rough ground with the wind knocked out of me and my side grazed and was sobbing when he found me and comforted me. It was almost worth the fall to get it. Mother was withdrawn and the best she could manage was an occasional peck on my forehead. Because of the lack of affection and emotional problems I had no one to go to. Instead I withdrew into myself and spent time alone in the bush.

Sometimes fierce fires swept through the bush and threatened our tiny homestead. One night we awoke to the crackle of a raging bush fire. The noise of an approaching bush fire is very alarming for anyone who may be in its path. This one approached at a deafening roar. What a sight! The flames leapt up tree trunks and licked the highest tinder-dry twigs, consumed the six foot grass and gave the night sky an eerie glow with sparks floating everywhere in smoke-drenched air. Dad called out the workers and with green branches and wet sacks they beat the flames. Mother had the pump going and hosed down the walls and roof of the house. Johnny and I did what we could by stamping out little flames that crept too close. At the end of an hour a weary blackened team eventually got control and extinguished the flames. What a dramatic scene of scorched earth. Fires were not only spectacular but could be interesting as snakes, spiders, scorpions and other creatures fled before the heat. In the daytime the crackling flames and billows of smoke drew flocks of kites and hawks that swooped in to catch locusts, lizards and mice. It was all very exciting.

A horse, a child and the Bush

Dad could not live without horses. They were too much part of his life and so he bought a couple going cheap. They were in poor condition but he had an eye for a good horse and could almost talk their language. It was not long before they were in superb shape. Dad taught us how to ride and I took to horses so he gave me my own pony "Boetie" which meant "little brother" in Afrikaans. This was a new chapter of life for me. I had curvature of the spine and not only did riding strengthen my back but also opened a new world. Boetie came from the sure footed, hardy breed of ponies that the Boers had used during the South African war. He was a sweet horse and became my close friend even though one day he kicked me unconscious. He did not do so with malicious intent, I had been brushing him and touched a ticklish spot on his tummy and he let fly clouting me on the side of my head and sending me reeling. Fortunately he did not get me in my face as I would have been seriously injured. I talked to him often and every weekend we were out in the bush which brought new experiences to me and an appreciation for wild animals. Dad and I were able to ride close to wild animals for they never linked a human with a horse and simply accepted the rider as part of the animal. We came across rutting Kudu bulls jostling among themselves, rode among flocks of Guineafowl and discovered Eagle nests and old mine shafts and all manner of interesting things as we rambled across the veld. On horseback we were able to cross the wide *vleis* and get to where brilliant Red Bishop Birds hung their little nests in tall reeds and brooded their delicate blue eggs and tiny chicks. It was on these rides that I first saw the effects of the poacher's snare. Far too often we came upon remains of antelope that had been caught and then died and left to rot. Snares were made from twisted mine cable and once caught no animal had a chance of breaking free but was doomed to die. As the cable bit tighter and tighter into its neck it would beat about the bush and eventually succumb to a lingering death through exhaustion. We would search for snares and remove as many as possible. One day dad stopped his horse just as it walked right into a snare and the noose started to tighten. We lost at least one dog to a snare. It went into the bush and did not return and was later found dead.

We had an exciting incident one day when dad and I came around a bend in the track and came face to face with a spirit medium clothed in all his paraphernalia. He looked aggressive and frightening in grass skirt, maize-cob headpiece and grotesque mask, with animal skins, skulls, bones and shells hanging from his waist. He was in a state of trance and began to prance around with a long spear all the time wailing at the top of his voice. Dad visibly stiffened in his saddle and visions of the musket shooter years before came back to his mind. With a voice of authority learnt from his police days he shouted to the man to surrender and then spurred his horse forward. The man suddenly came out of his trance and back to earth, turned and bolted, running through the bush like a springhare with dad in close pursuit. A short chase ensued with me bringing up the rearguard but the man ducked through thick thorn bushes and got away, not that dad really intended to catch him. I think dad enjoyed our rides, I think he was lonely.

After graduating from Infant School where mother was deputy School Mistress I attended Kennedy Junior School named after an early Prime Minister and eventually went for a few months to Jameson School named after our Rhodesian hero. The Queen's portrait hung in every school as well as a grand picture of her in full flowing robe. Every afternoon after attending school I pulled off my school clothes put on my bush clothes and roamed the bush. Living out of town I cycled to school on a path through the bush. Sometimes I bunked classes. I simply turned off the path and hid my bicycle under a tree and spent the rest of the day enjoying myself. The bush became a classroom. When I got to Jameson School I found my brother's reputation had gone before me. Even from a young age Johnny stood up for himself and could not tolerate bullying or unfairness. His reputation was well known and when bullies asked me if "Johnny was my brother" I proudly replied he was and they treated me with respect. However, when the teacher heard my name he went into a *"kadenza"*, the local term used for hysteria. He looked at me with his face distorted and panic in his voice and said "Don't give me any trouble or I'll get you." Johnny had obviously fallen foul of him but I thought he was over reacting and that it was not a good start and felt justified in staying away.

Mother encouraged us to read and we had more books than toys. I devoured the "Just so Stories" as well as other classics of Africa. I read about the "Roc," a bird big enough to carry away an elephant, and other fables. I read the Jungle Book in which I learnt the "law of the jungle." These stories shaped my fertile imagination and I believed they were all true for our home was filled with evidence of all kinds of exotic things from Mogadishu, Addis Ababa, Eritrea, Nairobi, and regions of unexplored Africa. I read about Mowgli growing up with the wolf pack and conversing with wild animals. It was natural for me to develop similar expectations and like him I spoke to them all. Animals, even the dangerous ones, were simply there to get to know. Considering the wealth of fauna and flora all around me it was not surprising that Africa got hold of me. It somehow got into my blood when I was very young and like a bug it didn't let go. Brought up on "Just so Stories" I was unable to recognise fiction from reality.

Storms and Lightning

During the wet season we sometimes could not get to school because the *spruit* (stream) overflowed at the drift and we were stranded. Summer storms were immensely exciting with furious crashes of lightning and reverberating thunder followed by torrents of water. Lightning kills hundreds of people every year in

Africa but as children we were not aware of the danger and ran unafraid in the driving rain. One day dad was thrown to the floor by a direct lightning strike and was lucky to survive. One moment he was leaning against a pillar in the stables and next, after a tremendous clap of thunder, he was on the ground ten feet away.

Africa was notorious for lightning strikes. There was an instance when three giraffe were struck by one bolt of lightning as they stood together. Many cattle were also killed every year. A lightning strike killed twenty-one people at Chinamora Kraal on the 23rd of December 1975. A zealous religious sect called the *Ma'postles* held all-night prayer meetings. To do so they often climbed a hill and could be heard praying for the "fire of God" to fall. One night a few days before Christmas a group gathered to pray and got more than they bargained for when their prayers were answered in a lethal manner. They had laid sheets of iron roofing on the ground in the shape of a large cross upon which they were all standing or kneeling in prayer. When the lightning struck twenty-one people were killed with one bolt. Lightning also struck huts. If a bit of metal, like a radio aerial, protruded from the grass roof it became a lightning conductor and the hut was likely to be struck resulting in the death of the occupants. Africans had a myth about a "lightning bird" called the Zimbabwe Bird and it certainly proved true.

Salisbury Shopping

Once in a while we went to Salisbury on a shopping excursion. Salisbury was hot and busy, a small colonial town that was to us the big "city." Memories of tramping around the bustling centre remain vivid. There was the Farmers Co-op where dad bought supplies, then we went to Sanders the up-market store for tea, then down to Ferraday's Gunsmiths to restock on shotgun ammo and then up to old Meikles Hotel for drinks on the balcony overlooking Cecil Square where the Pioneers raised the Union Jack. This was sometimes followed by a special treat, lunch in the old colonial dining room. Meikles was the gathering place for the whole of Mashonaland. People came and went and jovial greetings rang out as friends met and shared news and legions of waiters swept in and out with trays loaded with teas, scones and cold beers. The hotel had a rich history. It was situated on Second Street, which ran north to south and was at the end of the long cattle drive from Lomagundi district in Northern Mashonaland. Farmers would take many days to drive their cattle to Salisbury railway station which was just a couple of blocks away from the hotel. In the early days there were three main cattle pens located around town that secured cattle from lions that raided at night. One was near Avondale, another south of the railway line and the other at the *"vlei"* on Enterprise road. The farmers would bring the cattle in at night so as not to disrupt the town and at about 9.00 p.m. the cracking of the long *"rimpie"* whips with shouts and whistles told they were getting close. The cattle would be in a high state of agitation and the farmers driving them would be even higher. All of them were thirsty and the farmers often turned aside at the bar to slake their thirst.

Sometimes a *"mombie"* (cow) would run amuck and the whole place went berserk. On one occasion a farmer drove his prize bull right through the hotel's ground floor, with chairs, tables and crockery flying in all directions and guests and waiters running for cover. It was literally *"a bull in a china shop"*. On another occasion one of the farmers, having drunk into the wee hours of the morning, stumbled up to his first floor bedroom but could not sleep because of an over exuberant cockerel. He pulled out his rifle and bleary eyed from the night before fired several shots accompanied by appropriate language in its general direction. The shot missed the offending bird but crashed through a glass window bringing the long arm of the law to arrest the culprit. Many other stories could be told of that great hotel. Another well-known hotel was the Grand Hotel on First Street which was a famous place for grand balls with great bands.

Rise of Nationalism

The fifties were idyllic days in Rhodesia. There was a kind of camaraderie and optimism that pervaded Rhodesian society. People were starting again after the hardships of the forties. There was new hope and people cheerfully took on the challenges of developing the country. They worked hard and helped each other. Most people did not have much but what they had they shared. There was an unspoken code of conduct - one's word was one's bond. It was the days when civil servants were truly civil and when they would not so much as take even a paper clip. Everyone gave a good days work and within the business community there was a generosity and helpfulness even for one's opposition. Towards the end of the fifties things began to change. Some settlers had made a fortune in tobacco or mining and white society began to divide and African Nationalist movements began to rise. One could tell true Nationalists because they had what looked like a dead cat wrapped around their heads. The fur hat was a sign of allegiance to the Nationalist cause and hats were made from wild cats or mongoose skins that were often not properly treated and looked scraggly. Unfortunately when wild cats could not be found domestic cats were just as good and pets went missing. Another symbol of nationalists was the fly whisk. Every good nationalist had to have a fly whisk, also a pair of dark glasses, as well as a fur hat. Petrol bombs became the order of the day. These were easy to make. Just get a bottle, fill it with petrol, stuff a rag into the neck and light the end and throw. When the bottle hit the target it shattered and caught alight. It was very effective for burning down houses and woe betides anyone upon whom it sprayed. Mother moved our beds away from the windows as it was too dangerous to sleep near one and to this day I still find it strange to sleep by an open window. I find it easier to sleep out in the bush under the great African dome studded with crystal stars.

The whites called the Africans "natives" and the natives began to awaken. Aspiring nationalist leaders stirred up the masses and disturbances became regular. The Prime Minister, Sir Edgar Whitehead, would speak on radio and tell everyone there was trouble in the townships and announce he was calling up the

Reserve Battalions. Every part-time white soldier dreaded these radio calls as it meant they would have to drop everything and report for duty. Often they deliberately did not listen to the radio in case there was a call-up but then Military Police would hunt them down and bustle them off in no uncertain terms. These part-time soldiers were issued with five rounds of ammo and trucked in to trouble spots to quell the riots. However, if a round was ever fired a full report had to be submitted and the empty case returned.

End of Family

Dad loved his horses but mother did not and sure enough the time came when family life ended. As traumatic as this was I somehow coped as I was used to feeling alone and it was better than a home that seemed to lack joy. Johnny went off to boarding school and I was sent to stay with dad's police friends who lived on a farm at Golden Valley, a rich gold mining area west of Gatooma. I stayed in the outside *"rondavel"* (hut). They were kind to me. One of the perks was a cumbersome old valve radio that opened the world to me. Every night I tuned in to Radio Springbuck from South Africa and listened to the hit parade and the detective serial *"Dragnet."* I also listened to the BBC and heard the chimes of Big Ben. Over the weekends I would console myself about the lack of family by wandering off into the bush but they were lonely times and I missed Boetie most of all, my dear little horse and best friend. After that time in my life I never went near a horse again, I had found his loss just too painful.

This period passed and one day dad and I rode off for pastures new on his magnificent new BMW motorbike of which he was very proud. We sped down the road that led through the hills to the Eastern Highlands where he took a post in the Government Labour Department at Umtali (Mutare). It was a bustling little town with a vibrant community of English and Afrikaans speaking whites and several thousand Africans. The social life was good, for colonial standards, with theatres and clubs and numerous functions and dances. Dad found a pretty new wife and with two step brothers we became a family but I felt the odd one out.

Book 2

A Child in the Bush – Exciting Years

"Those who seek adventure find excitement. Growing up in Africa was a big adventure".

In the 1960s my life entered a new chapter. It would be a decade of exploration. I was glad I was born in Africa for I was growing up in the most exciting place on earth or so I thought. The angels that had watched my progress must have got concerned. It seemed I needed special protection. I attended a school in Umtali which had a good reputation for academics and sport. I did not excel at either. The school nestled at the foot of a forest clad mountain called Cecil Kop and overlooked a wide panorama of mountains. On a clear day it seemed one could see for ever, from the lofty peaks of the cool Vumba Mountains down to the hot sultry Mozambique plains. Wide sports fields planted by pupils on detention stretched in front of the class rooms and were watered by morning mists. The headmaster "Coney" was highly regarded by all. I think he may have got his nickname from the way he used his cane or else it was his bald head but it was an affectionate name and the kids liked him. Many tough colonial farm children attended school and they had to be kept in tight reign but he was fair. Not all the teachers were so popular. One teacher could swing his huge blackboard ruler with deft precision inches over one's head. We knew that if we moved a fraction we would very likely receive the full brunt of the swing and woe betides the head that did. Another teacher in charge of the cricket team practised his bowling in class and was pretty accurate with the blackboard duster. If we were not paying attention or closed our eyes for a second we could expect to be bowled out. We had singing lessons with a dear middle aged lady who simply could not cope with a class of rowdy kids who knew exactly how far to push her to screaming point all singing in perfect disharmony. However, there was something different about her and I wondered whether it had anything to do with the scars on her wrists and the number tattooed on her arm.

Umtali School was for whites only. We rubbed shoulders with children from different nationalities but no African children. Some children came from the mountains of Melsetter where Afrikaner families had settled after they trekked to Rhodesia in the 1800s. These were tough farming kids from pioneer stock. Others were Greeks and Italians. There were no African, Asian or mixed race pupils at school for each community had its own schools. One youngster had only one big toe. He had shot the other one off by mistake when he put his twelve bore on the cap of his shoe and it discharged. Talk about shooting oneself in the foot! There was Ant, determined to enjoy every moment of life and straining for adventure he could not wait to get out of school and see life in the big world. On one of his escapades he broke his neck but fortunately surgeons wired it together again and it healed. There was Tim who had an amazing affinity with nature and became a world-renowned naturalist in Botswana. There was Kobus who came from Boer stock and was an outstanding marksman and Paul who was good with a cricket bat. There was a good deal of mischief. Alec was a great one for "pulling the legs" of classmates. One day he decided to do this, literally, so he grabbed Nigel and hung him over the balcony. Fortunately one of the teachers came to Nigel's rescue. Tension sometimes ran high and arguments broke out. Boys who had an altercation and needed to settle their grievance sorted it out with boxing gloves during break time. However, free-for-all scuffles sometimes broke out. These were the days when school assembly started every morning with a Bible reading and a prayer followed by a hymn, "Onward Christian Soldiers" being a favourite.

The School anthem reflected the proud commitment the school felt for town and country and was all about guarding the border, Umtali being a border town. The song sounded good but in those days we could not foresee the cost to protect the border or the extent of our future scattering. There was another anthem we sang on regular occasions; the National Anthem, "God Save Our Gracious Queen." We all stood proudly to attention, even the Afrikaans pupils, and sang with pride.

It was difficult for me to settle in the new school. I found recent upheavals and the restrictions of town depressed me. Apart from being dyslexic, I suffered from hypoglycaemia that made me excessively tired and unable to concentrate. And I had my own inner conflicts. I sat at the desk gazing out the window at the hills. It was impossible for someone like me, who had known the freedom of a horse to be content with a classroom. The hills lured me, and my mind was miles away exploring *kloofs* (ravines*)*, and valleys, winging past distant ranges to those beyond, to unexplored places never seen by human eyes - and so I dreamt of wild places. The hills beckoned me and I determined one day to climb them all.

Fortunately, dad did not like town either and with great relief we moved to Fern Valley south of Umtali beneath the great towering Dangary Mountain. We had a little Dachshund dog named Moss. I do not know whether he was called after the racing driver Stirling Moss or because he reminded one of a mosquito but he was a precious link with the past having come from our previous home. I became more isolated from my family and took to the bush armed with nothing but a Matabele spear that dad had confiscated off a criminal. I would set off into the hills carrying the spear and followed by Moss waddling along behind. Also at

Fern Valley I met up with "Stretch" who became my life time buddy. We became inseparable friends and together we explored the world around us.

The Native Labour Department in which dad worked covered a wide range of activities and was the arm of Government that dealt with employment of African people. Rural people had to be convinced that new techniques were necessary and beneficial, things like dipping livestock, building contours on fields, stopping river bank cultivation that caused erosion, inoculation of dogs against rabies, draining swamps to prevent malaria and a host of other things. Part of dad's responsibilities was to ensure that labour had a fair deal and were not exploited and that employers met responsibilities towards work contracts. The notion that Rhodesians had slaves or slave labour is nonsense. There were laws that governed labour conditions but Africans were trapped in mediocre jobs with poor wages and no way to improve themselves and were at times exploited. I think for some it was like financial slavery. Dad was a mediator between employers and employees. He would travel to outlying areas to settle labour disputes and during school holidays he took me with him. He had a huge district to cover including the Honde Valley a remote area of tropical jungle that lay in a valley through which the beautiful Pungwe River flowed having cascaded out of the Inyanga Mountains. On one of its tributaries the Mtarazi Falls plunge 500 meters over the escarpment and are some of the highest in Africa. It was a most spectacular area with huge forest trees, sweeping mountains, mist and rain. The road dad used was a rough stone track that meandered down the escarpment and took hours to negotiate in his old Chevy truck. Today you would require a four wheel drive to go on such a road but dad could make his old Chevy go almost anywhere. Today, the forest has been destroyed. In those days it was magnificent and many rare animals, snakes and insects lived there. The forests should have been protected. There is little left of them now and it is hard to comprehend that so much was destroyed in such a short time.

Mountains of Myrrh and Mirth

During school holidays dad took children who could not afford holidays to camp in Inyanga Mountains (Nyanga). These mountains reminded Scottish folks of their home country. There was heather, bracken and bubbling mountain streams with magnificent vistas, cliffs and rugged peaks, all this in Africa with herds of Sable antelope, troops of baboons and leopards in the hills. The herbal scents of highland heather mingled with fresh breezes sweeping off the Mozambique Channel created an invigorating climate free of malaria and other diseases. In these mountains there are vast remains of ancient terraces that were constructed by clever people who cultivated the slopes. The terraces of Inyanga are some of the most puzzling mysteries of Africa. In times of antiquity the mountains of Africa were renowned for their spices which were highly sought after by Arabians, Romans, Greeks and other Middle Eastern people. In the 15th century BC Queen Hatshepsut of Luxur sent an expedition to the "myrrh terraces" of Punt.

Her ships returned laden with marvels from that land; fragrant woods and resins, with fresh myrrh trees, ebony, ivory and gold, with cinnamon, incenses, eye-cosmetic and all manner of animals such as apes, monkeys, dogs, and leopard skins. Punt was very likely Ethiopia and the culture of terracing spread south to the eastern highlands of Zimbabwe. A researcher who analysed Egyptian cosmetics concluded that the ingredient of antimony, used to darken the eyelids, could well have come from Zimbabwe.[3]

Dad organised a hike from Inyanga Village up through the hills to Troutbeck village a climb of over two thousand feet in about six miles, quite a walk for young children. It is imprinted on my memory as one of those great moments in life. We walked through a fairly land of lichen and ferns, trickling streams and beautiful forests full of birds. A troop of baboons protested our presence with barks that echoed through the ravines. As we climbed higher and higher the clouds descended with biting cold. We got to Troutbeck late and dad loaded us on the back of a lorry that drove to the village through driving rain and heavy mist. What an unforgettable day and we needed to thaw out with hot baths. I think it was this walk that instilled within me a lifelong love for hiking.

He also took us to see Great Zimbabwe Ruins. These famous Ruins have always had an air of mystery about them from when they were first discovered by explorers and as a child I remember a sense of excitement when we visiting them. Dad, Johnny and I explored the maize of ramparts, dad like an excited schoolboy. We squeezed through narrow confines of twisting passages and up steep steps to the Acropolis where panoramic views spread at our feet. Like others who visit the ruins we wanted to know who built them and let our imaginations run wild. They are clearly African in origin but there is no inscription found in the ruins and no explanation for them as if ancient unknown peoples had left without yielding their identity. Early traditions were cloaked in secrecy and a sense of ambiguity about them never left me. Since then much research has been conducted and later when I joined the National Museums and worked with renowned archaeologists I learnt more about them. These researchers wrote books to explain them; Indians, Persians and Arabs amongst others had for many centuries come to Central Africa seeking gold and ivory and Great Zimbabwe developed as a result of local trade with these merchants. Yet, the explanations, true and interesting as they were, somehow left me with a sense of inadequacy. The data seemed incomplete as if something vital was left unsaid. The ruins with their twisting passages and high walls convey something not fully explained by the politically correct theories of researchers. Do they hold a secret? Further study was done by a researcher that confirmed my misgivings as we shall see.

Fern Valley lay in the Vumba foothills which towered just south of where we lived and Stretch and I could walk cross country to their jungle clad slopes. These majestic mountains were shrouded in mists and received heavy downpours.

Looking east from the mountains one could look over the extensive tropical plains of Mozambique. The heat and sultry humidity of the plains were in sharp contrast to the cool mountain air. Dense forests with ferns and moss and tangled fields of bracken clothed the steep slopes and deep ravines. Fresh streams tumbled out of the forests which were home to a diversity of flora and fauna and every time we went exploring we discovered something new.

At a majestic projection called "Leopard Rock" it seemed a mountain had sheered in half leaving a huge cliff face exposed to the forest clad valley. The local people recall how long ago a wealthy village nestled beneath the mountain and strangers had come from distant lands seeking hospitality but had been rudely turned away. The tribal spirits became angry and wreaked awful retribution upon the village when the mountain crashed down killing them all. It was said that on stormy nights when the wind blew one could still hear wails coming from below the jagged cliffs of the mountain. A beautiful castle-like hotel was built at Leopard Rock and international guests came from all around the world to admire its beauty. The Queen Mother and Princess Margaret visited and brass plaques were placed on their room doors designating their stay. It was fitting that people from far off lands now were welcome.

I went to visit mother who gave me a special treat for Easter and we went to Gorongosa National Park in Mozambique. This was Africa in all its glory. Herds of elephant trumpeted through glades of flat topped thorn trees, thousands of antelope grazed on the grass, hippos lolled about in pools, and dozens of lions were everywhere - it was nothing short of amazing. One group of lions had taken up residence in a deserted tourist camp and lived like royalty. We counted over sixty lions; they lay on the grassy plains, big males, mothers and little cubs all enjoying paradise. These tremendous sights were beyond description and had a lasting effect upon me. One day, I decided, I would be involved with wild life.

The Winds of Change - 1960

In 1960 we heard disturbing news. A massacre had taken place in South Africa. The British Prime Minister Harold Macmillan had just toured Africa. He started in West Africa and ended in the South African Parliament in Cape Town. He gave his famous speech, "The Winds of Change" which deeply unsettled white people and badly knocked their confidence in the British government. It seemed the British intention was to give their colonies majority rule and apparently abandon the whites. Shortly after his speech a mass shooting in South Africa hit our news. Sixty-seven people were shot dead and another one hundred and eighty six wounded at Sharpeville. It was South Africa's awful answer to Macmillan. All this produced reaction among Africans who became even more restless and stepped up protests. Rhodesia considered it had good race relations yet overlooked regulations that restricted races from mixing and caused resentment and hardship. The Land Tenure Act apportioned large amounts of land to settlers and was a thorn in the sides of Africans. In South Africa the National Party that came to power in 1948 brought in harsh legislation to enforce Apartheid and during the early 1960s Rhodesians began to feel more and more uncertain of the way ahead being influenced by events both to the north and to the south. The state of emergency in Kenya had come to an end in 1958 but hardly had Mau Mau ended when the British government gave the country Independence. Some settlers saw it as betrayal and came south to Rhodesia. At the same time whites from South Africa migrated north to Rhodesia to get away from Apartheid. The Rhodesians felt caught between these opposing forces, the Black Nationalists in the north and the White Nationalists in the south.

There were many British army officers and ex-service men in Rhodesia; sergeants, sergeant majors, majors and even a few colonels and brigadiers many of whom had served in the Second World War. Some of them were flamboyant characters with long handlebar moustaches. They strutted about as if they were still in uniform and had voices to match. When Britain granted Independence to India whites fled from the "Jewel of the Crown" of the old British Empire. Some had lived there for generations and got out by the skin of their teeth and the clothes they stood in. The lucky ones came with suitcases. They now attempted to carve out a new life in the "Jewel of Africa." Some of my young friends were born in India. We listened with awe to the tales their parents told of old colonial India and the barbarism and chaos at Independence. Most of them were worried that it would happen again this time in Rhodesia but the locals said, "It can never happen here, we have self government".

Riots in Nyasaland compelled authorities to call up territorial soldiers to restore order. The Federal Government uncovered a plot by the Nyasaland African National Congress to overthrow the government and kill the governor. Sir Roy Welensky, Federal Prime Minister, decided to intervene. Reserve white soldiers were mobilised and flown to Nyasaland. Then came the upheaval in the Congo with sordid tales of terrible atrocities, nuns were gang-raped and men, women and children slaughtered. People fled across the border into Northern Rhodesia in a state of shock. Images of weeping women and children, clutching pathetic bundles filled the newsreels. Others came clutching their breasts and genitals which had been hacked off with machetes. In Rhodesia local nationalist movements held demonstrations that turned into riots. Nationalists were on the march throwing petrol bombs. Collapse of the Federation created a political vacuum and the prospect of the black majority gaining power unnerved the whites. We were entering a time of trauma that would last for years. In fact I cannot recall a time after early childhood when there was not a crisis. From now on "normal life" was to be abnormal. The colonial government was under threat and in perpetual tension – to act or abdicate - and it was becoming increasingly clear to everyone that Britain was about to ditch its colonies in Africa.

The Freedom of Youth

With pressures at home and in the country I tried to live as normally as possible and lost myself in my love for the bush. It exuded an unchanging, timeless quality that gave me a sense of stability and as soon as I was there I became happy, excited and safe. The hills and mountains radiated strength and confidence to me; they were immovable, secure. The land was a tapestry of ragged ravines, cliffs and waterfalls, springs, ferns and forests. There was abundance of wildlife from little shrews to lordly kudu antelope, secretive leopards, troops of baboons and many other creatures. The forests rang with the staccato cries of monkeys and the call of forest birds. The countryside was interspersed with granite outcrops rearing up in jumbled hills called *"kopjes,"* with massive expanses of unbroken granite called whalebacks or *"dwalas."* In few other places in the world are there such gigantic boulders of solid rock. They silently spoke about our smallness in the eternal scheme of things. At night my childhood buddy Stretch and I would sit on a great granite *"dwala"* out in the bush behind our homes and talk. It was an appropriate seat on which to expound the deeper mysteries of life. The nights were balmy and pleasant. Above us stretched the vastness of the universe with crystal clear stars in a pool of charcoal blackness that rolled from horizon to horizon. Stretch and I would stretch out on the granite and absorb the wonder all around us. The variety of animals was wonderful, there was always something new to see and learn. Bush babies, related to Madagascar Lemurs, called at night. They have a raucous scream, which is repeated in a series of descending cries and sounds like someone being tortured to death. Their little cousins the Night Apes are delightful little creatures. They hide in hollow trees and come out at night to leap around with incredible agility as they catch insects, all the time making little twittering sounds. We heard them as they moved around us. A rustle in the undergrowth disclosed the passage of some other night creature and behind us on the cliffs of Dangary sounded the soft rasping call of a leopard half cough half growl uttered gently and yet carrying far across the still night air. Troops of baboons lived in the hills and sometimes we could hear them screaming in commotion as a leopard harassed them. Nearer in the shadows a nightjar called its mournful but melodious prayer that sounded like – ***"Good Lord deliver us, good Lord deliver us."*** Anyone who has heard it will know it as the "Litany Bird" with its mournful but beautiful song. It is the prayer of Africa.

Growing up in Rhodesia was a time of extraordinary liberty. We roamed through a vast landscape in an environment in which we were completely free. Stretch became my close friend and together we explored the land. Not only did he become my friend but he also fulfilled the role of big brother Johnny having gone off to boarding school. Stretch lived up to his name. He stood over six feet tall and was as thin as a piece of string. Nevertheless his wiry frame was as strong as steel and he had an indomitable courage in the face of difficulty. He was never rattled and together we could take on any adventure. We climbed the mountains, explored the granite caves, went for midnight swims in the dam, played snooker at the Railway Club and dodged the bullies at school. With Stretch I felt part of an invincible team.

There is an African Proverb: *"If the tail of the mongoose is up, danger lurks near by."*

The Mongoose is a hunter of snakes. If a mongoose runs across your path and its tail is down then the animal is simply scurrying around on its daily chores. If, however, the tail is raised then the animal is alarmed and danger close. We had no horses at Fern Valley so I had to find something else to keep me occupied. Fortunately we were living in an area that had lots of wild life and it was to this I turned. Gerald Durrell's books influenced me considerably. I was an avid reader about his expeditions around the world to catch endangered animals for his zoo. He became my role model. Much later in life we met and I spent an enjoyable afternoon with him. He was a lovely man and lived up to my expectations. His books strengthened my love for wild creatures. Stretch and I learnt how to find animals seldom seen by others. Elephant Shrews, a secretive little creature with a sensitive trunk-like nose with long whiskers, lived in rock crevices. Another rare creature, the Giant Plated Rock Lizards that grew to nearly a meter in length were difficult to find and even more difficult to catch. We knew where mongooses lived and saw them scurrying through the bush. We knew where big Black Mambas had their holes and would creep up without disturbing them and hardly breathing gaze upon their lithe bodies as they dozed in the sun. Massive two meter long monitors and other exotic creatures all lived in our "backyard." It was like living in a vast zoo and it was all our very own paradise.

Snakes, Charming and Dangerous

At Fern Valley there was an abundance of snakes and they and other reptiles were the obvious answer when it came to something to do. Stretch was already an expert and we took to snake catching. Roaming the bush took on new meaning. Under logs and stones and in bushes there were snakes just waiting to be caught. They came in all shapes and sizes from huge Pythons five meters long to little Blind Snakes just centimetres. There were harmless House Snakes and dangerous Cobras, Adders and Mambas. One day we found an African Python, *"shauto"* in the Shona language. It was a magnificent and powerful snake with a reticulated pattern of greens, mauves, purples and browns. It was so large we had to commandeer two *"umfaans"* about our age to help us carry it home. They were scared to come too near but one of them named Robby was a brave young lad and encouraged the other to carry the dreaded beast. We became friendly with Robby who sometimes came around to Stretch's home and had tea and cake and Stretch got to know him. There were many Cobras over six feet long that were aggressive and highly venomous and required great dexterity to catch. They would rear up and sway with their wide hoods extended but in a flash we would grab them. We had our fair share of close calls and were sometimes bitten mostly by harmless types. One day I got a dose of venom spat straight in my face by a Spitting Cobra. This type of snake is very clever. Not only does it bite but also spits with accuracy up to about ten feet. When threatened it pretends to be dead by rolling onto its back. When approached it suddenly comes to life, rears up and sprays venom into one's eyes. If one is foolish enough to handle it under the notion that it is dead it buries its fangs in one's flesh before making a quick get away. This particular Cobra gave me the full facial treatment. I ran to a nearby pool and washed the venom from my face and went home and did the same with milk which helps neutralise it. Venom in the eyes is serious and can cause permanent blindness. Dad saw the evidence and told me I had to be more careful.

It was not just snakes we caught. Anything that moved was fair game. Monitors, also called Leguaans, were our speciality. They were extremely fast, had long whip like tails and horrible jaws. The way we caught them as well as snakes was to grab them by the tail. This was our general method of catching most things but it did not work well when we tried it on a big Mamba.

Bitten By a Black Mamba

Stretch and I knew where a big Black Mamba lived in the bush and so one day we took a couple of girlfriends to show them how to catch it. On arrival at the location it did not take long to locate the Mamba, over three metres in length, lurking in a favourite spot in a small tree. I grabbed its tail and began to haul. It locked its coils around the branches and held on tight. Then with its tail still firmly grasped in my hand it doubled back through the branches to have a look at who was on its other end. Mambas are not stupid and it summed up the situation fairly quickly. I was soon to learn that this was not the way to catch a Mamba but a way to commit suicide. A Mamba has no fear of man and this one came out of the tree like a bullet out of a gun straight at me with one intention, to end my days as quickly as possible. I leapt back, still holding its tail and now had a three meter, lethal, living coil of angry killing machine on the end of my hand and dared not let go. In the confusion of the moment Stretch yelled he was bitten for as the snake came out it lunged at him and bit him right in the middle of his back. I dared not lose concentration and still had it firmly by the tail. Then followed some of the most intense moments of life as I did the "snake tango" a rapid, highly erratic quick step with one main aim which was to elude its gaping fangs. The girls looked on aghast. Eventually after several minutes of ducking and diving, dodging death by a hair's breath I managed to grasp its head and holding it firmly by head and tail followed Stretch at a run for he and the girls had lost interest in catching Mambas and thought they should get back while they still could. A good bite from a Mamba can kill an animal in minutes and a person in not much more.

I overtook them, gave them a few words of encouragement, and ran on to get help. We were quite a distance from home and I ran all the way with the Black Mamba dangling from each hand like a large skipping rope. Dad was used to us bringing back all sorts of things but he looked a trifle shocked when he saw me running up with the snake. He got an even bigger shock when I told him Stretch was bitten and turned a deathly shade of white. For a moment I thought I was going to have another casualty on my hands for he looked as though he was about to collapse but pulling himself together he leapt into his car and wheel-spun out the driveway before I could get the snake into a cage. Dad was usually rather predictable and dignified, never had I seen him move so fast. He found Stretch walking down the road in a state of shock with two teenage girls also in a state of shock hanging on to each arm. Stretch got into the back seat, dad collected me on the way past and we flew into town. Usually dad stuck to the speed limit but this was the fastest I ever saw him drive all the time peering in the mirror to see if Stretch was still alive.

Stretch spent some days in hospital and complained that the treatment was worse than the bite. Oh well, never a dull moment. We had numerous close calls and were bitten by harmless or mildly venomous snakes but one night Stretch got another bite. The hot Odzi River Valley some twenty miles West of Umtali was our favourite snake catching area. One day we hiked there but were delayed on returning. Night came and we were stranded. We decided the best way to get back to town was to jump on a passing freight train and so we sat on the side of the railway track to wait. As we relaxed in the darkness Stretch lent back and placed his hand straight onto the head of a snake which promptly bit him. He yelled out and jumped up frantically waving his hand around with some kind of adder clinging on to it. Eventually he flung it off. Now what should we do? We were miles from anywhere in the middle of the bush. An old man was walking along the track, heard our commotion, and approached us to find out what the problem was. On learning what had happened he coolly pulled out a knife, slit Stretch's finger and sucked like crazy. Fortunately Stretch had no after effects from the snake, the knife or the saliva.

Some weeks after the Mamba incident we came home with another albeit smaller Mamba nicely wrapped in a cloth bag but dad felt it had gone too far and blasted it to pieces with his shotgun, bag and all.

How not to catch an Aardvark
Another time when our catching technique failed was when we dug up an Aardvark. An Aardvark is an African Antbear. They are usually harmless animals and are nocturnal so are seldom seen. They dig deep holes to get at ants which are their staple diet and they live in the tunnels they dig. These holes are used by all manner of other creatures so one can never be too sure who is resident, warthogs, porcupines, pythons and cobras are just a few common tenants. One can see if the hole has a resident or is abandoned by the entrance. If there are spider webs across the hole it will be empty of anything big but if there are no webs then an occupant could well be at home. I knew their interior with vivid familiarity and when I

recall how I used to crawl down them headfirst to see if anything was in them I shudder. One day we found one with the original landlord in occupancy and so decided to dig it out. An adult aardvark can weigh 70 kg and when cornered is dangerous because it has long powerful front claws that are used for digging and with which it can literally tear open the earth and also rip anyone foolish enough to tackle it. In African mythology they are considered with awe because of the notion that the little *"tokolosh"* of the bush rides on its back. The *"tokolosh"* is the equivalent of an elf, a little wizened dwarf who plays pranks on people and unless respected can turn quite mean. They are greatly feared. Folk law said that the little *"tokolosh"* used an Aardvark whenever he needed a ride which was quite regular.

We asked two local men who were brave enough to help and began to dig with all our might. Soon we broke through into its tunnel and saw the animal, its powerful muscles rippling as it clawed through the soil. We opened the tunnel some more and were able to grab its long, donkey like ears and pulled and heaved until it came out like a cork from a champagne bottle spewing us in all directions. Gathering ourselves we fell upon the animal with the idea of manhandling it into a sack. The Aardvark had other ideas. With a shrug of its powerful shoulders and a toss of its head it flung us away a second time sending us sprawling and made off into the bush dragging me along behind still holding on to its long thick tail until I lost my grip. It was the closest I ever came to riding an Aardvark and I think the men were suitably impressed.

Special Friends and Other Animals

We had special friends who had the same interests as we did. Two of our friends were twins, Alfred and Albert. They were big for their age and looked identical, unless one knew them very well. They were inseparable and went everywhere together and they were gentle, kind and happy. They were skilled snake catchers and we put on a snake show at the school fete to raise money. We constructed a snake enclosure with a wooden barrier that extended right across one of the classrooms from wall to wall. People paid to come in and we gave them lessons on how to dodge striking Cobras one of which promptly got its fangs through my trousers and nearly into my leg. We also gave demonstrations on how to stop snakes from getting over the barrier, which they constantly endeavoured to do to shrieks from school girls who fled in all directions. The whole performance was quite unforgettable especially when Stretch gave demonstrations on how to milk highly venomous cobras and adders. He wanted to try for a week's record-breaking stay in the pit but the headmaster put his foot down and forbade it. How we ever got permission in the first place was a mystery but due only to Stretch's incredible powers of persuasion. It was very exciting.

Ron was also our friend at this time and like us interested in all wild things but he was killed in the Liberation War when ambushed while working for the

Forestry Commission. Other pupils were to lose their lives in the coming conflict. But this was still in the future and the present was spent in all kinds of hazardous and enjoyable pursuits.

One day I was out in the bush with our little Dachshund. He was game for anything and could walk miles with me. It must have been quite a sight to see a child with a spear and a bag of snakes on one shoulder followed by a Dachshund hiking across the hills. On this day as I crept quietly through dense undergrowth the little dog suddenly dashed off having smelt some kind of animal foraging ahead. His barks receded into the distance and I ran after him as fast as I could, then I heard a scuffle and a howl of pain. When I caught up he was not visible so I began to call knowing something was amiss. After a while I discerned a slight dragging noise approaching me through the tangle of undergrowth and as I made my way towards it was shocked to discover him crawling through the bush towards me. He had been disembowelled from backbone to belly. A wild pig had got him with its razor tusks and opened him up like a tin can. His bowels bulged out and were covered in grass. Wild pigs are dangerous animals and will viciously defend themselves. Even leopards are wary of them. I carried Moss home cradled in my arms and we took him to the vet who cleaned his bowels and put them all back and stitched him up. Soon he was as right as ever but he bore a handsome battle scar.

It was a good thing that the majority of people were so congenial for we played tricks on them. A favourite pastime was to lie in wait by a path with one of our captured snakes. When an unsuspecting cyclist came down the path or perhaps people carrying stuff on their heads as they often did we would pull the snake out. The result was predictable, shrieks of fear as belongings tumbled and people fled. The poor people would turn grey with fear just seeing us holding snakes. They could not believe we handled them and were convinced we had special *"tagati"* (magic) and held us in awe.

Our days passed raiding orchards, swimming in the dam even though it was riddled with bilharzia, climbing the hills and generally enjoying life. The days seldom had a dull moment. We decided we would climb the sheer granite cliff of Dangary. We had no ropes or training but that did not deter us, we simply clawed our way up by our fingertips. About half way up we had a problem not knowing whether to go up or down. For a while we clung to the rock as if frozen but decided there was only one thing to do and that was to continue. We inched up and dared not look down although the view was magnificent and with the wind around our ears and the valley far below we had a sense of exhilaration and freedom that every rock climber must feel. When we reached the summit we could see for miles. The majestic, rolling, green-clad Vumba Mountains were near at hand, towering up to heights of several thousand meters. The dusty hills of Zimunya Tribal Trust Lands stretched at our feet and to the south we could just see the curved arch of Birchenough Bridge glinting in the sun. It was superb.

Discovering a New Species of Lizard

It was during this time that Stretch and I discovered a new species of lizard (*Cordylus warreni regius*). We found them in the rugged Dora Hills, a massive range of granite west of Fern Valley. We clambered around the hills which were a sanctuary for wild creatures and also contained many caves with Bushman paintings. On our visits we came across some bright coloured lizards about 25 centimetres long. They looked beautiful with bright yellow and orange bellies and spikes all over them. We caught one and took it to Don, the Keeper of Herpetology at the Umtali Museum. Don's main interest in life was reptiles and he became visibly ecstatic. We stood transfixed at his display of enthusiasm and were excited that we had discovered a creature new to science. He insisted that we take him to where we found it and the next weekend we all went out. He scrambled around the rocks like an exuberant schoolboy and together we found several more lizards. They turned out to be a species of Crag Lizard and this was the start of a long and rewarding relationship with the Museum. From this initial discovery we went on to unearth new frogs, lizards and snakes. It was the start of a new chapter that would lead me into an exciting career.

Alone in the Bush

There were some difficult times as a child and one afternoon after an upset I decided I was leaving so I walked off with nothing but the clothes I stood in. I suppose quite a few children think of running away from home and I kept walking until the sun went down and I was well and truly "lost in the bush". I had nothing with which to make a fire and no bedding. So I put my back against a tree and tried to make myself as comfortable as possible and pulled my hat down to keep my ears warm. It was a long night! Whenever a twig cracked or a leaf rustled I wondered what hidden danger lurked in the darkness and imagined leopards and other dangerous animals. The moon rose and bathed the bush in silver light blanketing it in shimmering softness. A pair of Jackals serenaded the moon with a beautifully emotive song composed of howls, whines and bays, a sound that seemed so poignant for the occasion and which drifted across the silver bush with a sense of ghostly sadness. It made me feel my utter aloneness. Later in life I grew to love that haunting song for it carries all the sad tones of Africa and seems to typify the vast loneliness of the bush. If one listens carefully with a bit of imagination one can hear the words of the song. It comes from one of the small weak and despised creatures of the veld and appeals to all the powerful creatures to let it venture forth in peace. However, it was the last thing I needed that night. There was no fire to throw a log on so I pulled up my knees and held them tightly. The gentle song of a nightjar comforted me with its clear notes, *"Good Lord deliver me, Good Lord deliver me."* They were repeated through the long hours and became my prayer. I dozed intermittently. At last the eastern sky lightened and the welcome sun appeared. I had survived my first night alone in the African bush. Later that day I found my way home and trudged back but never told anyone where I had been.

A friend and I went to Birchenough Bridge and spent our school holidays there. We spread our camp beds under the large trees on the banks of the Sabi River in a wild paradise. The abundance of bird life was just too extravagant to fully absorb and there were crocodiles and hippos in the river, rhinos in the hills and impala and other game on the river banks. Birchenough Bridge is a graceful steel arch that spans the wide, sandy river and is a small version of Sydney Harbour Bridge and designed by the same engineer. It rises a hundred metres above the river and from the top of its steel girders there is a majestic view of the surrounding bush. I know because one day my friend Ant and I decided to see the view even though climbing on the girders was illegal. Up and up we went until we stood at the highest point of the arch and felt like Hilary and Tensing on top of Mount Everest. The valley stretched away at our feet, mile upon mile of endless bush lost in a haze of heat. Whenever a large truck crossed below us the bridge shuddered and we clung on for dear life.

Elephants

In times past the maps of Africa were filled with elephants and little else. I had seen them in Gorongosa National Park but I still had to see them close up so some friends and I headed down to Odzi Valley.

About fifty miles south of Umtali in the hot, sultry, tropical Odzi Valley was a small resort known as Hot Springs where a subterranean spring of boiling water bubbled to the surface. A lovely swimming pool had been built and it became our favourite place during school holidays. The area was wild in those days. A narrow tarmac strip road meandered through the jumbled granite hills and dense jungles, through steep valleys and deep ravines with narrow bridges, on through glades of baobabs and thick lowveld forest until it reached the resort near the banks of the Odzi River. Here we camped, not at the resort but in the bush down near the river and cooked on open fires freshly killed "kraal" chickens purchased from the locals. Lessons from Rabson the cook on how to kill and pluck a chicken now came in very handy. We swam in the river and soaked in wild aromas. Elephants still roamed the area and it was here that I had my first close encounter with what were for me the most majestic of all African animals. The elephants moved from place to place and never stayed too long in one locality. They wandered in for a few days at a time and then melted away. Heaps of steaming dung marked their passage but sometimes we were fortunate to catch a glimpse of their huge, broad backs passing like ships through the thick bush. On one of their visits, knowing that elephants were close, I sneaked through the bush towards them, the sound of branches being broken and leaves being munched directing me. The bush was thick and as I crawled along I suddenly found myself looking at a pair of huge legs. It was awe inspiring. I fell in love with elephants and with all wild things.

Elephants are some of the most intelligent of animals. There is something supremely grand about a herd of elephants as they stride through the bush, head and shoulders above other animals and man. They are gentle giants for they harm nothing and move among their fellow creatures with an air of confidence, respecting each one whether large or small. They have a strong social structure and are very tender towards one another. They can become emotionally disturbed and grieve their dead even attempting to bury them by covering them with branches or dirt. Their great spirits epitomise the Spirit of Africa - vast, gigantic, uninhibited and free to roam the unlimited expanse of unfenced veld. They are the true Lords of Africa, absolute gentlemen, tender with one another, instilling awe and respect, yet when aroused a formidable foe. Only man has the audacity and insensitivity to harm them. For millennia they have suffered in the most heinous manner as hunters have decimated their numbers. Frankly, elephants only become dangerous when molested by mankind, their arch enemies.

Hiking the Country

Stretch and I hiked across the countryside and when distances were too great to walk we hitched lifts to wherever we wanted to go sometimes travelling hundreds of miles. Very often we had a weird assortment of baggage with us such as bags full of snakes or lizards, or perhaps an animal we had found in the bush. We had to tell all kinds of stories to convince people to carry us. Occasionally one of our captured companions would get loose and we had an emergency on our hands for they had a knack of disappearing into the car upholstery. The result would be a dismantled vehicle and sometimes we never did find them again. Our parents did not always know what we were up to but one day Stretch's dad found out when a friend of his gave us a lift. Laden with two bags of captives and a large monitor in a sack we clambered into his car. We sat looking as innocent as we could but in the course of conversation all was divulged. Our driver turned pale and became quiet for the remainder of the journey. Having recognised Stretch he promptly called his dad when he got home. Stretch had some explaining to do.

Local African superstitions were rich especially when it came to the strange creatures all around us and snakes were viewed with utmost dread. Some completely harmless snakes were considered deadly. For example the little Egg Eater is a placid snake and cannot even bite. However, it has markings that are similar to Night Adders and when alarmed they behave in typical adder fashion, hissing and striking in an aggressive manner. They are viewed with much dread. One night, many years later, this little snake was to play an important role in my life.

There is an amazing interdependence in nature. Many unlikely things happen in the bush. For example after a long hot walk I was resting under a tree when I felt gentle rain falling on me yet the sky was clear. It was a puzzle and I wondered how I was getting so wet. The secret was that I had sat down under a curious tree called the "Rain Tree." At a certain time of year it plays host to a species of tiny nymphs that feed on its tender shoots. As they munch leaves in one end they excrete a constant "rain" from their other end. This can become a deluge and very cooling on a hot day. Many of Africa's extraordinary insects are now no longer found having died from pesticides.

My friend Frank and I hitched to the new Kariba Lake on the Zambezi River. The gravel road went through hills so rugged that when the engineers attempted to access the site it was impossible to survey a road so they simply followed the elephant trails trampled over hundreds of years during their annual migration from the hills to the river. When the dam wall was finished it pushed back floodwaters that stretched a hundred and seventy miles and trapped thousands of wild animals. A team led by Rupert Fothergill rescued marooned animals, from elephants and rhinos to snakes and chameleons. Frank and I stood on the dam wall and looked down 420 feet to the gorge below and I determined to one day canoe the Zambezi River. We had no money to stay at the hotel but enough to have a meal and having not eaten for a couple of days we were famished. We booked in for dinner and ordered the whole menu and the main course twice and were so extended we could not move. We spent several hours lying on the lawn until we recovered and went down to the lake shore to sleep under the African night sky. We had no beds so we just curled up in the brush. We survived the night with lions, leopards and other animals all around us. A few months later Frank fell and hit his head and died within an hour.

As youngsters we got into mischief, mostly harmless but occasionally things went too far. One day Stretch and I "borrowed" the boats at Fern Valley dam, rowed them out to the middle and played pirates. Our art teacher Jock who taught me the rudiments of art also enjoyed fishing and unbeknown to us was standing in the reeds spying our antics. Unfortunately one of the boats was his. As we drifted closer and closer he suddenly appeared and in a thunderous voice and distinct Scots accent commanded us to surrender. Pirates never surrendered so I dived in and swam for my life and Stretch took off rowing in the opposite direction. Not about to miss the catch of a lifetime Jock ran around the lake to cut me off and I swam straight into his welcoming arms. He was usually a placid fellow but was fuming mad and I thought he was taking the whole incident way out of proportion. Next day at school assembly our names were read out and we were told to report to the Headmaster. We expected a good dose of the cane if not worse. Just before we entered his office Stretch whispered to me "Don't say a word, let me do the talking." I was only too happy for him to do so and had no idea how he was going to explain our little transgression.

"Well, what have you got to say for yourselves?" the headmaster asked, a foul look on his face.

"We were just having some harmless fun, Sir" Stretch replied.
"You stole the boats without permission" Coney challenged.
"No Sir, we only borrowed them, there was no damage" replied Stretch.

Coney was fuming mad and I was wondering whether Stretch had gone mad in defying him. This could only end in caning or worse but I kept quiet nevertheless.

"I'll give you a choice, you can either have a thrashing or you can answer to the police. Which do you want?" he said, thinking he could scare Stretch.

Stretch saw his opportunity. "Call the police" he replied, knowing that it was now out of the hands of the school, there would be no caning, and the police would only give us a mild reprimand. The headmaster was livid. He sat speechless as he realised he had been out-manoeuvred. After a while he calmed down and said good naturedly to Stretch, "When you leave school you had better join the police. Get out the both of you". Stretch later took his advice and his fast mind made him a very good policeman.

Jock forgot the incident and our relationship at art class did not seem to suffer. He persevered with me and instilled in me an appreciation for art that would pay dividends in later years. He had a young daughter who grew up in love with the bush, art and wild animals, all inherited from her father but in 1974 she was on assignment in Mozambique to study wild life when her vehicle hit a landmine and she was killed. More deaths of former pupils were to follow and Fern Valley eventually saw more than just harmless children playing mock battles for it became a war zone as trained killers wandered at will through our childhood haunts but that was still all in the future.

My school years closed upon me. In the final Afrikaans speech exam each student had to choose a topic to talk about. I chose to talk on reptiles and learnt my lecture off by heart and proceeded to do so stuttering and stammering until finally the examiner cut me short and told me to forget Afrikaans and just tell him in English. I had caught his attention and passed. The wonder of it was that I managed to pass any exams at all for hypoglycaemia caused me to fall asleep at my desk. Added to this were other personal problems. I left school having just turned sixteen. Coney wrote a glowing testimonial for me that I had been a very active member of the nature club. He could usually find something positive to say about most of his students.

Book 3

Freedom of Youth – Adventure Years

In Africa a story tells how the leopard got its camouflaged spots lying in the shade of a tree. As sun filtered through the leaves it burnt spots onto its beautiful coat. African Proverb: "You cannot see a leopard until it is too late."

With no prospects of continuing my education I left school and Don offered me a job at the Museum and I started the serious business of growing up. It would be a decade of adventure. The new museum in town had just been built but was an empty shell. It needed items for display so I was hired as a learner Display Artist and Field Technician. I started my new job on thirty-five pounds a month. The salary was not much but I was ecstatic. An exciting world opened for me. I was now meeting scientists of all kinds, eccentric personalities mostly, colourful characters who knew the secrets of insects, fish, reptiles and mammals as well as old bones, flints, pots and everything else imaginable. The Museum had galleries in which to display the natural history of the Eastern Highlands and I was sent out to the wildest corners of the mountains to collect that material and then construct the displays all in the name of science. My childhood years in which I had been busy observing and learning about nature were now put to good use. Although I could not further my education at university I had in a way already been to a university, the Bush University, and I knew exactly where to find everything needed. I also went on museum expeditions to the steaming jungles of Mozambique and to the dry Kalahari Desert of Bechuanaland to record and collect zoological specimens.

Kalahari Expedition – Exploring Africa

Our expedition to Bechuanaland was a great adventure. We loaded a couple of Land Rovers and a ten ton lorry and set out. After passing through dusty Francistown we turned west on the road to Maun just a track in those days. Here we saw herds of buck, elephants and giraffe. Then we headed south through the middle of the Makgadikgadi Salt Pans to camp near Kube Island an historical site where famous explorers had carved their names on baobab trees that cling to life on the edge of the vast white salt pans. These pans have a blistering white crust of salt residue, an inhospitable place especially in the midday sun when they reflect glare and heat in a dazzling, shimmering haze that gives no respite to travellers.

They are relic remains of a vast inland lake that once existed in central Africa when the climate was wetter and before the land elevation shifted and changed the course of rivers. In present years they only hold water for a short time and then become a sight of unsurpassed fantasy as tens of thousands of flamingos flock there painting a living picture of blue sky and white sand flushed with pink birds. Botswana has a beauty all its own with vast plains and tall palm trees, grasslands, wide open vistas stretching from horizon to horizon and limitless skies with the silence broken only by the call of a lark or some other rare bird.

Reay led the expedition. He was renowned as one of Africa's leading experts with a wealth of knowledge and could identify every rodent, bat and bird we came across. He was a tall, dapper man with a gentle face and greying hair. An absolute gentleman and totally dedicated to the study and conservation of nature he was highly regarded by everyone. Around the campfires the scientists discussed many things. One evening a pair of tiny Night Apes came to have a look at us. They twittered in astonishment as they looked at what must have been equivalent to aliens from space. They came nearer leaping with speed and agility from branch to branch and held us spellbound with a dazzling display of acrobatics better than any circus trapeze. We had ringside seats. Bechuanaland, now called Botswana, was very wild and uninhabited. At night the howl of Jackals floated across the Kalahari sands followed by the whoop of hyenas and the roar of lions, the most awesome sound of Africa. Their roars carried for miles. One evening when we went to bed the lions came to visit us coming closer and closer until their roars reverberated all around camp. We had no tents only stretchers and sleeping bags. We slept on stretchers so as to be off the sand where literally hundreds of large scorpions scurried about. Despite being off the ground scorpions managed to get into bed with me and in the morning were warmly cuddling in the folds of my sleeping bag. We learnt to gingerly slip out of our bedding so as to not disturb any uninvited bed companions. After a while the lions fell silent and we got to sleep but in the morning we saw their pug marks in the soft sand. Our beds had been in a circle around the fire and we were shocked to see that a lion had nearly got into bed with one of the team. It had walked up and sniffed the sleeping man with its great paws almost straddling his stretcher. From then on the poor man never slept in the open but insisted on sleeping in the cab of the truck. Who could blame him?

From the salt pans of Makgadikgadi we turned west and travelled via Orapa to Lake Xau. This was before diamonds were discovered at Orapa and it was a sleepy little African kraal. Lake Xau had been an important source of water for explorers including David Livingstone but when we saw the lake it was bone dry. From here we turned north and passed through the village of Rakops and on to Botletle River on the borders of what is now the remote and incredibly beautiful Makgadikgadi Game Reserve. Wrinkled stone-age San people still roamed the land and lived by their ancient hunting and gathering skills. We came across several groups trekking across the desert. Dressed in skin garments they carried bows and arrows and had ostrich eggs full of water. Bushmen, as they were then called, have an amazing ability to eat large amounts of meat and their stomachs extend to unnatural proportions. To allow for this the skin hangs loosely in huge folds upon them. There buttocks are extended and act as storage a bit like a camel's hump. It was a sight from another age. A Bushman accompanied us on the expedition. He knew the Kalahari intimately. One night I went with him into the dense thickets of the Botletle River where thorny acacias and creepers were so thick they blotted out the stars. We walked a distance, twisting and turning as we searched for rare nocturnal animals until I was disorientated and hopelessly lost but he knew exactly where we were and led me back to camp.

The Kalahari is a captivating place with many strange and beautiful wonders from Barking Geckos to majestic Gemsbok. At that time large herds of antelope roamed the plains but the government decided to construct cattle fences and these blocked migration routes and thousands of herbivores died of hunger and thirst. The legendary mass migrations on a par with the Serengeti in Tanzania became a thing of the past, an example of total disregard for nature. I must not romanticise the Kalahari too much. It is a vast dry, unbearably hot, dusty semi desert with miles of scrub. Today some of the wilderness and wildlife is gone but you can still fly in to a luxury safari camp and see beautiful unspoilt places. Diamond and other mines scar the desert and the Bushmen no longer roam the wide open spaces but the Botswana people are friendly and the Okavango Swamps are a superb wilderness area.

The Eastern Forests

In contrast to the desert the jungles in the eastern regions were beautiful and my zoological expeditions also took me there. We found rare dwarf chameleons, forest frogs, legless skinks, Sun Squirrels, forest birds and other exotic creatures. One expedition went to Amatonga Forest in Mozambique where we searched for rare animals. One night I saw a unique sight when I went out with a flashlight to search for night creatures. As I crept through the jungle I heard excited chattering and shrill screams coming from the canopy above. Creeping nearer I shone my torch up to see a pair of superb Green Mambas glinting emerald green in the light and badgered by a pair of diminutive Night Apes, the same species we saw in Botswana. They sprang from limb to limb just out of reach of the fatal fangs and all the time kept up an awful din. Every now and then the tiny creatures sprang against the huge snakes and caused them to lose their lodging in the branches. The snakes found the whole thing too intimidating and slithered away as fast as they could chased off by the smallest primates in Africa. Little dramas like this always enthralled me.

In the early 1960s Rhodesia embarked on building an oil refinery at Umtali and a pipeline from Beira port was constructed. Much of the pipe was buried six feet underground and this entailed excavating a trench right across Mozambique. Don was the resident Herpetologist at the museum and under his leadership trips were conducted to inspect the trench for reptiles that had fallen in and become trapped. The way this was done was for us to clamber into the trench and then walk along it. This was strenuous and exciting. Imagine coming face to face with a large Forest Cobra in the narrow grave-like confines of the trench? This sort of thing did not perturb Don one bit. He would trudge along the trench for miles with sacks of snakes, lizards, amphibians and rodents that he had caught. I had the dubious privilege to accompany him and came upon some dangerous captives. The idea was not to kill them but to capture them which made it even more adventurous. Gaboon Vipers were extremely dangerous' their venom being one of the most lethal in Africa. Thankfully these snakes are placid in nature and seldom bite and we kept specimens caught in the trench on display in the museum. However, a young herpetologist was careless when cleaning a cage and received a good bite. He was immediately injected with serum and rushed to hospital and hovered between life and death for some days before recovering.

We climbed the mountains of the Eastern Highlands. These are majestic and contain fauna and flora linked with the highlands of East Africa, Ethiopia and Madagascar. The Chimanimani are spectacular for their quartzite ranges which literally sparkle in the sunlight. Often shrouded in cloud they contain strange rocks weathered into weird shapes giving an eerie impression of giants encapsulated in solid stone. As one walks in the silence of heavy mist weird statues loom out of the vapour like guardians of an ancient way. It was along a narrow trail through these hills that slaves once marched from Great Zimbabwe to the East Coast where they were transported to distant lands. After the hot valley from where they had come many died in the frigid mountain air. In fact Chimanimani means "chilly". With dripping ferns and forests interspersed by grasslands these mountains were home to a diversity of animals as well as orchids, lilies and other wild flowers endemic to the region. Our expeditions into the mountains were memorable, exhilarating, never-to-be-forgotten experiences and after visiting them one felt spiritually and physically strengthened.

Politics in Crisis

In 1963 the Federation of Rhodesia and Nyasaland dissolved and Northern Rhodesia became Zambia, Nyasaland became Malawi and there was talk of Southern Rhodesia becoming Zimbabwe. The Southern Rhodesian Prime Minister, Sir Edgar Whitehead, had a house in the Vumba Mountains and regularly came to town. He was considered a liberal but lost ground in the political arena as fears grew among whites that Rhodesia would be sacrificed to the "communists". In most African nations to the north there were few resident whites left but Rhodesia had a fairly large number of whites who considered the country their permanent home. Britain seemed to have no policy for their future and offered no compensation for the losses they might suffer. Ian Smith of the opposition party also came to town but he said Rhodesia was going to stay

Rhodesia. He hired the old Railway Hotel and crowds came to hear him. He said Rhodesia had enjoyed self rule since 1923 so why should Rhodesians lose everything they had worked so hard for. It was true; the British government had granted self government to Rhodesia and people born there after that were no longer given British passports but Rhodesian. The British had also gave self government to the Boer Republics but changed their minds and taken it back. It looked like they were about to do the same to Rhodesia. At Smith's meetings the people cheered, "Good old Smithy". I went along to see the crowds but as youngsters we were more interested in the local disco than our political future. Rock and Roll was all the rage and things were swinging. Stretch grew himself a slick duck-tail hairstyle and hits from Elvis and Jerry Lee Lewis had everyone tapping toes and gyrating.

But there was anxiety among whites everywhere. There were some who supported a quick transition to majority rule but others felt betrayed. Many had come to Rhodesia encouraged by the British government and had poured their lives into establishing homes, farms and businesses. They felt deliberately deceived when the Federation was dissolved by the British government through a unilateral act by Britain on December 31st 1963. Sir Roy Welenksy was Federal Prime Minister and was highly regarded by many. He wrote, *"The Federation was destroyed, not by our avowed enemies but by those who called themselves our friends and said they believed in what we had built."* In his view the Federation was destroyed by British political expediency.

So it was that in the early 60s whites began to feel insecure as Britain dissolved the Federation and granted independence to two of its former colonies. Majority rule would mean the end of white controlled self-government in Southern Rhodesian. The African Nationalists wanted independence immediately without a period of preparation or an evolutionary process towards it. In several African states to the north there was confusion, corruption, military coups, bloodshed and anarchy but the British wanted Rhodesians to just step aside and let it happen to them too. Whites from newly independent states in the north came south to live in Rhodesia. Many had fought for Britain to save the world from anarchy. What they perceived as pseudo democracy and dictatorship were now offered to them and they were expected to go along with it. They were asked to abdicate to the very things they believed Britain had fought against albeit in their minds now disguised as democracy. Events elsewhere in the world were frightening. Conflicts in Korea and Viet Nam, the cold war in Europe and race riots in USA caused the local whites to get the jitters. This all confirmed the whites' deepest fear that communism was taking over the world. They saw African Nationalists as pawns in a communist agenda. Smith's fighting talk was not Smith's at all but was the consensus of local white thinking. The British government had lost the trust of its own citizens in Africa.

Hot Springs Resort

There was not a lot to entertain young people in Umtali. Weekend excursions to Hot Springs Resort on the Odzi River were one source of entertainment. A number of us had purchased cars. I had a lovely bottle-green Austin A40. What a car! It was immaculate for it belonged to Stretch's older brother and was his pride and joy before he sold it to me. It could go like the wind. Whenever there was a party at Hot Springs we loaded up friends in as many cars as possible and drove there. After the festivities we would race back thirty miles along the narrow road. Thinking back one realises how dangerous the whole thing was. The road twisted through rugged hills and wild animals as well as indigenous cattle and goats often strayed on to it. Low-level single lane bridges spanned the rivers. One notorious bridge over the *Mvumvumvu* River had hairpin bends on both approaches. The name means hippopotamus and is a lovely sounding name that conveys the grunts of hippo, a rich deep laughing sound once common along the great rivers of Africa. Any misjudgement approaching the bridge would have been disastrous. In our races the first car to get ahead had the advantage and held the lead with the others doing their best to keep up until we reached the broad highway of Umtali Main Street where there was an opportunity to overtake. The final bend past the old Customs House with its clock tower was often the last chance to win although sometimes the race continued up the incline and past the old Umtali Club which was about as far as one could go as a hasty disappearing act was then required having just roared past the sleepy little Police Station. The Umtali Club exuded colonial Rhodesia. Its cool corridors contained black and white photos of the early town and memorabilia of pioneer days. Its exclusive membership of whites with African staff dressed in starched tunics and an old red British Post Box standing in front was the embodiment of colonialism.

As mentioned, Umtali was a sleepy little town and any excitement had to be self generated. One day Eddie, his brother, and a friend decided to do just that. A recent spate of American gangster movies gave them a bright idea. Eddie had a sleek black Cadilac and he and his brother donned black suits, dark glasses and Mafia style hats. Their friend climbed into the boot and smeared his arm with tomato sauce and dangled it out the back. Then they drove slowly down the high street. The result was predictable. The town began to stir, the sleepy little Police Station was inundated with emergency calls and the trio were apprehended by youthful Police Officers who could not suppress a chuckle.

Portuguese East Africa - Mozambique

The residents of Umtali regularly crossed the border to Mozambique and drove to Beira for a weekend of prawns, beer and sunny beaches. The road descended several thousand feet and then passed through dense jungles until it emerged on the "Pungwe flats" a swampy area through which the Pungwe River flowed. This area was flooded during the wet season making further progress all but impossible. Beira was a dull place renowned for mosquitoes, heat and "Beira tummy," the "bug" that people invariably got from untreated water and badly prepared food. We endured all these discomforts. At peak holiday times thousands of Rhodesians camped along the beach.

Apart from a tropical coastline and coconut palms Mozambique held other attractions. Umtali residents only had to travel a few miles to taste the delights of Portuguese cuisine. Just across the border lay Villa Da Manica. It had seedy bars and lots of Manica beers, demijohns of cheap wine, curry with nuts, olives, Portuguese bread, shrimps and prawns. There was also a little jail without any basic facilities that quite regularly accommodated those who became over zealous. When an individual got into trouble too many times a prohibition order was put in their passport and they were banned for a season.

However, we discovered a way across the Mozambique border that did not require passports. South of Umtali in the foothills of Tsetsera Mountains nestled a picturesque farm called Helvetia, owned by my friend's grandmother. From there a rough track aptly named the Himalaya road ascended spectacular hills to an altitude of 2450 meters. It was here that it crossed the border, the highest track in central Africa. When the colonies were formed the colonial powers simply drew a line between two peaks on a map and declared it to be the border. There was a gate that opened onto a dairy farm run by a Portuguese farmer. There was no lock on the gate and all we had to do was under cover of darkness sneak through. The Himalaya road is one of the most spectacular roads I have travelled in Africa and as one can tell from the colonial names it was considered the equivalent to Switzerland and the Himalayas. It has incredible vistas of beautiful countryside with deep ravines and valleys. The massive granite bulwarks of Chinyamunda and Binga rear out of the Burma Valley and the Mozambique plains stretch below to distant horizons. Through a series of torturous hairpin bends the road descends 1600 meters in a few miles to emerge on the plain. Chikamba dam lies near by and at that time herds of antelope roamed in the bush.

With friends I often went to Helvetia where my friend's grandmother lived and we spent happy weekends there in the Tsetsera Mountains, camping, exploring, fishing and climbing the hills. A true pioneer she ran the farm on her own after her husband died. She was hospitable and welcomed us with home-made farm produce. A perennial stream rushed from the mountains and we made our camp on its banks and slept in the open air. The smell of venison roasting on an open fire and *"sadza"* cooking in a pot drifted across our camp and we swam in the river and lazed in the sunshine. It was an idyllic place. Mountain *kloofs* and forest glades abounded with wild animals and a profusion of birds including the majestic Black Eagles one of Africa's largest birds of prey.

Slaughter at Chipinda Pools
In 1963 the Museum organised a "research" trip to Chipinda Pools where there

was some of the most prolific wildlife in the country. The pools on the Lundi River were located in the magnificent "GonareZhou" National Park - "The Place of Elephants." Sadly, the Rhodesian administration got it into their dull heads that all wild animals in a wide corridor had to be eliminated because of Tsetse fly encroaching onto cattle ranches. The National Museum was given permission to have first choice of what would be slaughtered, for research purposes or so they claimed. Working with Tsetse Department we culled the beautiful wild animals of GonareZhou. Who ever thought it up should have been shot instead. It was terrible carnage.

Chipinda Pools was a beautiful area. Herds of antelope lived along the banks of the river and rare Hartebeest grazed in the grass and woodlands, Bushbuck and Nyala in the thickets, Impala were everywhere. We pitched our camp looking over the river. The situation was idyllic to say the least: huge evergreen trees shaded us and the river environs were alive with all kinds of bird life. That night a herd of elephant came out of the hills and crept past our camp on the way to drink at the pools. I will never forget the silent tread of that "ghost" herd creeping past our camp. Although so big and powerful they were afraid and moved as silently as ballet dancers on tiptoes. They were like silver ghosts in the starlight. There had been so much slaughter of elephants in that area that they were timid and easily spooked and some of them very dangerous. How sad that these majestic beasts should have to creep around the land of their birth as if they were trespassers. For centuries they have been hounded by man ever since the first traders came to Africa seeking ivory. These GonareZhou elephants now hated people. One day the National Parks Warden drove into camp with a smashed up Land Rover. An elephant had put a tusk straight through the front and pushed it off the road and through the bush and even though he was a committed conservationist he shot it at point blank range. Soon after this incident an angry elephant challenged me while I was out with an old Shangaan tracker. We had followed a Kudu into some thickets but unbeknown to us an elephant was within yards of us and we had not seen it. It let out an air splitting scream of rage. The old tracker began to tremble and so did I. The elephant expressed its rage once more and the shrill, piercing scream of its trumpet tore the air and sent a shiver right through us. The Kudu dashed off in one direction and we in the other. There is nothing quite like being close to an angry elephant about to charge.

Sounds on the river were captivating. The haunting cries of Fish Eagles rang during the day and Hadeda Ibis honked at sunset as they flew to roost. It was a wonderful wilderness but after our hunting teams had blasted away many beautiful animals were dead. They hung on hooks in rows and we dissected them with their blood and guts everywhere. We took stomach samples and measurements and did all the things scientists do. What a strange policy it was. We slaughtered animals supposedly to learn more about conserving them. This slaughter was nothing compared to the over-all destruction by the Tsetse Control

Department. Records kept for the Lowveld area alone indicate that 7000 Duiker and 5000 Stembuck were slaughtered every year for over twenty years. Many other species were massacred as well as magnificent trees cut down because they supposedly provided cover for the flies to breed or so the scientists said. This was the cost to eradicate Tsetse Fly. The destruction was appalling and sickened me and I became tired of the slaughter my work now required of me.

One night we heard a mighty commotion down by the river. The sounds of roaring chilled us to the bone. I was a novice with big game but Graham who later became Director of National Parks was an old hand and said it was a fight between lions which sometimes fight fiercely over territory. The roars shook the night air and it certainly sounded as if it were a clash of unprecedented proportions. We jumped in a vehicle and drove down to the edge of the sandy riverbed and switched on a spotlight fully expecting to see lions. To our utmost surprise two massive hippos were locked in mortal combat indifferent to our presence. They roared just like lions and their gaping jaws and massive teeth lunged at one another inflicting huge wounds. Graham was a bit embarrassed that the lions turned out to be hippos but the sight was just as spectacular. When we met in later years we had a quiet chuckle about the lions that turned into hippos.

Kariba Lake and Crocodiles

There was an opportunity for me to join National Parks and work with Rupert Fothergill but I decided to stick with the museum. Rupert Fothergill became famous when Lake Kariba flooded vast areas of bush and marooned thousands of wild animals. He led a team that conducted the rescue of animals, a project called "Noah's Ark". Although poorly equipped with only a handful of small boats he did an amazing job. It was the first serious attempt to save Black Rhinos and many other endangered species. However, I did not think I could keep up with Fothergill for more than a week.

I stayed with the museum and was sent to Kariba with Dave, an expert on crocodiles. After the new lake filled a fish explosion occurred due to abundance of food from flooded grass and vegetation and the fish reached monstrous sizes. The world-renowned Tiger fish of the Zambezi attained weights over thirty pounds. We caught fish all day and set nets to catch them at night. During the midday heat of the Zambezi Valley we cooled off with swims in the middle of the lake where we persuaded ourselves there were no crocs. It was exhilarating to leap off the boats into cool deep water but later we discovered that big crocs did in fact venture into these waters. Kariba became a breeding paradise for crocs and some of the biggest became so brazen that they followed boats to get fish offal cast off by fishermen. They also sometimes snatched humans off the boats when they carelessly draped their feet in the water or did washing on the back gangplank.

Over the years we grew to know Kariba and it became a favourite place to visit. The wild shoreline was home to elephants, buffalo and prides of lions and the islands had wild animals on them from the days of the flooding. Leopards were also common at Kariba. They were partial to the taste of domestic dogs and would snatch them, as well as domestic cats, right out from homes at Kariba town. Once while fishing in a quite inlet of the Sanyati Gorge we were captivated at the sight of a Leopard sitting no more than twenty yards away. Every time we caught a fish it would sit up, prick its ears forward and watch, and then afterwards lie back and relax until the next fish was caught. It seemed to be watching how to do it and some leopards do actually catch fish.

The rivers had a healthy population of crocodiles that sometimes lived on a diet of domestic livestock plus a human or two. We heard regular reports of women taken by crocodiles as they washed clothes on the rocks or as they knelt by the edge of a pool and stretched out an arm to collect water in an earthen pot. They would let just the surface water glide slowly over the lip of the pot so as not to gather any pollution thereby allowing plenty of time for a lurking crocodile to approach and with lightning speed snap the outstretched arm and drag the helpless woman into deeper water. I came to realise just how easy it was to be taken by a croc when on an expedition to the Lusitu River on the border of Mozambique.

This was a magnificent area lying in the shadow of sweeping mountains with primeval jungle and tall majestic forest trees known as Rhodesian Teak that reached heights of over one hundred feet. A large pool invitingly beckoned me to fling caution aside and enjoy a break from the sultry heat by wading in and swimming. But first I quietly strolled along the bank to observe what *"spoor"* was in the mud left by animals that came to drink. I stopped to admire the dainty footprints of a tiny Blue Duiker. As I bent down resting on my heels with the water's edge only about two feet from my back I heard a slight sound behind me and glancing over my shoulder looked into the gaping jaws of a large crocodile not more than a few feet away. Adrenaline and practice combined into a lightning reaction and without thinking my shotgun swung up and a shot of heavy lead was discharged into the mouth of the monster. I fell back and it slid beneath the waters leaving only a ripple to disclose its presence. If I had yielded to the temptation of plunging in to cool off I would have had a terminal surprise. It was a close call nevertheless.

I came to love the forests of Africa. They are full of fascinating and exotic creatures. Sometimes the best way to see wild creatures is simply to find a comfortable spot and wait patiently. On one occasion I was sitting quietly in the forest when I became aware of a soft rustle that gradually increased in volume as something approached across the velvet carpet of leaves and debris of the forest floor. I peered through the undergrowth too absorbed with curiosity to move. All of a sudden a river of army ants came marching through the forest. I had read about such ant columns that devoured every living thing in their path. I stood up causing instant excitement and hissing as the ants nearest to me broke ranks and spread out to search for the prey they sensed so near and I hastened away from them. For a while I followed them at a discreet distance as they marched along in a column of Black Death that was about two meters wide and twenty meters long. Everything they found in their path was quickly immobilised and eaten.

On another occasion I sat dozing under some huge trees when again I heard the soft movement of some creature. I waited expectantly to see what it was. Through the undergrowth came a large Boomslang, a type of tree snake, resplendent in newly shed coat of shimmering green. I sat dead still as it slithered past my feet. Some of the most memorable sights I have seen in Africa were while just sitting in the bush. Once a duiker antelope walked right up to me and sniffed my feet and at times I have been surrounded by baboons, monkeys, mongooses, guinea fowl and even big game so close as to almost touch them. At Mana Pools National Park a Buffalo bull walked up to within ten feet of me and a friend. We were seated as still and silent as statues and the old bull grazed towards us quietly munching grass and pausing to look around. He knew we were there and his inquisitive nature compelled him to gradually come closer until at no less than a few feet he stopped and looked us full in the eyes. We simply gazed back. There was no fear just curiosity as the big animal quizzed us and decided we were no threat and carried on munching. We were so close we could hear him chew and see every wrinkle in his massive hide. Much is made of animals being dangerous and at times they are but I have found they are usually so only when threatened by man. When one is not a threat to them and one treats them with the respect they deserve then all is at peace. If one wants to see animals one must be quiet and still. As soon as one is the bush comes alive.

The elephants at Mana Pools were renowned for their good manners. The campsite is not fenced and wild animals can wander in. Large evergreen trees grow along the banks of the Zambezi, gigantic Figs, tall Acacias, giant Sausage Trees and others. We camped under them and they gave shade by day. Often in the middle of the night the elephants would come through camp munching leaves and feeding on fallen acacia pods. They would step between the tent pegs and on some occasions gently around sleeping people without the people ever knowing. Elephants are not clumsy but can be as sure footed and dainty as ballet dancers. At night we put a tarpaulin on the ground and our bedding on top and slept in the open with the stars of Africa over head and the dust of Africa underneath. The sight of the Southern Cross hanging in the African sky was a comforting and beautiful sight.

Most of the forests have gone today except in conservation areas. In some places nothing remains as evidence that there once was a forest. It has all been hacked down. I did not know I would witness the destruction of entire forests in my lifetime. Eventually the day came when the museum was ready for opening.

The Prime Minister of Rhodesia Sir Edgar Whitehead attended the ceremony, I bought a suit and the staff turned out to have a photograph taken. It was a milestone in the history of the Museums.

The Congo Uprising - 1960

The general trends in Africa were disturbing. Riots in Nyasaland brought the Rhodesian Army Reserve out in full strength and rumblings from African Nationalists caused disturbances in the townships nearer home. In fact I can hardly remember a time when we were not subjected to disruption and unrest.

On June the 30th 1960 the Belgian government granted Independence to its vast African colony of the Congo. Taken in haste most whites considered it one of the most irresponsible decisions ever made by a colonial power. It was implemented without adequate preparation and within days the whole country slid into anarchy. The central government's Gendarmerie forces mutinied and went on a pillage of rape and killing. White refugees flooded into Northern Rhodesia and were airlifted to Salisbury. By July 11th thousands of men, women and children reached safety. Others perished. Whites who lived in Ndola were traumatised by what they witnessed when priests, nuns and others crossed the border terribly brutalised. Images of badly mutilated people shocked the world as refugees poured into Rhodesian towns. Horrific stories of rape and slaughter came with them. People were murdered and those who escaped lost everything. Thousands of Africans perished. The Congo uprising had a deep psychological effect on local people. The Rhodesians rallied and gave assistance with food and shelter but it left a deep emotional mark on local whites who believed the same thing would happen to them. More massacres were perpetrated in Angola. In March 1961 gangs moved across the Congo border and attacked a dozen villages in the northern coffee growing area. Rape, torture, and killing took place. Men, women and children were beheaded and had limbs hacked off. Living people were put through a saw mill and cut to pieces. Such horror of brutality was unleashed just when whites were thinking the "dark continent" had been tamed but it suddenly reverted to old ways of violence. Rhodesians began to feel their backs against a wall. Events in other places of Africa and the rhetoric put out by some African National leaders left whites shocked and dismayed.

Johnny joins the Mercenaries

The communist backed rebellion that took place in Congo persuaded Moise Tshombe leader of the copper-rich Katanga province that it would be better to secede from central Congo. It seems he had clandestine support from Belgium which had substantial interests in his mineral rich province. The central government disapproved and the first and only elected Premier, Patrice Lumumba, appealed to the UN to intervene. UN and Congolese troops poured into Katanga to take control of the provincial administration. Soon afterwards Lumumba was abducted, it was said by undercover agents supported by the West, and he was secretly handed over to Tshombe's men. He was beaten and then murdered and his body never recovered. He had made a serious mistake when he expressed approval of Russia whereas Tshombe seemed to stand against communism. Tshombe was pro-west or so he said and appealed to the West including the Federal Government for help. The Federal Prime Minister, Sir Roy Welensky could not act without British authority and thankfully the UK refused military assistance. In the absence of help Tshombe put out word that he would pay for assistance and Mike Hoare raised an "army" of about two hundred mercenaries to help him. Unfortunately for "Mad Mike" the rest of the world did not view this favourably and a prolonged conflict unravelled the country even further. The mercenaries got bad press as the situation degenerated with atrocities committed on all sides even the UN.

My brother had recently finished school and this happy event coincided with "Mad Mike's" recruitment of mercenaries to fight in the Congo. Johnny all grown up now enrolled and found himself in his teens as a full combat soldier in one of Africa's particularly nasty wars. He thought it would be a grand adventure. Dad knew nothing about it for he simply enrolled before anything could be done to stop him. Some mercenaries were hardened soldiers and ex servicemen and came from South Africa, Britain, Europe and USA. Some like Johnny were hardly adults and had been lured into joining. These mercenaries were much maligned by the world press and had a tough time in the battlefield. They found themselves fighting Congolese Government troops on the one hand, rebels on the other and United Nations troops as well. It was futile and tragic but they did liberate Stanleyville and rescued missionaries and civilians.

Missing in Action

Johnny was involved in the thick of the fighting and the stories he recounted on his return were enough to make one turn pale but at one stage it seemed he wasn't going to return at all. For several months we heard no news of him and feared the worse. When news did come it was not the kind we wanted to hear.

The following curt communication arrived:

Kangolo, Katanga, Dec.1962
Monsieur,
It is with regret that I am inform you that your son is missing after attack with Manono last week. He is a good son and trying to find him we are, but it is not certain that we find him but we do all we can. Possible he is dead, possible he is live, I not no. We hope so. If him we find I tell you.
    I reste,
            Jean Piere Barteien

No further news came and weeks passed into months. What had happened to him in the Congo jungles we wondered? Eventually rumours filtered through that he was alive.

He had been fighting his way out of Congo. After a skirmish with Congolese troops he and a couple of mates were unable to rejoin their men. Under cover of darkness they hid in the jungle and kept a low profile for some days until they found a United Nations contingent and an opportune moment to steal a vehicle from the convoy. Living off their wits and with help from local people they set off through the jungles. Using rough bush tracks they travelled several hundred miles all the time trying to dodge the real UN. The local people were patriotic towards Tshombe and assisted Johnny and his mates who narrowly escaped death on several occasions at the hands of Central Congolese and UN forces. They clashed with the famed "Gurka" troops and eventually crossed into Northern Rhodesia. I think the things he saw seriously affected his young mind. "Mad Mike" was apparently considered a good soldier but he couldn't save Tshombe. The United Nations moved in and appalling atrocities were committed. Tshombe's regime fell and eventually in 1965 Mobutu established a non-democratic and brutal dictatorship that lasted nearly thirty years. There was war in the Congo with millions of casualties. It seemed to suit the West who went on trading with the Congo during this time.

Slowly the surviving mercenaries filtered back home and Rhodesians became even more insecure. In 1963 John F. Kennedy was gunned down supposedly by communist agents and racism showed its ugly face in the United States. The Vietnam War raged and it all looked pretty bleak to white Rhodesians.

Terror came to the Land
In June 1964 communist trained insurgents set an ambush on the road near Melsetter in the beautiful hills of the Eastern Highlands. As a local white family drove home in the evening they came upon a barrier of sticks and stones. The man stopped the car and got out to move them and was immediately attacked by armed men. Knocked on the head with knobkerries he sustained fractures in four places as well as being stabbed sixteen times in the face and neck. Bravely he managed to fight off his attackers and claw back into the car and drive full-tilt at the roadblock which he crashed through, but he was dying. The car careered down the road and hit a tree. The gang ran up and poured petrol onto the car and the occupants but fortunately were not able to get a match going to ignite it. The arrival of another vehicle disturbed them and consequently the mother and daughter were saved from certain death. The gang that did the deed called themselves the "Crocodile Gang" and left notes at the scene saying *"The Crocodile Group will kill all white men in Zimbabwe."* It was blatant racist murder but then crocodiles are not known for their gentle ways.

It seemed the Congo uprising had ignited long-standing grievances. Images of frightened whites had stirred the aspirations of "freedom fighters". The perpetrators of this murder were hunted down by Rhodesian police and brought to trial. They were sentenced to death by the Rhodesian courts but a legal wrangle with the British government which was theoretically sovereign over the country took place and Britain issued a Royal pardon. The veracity of this decision completely flummoxed Rhodesians who went ahead and executed them anyway after the High Court declared the Queen's pardon illegal. In the meanwhile the question on everyone's mind was what had happened to British justice? Why had they granted a royal pardon to murderers?

At about this time the OAU put out a statement of intent that they would destroy all vestiges of white civilisation in the south and that the rivers would turn red with the blood of the tyrants and their children.

Meanwhile, Johnny decided to go for tamer thrills and he and a friend set off on a marathon non stop motorbike ride from Salisbury to Cape Town a distance of about one thousand four hundred miles. After that he took to sky-diving. His great search for adventure was an example I admired and his quest eventually took him out of Africa but not before he did me one "last favour."

Soldiers of the Queen - 1964

The Rhodesian Government had passed a bill to make military training compulsory and in 1964 at about the time of the killing my call-up papers arrived and I had no option but to board the official train to Llewellyn Barracks located near Heaney junction near Bulawayo. The scene at Umtali Railway Station was reminiscent of men going to war. Fathers and mothers, brothers and sisters, shed tears and clung to teenage lads hardly out of school. Johnny, who had evaded military call-up by going off to the Congo as a mercenary and who was in Bulawayo met me on arrival and thought it was his brotherly duty to spare me the indignity of the military trucks sent to collect us and instead to take me to the army depot. On arrival we stepped into the reporting office and Johnny's appearance in untidy clothes, long hair and casual manner was like a red flag to a bull. It was not a good start. The officer reacted predictably.

"Get your hands out of your pockets and stand up straight" he bellowed at my brother, sounding a bit like a hippo.

No reaction came from Johnny who pretended not to hear which infuriated the man even more for he was used to people jumping the moment he opened his ugly mouth.

Again, "You lazy no good lay-about when I speak you jump," he shouted. Again there was no response from John.

The officer was about to get physical when Johnny decided it was time to tell the man he was not reporting for duty and coolly walked out leaving him angry and me to take the brunt of his rage. It reminded me of my school experience when the teacher heard my name and threatened me with dire consequences simply for being Johnny's brother which I thought very unfair. As I said, it was not a good start.

The army did not impress me much but I had to grow up fast having left school at sixteen and now a soldier at barely seventeen. Some of my friends had got out of army by going off to university. Unfortunately I did not have that advantage. One of the first things we were required to do when we enlisted in the army was to swear allegiance to the Queen of Britain. We were "Soldiers of the Queen."

Army discipline was not entirely new to me having been a school cadet. As cadets we marched around the school fields carrying old 303 rifles and with our wide brimmed hats turned up on the side. It was all a bit of a joke. On one parade I fainted. After that I got tired of it. Thankfully, living out of town, I made sure that there were all manner of reasons why I could not attend regularly. After school Stretch and I had to catch a lift back home so we were excused afternoon activities. When there was no lift available we walked several miles to the bus terminal and caught the local African bus to the nearest drop off point and then walked the remaining miles in the heat of the African day. In Rhodesia there were two kinds of buses, the kind used by people around town and the long distance kind used by Africans. By catching the African bus we were breaking all the norms but they were very polite to us. We would sit among the mothers and their screaming babies in the crowded seats and endure the long hot haul over the hills to home. This got us out of cadets and the rest of the afternoon was free to roam the bush.

The Royal Rhodesian Army, however, went beyond a joke. Led by instructors who had fought in various campaigns in Europe, North Africa and Burma, they claimed to be a reflection of what they considered to be the real thing, the British Army. They required our boots to reflect the sunshine as well as our brass and buttons. We spent days polishing them into the small hours of the morning. The first few hectic days after arrival were intended to be a shock to our system. Stripped naked we were paraded before a panel of medical officers who scrutinised each one of us for possible defects and passed comments amongst themselves as they did so. I got the distinct impression I was a piece of merchandise and began to empathise with slaves paraded before their captors at a slave market. I gathered from what they said that my crooked back was not crooked enough to prevent me from doing my duty which was a pity. Then there were the jabs, the dreaded three in one for typhoid A & B and Tetanus sadistically given into the arm by an army medic and causing severe pain for the next twenty-four hours. Some men fainted just at the sight of the large needle and it was not uncommon to hear men groan because the injections were so painful.

Then there was kit issue each item thrown at one with callous humour. The boots, tied together by their laces and thrown with special venom, had to be polished and broken in. The toe caps had to be smoothed and this required a special technique using a heated spoon which when pressed down on the leather together with melted black polish resulted eventually if done correctly in a mirror like surface. Anything less was not acceptable. Endless weeks followed in training, drilling, running, polishing, running, drilling, training and far too little sleep. In fact we were no better than slaves as we had no life of our own. Eventually I got the routine down to a fine art and by getting organised with a good batman began to enjoy my sleep again. The batmen were African staff employed at the depot for various tasks and who did work for us on the sly. Batmen were forbidden but from our point of view were necessary. It was impossible to do what the army required without a little help. The penalty for being caught was severe but we all used them anyway. I must have inherited something of dad's military organisation for I found I was able to get everything ready the night before and on the morning of inspection while everyone else was dashing around in mad panic I would lie dozing to the last possible moment and then rise, slip into my uniform, pull up my bed and stand by. To the considerable consternation of the rest of the soldiers I won the coveted "Stick Medal" of the barracks which meant I could enjoy full weekend passes. Weekend passes were spent mostly in certain pubs in Bulawayo and we became familiar with their nightlife. The Palace Hotel was a favourite watering hole for those in uniform. The Military Police also knew this and one had to keep a sharp eye open for them. We all began to drink, what else was there to do?

The Rhodesian Army used surplus Second World War equipment and most of the instructors still seemed to be fighting that war or pretending to. After the initial training I applied to signals corps and was transferred to Brady Barracks in Bulawayo. We battled away at Morse code tapping out messages until our heads rang. If only my old grandfather from Marconi's wireless company could have seen me. I never did grasp radio techniques and half the radios only worked intermittently anyway and would not have coped in a real war. That was still to come. We had basic lectures about the methods used by "terrorists" and were informed as to how the army combated them with "anti-terrorist" tactics. The term "terrorist" was the term used by the army in those times for anyone who might attack them and came from past experience of the British in Burma and Kenya.

Lectures were dull events especially after sitting up all night cleaning kit. At times even the bellowing insults of the staff were not sufficient to keep us awake. A special punishment was reserved for those soldiers caught nodding off. It was a bit like the old practice of sitting in the corner and wearing a dunce's hat but instead of a chair and hat a bucket of water was kept in the corner. Anyone caught dozing had to duck his head into the bucket and keep it under for a prolonged period of time. Having been thoroughly awakened in this manner he would then have to lecture the class for five minutes on any subject of his choice. The ducking was some-what unpleasant and the opportunity to talk very embarrassing for those inept at public speaking especially in front of a class of rough, taunting soldiers.

I experienced first hand the benefits of army nursing. It was the year of Hong Kong flu and lots of people were getting sick. A number of us went down with bad bouts and ended up in the army hospital where we lay in rows with our bums up for jabs. The army Doc thought it a good opportunity to let medical recruits practice giving injections. He chose me as the pin cushion and using a ball point pen carefully divided my bum into sections and then proceeded to explain the method and place for giving the jab. I felt awfully exposed and my bare bum was having spasms at the dreaded thought of a dozen recruits practising on my tender flesh when fortunately the Doc decided to show them how to do it and before I knew it gave me a perfect injection. I felt nothing. Then it was the turn of the others and down the line the learners went jabbing at bare backsides accompanied by appropriate grunts, groans and squeals. It was a bit like one of the British "Carry on Movies."

One of the most difficult times was when we had "Change Parade." This entailed changing quickly from one uniform to another and after parading changing again into another set of uniforms. There was the "Stick Uniform" which was the posh one with all the brass and shiny boots and puttees. Puttees were long khaki bandages that wrapped around our ankles. They had to be perfectly spaced with about ¼ of an inch between each wrap, not easy to do in a hurry. Then there was Combat Uniform and Physical Training and so on. A Change Parade meant one had to dress and undress rapidly sometimes on the run. All kinds of mistakes could be made. On one parade a soldier in haste pulled his webbing on back to front so that the two back straps were on his chest instead of his back and the two pouches were sitting high up instead of low on his belt. The staff officer looked at this and took the cue. Walking up to him he said, "Let me adjust your bra darling" and fumbling with the pouches neatly arranged them for the rest of the parade. He never lived it down.

The monotony of barrack life was relieved by the music of a soldier who had a guitar and in the evenings we gathered around and listened as he crooned. He wrote his own music and we enjoyed his songs for radios were banned in the barracks. Sitting in the austere barrack room he worked his fingers over the guitar strings plucking each note and crooning out the words until the tune and song were perfect and we all sat around and crooned with him. Our battalion had men who came from all walks of life, farmers, accountants and dropouts. One man, I forget his name, took exception to the songs and for no apparent reason decided to put an end to the singing. He was solidly built and when he hit our crooner there was no give in his fist so it was his cheek that crumpled. Our singing friend was shocked but he was a gentleman and controlled himself admirably. His face swelled and his singing stopped and we all had to cover for him as fighting was punished with stiff penalties for all in the barrack room. However, he gained the respect of the whole barracks and was soon singing again. In fact our crooner later became son-in-law to the Prime Minister and became quite famous with his songs. At the time we could not foresee the terrible future awaiting some soldiers who would perish.

Most of the regular army officers were a bad tempered bunch of fairies. They wandered around with their wands clutched under their armpits always ready for action. These were used at appropriate times to wave in front of one or under one's chin so as to apply upward pressure or in extreme cases to poke up one's nostril. All this was done accompanied with screams and threats. The spell worked wonders. The more abusive and derogative the language the more wonders it worked. It placed the fear of the army in us and transformed a normal rational person into a walking talking "yes sir - no sir" mindless machine. A favourite saying was "Hurry up, and wait." We would be given urgent commands to be carried out on the double only to spend the next hours sitting around while the staff decided what to do next.

The army had a special language all of its own such a *"jollers"* and *"scabangos"* and a whole lot more that cannot be repeated. Perhaps the most unforgettable language came from the rifle range. Target shooting was always a pleasure for me and having had past experience I won the coveted "Battalion Medal." The competition entailed shooting, first from a lying position followed by sitting, walking and running and shooting at stationary and moving targets. We also had to take a turn in the "pits" holding a target above our heads and running like crazy with bullets flying above us. It was quite exciting.

Our final exercise will never be forgotten. It was decided that the entire company would partake in a war game. We were split into "soldiers" and "pretend terrorists." The "terrorists" had the easy part for they went off and took possession of a *"kopje"* where they were instructed to wait in ambush. We, the "soldiers", then assembled miles away and under the guidance of our officers set off on a forced night march with the intention of locating and surrounding the terrorists so as to launch a dawn attack upon them. Having one of the lightest physiques in the company I was given the task of carrying the MAG or Heavy Machine Gun. I was chosen intentionally to carry this heavy gun for it was thought that the lighter the person the better able they were and heavier larger soldiers often collapsed when given yet more weight to carry. As we marched through the night several sly remarks were made as to my capabilities so I was determined to keep up. We marched till the small hours of the morning when a halt was called. As I was also the medic I then had to nurse the toes and heels of the men who had blisters. Their mocking turned to expressions of appreciation. After a while we were given instructions to move forward and with the utmost caution we surrounded the designated kopje. As the eastern sky lightened we were given orders to storm the summit which we did. As we reached the top a great commotion broke out from the adjacent kopje and we came "under enemy fire" from the "terrorists". Confusion took over and a hundred men were humbled and the officers went off to discuss who was responsible for the blunder. It was a good thing they were pseudo terrorists and not real. Unfortunately the real thing was not far off.

The incident brought images to my mind of the British blunder in January 1900 at Spioenkop in Natal during the South African War when British troops came under Boer bombardment. The British military contingent far outnumbered the Boers and with some arrogance the army leaders boasted that the Boers would soon be defeated. From the peak of Spioenkop the Boers watched the approaching British. Then under cover of darkness thousands of British soldiers clambered up the steep hill to take the summit only to find at dawn the Boers were not there. They had repositioned themselves on adjacent peaks and were now able to rain fire upon them. It was one of the most awful British defeats during the war. The official British figure of three hundred and twenty two men killed is still debated but whatever the exact count hundreds of Britain's finest fighting men died that day. It was a beautiful place to die but the cause was questionable. Spioenkop is considered by many as the end of the era of invincible might of the British Empire defeated by a handful of Boer farmers.

The hill of Spioenkop is not too far from the hill of Isandlwana where the British army was massacred in 1879 when they faced massed Zulu Impis. Again, in typical imperial arrogance the commanders underestimated the skill and courage of the "inferior" Zulus and paid the supreme price. British troops faced the full brunt of Zulu warriors and were overrun and massacred even though they fought bravely as British soldiers always do. At the end of the battle over thirteen hundred British troops lay dead. A few miles away at Rorke's Drift another battle raged. A small group of British soldiers made a heroic stand against the Zulus. They fought all day and withstood the attack. Eleven Victoria Crosses were awarded. Was this to somehow balance the high casualties? What British officers lacked in intelligence the soldiers made up in courage but it just seems another unjust war fought in Southern Africa. During the Victorian era Britain actually had a "Minister of War" instead of a "Minister of Defence" and during Victoria's sixty four year reign there was not a single year without a conflict.

In later years Rhodesians made their own blunders but if they had been recognised as "soldiers of the Queen" they would have won a few medals also. Unfortunately, although Rhodesians considered themselves loyal to the Queen it did not seem anyone in the British government thought they were even though we had sworn allegiance to "Her Majesty." At the end of our training it was with a sense of joy that we marched on to our final parade. We certainly looked the part, we had come in as kids, we were going out as a disciplined unit of soldiers or so we were told. We were supposedly upholding the fighting traditions of our forefathers. We were inspected and given a little talk about doing our duty and how Rhodesia must stand against communism and terrorism and several other isms. With a final bellow and to the tune of "When the Saints Go Marching In" and led by the regimental mascot, an old goat wearing the battalion colours, we marched off the grounds and thankfully out of full-time army life. It was one of those rare moments of true ecstasy. What relief! I breathed a silent rebuff to the Regimental Sergeant Major and left. Years later I was to meet the man and he did not seem very intimidating in fact he was quite human. Time must have mellowed him and circumstances had changed. And how were we to know that so many "saints" truly would "go marching in," wounded, maimed and broken lives given to "save" our country. Most of us were still in our teens, young enough to die, not yet old enough to vote.

Although I had left the army the army had not left me for there was a system of call-ups and every one was expected to fulfil quarterly camps. I was posted to 4th Battalion Royal Rhodesia Regiment. In fact I was to be in the army off and on for the next sixteen years during the long and painful Liberation War.

The Fairest Cape

When I came out of the army I needed a break. Mother was in Cape Town and invited me to join her. I don't think she really expected me to make it but undaunted I set out to hitch nearly two thousand miles. On the way I stopped off to see my brother who had not yet left to go overseas. He was a surveyor and loved every minute of it. He worked in a rough shanty town called Triangle very much like a wild western frontier camp. It was the last I would see of him for thirty years. He embarked on a career in engineering that took him all around the world. I stayed at home and ended up having the wrong kind of experience; war, dictatorship and revolution.

The long journey to the Cape was exciting. One night I was tired and unable to get a lift. Darkness fell and I was left standing on the side of the road in the lonely bush. A twinkling light in the darkness marked some human habitation. I found a track that led to it and eventually knocked on the door of an isolated farmhouse. The people were shocked to see me but welcomed me and gave me a meal and a room. It was a large dusty room with an old wire bed in the corner. Heaped in piles and filling the room were thousands of second hand shoes of all shapes and sizes with worn out soles, torn buckles, broken heels and open toe-caps. "Where had they all come from?" I wondered. The pungent aroma of a thousand shoes that had walked an accumulated sum of thousands of dusty miles filled the room.

Can you imagine the smell? It was an unforgettable night! All kinds of thoughts filled my mind. Perhaps these were the shoes of hapless travellers who had stopped off and slept in this very room and been murdered during the night? It brought images of the holocaust to mind and I had nightmares. I was relieved to survive the night put on my own shoes and leave as soon as I could.

I don't remember how many days it took but reaching the border I crossed the Limpopo River and sped south through Transvaal, Natal, Transkei and on to the Cape of Good Hope. Sometimes I was offered accommodation but some nights I slept on the side of the road. It was not the broad highway of today but a narrow winding road twisting through the hills. On I travelled, through the Wild Coast through forests and across deep rivers down to wet windy Cape Town and a bit of culture. After the long journey I looked rough and when I knocked on her door mother nearly fell over backwards. I don't think she ever thought I would make it. After the tough time in the army I enjoyed the break. The beautiful shores and majestic mountains of the Cape lifted my spirit. The long rail journey back through the Karoo, Kalahari and Bechuanaland was itself one of those unforgettable adventures of colonial Africa, the train chugging along with soot pouring from the engine and steam from the funnel, stopping at sidings to top up with water and sounding the whistle at road crossings. It had all the trimmings of old colonial luxury with fresh, starched linen, a posh caboose and smartly dressed waiters rapping on coupe doors bearing morning coffee. The train stopped at Kimberley where Rhodes got rich through diamonds. We were told by the conductor that we would be stationary for a couple of hours so I decided to take the opportunity to see the "Big Hole", the biggest man made excavation in the world and out of which many diamonds were dug. I trudged off down the tracks and eventually came to the very brink of the gigantic hole. Swallows, falcons and eagles now inhabited the hole and I spent a while admiring it then traipsed back. When I arrived at the station my heart missed a beat, the train was gone. Panic rose in me. Here I was in the middle of the Northern Cape with no money and only the clothes I stood in. I had no idea what to do except start hitching north but with no passport or funds it looked bleak. Then I heard some shunting and saw the north bound train starting to move off from a side track. I ran for my life and managed to haul myself on board.

It was soon back to work and I was eager to start. There was never a day when I was reluctant to go to work but at about this time I had a breakdown. Difficulties of childhood, leaving home and then the army all contributed to it. One thing that came out of it was that I joined a small church and began to attend regularly.

1965

In 1965 Winston Churchill died. Churchill was admired by Rhodesians. There was no TV so we listened to the funeral on radio. Later we saw the cinema newsreel and watched the procession as it made its way through the streets of

London. An era had ended and for us another era was about to start. Churchill had declared in one of his "pig headed" speeches: *"I have not become the King's First Minister in order to preside over the liquidation of the British Empire"* but the final liquidation of that Empire was not far off as we were about to find out.

The turmoil in Africa had a profound effect upon whites. At the end of the Second World War communism was portrayed by the West as a deadly foe and the Russian invasion of East Europe seemed to prove it. The Russians and the Chinese we were told, were known to support revolution all over the world including Africa. After the collapse of the Congo numerous coups took place throughout Africa and democracy went out the window as dictators took power. Russia and China seemed to be invariably implicated in the events. This did not help to create confidence among whites, to the contrary, it persuaded them more than ever that they must resist a quick hand over to majority rule for the alternative was complete anarchy.

A few months after Churchill's death in November 1965, I was in the Sabi River Valley. My task was to conduct a zoological survey of the area with special attention to certain specific animals one of which was the rare Suni, a diminutive antelope that lived in isolated thickets. This little animal was scarce and zoologists were particularly concerned about its status. It is one of the smallest antelope in the world and only stands about as high as a hare and is very shy. I investigated likely spots but was unable to find any evidence of the animal. However, I bagged a common duiker for "pot roast" and cut some meat into strips to make biltong and salted and hung it under trees on the banks of the Sabi River. My camp was in a beautiful setting of large shady trees under which I placed my stretcher. November is a hot month and the valley was hotter than most areas but the breeze under the cool trees soon turned the meat into some of the most delicious biltong I have tasted.

Rhodesian Rebellion

November the 11th 1965 was for Rhodesians one of those days that would not be forgotten. If you ask an ex-Rhodesian, "Where were you on November 11th 1965?" they will tell you exactly what they were doing. I was sitting on the banks of the Sabi River eating biltong. For some days before there had been rumours of an impending announcement of importance so I switched on my portable radio to listen to it. The monotone drone of the voice of the Prime Minister Ian Smith drifted over the air of my peaceful camp as he made yet another speech. I became captivated by what he said not fully realising the consequences of his words but knowing that they would change my life. They were stirring words about fighting for civilisation, counting the cost, making the sacrifice and resisting the tide of communism that was overtaking the world. Rhodesia, he said, was a little nation with great stature and courage, a nation chosen for this very hour to stand against communism. Britain, we all knew, had let us down badly. Now we were compelled to declare our independence. The speech droned on and Rhodesians believed every word of it. The Prime Minister certainly believed it for he could not have been more sincere. He believed it and so did everyone else, well almost everyone. After all, we had been brought up on stories about the Second World War. Had not Britain fought to save the world and were we not also British? We were told that the communists were bent on taking over the world no matter what. The Nationalists were in the pay of the communists and Rhodesia had to stand where Britain had surrendered. Rhodesia would stop communist instigated terror sweeping through Africa, or so it was said.

So the Unilateral Declaration of Independence of Rhodesia was proclaimed at 11 o'clock on Armistice Day, 11th of November, 1965. It was the first rebellion by a British territory since the American Revolution. Yet the Prime Minister who had himself fought in the RAF during the Second World War emphasised that there was to be no break with the Crown. In fact he ended his speech with "God Save the Queen!" I reached for another stick of biltong and tried to understand the complexities of the situation. It was quite beyond me but I was proud that Rhodesia would keep British honour alive. The threat made by Rhodes's long ago when he addressed his troops after they had occupied Bulawayo, that Rhodesia might rebel, now seemed prophetic. In 1956 the Rhodesian Prime Minister Godfrey Huggins had also hinted at it and Welensky too in the troubled days of the Federation. It seemed to be a deeply entrenched concept in the minds of Rhodesians for they were unable to grasp the times in which they lived and that ultimately the country did not belong to them. However, they were not going to give up what they had without a fight. My African co-worker Leonard did not seem too interested in the announcement and together we enjoyed the rest of our venison.

There are many beautiful birds in Africa. Among the family of Doves is the Laughing Dove which is widely distributed. One can often hear their beautiful melodious calls wafting across the bush. It is a gentle call that sounds like soft laughter. But the Mourning Dove which is not as common and lives along the fringe of big rivers has a call that sounds like a rough guttural growl and very sad. The most mournful of all is the call of the Emerald Spotted Wood-Dove. It starts with two muffled notes followed by notes on a descending scale and diminishing in volume. It is repeated monotonously and is interpreted in some African languages as, *"My mother is dead, my father is dead, my relatives are dead! Oh, oh, oh, oh, oh, oh."* The calls of the bush doves are the most haunting melodies of Africa and seem to epitomise the spirit of the land and people, laughter in the midst of sorrow. Their calls rang through the trees of the great Sabi River. Great sadness would follow the announcement I had just heard and many would perish.

November is the time when the wet season starts, in fact in the "old days" one could predict the start of the rains on the 16th of November. Sure enough in the next few days the clouds gathered darker and darker and then the rains broke with vengeance pouring down tons of torrential rain. Fearing that the cloud burst would isolate us we hastily loaded everything into the Land Rover and hurried to get out of the valley. The Sabi Valley is surrounded by steep ranges of rugged hills off which water rushes in great torrents during tropical storms. Our dash was dramatic as we rushed to get across each gully before they flooded and became impassable. At one gully the water engulfed the vehicle up to the doors and rose higher flooding the electrical system but the momentum of the vehicle carried us through and it emerged spluttering on the opposite bank. Vehicles are carried away by torrents like this but the engine revived and on we sped skidding and slipping until at last we emerged onto higher ground and safety. I will always remember November 1965. It unleashed a storm of massive proportions and a bitter struggle that swept many lives away.

River Tramps on the Rio Save

In June of 1967 my friend Phil and I embarked on a canoe trip down the Rio Save to the sea a distance of about two hundred miles. Save (pronounced Sarvay) means "to trade" and the river was once an ancient trade route to Great Zimbabwe. The Phoenicians, Persians, Indians and Arabs all came to East African shores to trade. The river flows across Mozambique to the Indian Ocean south of Sofala which was a coastal fort near the southerly limit that boats could reach on the trade winds. From the delta boats sailed up the river propelled by coastal winds and then returned to the sea on the river current. In ancient times the river flowed much stronger than today and allowed small vessels to navigate it. Traders came with their wares of cloth, porcelain and beads and took away gold, ivory, and slaves. These traders used Sofala as a base and conducted expeditions into the interior. Research has revealed that the origins of Great Zimbabwe were linked with this trade.

Phil and I decided we would explore this river. Phil was short in stature but in life was larger than any man I knew. He was a driver on the Railways. His parents had come from India of British stock. His father had been in the British Indian Army following the tradition of his father before him. For three generations India had been their family home but when Independence came they left in a hurry as thousands of others were forced to. Phil was a child when his family fled but he could still recall his infancy and those frightening days of violence. They landed on the shores of South Africa with nothing but a couple of suitcases and made their way north to the British colony of Rhodesia to start again from scratch. The upheaval of those early years had a profound affect upon Phil yet he retained a mischievous sense of humour and a warm heart of compassion towards those in trouble. Phil and I became friends.

We bought a sixteen-foot fibreglass canoe and got our friend Piet to drive us to the confluence of the Sabi and Lundi Rivers where the river becomes the Rio

Save. This was itself a remarkable journey along rough bush tracks. We lashed our canoe on the top of Piet's old 1940 Ford van of which he was very proud. It had headlights on the front mudguards, was painted a deep royal blue and was his pride and joy. We left Umtali in the early hours of a morning in June and drove through the rugged hills of the Odzi Valley and on to Birchenough Bridge where we stopped for coffee and breakfast. From there we continued past Middle Sabi into the remote country of the south. Here the bush was thick and the road an overgrown track. The sun set and on we drove twisting through thick undergrowth on what had now become a rocky pathway. In the late hours that night we called a halt and rested. As dawn filtered through the trees we pressed on with the rising sun. Eventually the track entered dense forests that indicated we were approaching the river. Huge evergreen trees towered above, thick lianas and creepers hung across the forest track. The front headlight crashed against a protruding stump and shattered. The canoe lurched from its place on the back of the vehicle and we sprang to support it. Antelope sprang away in panic. Parrots flew above screeching at the sight of us and at last we emerged on the banks of a wide and lazy river shimmering in the morning heat.

We collapsed on the sandy bank and viewed the river for the very first time. Piet was mortified at the sight of his broken headlamp and crumpled mudguard. We kindled a fire and cooked *"sadza"* porridge and coffee. After eating we waved goodbye to Piet and shoved our meagre supplies into the canoe, squeezed ourselves in and set out on what was to be an epic trip. We had a kilogram of rice, a packet of sugar, a little salt, some coffee and that was about it for a trip of several weeks. We hoped to live off the land. The river flowed through some of the wildest areas in southern Africa that abounded with animals including the "big five," as well as big crocs and big hippos. During the day we paddled and at night slept on sandbars or under huge trees on the banks. Paddling the river was exciting. We dodged hippos that congregated in family pods. They snorted in surprise and flicked their ears at the sight of our tiny vessel bearing down upon them. Other hippos slept on the sandbars. When we got near they plunged into the water. Massive crocodiles also slept on the banks and as we approached they too dived into the water just as one sees in Tarzan movies. Buck grazed on the grassy shores and baboons romped along the banks. Herons, Guinea fowl, Eagles, the profusion of wildlife around us was marvellous. We cooked fresh fish over open fires and ate them with rice and "monkey nuts" that we had got from a man we met on the river. What a paradise! Days slipped into weeks.

The River traversed an extensive hunting concession called "Safarilanda" controlled by a German, the legendary Baron Werner Von Alvensleben, whose trademark headgear was a bright red bandanna. Part of the area was administered by a well known hunter from East Africa called Wally who I had met some months prior when he brought a lion's foot for me to process. The wounded lion had nearly clawed a hunter to death when it sprang on the hunter and sank its teeth into his shoulder and raked his chest with its claws. Fortunately it was in its dying throes and the hunter was rushed to hospital and survived. Wally had no time to skin the lion but instead cut off its foot as a memento and I tanned the massive paw and mounted it on a wooden plaque which was presented to the hunter.

This area was later proclaimed Zivane National Park. When we got to Wally's camp on the river banks he welcomed us and we slept in starched sheets and ate the finest cuisine in Africa, braised Nyala steaks and fresh vegetables. A pet lion strolled around the camp and staff in starched white tunics waited on us. We left such luxury reluctantly. As we progressed further along the river we stayed at several other Safari camps comprised of neat whitewashed *"rondavels"* or sometimes tents under shady trees. At other times we just made camp where we arrived at the end of the day. Sometimes we slept in hammocks strung between trees in the undergrowth. At night animals moved through the bush and hippos grunted in the water. In the mornings we awoke to the call of guinea fowl and troops of monkeys leaping in the trees around us. At other times we slept on the cool, soft sand of the riverbanks. One night we had to dodge a hippo that came to investigate us. In the light of the stars it strolled across the sand to where we lay hidden behind our upturned canoe. We slept one night in the hot tin hut of the engineer who was constructing a bridge over the Rio Save. He showed us the plans of the massive arches that would span the broad river and link the new highway from Lourenco Marques (Maputo) to Beira. Then he gave us Portuguese wine, rice and fresh fish all the time smiling graciously and nodding amicably as none of us could speak the other's language.

We were nearly killed by a rogue hippo, came perilously close to massive crocodiles and saw some of the most incredible areas of pristine wilderness left in Africa. Sights of exquisite grace and beauty were imprinted forever on our minds; a bushbuck caught in shafts of sunlight as it stood in morning mist at the water's edge, a glistening python curled on driftwood in the river's current, baby crocs all lined up on matted reeds, a brilliant kingfisher plunging in to the water, a solitary Fishing Owl staring down from an overhanging branch, a huge crocodile slithering into the water and slipping beneath the surface. The haunting call of African Fish Eagles rang on the river. This canoe trip was one of those enduring never to be forgotten experiences of life while the encounter with the rogue hippo nearly ended our lives. As we entered the pool where it and its mate were cavorting it decided it did not like us disturbing its private love life. We found that hippos would usually flick their ears and snort and then submerge at our approach. This one fixed its gaze on us and rose out of the water with a mean scowl on its face and an evil look in its eyes. Then it charged plunging beneath the waves as it lunged towards us. Propelled by the river current we bore down upon it but it is amazing what adrenaline can do. We dug our paddles in and paddling with all our strength reached the steep bank which we scrambled up clutching desperately at exposed roots and creepers. The canoe floated in the tangled undergrowth beneath us hidden from view and the hippo snorted in surprise wondering how we had disappeared so quickly. It spent a while looking for us but we kept our heads down and it went back to its overweight sweetheart. After a period it seemed to have settled down and we took this opportunity to sneak down the bank, creep into the canoe and strike out for the opposite bank. Then it came a second time and it was even more upset, a massive bull intent on killing us. It was a race with death as we paddled for shallow water and the sandy bank. With mere metres to spare we made it onto the sand and pulled the canoe to safety. What happened next was truly awesome for with unbridled anger it reared up in the shallows and flung its massive head back and forth with gaping jaws in a display of uncontrolled fury all the time roaring like a lion and bellowing with rage. It made me recall the dreadful battle I had witnessed at Chipinda Pools except this time we were not seated in the safety of a vehicle. Fortunately it did not venture onto the sand and we watched in silence. When it was all over we sat shocked. We had witnessed an indescribable event and escaped a truly dangerous animal bent on our destruction. We had been very, very lucky. Hippos are responsible for more deaths in Africa then any other animal.

After several weeks on the river we arrived at the sleepy malaria infested town of Nova Mambone near the delta where local Portuguese officials were astounded to see us. With worn clothes and a shotgun we looked like a couple of desperadoes and they were apprehensive as to our intentions. They interrogated us in a hostile manner aware of the activities of liberation fighters in the country. They found it hard to believe we had come down the river from Rhodesia but we showed them the letter of authority issued from the Governor of Manica Province and convinced them we were legitimate explorers and then they shook our hands with gusto and congratulated us. Then all the officials came to meet us shook our hands and slapped our backs. They loaded our canoe onto a small weather-beaten wooden boat that ferried people and merchandise across the sea from Mambone to Beira about seventy five miles up the coast. There were no life jackets and no life raft. We set out and almost immediately struck a sandbar and had to wait an hour for the tide to lift us off. As we left the mangroves of the delta a school of dolphins escorted us into the open sea. They danced and leapt around the bow in playful exuberance, a fitting conclusion to our river journey. It took us the whole day to cross the sea and we clung to the vessel as it pitched about on the ocean swells. We felt a bit like boat people must feel for the boat was old and rickety and laden with produce and people, goats, chickens and other paraphernalia. A wind brought up the swells and we lurched around deck until eventually we got on our tummies and simply clung on. As the sun sank beneath the horizon we were relieved to see the lights of Beira glimmering on the ocean waves and at last we crawled into harbour under cover of darkness. The next day, after seeing more government officials and clearing immigration we toured the town including the Grande Hotel the most impressive building there was. After this we went to Estoril beach where we slept under the stars near an old wreck that lay marooned beneath the lighthouse. What a time we had experienced on the river. While we were away the Six-Day War in the Middle East had come and gone without us knowing. We had not heard a radio during the entire trip except for the first night when we camped near a village and one of the workers from the South African mines had a transistor radio which blared out its "penny whistle" music. African music is a genre of its own and by the 1950's Southern African music had taken on its own special sounds. The world famous song "The Lion Sleeps Tonight" originated in South Africa. A well known piece called *"Skokiaan"* contributed largely to the African genre and originated back in my hometown of Bulawayo at about the time I was growing up when it was the popular sound coming from black townships. This music became popular in the mines of South Africa where workers from all over south and central Africa mixed in a melting pot of tribes and languages. It was also on this first night when Phil thought I was about to die for we had shot a wild goose and cooked it but it was as tough as old boots. My tummy took a serious dislike to it and went into horrible cramps and all I could do was roll around groaning and moaning. Phil had visions of carrying my body out of Mozambique, much like David Livingstone's body was carried out of Africa by his faithful companions, but he was unable to do much but listen to my groans and the wild serenade of jungle music. It was a sleepless night but in the morning I recovered.

We were to learn later that even in those days guerrilla activity had begun in Mozambique at the start of the long gruelling war for Independence. In 1964 one of their first acts of sacrilege was to chop off the head of a Catholic priest and leave it on his church altar. In 1967 there were already 8000 "freedom fighters" in Mozambique. They fought the Portuguese and after "liberating" the country in 1975 a civil war developed between two factions, Renamo and Frelimo, and they fought each other. The fragile economy of the country collapsed and the Port of Beira became a dismal, poverty stricken, disease ridden town. The Grande Hotel was no longer grand for it was buried in obscene filth. Pawpaw trees grew on the once prestigious balconies and the marble dance halls were blackened by cooking fires. At the time of our visit world opposition against Rhodesia continued to mount and British warships blockaded the Mozambique Channel enforcing a fuel embargo that Britain had slapped on the country yet several tankers ran the gauntlet and got through to offload their precious cargo.

Exploring Mozambique

At about this time I made friends with Angus a member of our church youth fellowship. Angus had the strong features of his Scots ancestors and a thick red beard that highlighted his youthful face. An explorer at heart he was a great adventurer. We explored Mozambique driving everywhere in his bright red two-seater 1949 MG sports car and camping on the beaches at Inhassoro and Vilanculos. The water was warm and clear. Coconut palms gave shade to our camp and we caught fresh fish and cooked them on an open fire on the beach. We spent our days swimming and sunbathing. What a time! One day as we relaxed in the shade of coconut palms after having dined on such delicious fare as freshly grilled fish we saw a chilling sight. We had just enjoyed a swim and the sea was calm with gentle waves on a post-card beach when our attention was drawn to something surging through the shallows and pushing up a torrent of water and spray as it moved. We were shocked to behold the form of a massive shark idly swimming in the shallows from where we had just emerged. Apart from the sharks, however, it was paradise.

Canoeing in Mozambique - Buzi River Adventure

Angus and I decided to canoe the Buzi River and with the help of Phil as driver we set out from Umtali in my VW Kombi with our canoe lashed on top. The Buzi River gushes out of Chimanimani Mountains and flows through primeval forests to emerge at the sea near the ancient port of Sofala. Having canoed the Rio Save I was keen to do the Buzi as well for it was the other route followed by ancient traders when they came to Great Zimbabwe. We knew it was navigable for some of its course but had no idea what the rest was like. Phil drove us into Mozambique. We crossed the border at the tiny border post of Cashel and then dropped thousands of feet along a narrow bush track through rolling hills of woodland and jungles until eventually we arrived at the river. Here Phil left us in the middle of Africa and returned the way we had come and we set off for the Indian Ocean.

The Buzi River must have some of the most splendid scenery in central Africa and we were enthralled by its pristine beauty. It meandered through unspoilt jungles with a profusion of ferns and tropical plants on the banks and huge forest trees that formed a canopy above us under which we canoed. Wild Date Palms and dense clumps of Bamboo grew everywhere. Dragon Trees attained a height of twelve meters with palm-like leaves sprouting in rosettes from the branches and cascades of bright red fruits hanging in clumps. The river flowed through long open pools broken by boulders and rapids as the land descended to the coast. It abounded in fish and crocodiles and in later years the crocodiles of the Buzi became infamous as man eaters for when Mozambique slid into war and poverty the local people depleted the fish on which the crocodiles fed causing the crocs in turn to eat the people. However, that was still in the future. We canoed for several days and the further we went the greater the rapids became until we found ourselves negotiating long stretches of white water. Eventually we could go no further. We had overturned so often and swam and waded through so many rapids that we were exhausted and our canoe was the worse for wear. There was nothing for it but to stop and get assistance. We were stranded miles from anywhere in the middle of Africa. We would have to walk through the bush but first we had to cross to the other side of the river. We chose a narrow section and safely swam across and then set out to look for help. We walked for miles through dense bush. Angus had lost his shoes in the river when we flipped so he tied some rags around his feet but this was make-shift protection and did not last long in the rough terrain through which we walked. Soon the rags were in shreds and his feet were too, scratched, torn and bleeding. Eventually we found a remote village and a man seated at a small table with an open book from which he was reading. It was the Bible! He could not speak English and we could not speak Portuguese but we communicated through *"Funaggalo"* the international language from the mines of South Africa. We shook his hand and felt like David Livingstone might have felt when exploring Africa. Here in the middle of Africa we had found a Christian. He was more like an angel. Actually, he was a tall Shangaan with the physique of a Greek god and he gladly offered to help us. The Shangaans are an off-shoot of Nguni people who centuries before fled from the Zulus in the south. Angus made repairs to his footwear and we retraced our steps to our damaged canoe. Our new found friend swung it effortlessly onto his head and led us back along twisting paths to a small Portuguese settler's farm.

The farmer welcomed us into his home. He was typical of so many struggling Portuguese settlers in Mozambique. Tanned brown he was a wiry, tough little man who had left Portugal to build a life in Africa. The Portuguese Government offered incentives to attract settlers to the colony and he and his wife and three beautiful teenage daughters of whom he was very possessive had come to farm in the jungle. None of us could speak the other's language and so we shook hands, smiled and nodded. We had a pleasant but simple meal with the rudimentary trappings of Mediterranean cuisine. Seated around a large table and unable to communicate we simply pointed and nodded enthusiastically constantly murmuring *"obrigado"* interjected by giggling from the girls who coyly caught our eyes and then hid their blushing faces behind their long dark curls. All the time the father was becoming increasingly aware of the effect we had on his daughters and was becoming upset at the way they smiled at us. They probably never had company and we were the answer to their wildest dreams.

When it was time for bed we were shown to a very large room furnished with two single beds and the door was firmly closed behind us. The house was a huge colonial building with large rooms, rambling passages and no electricity. We were left in darkness and soon fell asleep but in the small hours of the morning I awoke with tummy cramps and an urgent need to get to a toilet. The cuisine had had an adverse effect on my bowels and it was an emergency. I opened the bedroom door and peered into darkness. Where was the toilet I wondered? I crept down the passage and opened a door only to hear the muffled sounds of deep sleep. Quietly closing it I tried the next door with a similar result. I sneaked around the house for twenty minutes trying to locate a toilet all the time getting needier of it and more concerned as I contemplated what the father would do if he caught me sneaking around the house or God forbid in his daughters' bedroom. Despairing of ever finding a toilet inside the house there was nothing for it but to get outside as quickly as possible and I attempted to open the front door but it was firmly locked with no key available. Every door to the outside was locked. The farmer had well and truly locked us in. I gingerly attempted to open a window. It was fast shut. I tried some more and succeeded to force the catch on one, half lift the lower pane, crawl through, tumble out and then bolt down the driveway. What relief I found at the end of the road! After a while I had to repeat the whole process as I sneaked back all the while wondering whether I would be mistaken for an intruder and get a blast of buckshot. It was with relief and exhaustion that I found my bedroom and collapsed into bed. Talk about going down the garden path to the PK, this beat it all.

The next day we bade farewell to our host and his shy daughters and left on a truck that took us to a larger road from where we managed to get a lift the one hundred miles or so to the Rhodesian border but on arrival were aghast to find we had lost our passports somewhere along the route. We wondered what to do. I was all for walking through the bush under cover of night for I knew the area well but Angus insisted we must go the right route and explain what had happened. One never ceases to be surprised in Africa or by human nature. I am sure we got through quicker without passports than if we had had them. The officials could not have been kinder. They simply stamped a piece of paper and waved us through. Within days Angus was to set off on a world tour but now had no passport. Through a strange coincidence our passports were found by a man who just happened to have a relative living in Rhodesia who also knew Angus. How extraordinary!

Mauled by a Leopard

Angus had a good time touring Europe and returned to Rhodesia and after a while working in National Parks went to work on the Cold Storage Commission ranch at West Nicholson very near where I had grown up when dad was a rancher. One night he was out culling Impala when he was himself nearly culled. Every year culling was done of certain species of antelope that multiplied quickly. It was carried out at night by a team of workers. On this night Angus had walked after an Impala when he came face to face with a full-grown leopard that had been lurking nearby also after Impala. It snarled menacingly and Angus lifted his weapon and got off a quick shot. The leopard promptly disappeared into the shadows. Angus decided it was safer to come back in the morning.

The circumstances were similar to an incident I had years before when working with the Museum and authorised to cull at night. I and a friend had walked after a bushbuck only to walk straight into a leopard which sprang at us. I had fired a hasty shot from my shotgun and the leopard turned in mid air. Angus was not so lucky.

In the light of early morning he and his gun bearer who carried a second weapon approached the spot with utmost caution. Suddenly in a blur of yellow the wounded leopard launched itself at him with deadly intent. His mind raced as he braced himself for the impact. "What a majestic animal" he thought. He had always admired leopards. With the ease and familiarity of years of hunting experience he swung his rifle into his shoulder where it fitted snugly. In his career with National Parks he had shot everything from hogs to elephants but this time the leopard's charge was just too fast. The force of the impact felled him before he even pulled the trigger. The rifle spun from his hands and the animal flew at his throat.

"Shoot, shoot" Angus screamed to his faithful gun bearer but there was no reaction, the man had absconded as fast as his legs could carry him. Angus kicked out with both feet desperately keeping the animal away from his throat and belly. A vice like grip clamped around his thigh and its fangs sank to his bone. He tried to crawl away but he had been immobilised by the weight of the animal and its powerful jaws. Thrashing paws clawed his trousers but he got in a couple of solid kicks with his free foot. With eyes blazing and lips curled in a frenzied snarl its claws and teeth held him tight and the vice-like hold on his leg tightened. He fumbled frantically for his 9mm pistol that he always carried on his belt. He was fighting for his life.

"Why won't the holster open?" he wondered.   Time slowed down.

Rolling over he kicked the beast again with his free foot and managed at last to get the pistol out. The animal was chewing his thigh higher up and the smell of its rasping breath and sound of snarling was terrifying. Deep grunts came from the beast each time Angus got in a kick. The strength of the animal was amazing as fluid muscles seethed beneath the dappled coat. He felt his own strength failing fast. Fumbling with the pistol he managed to cock it and summoning his strength he leaned towards the fearful animal, placed the muzzle of the weapon on the leopard's chest and pulled the trigger. It was a fatal shot straight to the heart. The animal's pent-up rage petered out and it collapsed on top of him. All went quiet and he swooned under its heavy weight. Gaining consciousness Angus pried open its jaws to release his bloodied leg and lay exhausted.

Mustering all his strength he crawled to the vehicle where he managed to get a cloth to stem the bleeding. The fangs had narrowly missed his main artery but he had lost a lot of blood and he was covered with both his own blood and that of the cat. He called weakly for his gun bearer but had no voice so he pulled himself up and pressed his hand on the horn. His faithful gun bearer came running through the bush and together they bandaged him and called for help by radio. After some time a neighbour arrived and bundled him into his Land Rover and drove flat out to Gwanda hospital. Although weak from loss of blood and badly torn he made a full recovery despite having a course of rabies injections. The skull of the animal sits on the mantle piece in his ranch house in the Cape where he ranches cattle.

Periodically he loses a calf to a passing leopard but is reluctant to shoot the culprit out of a desire to conserve the dwindling wildlife of Africa.

He and I spent enjoyable days in Mozambique. It was wild and filled with animals and primitive people. He had a superb butterfly collection and I accompanied him on trips to remote areas to catch exotic species. The land was lush and tropical with beautiful jungles and huge hardwood trees. We climbed its mountains and spent days swimming and camping. They were hot lazy days in the sun, eating fish and living on Portuguese bread, wine and fresh fish. At times I was with other friends. I had fitted out the back of my VW Kombi as a camper van and with a little nursing it could access the roughest roads. On another trip down the coast near Inhassoro we drove the Kombi twenty five miles along the beach at low tide to the end of a peninsula of sand named Bartolomeu Dias. Here the sand narrowed to a few meters and waves broke on either side. Then the tide turned and we had to race back but got stuck instead. We fought the incoming tide inch by inch and eventually got the vehicle a metre above high water mark. What a triumph it was. We spent the night on the sand bar with the waves crashing all around us as if we were at sea and when day came and the tide went out we drove all the way back again. Bartolomeu Dias no longer exists having been entirely washed away.

Angus was to lose all his priceless butterflies when the Lundi River flooded and washed his home away. There was never a dull moment in Africa.

The Shooting Starts

We had vibrant youth groups in our church and lots of fun with enduring friendships. The group was a match-making club and a dozen or more young couples got married. The young people got up to good natured pranks. One evening a skit was planned depicting a bank hold up. It turned out a little too realistic when a new recruit from National Parks brought his rifle and let off a couple of blanks. The girls screamed and the church was filled with shouts. Neighbours heard the shots and called the police who arrived ready for a gun battle. The priest was furious.

It was at this time that Stretch was involved in a real gun battle in one of the first incursions by trained "freedom fighters". The "shooting war" started in 1966 when a group of insurgents crossed from Zambia into Rhodesia. They split up and some headed down to Hartley town. There they burst into a farm home and killed white farmers but the terrified children escaped through the window and ran for their lives into the bush. Another gang infiltrated into the Sinoia region where they fought Rhodesian security forces in what became known as the "Battle of Chinhoyi." They were all killed but shortly after this event grenades were hurled into a crowded restaurant in Salisbury and dozens of people injured.

Then in 1967 a gang of seventy crossed the Zambezi and Security Forces clashed with them in the Wankie Game Reserve. Stretch was among the forces. He had joined the police a few years earlier and was stationed in Matabeleland and was part of a Police unit attached to the Rhodesian African Rifles and the Rhodesian Light Infantry sent to track and combat the incursion. A battle took place and several servicemen were killed including the first Police casualty of the war. Although Stretch had been through Police training he was hardly out of his teens. He was one of many who faced death in the coming bush war, had numerous close shaves and was involved with the capture of insurgents. During the course of his work one day he had to interrogate several prisoners. As he looked them over, sorry looking individuals in irons, one young man's face brightened in a smile of recognition.

"Sir, I am your *"shamwari" (friend)*, do you remember me?" the young man blurted out.

Stretch peered more intently at him. The young man looked vaguely familiar but captive combatants tried many tactics to win favour and Stretch was not going to be fooled.

"Who are you?" he asked.
"I am Robby," he said, "do you remember the big *shauto* (python) we caught?" and a broad grin broke on his face.

Stretch was taken aback and looked closer, peering into the hardened face of the young fighter. Sure enough it was Robby the *"umfaan"* who had helped carry our big python and had become our young friend but now older and wiser, a man who knew war and violence. Stretch was shocked. What could he say? He wanted to welcome him as a friend but now they were enemies although still with memory of that friendship in their hearts. Stretch questioned him, "Where did you get your training, where are your leaders, why did you become a terrorist?"

"All I wanted was a small house, not a big one like your house" Robby explained recalling the days he came for tea "but I could not even get a job. I wanted to get on in life but you whites had all the money."

Robby was taken away by the "Special Branch" Rhodesian Police and after a trial was found guilty of terrorist activities and hung. In a few brief years we had moved from a tolerant society to one in which we were killing one another. The second *"chimurenga"* had begun.

Book 4

Soldiers of the Queen – War Years

African Proverb: "Beware the bird that leads to a lion."
In Africa there is a little bird called the Honey Guide and it helps people to get
honey. It will flutter before a hunter and lead him to a beehive. After the hunter
has smoked the hive and eaten his fill of honey the bird moves in to eat some of
the remaining honey and larva. Woe betides the hunter who takes everything
and leaves nothing. Next time the little bird will lead to a lion. Beware, our
deeds will find us out!

The War Years

Men who had once fought for Britain commanded the Rhodesian army. The Supreme Commander in Chief had been with the British SAS in the Far East Volunteer Unit and with a hundred other Rhodesians had learnt fighting techniques there. In those days the British called all communist fighters "terrorists" and they eventually overcame the communist threat in Malaya by using military strategies which the Rhodesians now also used. The Rhodesians called all African Nationalist fighters "terrorists" and many of them were indeed trained in communist techniques of war. Among these fighters there were those who were both brave and sincere in their battle against white control but regrettably there were those who used their training to bring death to civilians black and white. The Rhodesian Army small as it was became a force that held at bay thousands of communist-trained insurgents. Rhodesians will say they were never defeated. They lost brave men and they lost skirmishes but when Rhodesia was handed over it was not because the army was defeated but because of overwhelming world pressure. Having said that, it was obvious at the end of fifteen years of standing alone that Rhodesia was battle fatigued and could not continue to hold out much longer. In fact some people thought they probably handed over just in time to avoid a bloody rout. Despite having recently received some new weapons they were short of supplies, equipment was old and their fighting men suffered from mental and physical exhaustion.

It was the British government that originally connived with Rhodes to annex central Africa and then encouraged British settlers to come to the land. When self government was granted in 1923 Britain encouraged whites to take up permanent settlement and promoted the notion that self-government gave them control of their destiny. It was Britain who decided to take self-government away. Before Rhodesians had ever picked up a gun to defend themselves the British government had declared its intention of sacrificing them to the chaotic conditions of African Independence. When Rhodesians declared Independence in 1965 they did so out of desperation not to lose what they had given their lives to achieve. The British Prime Minister of the time, Harold Wilson, immediately slapped sanctions on Rhodesia and declared with typical brash insensitivity that he would crush the Rhodesians within weeks but he had not bargained for that tough, resilient quality they had inherited from their British forebears. It would be a long fifteen years before the white rebellion would be over. It would be a bitter struggle and Rhodesian soldiers displayed great bravery but unlike the 1896 rebellion there would be no Victoria Crosses awarded this time. Rhodes's veiled threat that his new nation might rebel against the "home country" had come true 72 years later. Rhodesia was a nation that dared to stand against Britain and the power of African Nationalism. Rhodesians must have been very brave or very naïve, maybe both. They had a mentality that came from old British thinking and were convinced they had a noble cause - to save Rhodesia from communism and all the other things happening to the north of them - mayhem, anarchy and bloodshed.

I was to be a soldier of the Queen for sixteen years. During my army training all recruits swore allegiance to her. After the Smith government declared Independence this was never rescinded and the question of loyalty did not seem to occur to any of us. In our minds we were still loyal soldiers only doing what her Majesty's Government should have been doing and that was fighting communism. Rhodesians saw themselves in some strange way as fighting for British honour and British standards. In his Declaration of Independence Smith insisted that Rhodesia was still loyal to the Crown and our altercation was not with Queen or people but with political decisions. After initial training I was posted to 4th Royal Rhodesia Battalion in Umtali. As the threat of insurgents became real we were called out often and I found myself roaming the mountains not this time in pursuit of nature but in pursuit of what the government called "terrorists". We did night marches, ambushes and patrols into rural areas. I had an advantage over some of the others because I knew the area so well and was familiar with the bush. Nevertheless it was not as pleasant as the carefree days when I was free to roam at will. Now I had to watch my back.

In 1968 I took a post of display artist in a commercial store in Salisbury. Despite international sanctions the shops were full of imported goods. I enjoyed working at the store but the one draw back was my involvement with the army. I had to report for duty whenever the authorities called and that was often. Once again I had to draw kit and once again I was allocated the MAG. This time however my strength did not stand up to forced marches and clambering in and out of army trucks and the general vigorous activities forced upon me. On one of frequent call-ups the officers decided to see how fit we were and took us on a long run, of course they followed in a Land Rover. I did my best to finish the course but collapsed. Soon afterwards I was in hospital having damaged my back, strained my heart and got a hernia. I ended up in the old wing of Salisbury hospital. Afterwards, I was given recuperation leave with light duties but I determined that it was the end of the army for me and did not report back. This ultimately got me into trouble with the authorities.

I filled my weekends with what I felt was more constructive activity and started a youth movement for kids in a suburb that was considered the sleazy part of town. Kids here were poor but the people were hospitable and receptive. Poverty, alcohol, violence and divorce wrecked many homes. Consequently children were disadvantaged and only too willing to join our youth club. There was a weekly attendance of fifty children and we attempted to develop meaningful life values that would help relieve their problems. A large Sunday school grew out of this youth movement.

Famous Missionaries

I was fortunate to see a little of Africa that one only reads about in history books, the Africa that people gave their lives for in sacrificial service. Although some early settlers were undesirables some were true heroes. Among them were some notable missionaries who came to serve the people. Many of them died from disease, wild beasts and murder. The church I attended had close links with missions and I was privileged to meet several from the early days. One famous missionary was William Burton who came from Preston in England. He was a dour man who seldom smiled, the rigors of pioneering in tropical Africa having knocked all jest from him. Yet he was compassionate and gentle. He came to the Congo in about 1914 and spent his entire life there. He and a friend started the Congo Mission Churches deep in the heart of the jungles. This grew into a large and vibrant church mostly in the Katanga Province. Burton recounted amazing experiences about cannibals and wild animals in an era that saw the Congo emerge from medieval darkness, experience a short lived season of comparative order despite colonial abuse and then plunge into anarchy after Independence.

One account he told was when he arrived at a village that he had not previously visited. There were no roads so the missionaries travelled on the rivers in dug-out canoes. As he stepped from the canoe onto the bank men surrounded him and began to gesticulate, prodding him with their spears. He could not understand their language but their intentions were plain and by the way they looked at him he knew he would soon be in the pot. He began to shake violently and tried to stop for he did not want them to see he was afraid but the more he tried to stop the more he shook. Then he came to realise he was not really afraid and boldness came upon him. He suddenly felt compelled to speak but in a language he had never learnt. Whatever he said the tribesmen seemed to understand him, laid down their spears and backed away. On another occasion he was given poisoned food but when he ate it and did not die the people were convinced he was invincible and the community welcomed him. Burton lived most of his life in the Congo. His wife died there and he survived cancer there too. Eventually during the uprising in Congo he was very ill and carried out on a stretcher. It probably saved his life for he would not have left of his own volition. When he recovered he went back and travelled throughout the whole of his extensive parish to gather scattered people who had survived the horrors.

Another missionary was Fred Johnston, a small man but full of gallantry and fortitude. He too had served the mission field for most of his life and was gifted with a wicked sense of humour and could tell many tales about the Congo. One account was when he came to a hostile village where the people reacted violently when they saw him. One must bear in mind that in those days many of the indigenous people had never seen a white person and rumours were rife that they were slave traders, murderers or demon spirits. Fred rode a bicycle on the narrow twisting paths through the jungle to visit communities. He had just arrived at this village when the occupants lurched towards him with blood curling screams and an assortment of weapons. Fred jumped on his bicycle and fled down the path he had just come up with a large contingent of angry people led by a heavy, large bosomed woman wielding an axe in close pursuit. Because of the twisting path he was unable to get up speed and realising they were gaining on him he knew his only chance was to stop and confront them. He slammed on brakes and skidded to a halt, swung the bike around as a barricade, put up his hand like a policeman and with a voice of authority commanded the woman "Stop." She skidded to a halt and the crowd stumbled into her. The heavy bosomed woman towered over Fred who stood peering up at her with his moustache quivering. The two of them looked each other in the eyes both puffing wildly. Slowly she calmed down and then turned away like a meek child. Fred concluded that it was the first time any man had ever stood up to her and she simply did not know how to react.

It was men and women like this who gave their lives to Africa. At one time the average life span of early missionaries in the Congo after their arrival was about three months. David Livingstone and many others sacrificed to bring Africa out of darkness. After years of hardship and months of suffering Livingstone died on his knees with a prayer on his lips, "God Save Africa" was the cry of his heart. He had walked across the entire continent several times over.

Old Timers

In Salisbury I boarded with Elsa an elderly lady from a pioneer family. Her husband, Joe, did not live at home as he was a prospector and came in for brief visits at the end of the month. He had lived all his life in the great outdoors of Africa and could not tolerate town. He was born in the mine village of Shamva and as a lad could remember rolling into Salisbury town on the back of an ox wagon. Every month wagons trekked up the long twisting track from Enterprise district to bring in fresh produce and take supplies back for the mine. They outspanned on the *"vlei"* near Newlands shopping centre where the Gremlin restaurant used to stand. This was the furthest from town centre where they could camp without being troubled by lions. Joe had explored the whole country and prospected almost everywhere. He found significant deposits of minerals but the big strike always eluded him. Everyone in the mining industry knew him for he was one of the last of the old timers. His hair was snow white, his weathered face had a thousand wrinkles and he had a thousand tales to keep us enthralled whenever he came home.

Elsa had seen many things. She was born in South Africa and came to the country as a young girl. She married Joe and they lived one of those fairy tale lives filled with adventure, hardship and courage. Elsa's brother joined the RAF and died in the Battle of Britain when he went down with his Spitfire in the English Channel. One of her cousins was blown apart in a bush fire. He was out hunting when a fire cut him off. An *"umfaan"* who accompanied him as a porter was caught in the flames and he dashed in to save him but the heat exploded the ammunition in the belt around his body. He died with the lad in his arms but the child's brother climbed a tree and survived although burnt by the flames.

Elsa's friend "French Marie" was one of those eccentric almost fictional characters one hears about from time to time. Stories about her were legend. Back in the 1930s she lived on a farm outside Gwelo near where Joe and Elsa lived. The local police had an initiation test for all new recruits who arrived at the Gwelo Police Station. They would send any new comer out to French Marie on some trumped up complaint about her. She viewed most men with utmost contempt. She had never been seen in a dress but wore breeches and was always armed with a long whip and was not afraid to use it on anyone who crossed her path. The inevitable outcome of the new recruit's visit was a sound lashing. Only afterwards was he told amongst much hilarity that it was her custom to soundly whip every new policeman in the district. One night she was sitting in the bar drinking her nightly sun-downer when an ignorant man foolishly mumbled something under his breath about women in bars. A deathly hush descended upon the place as everyone became silent and waited to see what would happen. She did nothing at first but when she had finished her drink she laid into the man and whipped him right out of the pub. Then on a roll she cleared it of everyone else including the barman, locked the doors and held a one-night concert and no one dared interfere. Later she moved to the district of Lomagundi where she illegally sold meat for trade. No one had the courage to stop her. She lies buried in Harare cemetery together with many other frontier men and women who opened up Central Africa.

Back in the Army

The policy of army call-ups continued as the war intensified. The authorities were very efficient in tracking down all who tried to dodge their duty. The more call-ups one missed the more one had to do. After my recovery from surgery I managed to keep ahead of them but they caught my scent and were hot on my tracks again and I was in trouble. The white government needed every last white soldier they could get. It became an endless routine, parading at the Drill Hall and then stiff marches to the army barracks about thirty miles from Salisbury or else running around the hills trying to find terrorists who did not want to be found. When we reported for duty we first had to sign in and then were made to sit and wait until the officers decided what to do with us. This was usually dismantling, cleaning and assembling weapons. After that we were issued with "rat-packs" (food rations) and made to await the next instruction. It went on for hours and was hard to tolerate. Then we were bundled into trucks and headed for the hills to track down terrorists who did not want to fight us and who ran circles around us in a game of cat and mouse.

Unfortunately casualties began to mount. My friend, Brian, was in the back of an army truck when it went out of control on the "Alpha Trail" and plunged over the edge of the Zambezi escarpment into a ravine. The Alpha Trail was a notorious descent from the fertile Centenary farming district into the hot sweltering Zambezi Valley. From the top of the trail the view was impressive with the vast floor of the valley shimmering below in heat haze. However, in those days the torturous, twisting gravel track down the steep escarpment was littered with the mangled wrecks of trucks that had not made it. A similar descent near Chirundu was just as hazardous and was called "the Truckers' Graveyard" and wrecks littered the side of the road. On this occasion as the military convoy eased down the trail the brakes on Brian's vehicle failed and it careered over the edge. Some of the soldiers jumped for their lives, others were flung out and several were killed. Brian landed across a log at the bottom of the ravine. He survived, but only just. When he regained consciousness none of his body wanted to work. He had survived a previous fall when he and Angus were mountaineering and he had fallen seventy feet over a cliff. This time it was worse. When they got him back to hospital there was nothing they could do, he had a broken neck. He had some movement in his two arms and slowly he learnt to use them a little. Brian was an accomplished artist and wildlife enthusiast. He, Angus and I had at times photographed eagles at their nests and also caught rare butterflies. Brian was a great outdoor sportsman, hiked extensively and a mountaineer. That was all over now. His spirit never broke and he learnt to paint holding the brush in his mouth. He never lost courage but as his body wasted away so his enthusiasm waned. Brian died at Victoria Falls a few years after Independence in what some people considered suspicious circumstances. Every day Brian was taken in his wheel chair to his favourite spots and one day his helper pushed his wheelchair near the edge of a steep incline by the gorge where he could watch the world and perhaps do a little sketching. He left Brian there to do other chores and later Brian was found at the bottom of the gorge, his twisted wheel chair testimony to his fall.

This time he had not survived. How did he get there? The question was never resolved.

The 1970s

The seventies were a time of hardening attitudes in our country. British and American propaganda since the Second World War encouraged resistance to communism. Rhodesia supported this stance but no nations supported Rhodesia. We were brought up with the Union Jack and the National Anthem but when Rhodesia became a Republic in 1970 all that ceased. For many Rhodesians a republic was not what they wanted but was a reaction to what they perceived as British hostility. Rhodesians had expressed their loyalty to the Crown through both World Wars and after UDI had insisted their quarrel was not with the Crown or people. However, there had been no healing of the rift with the British government and now Rhodesians felt abandoned. The world forum, led by Britain, had slapped sanctions on the country and a lot of acrimony was exchanged between the two governments. There seemed no way forward. Now, for the first time in eighty years the British National Anthem was no longer played. In its place came a new anthem to the tune of "Ode to Joy." It was quite pleasant and had stirring words but Beethoven probably would not have approved.

I had resigned my employment in order to go on various canoe trips and other bush outings but money ran out and I needed a job so I joined the bank. For about a year I put on a tie and went to work behind the counter at the Foreign Bills Department. The international community had slapped sanctions on Rhodesia but at the bank I learnt how to channel transactions through various unnamed international banks that were willing to handle Rhodesian finances. I was posted to a branch in the heart of Salisbury and became a small cog in the wheels of finance. It introduced me to the world of sanction busting that I had not known before. Everything was very confidential. Long hours of daily monotony were depressing and I endured it only as a means to my own economic requirements until such time as something else materialised. The only relief from the daily routine was when the "forces sweetheart" came in to visit her husband. Sally was well known and greatly admired by the soldiers and when she stepped through the doors a kind of hush fell on the place as every male eye gravitated towards her. She spent lots of time visiting "the boys in uniform", organising radio talks, troop shows and general morale boosting programmes. Bank life was not for me and I was relieved when one day I received a telephone call from the Director of Museums. "Would I come back to the Museums?" he asked. He had heard I was in town and had tracked me down. I was glad of his confidence in me and jumped at his offer to join the Queen Victoria Museum in Salisbury. I handed in my resignation. Things were looking up.

My time at Queen Victoria Museum was pleasant. I had opportunity to embark on more zoological expeditions. I was constantly called by people who had snakes in their gardens and had endless escapades catching Cobras, Boomslangs and Adders. I felt that I should be paid "danger money" for every snake I had to catch. Once again I was working with interesting scientists. We dug up huge dinosaur bones, discovered new species of mole-rats, installed displays in the galleries and did a hundred other fascinating things. A famous bird artist from UK, David Reid Henry, came and worked at the Museum and inspired me on a career as a wildlife artist. Other interesting people came to visit. However, as exciting and enjoyable as the Museum was another calling took more and more time, that of Christian care. There were so many people in need.

I was a member of a church in Salisbury and was active in youth groups and social work. It was in about October 1972 that after a time of consideration I came to an awful conclusion concerning our nation's future; war was coming. It was so real that it became a constant burden upon me. Such was the weight of conviction that I shared it in a large congregation in Salisbury, not an easy task but I knew I had to speak from my heart and did so with trepidation. I spoke about coming conflict and warned that it would bring death and suffering to thousands of people. It would need changed attitudes to avoid. The message was out of keeping with those days. It was hard for many whites to know how to change the direction things were going. Most could not understand what I was saying and leaders in the church quickly downplayed my sermon. But the country was heading for conflict and one had to be blind or dim-witted not to see it. Yet the political leaders assured us all was well and if necessary we could take on the whole world.

Border incursions by armed gangs occurred in the latter years of the 1960s. Most of these groups were either eliminated or captured by security forces but on December 21st 1972, just before Christmas, an attack took place on an isolated farm in the north-eastern part of the country and signalled the real start of the "Liberation War". Insurgents using rocket launchers for the first time attacked Altena farm in the Centenary district followed shortly afterwards by attacks on Whistlefield and Charmwood farms. One of the first casualties was an eight-year-old girl who died under a hail of bullets as she slept in her bedroom at Altena, a picturesque farm nestling in hills over looking the Zambezi escarpment. The Rhodesians responded to this attack with "Operation Hurricane" a full scale mobilisation of army, police and air force. The unleashing of violence indeed became a hurricane and engulfed the whole land. Later I visited these farms. They had once been home to young and vibrant families willing to take on the challenge of farming in Africa. Now there was no charm left for they were deserted and derelict. How sad, I thought, as I stood in the bedroom and looked at the walls pitted by bullets. Here nightmares replaced dreams, terror replaced happiness. In the years to come we were to experience that terror in ever increasing measure.

Que Que

In January 1974 I left my beloved museum work and was posted to a small church in Que Que (KweKwe), a town in which the old Globe and Phoenix mine once operated as the largest mine in the country and the richest gold mine in the world. The mine was now exhausted but the extensive dumps were being reworked. We held Sunday services in the Globe and Phoenix Mine Club as huge buckets carrying tons of rock rattled above the building on overhead cables. Parties were held every Saturday evening and early Sunday morning the hall needed to be cleaned. Sometimes the last reveller was leaving as I arrived. The place was a mess with broken bottles, cigarette stumps, crumpled paper napkins, shattered glass and other rubbish lying on the floor and the overpowering smell of smoke and booze saturating every corner. Out would come mops and brooms and after a vigorous hour or two it was transformed into a place of worship. Nothing could disguise the smell but it was in this hall that we had some memorable church services. The sweet aroma of heaven seemed to descend upon us and at times I was sure I could hear angels singing with us. It was as if we were seated at the very gates of heaven. Church work exposed me to terrible tragedies and also great triumphs of courage.

The conflict was gathering intensity everywhere. About thirty miles east of Que Que lay Katanga Range, the official bomb range of the Air Force. We knew the officer in charge, in fact he was a member of our congregation and he invited us to see the planes in action. The Air Force was a tiny force but very impressive and we went to the range to watch. The Canberra bombers flew high over head and then the Hawker Hunters dived in and let rip with cannons and bombs. It was better than any air show but disastrous for those on the receiving end. After the display the OC radioed the pilots and requested a low-level fly past as he had some VIPs in the control tower. Down came the Hunters throttled back and eye level with us and the pilots gave a salute as they flew past.

Katanga was not only a bombing range but a wild life sanctuary for our friend kept it as his personal game park. It was many thousands of hectares in area with kudu, zebra, wildebeest, warthog, a couple of buffalo, cheetah, leopard and even some wild dogs. Antelope often grazed on the range but would invariably move off a few minutes before any action began. How did they know, did they hear the approaching aircraft when no one else could?

Funerals
I was called upon to conduct funerals, some through tragic circumstances, servicemen killed in action and civilians caught in farm attacks or ambushes. One was the dreadful death of our childhood friend, Wendy. She was a young, vibrant woman seven months pregnant. Her husband was Harry who was a platoon commander and like so many other loyal Rhodesians was fighting for home and country. On this occasion he led his group of men through thick undergrowth as they followed the tracks of a band of insurgents. Suddenly all hell broke loose and no one could see even ten meters ahead or make out who was firing. They had

walked straight into an ambush and bullets flew in all directions as soldiers behind Harry opened up. He got hit in his thigh, not by the enemy but by his own men. After the firing ended he and another casualty were taken to a small field hospital and made as comfortable as possible. Army HQ decided to fly their wives to where they were recovering. Unfortunately the light aircraft they flew in crashed and all on board were killed and it was gutted by fire. Harry lay in hospital waiting to see his wife when in walked a messenger to tell him the terrible news.

I was asked to do the funeral. It was a difficult task but someone had to do it and it might as well be me. We knew Wendy from school days and they had both attended church. The service was packed. Harry arrived on crutches and hobbled up the aisle with his leg in plaster. I cannot remember what I said. I struggled through the service and hardly managed to keep my emotions controlled. After the service we went to the cemetery to lay her charred remains to rest believing she was in the presence of her Lord and Saviour. That, however, did not bring comfort to many who attended for it was too hard a blow. We were all hurting too much. We wept bitterly. After the prayers at the graveside the white men took off their dark jackets and ties, rolled up their long white sleeves, picked up the spades and shovelled in the grave. The paid attendants, all blacks, hung back in silent respect. I feared then that nothing was going to stop this conflict and that it would tear the country apart. There would be more tragedies.

Grandfather

My grandfather was laid to rest in this very cemetery many years before. As I have mentioned Robert like so many loyal British of the time answered the call of duty and enlisted for service in the South African War. Robert was born in Scotland near Aberdeen in 1876 and came from a poor family. At the outbreak of the South African War he joined the "Scottish Highland Brigade" and found himself in South Africa far from home and exposed to all the horrors of war. The war was a catastrophic saga of British blunders, imperial arrogance and crimes against humanity. Two of the smallest republics in the world, the Free State and the Transvaal Republic, stood against the most powerful imperial army of the time. The Boers were fighting for land and homes, the British were fighting for financial gain.

The Boers had a difficult history having trekked away from British administration in the Cape. The introduction of British rule there in 1806 resulted in widespread dissatisfaction among the fiercely independent Afrikaner people many of whom had left Europe because of persecution. The British were insensitive and at times harsh. South Africa was vast and empty so the Afrikaners loaded their wagons and trekked north. Things were not to be easy for they found a new enemy in the fiercely independent Zulu nation. The Boer leaders requested a meeting with Dingane the Zulu king in order to negotiate for land on which to settle and a number of them were invited to his royal kraal. Once inside he disarmed and killed them, 102 in all. Immediately after this he sent his army to kill isolated "Voortrekkers" out on the veld in their wagons. Dingane must have had his reasons for killing his guests but the Boers felt they had a legitimate gripe with the Zulu. They regrouped and at the Battle of Blood River on 16th December 1838 a few hundred Boers were surrounded by 10,000 Zulu warriors. The Boers moved their wagons into the famous *laager* formation and faced the full brunt of attack from the warriors and although the Zulus were brave they could not withstand Boer guns. Three thousand Zulus were killed until the river flowed red with blood and Dingane's army was defeated. A handful of Boers had defeated the might of the Zulu army. It was one of those epic battles of history.

The Boers founded the Free State and the Transvaal Republics. Meanwhile the British established a colony in Natal. In 1880 the Boers now found themselves fighting the British in the First Anglo-Boer War. At Majuba Hill in 1881 they inflicted severe casualties on the British who then made peace but it was always a dubious agreement and in 1899 the Boers faced their old enemy again. As already mentioned the historical events that brought about the Second Anglo-Boer or "South African War" seem to have been largely contrived by the British to win control over gold regions in the Transvaal. The attempt by Rhodes to win control of the wealthy mines when Jameson marched on Johannesburg with a rag tag force of Rhodesian settlers had failed. Now in October 1899 three years after that fiasco a bitter war broke out between Afrikaner Nationalism and British Imperialism. At first the British suffered severe losses but after initial setbacks they got the upper hand by sheer weight of numbers. They eventually controlled much of the land but at tremendous cost. The trench warfare initiated during this conflict was fore runner to the horrific trench wars of the First World War. After the Boer Republics surrendered three Boer armies led by Generals Botha, De La Ray and De Wet still remained in the field undefeated so a scorched earth policy was implemented by the British who rounded up Boer women and children and put them into camps, the first concentration camps to exist in modern times and in which thousands of Boers died due to disease and malnutrition. The Boers never forgot.

Hostilities eventually ended in 1902 and the Union of South Africa was later formed in 1910 under General Jan Smuts an ex-Boer general who after the war worked with the British. He knew that South Africa had to unite to survive. Despite their sufferings South Africans remained loyal to Britain in both World Wars but when the Afrikaans National Party won a resounding victory in 1948 all that was over. Separate development of races came and the years turned bitter. Actually, it was back in Kimberley that apartheid became entrenched. Many Africans flocked to the diamond fields and at first the white miners tolerated them but soon this changed and it was legislated by the British Cape Colony that no African could own a claim, they could only work for whites, they also could not vote. What brought about this attitude; probably a number of things, greed and intolerance being some of them.

Grandfather's war was over when the last Boers surrendered in May 1902 shortly after the death of Rhodes in March. Rhodes had died of heart failure at the age of forty-eight. A special train transported his body on his new railway from Cape Town to Bulawayo. It was then placed on an ox wagon and hauled out to Matobo Hills. The route was lined with faithful Matabele warriors many of whom had fought against him and his settlers but they gave him the royal salute reserved only for a chief.

Boer War Statistics

The Boer War sizzled out shortly after the death of Rhodes. It left South Africa a land of sorrow and destruction, of mourning and hatred. British troops numbering 440,000 had been mobilised to fight a Boer army of no more than 35,000 commandos at any one time. The British army was larger than the entire Boer population. In all, the British lost 22,000 men during the war of which nearly 6,000 were killed in action and over 16,000 died from disease, 31,000 returned to Britain as invalids. The Boers lost over 7,000 commandos. The war was costly in other ways. Over 400,000 thousand horses perished. The harshness of the British had been excessive for Lord Kitchener was a ruthless man. In a previous campaign in the Sudan he had put down a rebellion by killing over 30,000 peasants and in South Africa he implemented a "scorched earth" policy. Many thousands of Boer farms and over 40 villages were looted and burnt to the ground. Pianos, books, clothes and heirlooms were destroyed. Several million cattle and sheep were killed or looted. Horses were shot in the paddocks. Boer prisoners were sent into exile. The worst suffering inflicted was on women and children. Some women were raped by Her Majesty's soldiers and it is estimated that between 28,000 and 30,000 Boer women and children died in the concentration camps, twenty thousand of them less than 16 years of age. This was nearly 15 percent of the entire population. A whole generation of young people was wiped out. With an active army of British soldiers numbering 240,000, a Boer population numbering 235,000 and with 130,000 interred blacks there were over half a million people needing daily food. Yet the British administration burnt the farms and stopped food production. Food rations and medicines were inadequate and hygiene was appalling. Boer women whose husbands did not come in from fighting had their pitiful rations halved. All this in the name of Queen and Empire! It broke Boer moral and forced their surrender. That Rhodes and Jameson and other entrepreneurs should have connived to gain the wealth of South Africa might be forgiven, that British administrators had manipulated the entire fortunes of the subcontinent and destroyed a whole generation was not forgivable. It left deep bitterness amongst Afrikaner people who had suffered so badly. Africans also suffered and many were displaced and many died. If someone today did what Kitchener did then they would be tried for war crimes. It was this treatment of Blacks and Boers that sowed the seeds of apartheid in South Africa. The Boers withdrew even more into their own cultural laager and the cost to Africans was appalling. No one bothered to keep records of their deaths. Many were interred and the unofficial estimate is that at least 17,000 died; it is almost certainly much higher. Afterwards they received no compensation and nothing was done to alleviate their sufferings for they were mostly ignored in the new order. After the war both Blacks and Boers were destitute and impoverished. Within a few years Britain handed self rule to the Union of South Africa significantly not to majority rule but to a white controlled government sympathetic to Britain. Under this government Afrikaans people were often marginalised and excluded from jobs. When the Afrikaners eventually won back power in 1948 they opted to leave the British Commonwealth and none could blame them. They then pursued a policy of separate development but this began long before when much of South Africa was under British influence. It had been a time of madness.

Lonely Mine

At the end of the war grandfather decided that he did not want to leave Africa and go back to cold Scotland. The things he had seen and experienced changed him and he could not go back and masquerade as a hero. Neither did he feel that he could stay in South Africa where there was so much bitterness between Boer, Brit and Black. The war had traumatised him and he wanted to get away from it. At Magersfontein the Scottish Regiments had taken a whipping from the Boers and over 700 were killed and many injured. Pinned down under fire and lying exposed to the fierce sun they suffered severe third degree burns on the back of their legs which were not covered by their kilts. It left their legs badly blistered and made them as useless in battle as if they had been shot. A large stone monument to the Scottish Regiments stands on the top of a low hill and on it is engraved the words, *"Scotland is poorer in men but richer in heroes."* It seems to leave a lot unsaid.

Grandfather did not want to be a hero and had experienced things that left deep psychological scars in him so rather than return to Scotland he chose to lose himself in Africa. He decamped and absconded. He changed his name and after a short spell moved north to the land of Rhodes. Grandfather came to seek a new life in the great expanse and lonely bush of Rhodesia. He found employment at a place aptly named "Lonely Mine" and was there for its initial development. Lonely Mine, as its name implied, was a lonely place in the middle of thick thorn bush north of Bulawayo. It was discovered in the early 1900s from evidence of deep trenches left behind by ancient miners who had worked the gold reef. The mine developed rapidly and was at one time the deepest mine on a quartz reef in the whole of Africa. Grandfather was a keen prospector and forever pegged new claims but he never hit the "big one." Like other prospectors he moved around the country in search of his El Dorado. In 1910 he was in Bulawayo and met a beautiful young woman out from Scotland, Anne. She was born in 1875 and came to Cape Town as a nanny for a family called McKenzie. After a time she travelled north to Bulawayo and it was here she met Walter and they were married. In those days there was a shortage of eligible women in Rhodesia so Walter was exceptionally fortunate to win this fair maiden and carry her off to the lonely wilds of Africa. He had nothing to offer her but a mud hut. She must have been in love! What made her leave home and family and travel to Africa and then settle in the remote bush? Was she running away from a sad past? What were the real reasons that made grandfather change his name? He obviously did not want to be found. Had he committed some misdeed in the army, or broken the law? We will never know but two lonely people found each other in the wilds of Africa.

They lived at Lonely Mine for a few years in a little pole-and-dagga hut they called home. It was the roughest of homes with no running water or electrical power, a clay floor and packing cases for furniture. The outside kitchen near the back door contained a wood-burning Dover stove their sole luxury. Wild animals were abundant and so were snakes. Baboons regularly raided the kitchen and stole the food. Grandfather had a pack of faithful hounds of mixed blood, mostly terriers - and that was about all the company they had.

After a while my grandparents trekked to Messina in the Transvaal to work on the copper mines but did not stay long and moved back to Lonely Mine. During the return journey lions followed their wagons which were hauled by donkeys as oxen were in short supply after the Rinderpest plague. Lions were very partial to donkeys and each night they circled the camp and roared until the veld reverberated. This was a favourite method used by lions to panic animals and make them bolt from the safety of the camp and become easy targets. One day the water ran out and the party walked miles to a river. On their return they found the lions had stampeded the donkeys. They were now in danger of being stranded in the bush. After much searching they managed to round up some of the strays and get moving again but the lions had eaten well.

Their first child, Dorothy, was born in Bulawayo and spent her first few years at Lonely Mine. The family moved once more when grandfather was employed to open Mashaba asbestos mine. He had about a hundred workers under him. Leopards abounded in the hills and one evening one caused panic. Little Dorothy was asleep in her cot draped with a mosquito net and the family cat was also asleep at its foot. My grandparents were having dinner in the adjoining room when all of a sudden a leopard slid through the open door and into the bedroom. By the time grandfather had grabbed his rifle the leopard had sprung out of the window with the family cat in its jaws having failed to claw Dorothy from under the net.

It was a primitive existence not for the faint hearted. Tropical diseases abounded. Malaria was rife and could develop into Black Water Fever from which there were few recoveries. There were other dangers such as crocodiles, snakes, lions, poisonous insects and disease. Work conditions were harsh and the world financial depression hit many men out of employment. Government started building strip roads and white men worked for food. They were hard times. During the First World War asbestos was banned as other supplies had priority for the war effort so the mine was abandoned and the family moved yet again, this time to Connemara Mine near Hunter's Road. A second daughter was born, Sheila my mother. Hunter's Road was the old track used by Selous and other hunters when they trekked to their hunting grounds in Mashonaland before the land was occupied by whites. The Mine was later converted into a prison and still stands on the main road between Kwe Kwe and Gweru and whenever I drove past it I wondered what life must have been like there for my grandparents.

Dorothy could remember an incident that took place at the mine when she was about four years old and my mother hardly a year. It was during Christmas lunch when the workers got out of hand with wild celebrations and the whites had to dash for cover at the appearance of a frenzied crowd wielding clubs and spears. Spears landed on the thatched roof of their home and for a while it looked as though they would all be butchered. Eventually the mob dispersed, the family emerged from hiding and Christmas lunch resumed. It was while the family was at Connemara that the influenza epidemic of 1918 struck twenty million people world-wide. It was known as Spanish Flu and thousands perished in Rhodesia. At the mine one hundred and forty two African staff died and three hundred and twenty others fled into the bush most of whom never returned. Grandmother nursed the whites while grandfather did the best he could for the Africans. Dorothy ended up with double pneumonia and wrapped in blankets was taken to Gwelo. The tiny hospital was full so she was taken to the hotel where grandmother had the freedom of the kitchen and nursed her back to health.

After this the family moved to Wankie. Grandfather went first to organise a house and the family travelled there by train. Dorothy got "lost" during the trip. It happened when the steam-train stopped at a tiny siding to top up with water. All the passengers got down to stretch their legs and walk among the crowds of people selling curios and begging for *"scoff"*. When the train was ready everyone embarked but young Dorothy got separated from her mother and could not find their compartment so she climbed off again in order to get on at another carriage. It was at this inopportune moment that the train pulled off, leaving her stranded, surrounded by strangers and wailing for her mama. Dorothy ran down the track after the train but it disappeared and she found herself abandoned. Grandmother was frantic when she did not find Dorothy and eventually the guard stopped the train and the driver shunted back several miles to where she was stumbling down the track in a terrified state of shock and sobbing. It was a harrowing experience for such a little girl, much worse than my Kimberly experience.

After Wankie they moved to Queens Mine in Matabeleland where the whites had been slaughtered in 1896. Queens Mine was one of the very first mines opened in the colony. By the time grandfather moved there the mine had been extensively worked and was in severe decline because of an acute shortage of labour after the influenza epidemic. The mine closed in 1930 and once again the family moved, this time to the Globe and Phoenix Mine at Que Que, and this is how grandfather came to be buried in the cemetery. Many miners in those early days ended up with emphysema because of the primitive conditions in which they worked. Grandfather was no exception and as he got older he suffered terribly with difficulty in breathing. At the time of his death in 1936 he was the only European working with a gang of Africans at a smaller shaft. One morning a worker raced to the main office with the news he had died, but not of emphysema.

Poison in the tea

Grandfather took morning tea at about nine every morning. He liked it strong and this day it was prepared as usual and brought to him by an employee. Shortly after drinking it pain gripped him, he fell to the floor in convulsions and within a short while was dead. There was a post-mortem and "death by poisoning" was the conclusion. At the inquest a verdict of murder was suggested; a recently reprimanded worker had poisoned him but it was never proven. It remained unresolved but the circumstances were certainly suspicious and people considered it murder by poison. His funeral was dismal, just two daughters, Dorothy and Sheila, about four friends, two policemen and the vicar. The shock nearly killed grandmother who was admitted to the Globe and Phoenix hospital. I don't think she ever got over it. Grandfather was a member of the "British Empire Service League" and so two policemen attended and fired a volley over his grave and then sounded the "Last Post."

However, the murder had a happy ending. A young Anglican minister named Humphrey was Rector at St. Luke's Church, attended the inquest, gave solace to the family and conducted the funeral service. He fell in love with Dorothy and about a year later they were married and soon afterwards they left for England. Humphrey had come to the colony on what was called the Manchester Scheme. The Rhodesian Midlands was a cotton growing area and so the Manchester Diocese in England which was also in the cotton industry undertook to maintain four priests in the parish of Gatooma and Que Que, paying their stipends and travelling costs. So it was that Dorothy said farewell to family, friends and the land of her birth and left for the "home country" - for good.

Grandmother couldn't take the rigours of life on the mine anymore and moved to Bulawayo where she established a small boarding house. During the Second World War she knitted for the troops and after the war returned to England where she died in the 1950s. Dorothy wrote of her, "She was a truly brave woman who helped to build the Rhodesia I remember."

The Night of the Shining Messengers

So here I was in the same town where my uncle had been vicar and my grandfather murdered. Late one night I had a dramatic and strange experience in a large field right next to the cemetery where grandfather lay. It was my custom after the day's work to spend time walking and as I did I would unwind and meditate. I lived in a house just around the corner from the cemetery and one night after my walk instead of going home I made my way to the middle of the field, knelt down on the soil of Africa, and began to earnestly pray for the nation. It was near midnight. The southern hemisphere spread above me in a majestic display of grandeur. It seemed the whole universe with billions of stars stretched to the furthest horizon and above me the sky was black and crystal clear. The burden of an awful future weighed heavily upon me. I felt we were entering a time of trouble and that only some kind of miracle could save us. As I knelt in the field something strange happened. A group of beautiful translucent, massive orbs appeared in the night sky to the south and flew towards me in glowing formation with radiating auras. I stopped in the middle of prayer and my mind began to race. What on earth was I seeing? At first I thought an immense Jumbo jet was coming in to land right on top of me in the tiny field on which I knelt but there was total silence and no sound of engines. The orbs were enormous, larger than any normal jet but they did not appear solid, more like something out of a science fiction movie. The huge orbs flew above me and then broke formation and shot off over the northern horizon at great speed. They had come and gone and I had not moved off my knees. Was I hallucinating? But I was not on drugs and was quite sober with my eyes wide open. What were they? All through history strange flying objects have been seen. There are different theories as to what they may be; some people think they are aliens, others that they are aircraft like the Stealth or other highly secret man-made flying craft, yet others that they are natural phenomena. What I had seen was in my mind certainly not natural. In different cultures "angels" sometimes appear as shinning "stars" that shine iridescently. Whether aliens or angels many people think they are messengers of some kind. From that night I began to research flying objects and similar strange events and their meanings. They often seem to be portents to significant events. I believed we were going into a long, arduous and dangerous period and I was to have several more strange experiences during the years to come.

Revival

We had a revival in the church in Que Que. It soon became known around town that things were happening at the Globe and Phoenix Club and all types of people came along. We were a lively church and it was often difficult to keep some of the more exuberant members from expressing themselves in eccentric ways. We also had drunks and drop outs come to church to "give their hearts to Jesus" which they did in the most demonstrative manner. Often they would be back the next week to do the same again. Que Que was a rough-and-ready mining town with many "rough diamonds" but among them were genuine kind people.

One night as the people gathered and the church was a hum with conversation before the service began a young lady with the shortest skirt and long black hair stepped through the doors. She was a striking woman and as she walked up the aisle every eye in the church followed her. The place became very quiet. One could almost hear the criticism that some were thinking: "who does she think she is coming to church dressed like that, why doesn't she dress properly for church?" It happened to be the same night that a delegation from a very conservative respectable church came to spy what was happening in our services. All went well but in the middle of the service all of a sudden she began to tremble, threw up her arms and began to pray. Right there in the pew her heart was touched. I walked down the aisle and gently spoke with her and she became quiet but her life was transformed. She eventually married a young man in the church and became a member. We had been seeking a measure of respectability and acceptance but in Africa people often tend to be demonstrative in their religion.

Near Que Que was a town called Redcliff and I had services there on Sunday evenings. It had grown around a steel mill and the people were rough and tough. I used to visit members at home and had some close calls with unruly people not to mention vicious dogs. One night I drove up the hill and parked to overlook the town. I liked this spot because it was quiet and I could see the twinkling lights below. I used to pray up there and this night was a glorious balmy night like so many are in Africa. The Milky Way stretched above like a jewelled necklace and the sounds of familiar night birds called softly. It was very still. Suddenly a strong wind came along the road in a kind of muffled roar, sweeping past me and rocking the vehicle back and forth as if by some unseen hand. It was as if an invisible being had passed in the dark African night. All was still again. The stars above were crystal clear in their profusion. A revival came to Redcliff and we saw rough, tough miners and their wives and families changed in meaningful ways.

Some servicemen broke down under the stress of war. They behaved irrationally, drank excessively, became violent and sank into depression. They were constantly exposed to the horrors of war always living near the edge of death and seeing terrible things impossible to forget. I spent more and more time counselling and what they shared gave me insight into what was happening in the war. There was cruelty on both sides and terrible deeds were committed. A soldier went crazy in Redcliff. He shut himself in an apartment on the top floor of Redcliff's one and only "skyscraper", about six stories high. From there he discharged rounds from his army rifle. People ducked for cover as bullets flew at random across town. Because I knew the man I was called to help, together with Eddie an ex-policeman in our congregation. We cautiously snuck up the stairs and called to him through the door. The reaction was swift and furious as he let off more rounds and told us to *"foetsek"* (go away). Eddie was trained in this kind of situation and continued to speak through the door urging him to calm down and to let him in. Eventually after a good deal of cajoling the man gingerly opened the door and Eddie slipped in whereupon it was quickly locked behind him. My heart sank as I thought "That's the end of Eddie." For what seemed hours I sat on the steps and waited and held my breath and at last out they came, the soldier disarmed and held in the big arms of a truly great man.

The Ways of Witchcraft

Manifestations of witchcraft also occurred but were not easy to handle and sometimes ended tragically. Sadly, people were held in the grip of superstition which had intruded into their religion through witchcraft. Ancestral veneration was at one time a meaningful way to honour traditions and maintain family and community bonds but too often it degenerated into a means of manipulative control through witchcraft. Witchcraft was outlawed in Rhodesia but we heard of ritual murders of children who were killed for body parts to make *"muti"* (magic). Bodies were sometimes found without hearts and other vital organs. Such was the power of witchcraft that if a curse was placed upon an individual that person would inevitably die unless they were able to obtain the services of another witchdoctor who could neutralise the curse.

African ancestral religion developed in the ancient land of Egypt where the power of the Pharaohs was perpetuated after death by being elevated to the status of divinity. Their bodies were embalmed and placed in plush tombs together with their worldly riches and at night the spirit of the Pharaoh was free to travel through the land and visit the people thereby perpetuating the control of the deceased ruler. Of course this strengthened the hold the priests had for they claimed to speak for the deceased rulers. Researchers believe that Southern Egypt known as Nubia was the ancient area from where many African people originated before migrations into western and southern Africa. As they moved they carried with them the influence of Egyptian religion and African spirituality developed through elevation of ancestors. These ancestors are believed to take a continuing interest in the activities of their descendants, to punish them for breaches of conduct and to require sacrifices and rites to be made to them. The mediums had authority to approach the ancestors and this in turn gave them influence and power over the people. In this way ancestor veneration became an extension of political control. This power still influences top echelons of African society and mediums are still called upon to advise and empower leaders in countries were ancestral religion is practiced and where leaders are elevated to ancestral status. Thousands of years of spiritual manipulation in Africa developed a mindset in the people of either subservience or dictatorship and the people slip easily into either one or the other. It is this mindset that has plagued Africa for decades and is evident in the way that dictators have meteoric rises over independent nations and why Africa is still so divided in tribal ways. In the days of the 1896 *"chimurenga"* the mediums played a large part in the uprising and during the liberation war some mediums worked with insurgents and motivated the people to fight and even promised "freedom fighters" that bullets could not harm them.

Unfortunately this did not help those who died in combat.

We noticed that whenever there was a turning in a community to the church there was an outbreak of what appeared to be spirit activity to counteract it. Sometimes individuals were subjected to poltergeist activity. At times we were called to help and when we prayed for someone that person experienced a release but they then needed to renounce "the spirits" to remain free. For example, a new Christian said she saw a "spirit" sitting in her home hunched in a chair. She remembered some voodoo carvings she had in her house and when she removed them she had no further problems. This might sound strange to western people who have not been subjected to it.

During these years I teamed up with my friend Eli (short for Elisha) and he helped me to relate to Africans in ways that would not be offensive. African and white culture is quite different and one can unwittingly cause offence. For example the way whites give respect to others is often by standing when someone enters a room. However, in Africa this is quite the opposite and they remain seated. To be in a Church service in Africa is an unforgettable experience. It is not like a conventional church in Britain or Europe. It is African and filled with strong emotions and expressions of exuberance with powerful and emotive singing, crying, laughing and dancing. People sometimes fall down, others shake and there are volumes of music, clapping, stamping and swaying. Time means nothing in Africa. Such services can go on for hours. Africans can be very enthusiastic about their faith. Their enthusiasm is catching. I have been in many such services often in isolated places with the dust and heat of Africa all around and flies buzzing and people sweating and yet with a sense of blessing. If held at night then the vastness of the African sky is spread above like a jewelled curtain punctuated by the Southern Cross and the sermon is given by the light of a paraffin lamp or candle to the drone of mosquitoes buzzing in the air. When one has been in such a gathering one comes out invigorated feeling it has been worthwhile.

Robert worked for me but fell foul of the spirit world. He told me of several visitations he had from spirits. Eventually he had a total breakdown. Then there was Jeffery. He was well until one day he heard voices and tried to burn down our house. Another was Rosemary, a happy woman who worked in our neighbour's house. She went to pieces when apparitions appeared in her room. This became a regular occurrence and she had a total breakdown. I have seen people apparently possessed, whirling and twirling, falling in a trance and then acting and speaking as if controlled by another power. Sometimes "spirits" manifested in strange ways; people spoke in strange voices, screamed, rolled about making guttural sounds and went into trances. Witchcraft still survives in Africa.

There were times when we saw the conversion of "witchdoctors" for when they saw that Christianity was affective against their spirits they sometimes renounced their profession. Whenever a "witchdoctor" made a confession of Christianity it was a significant event for they would bring all the "tools of their trade," their charms, divining bones and other paraphernalia and burn them in the presence of the congregation and then kneel down and pray. One knew it was real when done like this in front of the whole community and they publicly renounced their past way of life. I am referring to those who practiced voodoo and not herbalists. The term "witchdoctor" is no longer in vogue today but it was the term used at that time. I witnessed an extraordinary conversion of a witch doctor in a remote area where a colleague and I conducted a mission. One night a crowd gathered in front of a local country store to hear Bible teaching and I stood on the steps with a paraffin lamp that caused eerie shadows to fall in distorted shapes. A mass of bodies crowded around us and the dark African night pressed in. Suddenly in the middle of the sermon a commotion broke out among the people seated in the shadows before the steps. Screams of fear erupted as people began to squirm and fall over each other as they scrambled for safety with yells of *"nyoka, nyoka,* snake, snake.*"* Quickly lifting the lamp high and stepping over the writhing bodies I saw that the cause of the confusion was a diminutive Egg Eater slithering around among the panic stricken people. This was a bad omen for it was one of the most feared of all snakes and caused terror yet it was entirely harmless.

In one easy movement developed from years of snake catching I gathered up the offending culprit and without a backward glance strode into the darkness where I released it some distance from the people. Well if they weren't believers before they certainly were then. A hush fell upon the crowd behind me broken by exclamations of awe and astonishment. They had witnessed what they considered to be an astounding miracle. The preacher had done what the Bible said could be done, "to take up serpents without suffering harm." Now we had a captive audience and our reputation spread like wild fire. It was not long before the whole district heard about the event and, not to be left out, the local *"nganga"* or "witch doctor" claimed it was his personal snake that he had sent along to the meeting to see what was going on. This extraordinary event brought more people to our services and the witchdoctor also came and wanted to be a Christian. He brought all his charms and bones and other things and burnt them before the congregation. Before all the people he knelt down and prayed. The whole district heard about it.

Mission Work

Eli built a mud and thatch church on the top of a hill in the remote area of Goradema near the wild Chisarira National Park. There were lions, elephants and other wild animals in the surrounding bush. The church was like a beacon that could be seen for miles around. Over the years even during the war we went out there to help. The enthusiasm of the locals inspired us to give our best and we found it easy to share with them for they were keen to learn. Another man I knew was Morton. We travelled together to wild areas in the Zambezi Valley where he conducted teaching and established churches. One significant occasion was when

I accompanied him to some villages on the banks of the Zambezi River. At the conclusion of several days teaching a large number of people wanted to be baptised. As there was no beautiful church in which to do this the answer was simple for there before us stretched the broad Zambezi. That it was notorious for having some of the biggest crocodiles in Africa did not seem to bother them. The people chose a spot where they could look out for crocs and Morton conducted a service. We sang as they were baptised in the Zambezi.

A "Near Death Experience"

On one of our bush trips during the height of the armed struggle a colleague and I had a "near death" experience. We were with Eli for several days of teaching far away in his bush parish. As I said, Eli had built a pole and grass church. It was no cathedral but crowds crammed into his rough bush chapel. At night it was lit with paraffin lamps that threw dull light with long shadows. The sides were open so as to allow fresh air and crowd expansion. The people did not sit in nice pews but on the ground wherever they could find space or on rough log benches. Standing at the front and peering out at the sea of faces, the old and young from tiny babies to wizened, wrinkled grey-haired ancients, was quite an experience in itself. The people were so keen that they walked for miles along the twisting paths of Africa to attend the sessions. All went well with large numbers attending and we were pleased with the way things were going.

Then a foreboding fell upon me and I became deeply troubled. In the evening service I had noticed two rough looking men sitting in the back of the congregation who appeared detached from the rest of the people as if somehow they did not belong. It was dark and impossible to clearly see their features and afterwards they melted away among the crowd. But I was troubled for I knew that numerous missionaries had been abducted and killed by "freedom fighters". I could not shake the feeling off and said to Eli that we should cut short our visit. He agreed and we left immediately. Later he told us what happened. Very soon after our departure "the boys from the bush" came looking for us, a polite way of saying "terrorists came to kill us". In fact the two men were indeed spies who had gone to call their comrades and a group of them arrived ready to deal with us. We got away in the nick of time and I shudder to think of the brutal death we would have suffered if caught by them.

The Fall of Portuguese East Africa

Portuguese East Africa was that vast tract of tropical forest and coastal bush that stretched for many miles along East Africa and was what Mozambique was called before independence. It was controlled by Portugal, on the other side of the world. In about 1974 the army General Antonio de Spinola staged a coup in Lisbon and overthrew the Portuguese government. This had profound consequences for the new military leaders made a decision to withdraw from their colonies in Africa. It was another of those hasty decisions that brought great tragedy; after nearly four centuries in Africa Portugal suddenly decided to pull out. Within a few months they handed Portuguese East Africa and Angola over to a band of bush soldiers. The result was predictable, the nations plunged into anarchy and the local whites lost all they had. Many white farmers had been encouraged by the Portuguese government to come to Africa. They had left their homes in Portugal to brave the rigors of primitive life in the jungles of Africa where they carved farms out of wilderness only to lose everything. Images of the Congo were repeated as whites fled. With tear-streaked faces they poured across the border into Umtali clutching one another, people who had escaped with their lives and now faced an uncertain future. I couldn't help wonder whether our Portuguese friend with his wife and daughters had managed to escape. Africans and other people also fled and soon Mozambique and Angola slipped into long and cruel civil wars. Instead of fighting the white administration they now fought each other for the spoils.

In 1976 I returned to Umtali as minister in the church. It was nice to be back in the town of my youth, back in the land I knew so well. But now things had changed. There were no happy border crossings into Mozambique to enjoy the Mediterranean cuisine for now it was controlled by Frelimo forces. The Rhodesia Army patrolled the district and the town was full of army personnel and vehicles. These vehicles were designed to deflect landmines and withstand ambushes and had heavy reinforced metal. They came in weird shapes and sizes and were called all manner of names: Hippos, Crocodiles, Pumas, Rhinos and so on. The town bustled with men and women in uniform and had the feel of a frontier border town.

Our church was linked to a mission in Inyanga North so one of the first things I did was to visit the mission to see friends there. Peter was in charge. The mission had been established years before and was staffed by dedicated missionaries from England. Over the years they had achieved great improvements in education and health among the people. They had a strong local following but the missionaries were having a tough time for "freedom fighters" had infiltrated the area and were causing havoc amongst the peace loving community. It was a long drive through majestic hills. On every side there were signs of war; burnt out stores and deserted villages, derelict army trucks and vehicles.

Umtali Bombed - 1976

I kept fit by running in the cool of night. African nights are beautiful and temperate and I ran along Main Street where once we used to race our cars and then on through the suburban hills. When tired I would stop and pray a while. The war was escalating. In the second week of August 1976 in the early hours of morning Frelimo forces in Mozambique bombed Umtali. Our sleep was broken with reverberating shocks of exploding rockets and mortars. I awoke to what sounded like rolling thunder followed by loud detonations and ran outside as rockets flew overhead and landed haphazardly around me. Looking towards the east from where the rockets came was "Cross Kopje" silhouetted against the sky. It was a memorial to African servicemen who had died for Britain in the First World War and a huge cross was constructed from granite blocks and stood on the pinnacle of the kopje. It was a beacon over Umtali prominent during the day and night, the symbol of loyalty and sacrifice. Every night the cross on the kopje was lit with spotlights and stood like a lighthouse giving comfort to town residents. Now it guided Frelimo bombs. The rockets were interspersed with the rattle of spasmodic small arms fire. I watched and wondered, "Where will it all end?"

Just after daybreak jets of the Air Force flew low over town in a show of force but that night the light on the cross was switched off. It seemed to be a sign of the darkness falling over the country. Rhodesians were beginning to realise the whole world was against them and still could not understand why. Had the world lost its mind, they asked. In Uganda a dictator committed horrendous atrocities and they felt they were trying to stop such a situation occurring yet faced the venom of the world, nothing made sense to them anymore. Idi Amin came to power in Uganda in 1971 after an army coup. He was an army sergeant but bestowed upon himself the illustrious titles *"Conqueror of the British Empire"* and *"King of Scotland"*. Uganda was once called the *"Pearl of Africa"* for it was the most beautiful and fertile of African countries. However, Amin's brutal eight year rule resulted in the deaths of hundreds of thousands of people and the cruel persecution of Christians. In 1977 it was rumoured that Amin had personally killed the Anglican Archbishop during a torture session. It was also rumoured that he enjoyed eating his victims and that he kept choice pieces of them in his fridge. Whether true or not he did expel Asians and whites and was said to have committed other deeds too obscene to mention. Something like three hundred thousand people perished under his dictatorship. He eventually fled to Libya and was never brought to trial. It was this kind of thing that Rhodesians feared most. The world did very little to stop this madman yet did everything possible to bring about the downfall of Rhodesia. Uganda had been the show piece for British policy on African Independence. Could Rhodesians be blamed for not wanting something similar to happen to them?

Over the next four years Umtali was bombed several times and the people of the town and district took a tremendous beating as farmers, missionaries, Government Officials and Security Forces were killed and rural people intimidated, abducted and exposed to great suffering. Communist trained insurgents ran rampant throughout the province for it was a rugged country interspersed with granite kopjes and dense jungles ideal as hide outs. Farms, forest plantations and towns were all attacked. Ambushes were set on roads. Tractor drivers and farm staff were killed. Some whites were abducted and taken into Mozambique.

SA border closed

The Rhodesian conflict worsened and in response to pressure from USA Secretary of State, Henry Kissinger, South Africa suddenly closed its borders with Rhodesia in 1976. Fuel and strategic requirements were instantly cut off. The "Kissinger agreement" as it was called was not an agreement at all but a move to "checkmate" Rhodesia which was reduced to 19 days of fuel and very little ammo. Men were sent into the bush with two magazines of forty rounds. What they did not lack in courage they now lacked in resources.

The vulnerability of farmers worsened. The slogan of the insurgents was "one farmer, one bullet." Every farm homestead had a radio network open twenty-four hours a day. If in trouble the farmers could call for assistance. Our friend, Barry, responded to numerous calls from isolated farmers. He lived in the Mtoko district a hot spot in more ways than one for not only was the area hot in climate it was also hot in violence. As war intensified the regular army was stretched to the limit and so local farmers formed reaction teams and were armed with rifles and ammo. When farms were attacked the nearest farmer would jump in his vehicle and set off irrespective of ambush or landmines that may be set on the narrow farm roads. Sometimes he would collect a friend on route. They would dash down the winding tracks often straight into a "contact", a term used for a battle with insurgents. Usually they were outnumbered but they got away with it because the insurgents simply could not believe that just a couple of men would attack them. All they saw was a Land Rover speeding towards them and very often they fled. This was how the farm war was fought with very little else but bravado. The 1976 blockade by South Africa shocked Rhodesians who considered South Africa an ally. The two countries had a close but not always harmonious history. Although many white South Africans were of British stock the Afrikaans people were descended from Dutch and French Huguenots. The British administration in South Africa had made things very difficult for Afrikaans people. Rhodesians always considered themselves to be British but when a Republic was declared in Rhodesia any gripes between them and South Africa were forgotten and they drew closer. South Africa assisted Rhodesia by providing both men and arms for the bush war. However, after Kissinger brought pressure on the South African government they became just an American pawn. At that time America was involved in its own nasty war in South Vietnam yet chose to crush the small nation of Rhodesia. The Rhodesians found this somewhat inconsistent. Barry survived the Bush War but later he and his wife were attacked on their farm in Zimbabwe when Mugabe decided once and for all to get rid of white farmers. They survived this too but left soon afterwards. They lost everything, a lifetime of hard work and commitment.

Before the SA embargo and out of sheer frustration and defiance Smith had made a hasty statement that majority rule would never happen; *"never in a thousand years"* were his words. It was a bit like Churchill's statement that the

British Empire and Commonwealth might last a thousand years. After talks in South Africa with Kissinger Smith had to eat his words and announced majority rule within a couple of years. It was a great turn about.

Albert's Funeral - 1976

It was August 1976 and another routine bulletin by Rhodesian Broadcasting Corporation announced the death of four soldiers. These announcements were given daily and listed war casualties, the dead on "our side" and the dead on "their side." The four dead men were from my 4th Battalion Rhodesia Regiment and died when their camp in Burma Valley near the border with Mozambique was bombed. Another man was killed in follow-up action. The names of the deceased were given the following day in the newspaper under the death column. I bought a paper. There he was among the names of the others who died, "Albert ..., killed in action". Albert, our dear gentle friend from childhood days, was dead, killed in the place he loved, the thick, tropical, sweltering Burma Valley which lay in the shadow of the Vumba Mountains and was full of exotic birds, snakes and other wild animals.

I had known Albert as my big, happy, harmless friend. Now I had to bury him. A group of distraught people gathered around the hole in the ground at Umtali cemetery. A small contingent of soldiers stood to one side of the grave and fired a volley of blank rounds and the reports seemed pathetically inadequate against the great backdrop of mountains and awful grief. The clear blue sky overhead was like polished bronze. Family members supported his identical twin Alfred. Normally he would have stood head and shoulders above the others but now his body was shrunk and shook with spasms of grief. The twins had never been parted; they went everywhere together and were the closest friends. Now they were separated as they had never been before. The hills looked down that day like brass, cold and indifferent to the sounds of the plaintiff notes of the bugle as it sounded the Last Post. The notes hung in the still air then died away and were replaced by wails, cries of anguish and deep sobs until eventually silence settled on us broken only by whimpers of despair. I surveyed the scene in dumb shock. Those beloved hills of mine that once charmed me with their delights and where I spent happy hours exploring were now fearful places to be avoided at all cost. They hid the unseen enemy that lurked in the shadows to strike at the helpless and unsuspecting. We were learning to live with fear, an insidious uncontrollable fear, daily and constant, always just beneath the outward calm, waiting to rear its head; fear of attack, of rape, of theft, of violence, of ambush, of abduction, of death – the fear of terror. It slowly ate its way into us without us knowing it was there until suddenly it rose and strangled us in its suffocating grip. And so we began to die on the inside, as friends and loved ones died we did too. Some of us died quickly, most of us died slowly.

Within days the army attacked a large camp in Mozambique from where many insurgents came. It was reported that over a thousand people were killed. Then in December militants hit Tea Estates in the Honde Valley where dad took me as a child and where I had spent enjoyable times on Museum expeditions. They rounded up twenty seven men who worked on the estates, lined them up against a wall, and gunned them down execution style for no reason other than they worked on the tea estate. Others were burnt alive in huts. They then herded the older children together and marched them into Mozambique to join other "volunteers" in the Liberation Struggle. Many hundreds of child soldiers were recruited in this manner.

I bought a 9mm semi-automatic machine gun. It had a folding butt and looked like one of those machine guns used by gangsters in American films. Its magazine held 25 rounds and I bought two so I had 50 bullets to let fly if needed. It was made in Rhodesia and locals complained that it had a tendency to jam in a crisis. I prayed that I should never have to use this dreadful weapon and fortunately although I carried it everywhere I never fired a shot.

War Casualties

The trauma experienced by men on active duty was hard to deal with. Some were badly shaken at what they saw and experienced. They could not talk about these things and sank into an inner world of guilt, shame and sorrow. How do you counsel a man who has sat through a night punctuated with shrieks of torment as armed killers moved into a nearby village and conducted indoctrination sessions including the killing and maiming of those who were considered "sell outs"; sometimes the helpless aged and women. Nights filled with pitiful sobs and screams, broken by harsh male voices and wailing women and children, intermingled with *"chimurenga"* songs accompanied by crackling flames of burning huts, followed by long silences of terror, people ravaged by the vermin of the night. Government soldiers were unable to protect these defenceless people and could not intervene in the darkness and just had to wait till morning. They endured, too afraid to sleep, to move, to breathe, to make a sound, and then in the dread of first light they would move in with guns cocked, fingers on triggers, and see the smouldering shells of huts, bayoneted bodies and smell the smell of burnt flesh. What do you say to people who have seen things they should never have seen? How do you comfort a man who has just seen his best friend killed or innocent people shot down before him in cold blood? How do you explain such things to men sick in their spirits, smouldering with anger? Words were inadequate and men sank into the silence of hate. Some Rhodesians may indignantly deny that Rhodesia did anything wrong but torture and atrocities did happen. In our church we had several soldiers and I also knew others. They were not supposed to talk of their experiences but as I maintained strict confidentiality they did talk to me. Such men needed to talk, to confess, to cry, to agonise. Too often they could not. Many were so badly demoralised that they became hardened and bitter seething with inner rage. Witnessing brutal acts made some turn with vengeance on those they believed perpetrated such ghastly war deeds. When they found them they showed no mercy. Afterwards, they came back in silence too appalled to speak of things they saw. By committing acts of war they succumbed to the guilt it brought. This is the way of war, all sides suffer. Some soldiers were exhilarated and celebrated every kill. Others turned to religion. Rod was one. He was in the Rhodesian Light Infantry and decided God must be speaking to him after he had several scrapes with death; twice wounded in skirmishes, twice had his parachute fail to open properly and once an elephant nearly kill him.

It was when he was with a group of soldiers battling insurgents in a dry, sandy river in the Zambezi Valley that an enraged elephant, upset because of the commotion of shooting, charged him. It grabbed him with its trunk and threw him on the sand and then proceeded to stamp on him. Every time a foot came down he rolled to avoid it but without success. What saved him was the softness of the sand and he began to be compressed into it. Then the great monster knelt down and thrust his ivory towards him. A tusk went on either side of him and he found himself eyeball to eyeball with the huge animal. All this time he was screaming but did not know it. One of the other soldiers plunged his bayonet into the animal's backside whereupon it left him and turned, grabbed the offender and threw him through the bush. Branches broke his fall and saved his life and the animal dashed off. Rod was airlifted out with massive bruising. The soldier who saved his life was awarded a medal but Rod believed God spared him.

In urban areas more people came under attack. There were bomb alerts at schools and bag searches when entering shops and buildings. People were cracking under stress. Garth was a young man who attended church regularly. He was full of enthusiasm and greeted everyone with great gusto, throwing his arms around the men and plonking holy kisses upon the "sisters", from teenagers to grannies. This caused great consternation amongst the ladies but he had a good heart. With the increasing difficulties in the country he came under pressure at home and at work. He had an ailing mother and extended family to support and he spent long hours working in a local cafe in order to do so. One day he cracked under the pressure and arrived at church ready to shoot the minister whom he accused of preaching heresy. He walked down the aisle brandishing a loaded gun. Where he got it from is uncertain but many people had guns during the war. The congregation ducked under the pews and the minister hid behind the lectern. He proceeded into town threatening to do battle with heretics and antichrists. The police got him and took him to the mental hospital. I had to go there from time to time to visit patients at Ward 12, as it was called. These were the casualties of life, destitute old timers, alcoholics, youngsters, all with shattered lives walking in a world of dumbness and pain. As the war intensified their numbers increased.

The telephone rang. "Are you able to visit a man in jail awaiting execution?" was the request. I thought for a moment and replied, "Yes."

Together with an official from the Christian Prison Fellowship we drove to Salisbury central jail, a sombre complex surrounded by high walls with watch towers and barbed wire. A small metal door marked the entrance and we pressed the bell. A few moments later a narrow peep latch slid open and a pair of eyes appeared. We explained who we were and that we had authority to see a prisoner and keys rattled as the door swung open and we were led into the reception area where we went through the formalities of signing in. From there we went into a cubicle where we were searched and relieved of everything; car keys, pens, wallets and money. Having signed for it all we were ushered through several narrow iron gates into another waiting area. After several more minutes we were escorted down a long corridor into the bowels of the building. I began to wonder whether having got in we would ever get out again. The corridor eventually led towards a row of cells and we were shown into one. Sitting in the cell was a small, neat black man. He looked up and smiled. This was our killer, a man under sentence of death for committing acts of terror. He did not look like a terrorist. We greeted one another and exchanged pleasantries. He expressed his faith in God and requested prayer for himself. He knew he would hang and had resigned himself to that fate. What he wanted was just to speak to a white priest and have a prayer. We prayed for him, black and white sitting together in the austere surroundings. We asked if he had a family, shook his hand and left. It was so complete. I will never forget the long walk out of that jail.

"A naked man came to church on Sunday." This is the entry in my diary. He turned off the main road and came walking down the driveway, stark naked. Our eyes nearly popped out of our heads. Maybe he thought he was Adam. In the Bible it says that Jesus delivered a naked man and afterwards he was clothed and in sound mind, sitting at his feet. Our faith failed to meet the challenge. Instead, some of the men blocked the path of the naked visitor and the women hid inside. Then someone called the police who came and took him away.

Inyanga Mountains

I sometimes went to Inyanga Mountains to stay with Ted and Bon. They had a lovely cottage near the little hamlet of Juliasdale. Their home looked over miles and miles of rolling hills, cascading waterfalls and a great placid panorama of beauty. My weekends at Juliasdale were spent roaming the hills, exploring caves and forests, and generally enjoying the superb beauty of the area. There were so many interesting things to see and do. Bon had created the most beautiful garden filled with wild succulents, aloes and other unique flora. Birds flocked there, Robins, Bulbuls, Sunbirds and many more. Dawn in Africa is a glorious event and always heralded by bird song. The first birds to awaken are the Bulbuls who welcome the new day with great excitement. They are the "middle class' in the bird world and have an exuberant song and are very vocal at dawn long before other birds. The evenings are just as beautiful but are usually punctuated by Hueglin Robins. They are "aristocrats" and do not mix with others but are found in pairs skulking around thick bush. As afternoon wears on they come out and display their beauty both in colour and melodious song. It is a song that once heard rests in the heart of everyone who has lived in Africa. As dusk approaches out come the noisy Babblers. They are the "working class" and babble they do, usually in a raucous crowd laughing in the most outrageous manner.

Ted was with dad in the BSA police and also stationed at Fort Rixon. He had known dad's favourite horse, Kit, from whom one could shoot from the saddle without him even twitching a muscle. Ted had lots of stories about those early days for he had joined the Police in the 1930s. At that time horse patrols were the order of the day and he had tramped almost every part of the country. He had a great sense of humour and always saw the funny side even when it was sad and bizarre. Once he had to cut down the body of a man who hung himself in the bush. When Ted got to him he had already been in the sun for some days and was very ripe. He tried every possible way to get up the tree and cut the rope but found the angle would not allow it. So he rode his horse under the man, got the man's dangling legs down on either side of the saddle and then by standing in the stirrups managed to reach up and cut the rope. The body tumbled down on top of him, the horse got spooked and took off and he found himself galloping through the bush clutching the smelly body. He flew though tall grass with thorn branches whipping against his knees and the smell of the deceased in his nostrils. Ted managed to get the horse under control just as he approached the local village whose occupants took one look and ran screaming in terror at the appearance of the apparition. As he pulled the horse to a halt accompanied by shrieks from the people the body slid from the withers with a sickening thud. Ted swung his horse around and spurred it down to the river where he jumped in clothes and all. It had been the ultimate ride with death.

Ted left the police and became a guard on the railways where he knew a guard called Sandy. Animals transported on the trains were put in the guard van and on one journey in which Sandy was on duty there was a beautiful pedigree Poodle on route to Ndola in Northern Rhodesia. All went well until the dog began to yelp and whine. Eventually Sandy let it out into the van and it settled down. He had forgotten about it when they arrived at a siding and he slid open the door and the dog jumped out and disappeared among the throng of hawkers and disembarking passengers. Now Sandy was in a quandary but had a "bright idea" when he saw a scruffy, flea bitten, mangy indigenous dog with hollow ribs and curved tail. He enticed the dog over with some good food, pounced on it and put it in the dog cage in the van. He checked the consignment note which simply said "one dog" and covered the cage with a blanket. A few more sidings up the track he ended his duty and another guard took over. What happened at Ndola when the owners came for their prize pedigree dog must have been entertaining to say the least.

Our idyllic days tramping the hills came to an end when the bush war reached

Inyanga. The district exploded and fighting took its toll. Isolated and defenceless homesteads were attacked, burnt down and the occupants killed. Some were lucky to escape, others perished. A tide of killing swept through the Eastern Highlands. Forest Estates came under attack. At one estate a man and his wife were publicly decapitated for no other crime than their daughter was married to a policeman. The good days were over and our friends moved to town.

Renewal

During those difficult days renewal broke out at church in the small town of Marondera in the centre of a farming district. Our services were full of both young and old. It started with school children who then brought their parents and soon business people, farmers and others were coming to church to seek spiritual renewal. Farms were attacked on a weekly basis. As minister I was expected to visit the farming community and give encouragement and so I found myself travelling into rural areas often on my own. Farmers were attacked, families ambushed and farm workers intimidated and killed. It happened throughout the country. It was farmers and their labour who took the brunt of the terror and they had little protection from roving bands of insurgents. I travelled to farms and held services and prayers. I felt it was a privilege to be able to help in some way. A spiritual awakening took place among both white farmers and their African labour force. The people were hungry for Christian teaching and they all attended without coercion, from the aged to children. They would express their faith by singing and dancing, praying and clapping with exuberant rejoicing. The services could go on for hours and it was great to be among these happy people. They were all part of an extended family and enjoyed benefits of farm life with fresh produce and rations. Many farms also had a school paid for by the farmer and provided with a government teacher. It was a simple lifestyle but wholesome. These worship meetings were in direct contrast to the fearful meetings held by insurgent gangs who forced all, both young and old to sing "freedom songs" and denounce one another and where innocent people were brain washed, sometimes tortured and even killed.

In the midst of war, with our fate in the balance, I got married; joy in the midst of sadness as dark clouds hung over the country. It was hard to celebrate when friends were dying. It reminded me of a "monkey's wedding", a rainbow against a dark sky of suffering. It was a wartime wedding; with no luxuries, no celebrations, no invited guests and no cake. To add to our sorrow some in church hierarchy took umbrage at our marriage. My spouse had children from a previous marriage who were currently with their father. Even though the church had blessed our proposed marriage some decided that because I was a minister it was unacceptable. There was such dissent we were unable to establish the home we wanted and I found out how harsh some people could be. I lost a lot of friends and very nearly my job too. After our modest ceremony we went to the shores of Lake Kyle where we hoped we could escape the violence that stalked the land and the acrimony of so-called friends. Rhodesia had become a nation in crisis. Around every bend in the road there was the possibility of being ambushed. That very week a six-month old baby, Natasha, was cruelly bayoneted to death by "freedom fighters." The killers invaded a farm house and in order to protect the white baby the family nanny, an African woman, wrapped little Natasha in a blanket and put her on her back as if she were her own baby but the murderers demanded to see the child. When they saw she was white they ripped her away and flung her across the room and then stabbed her to death. It was not the first time white children had been killed. In March of 1977 eleven year old Sharon was killed. In June the same year five year old Ray was killed and his four year old brother Manie died later of wounds. Then in July three year old Lianne was shot dead. The list went on. The "shadow of death" lay on the land.

Grandparents

My spouse came from a South African family. Her grandparent's were caught in faction fighting in Zululand in the 1920s and her mother as an infant was carried out of Zululand on the back of a nanny. Fortunately she was not discovered and survived. There had been trouble in Zululand and gangs of Zulu warriors, crashing their spears on shields and stamping their feet, surrounded isolated dwellings and threatened to drive the whites out of Zululand. Some African servants were killed by the Zulus. Her grandparents were mining in Zululand at the time and decided to leave for their own safety. They loaded a few supplies onto their ox wagon and joined other families trekking out. It was tough going. Each night the wagons formed a laager with the oxen in the middle and thorn branches stacked around the wheels to ward off attack. It was customary when trekking to carry the embers of a fire in a cauldron suspended on the rear of the wagon. The embers remained hot and at the end of the day were used to rekindle a new fire for the night. Her mother was only a few years old and at a particular severe jolt she tumbled out of the back of the wagon and landed on the glowing fire right on her bottom and was badly burnt. From then on she had to be carried right through Zululand on the back of her nanny. On a number of occasions she escaped being noticed on the woman's back which may have saved her life. It took months for her to recover but her younger brother, little Thomas, fell ill with pneumonia and died during the trip. His little body was buried out on the lonely veld somewhere in Zululand. Three other sisters survived but with the loss of income from the mine the family could not hold together and broke up. The children were left at the doors of a Catholic orphanage where they grew up until their teens. Her mother then started work as a waitress and after a while got to know a young man, Robert, who came and ate regularly at the restaurant. He was a widower with two lads. One day he asked her to marry him and she did but soon afterwards the Second World War broke out and he went off to fight under Montgomery in the North African desert. After the war, when South Africa fell to the National Party he was not prepared to live under Apartheid and moved his family to Bulawayo.

Victoria Falls

During the liberation war foreign tourists dwindled and hotels embarked on a policy to get the custom of local residents. This meant reducing tariffs to suit the local pocket and we found for the first time we could afford a holiday and we set off on the long road to Victoria Falls despite the dangers of the war. We felt the remoteness more and more as we travelled through mile upon mile of Mopani forests. People had recently been abducted and killed on this road and the posh Elephant Hills Hotel at Victoria Falls had been reduced to a pile of ash by a rocket fired from Zambia.

When David Livingstone saw the falls in 1855 he wrote *"angels must have gazed upon them in their flight"* but now soldiers glared through the spray and elephants were blown up by land mines placed along the river banks. Friends and I walked the full length of the falls, over a mile wide, to the famous bridge built by Rhodes to span the yawning chasm of the Zambezi Gorge. Because of sanctions the bridge was now closed to traffic, however, a troop of baboons, not needing passports, crossed the bridge from Zambia. They strode along in a casual manner and some jumped on top of the train parked half way across the bridge. This was how Rhodesians and Zambians exchanged trade by shunting loaded trains half way onto the bridge and letting the other side collect them. We watched the baboons as they lifted the tarpaulins on the wagons and peered inside them and we joked that they looked like customs officers checking the contents. Hardly had we said it when a troop of Zambian soldiers in a truck lurched onto the bridge and screeched to a halt. Soldiers sprang out and spread across the bridge at a run pointing their guns towards us in a menacing manner. We quickly ran to the undergrowth not wanting to be casualties in the way two young Canadian girls were in 1973 when they were shot dead by the Zambian army. We ducked into thicker foliage as the soldiers made hostile gestures towards us. After a while when they could no longer see us they grudgingly left and thankfully we emerged from hiding and headed to the Victoria Falls Hotel, one of the great colonial hotels of Africa, where we relaxed in shady gardens with refreshing cool drinks.

However, danger was not entirely over for the baboons had fled and now also visited the hotel. Food was scarce in Zambia and they had learnt that it was abundant on the Rhodesian side. People fed them with scraps from the tables despite the signs saying "Do not feed the monkeys." Consequently they would jump on tables and steal what they could. Periodically the waiters, dressed in starched white tunics and with beads of sweat running from their brows, chased them across the lawns. It was entertaining but dangerous. Nevertheless, as we sat in the cool gardens we felt we preferred the dangers of baboons to soldiers.

The Political Climate

Rhodesians responded to sanctions imposed on them with a resolve to show the world that they could "go it alone". They were resourceful people cut from the old block of British ingenuity and resilience. Sanctions only served to strengthen their determination not to give in despite hardships. People found ways to import vital commodities and also began to manufacture things previously imported. Despite fuel rationing and other difficulties Rhodesians maintained a sense of humour and fortitude. It was only later that they became demoralised – the constant killing, the lack of international understanding and particularly the realisation that the West had turned from them and they were expendable caused more and more despair. They became disillusioned with what they perceived as double standards in the world. Africa was in chaos with coups and counter coups, rebellions and war yet they were expected to just stand aside and let those conditions prevail. As things deteriorated the government resorted more and more to tactics of repression and the brutal methods used by some so called "freedom fighters" trained in North Korean continued unabated. Some whites began to realise the war had gone terribly wrong and left the country.

Red Cross workers were killed even though their vehicle was clearly marked with a large emblem. Missionaries were targeted and defenceless citizens killed. We continued to move from shock to shock and world media portrayed Rhodesia in poor light. Blame for the violence was placed entirely on Rhodesians without any historical context or coverage of horrific tactics used by some communist trained insurgents. Something we all found very strange was how our mail to UK did not get through especially if it contained local news with local perspective of what was happening. Aunt Dorothy mentioned that mail from us was opened. Other people noticed the same thing. There was no doubt that someone was preventing our side of the news from getting through to family and friends in the UK. Some events that were reported as factual were in fact fabricated. Photographs depicting racial violence in South African were ascribed to Rhodesia, a blatant untruth. Journalists threw sweets into dustbins and when children dived into them they took photos which were published under captions of "Starving children." Yet in the days of Rhodesia even though people did suffer there was no mass starvation. Movie archives of that era will show how robust many people were in the 1950s and 60s. Life expectancy was high; there were many elderly people and child survival good. I am not saying it was easy as conditions were at times harsh but these were comparatively good years in contrast to what would come. Between 1897 and 1960 not one shot was fired by police or soldiers in Southern Rhodesia. The people were good-natured and there was a lot of good will. It was when nationalist movements started that violence broke out with police trying to quell riots. When the Liberation War began many rural communities were devastated. The big mistake the colonial government made was to think they could continue indefinitely as big white chief and not put into place mechanism to uplift and empower the people. Even though some whites were sympathetic towards local people they never seemed to realise the extent of discontent or their legitimate demands. Legislation that had moved thousands off their traditional land caused untold harm as did other laws of segregation. Instead of addressing injustice the government simply banned nationalist movements. The white administrative was arrogant whereas Africans generally remained submissive. Now it had all come to a head.

As barbarity was perpetrated two things happened. Firstly, local people succumbed to tactics of terror and submitted to the goals of those who intimidated them. Secondly, the administration, unable to apprehend the perpetrators, vented its frustrations upon the people. Instead of being their protector it was increasingly seen as their oppressor. When the administration brought in collective punishment the tide turned in favour of the nationalists. If individuals were found to harbour insurgents then the whole community was punished by having food confiscated and cattle impounded. We had moved from an administration generally marked by justice and good governance to a Police State with harsh legislation to cope with war and violence. Some soldiers reacted out of fear and anger. One soldier came back from the bush depressed and angry. His officer had ordered him to "eliminate" a wounded insurgent. "Don't shoot, don't shoot, I'm already dead" the wounded man cried to his captors but it did not help him and soon he was indeed dead. Another soldier returned from duty having seen a defenceless civilian shot dead as he rode his bicycle past an army patrol. Similar incidents occurred as soldiers grappled with an enemy they could not find and who were indistinguishable from innocent people. It had now become a war against the people and caught in the middle the people were terrorised by one side and abused by the other. Thousands fled to neighbouring countries and enrolled in the armed struggle, others were abducted for communist training.

The increase of violence caused attitudes to harden. Not everyone actively supported the struggle yet neither were they in favour of continued white control. Rhodesians were also caught, in a time-warp. They wanted to stop change for they perceived change would be disastrous for them. Rhodesian soldiers had success in winning battles but the bush fighters had the advantage of moving freely at night, visiting villages and mixing with the people and winning their minds. They held rallies or *"pungwes,"* the term given to all night re-education sessions or "brain washing." They sang freedom songs and won the people over with promises of land and that elusive thing called freedom. Anyone who did not submit was intimidated or even eliminated. Some horrendous atrocities took place. People had their lips cut off, their ears and noses, sometimes their hands and feet. Some people had sticks shoved up their genitals. They were herded into huts and burnt alive.

With no political progress towards a solution and long periods in army call up whites became despondent. Men were called up for long periods. More than a tenth of the entire white population was on active duty of some kind and almost everyone was in some way involved in war. Many were leaving for foreign shores, leaving with a few dollars in their pockets after the government clamped down on how much they were allowed to take out of the country. Those leaving were referred to as taking the "Chicken Route." In hindsight it might better have been called the "Wise Owl Flight." Perhaps the term "White's run" might have been appropriate. The government found their options reduced with less room to manoeuvre. They had hoped to bring moderate African leaders into government but most insisted on immediate capitulation by whites, the very thing whites feared most. Even moderate African politicians were not going to align themselves with a white government that was increasingly loosing control and could not win the minds of the people. When we were children we had got on well with our African friends despite our differences. We played together and ate together. As we grew older and because of the social structure relationships usually degenerated into one of employer and employee and although we were civil we were reserved. Politics and race became divisive issues. People tended to take sides, many whites wanted the status quo to remain while Africans supported one or other nationalist movement. Tension increased.

"Contact"

Some friends decided to go fishing at Sebakwe Dam and I joined them. The dam is set in the Midlands Province and is picturesque and peaceful. The weather was idyllic, fishing was good and we relaxed at the water front. The gentle lapping of water, the sound of bird songs and the beautiful scenery created an air of peace and security. In the afternoon I wandered off to explore the hills and spent the next couple of hours on my own in the bush. Suddenly all hell broke out around me with what sounded like gunfire, automatic weapons and mortars. I dived for cover among granite boulders but was unable to see the combatants. It seemed as though I had walked straight into a "contact" between security forces and a gang of insurgents. I didn't know where the enemy was or where the troops were and kept my head down cowering among the boulders. Then as suddenly as it started it ended and all became quiet. After a while I cautiously peeped out but could see nothing. A few more minutes and I crept through the bush to where I could see the water front. All had returned to normality, my companions were back to their fishing, the soldiers had gone and any "terrorists" had melted into the bush. This was how deceptive the conflict had become.

As the conflict intensified so did the level of intimidation that local people were subjected to. Under cover of darkness insurgents infiltrated rural communities and held "pungwes." Anyone who did not attend or refused to co-operate was labelled a "sell out" with dire consequences. To try to stop this government embarked on "protected villages." The reasons for establishing them were two fold, to protect the local civilians and to isolate the insurgents. The concept had originally been thought up by the British in Burma. During the day people were free to come and go but at night they had to sleep within the confines of the villages with security forces standing guard over them. This prevented insurgents getting food or intimidating the people. The overseas press dubbed them Concentration Camps. This was not true for although they were forced upon communities the intention was to protect the people. The guards were supposedly there not to stop people getting out but to stop terrorists getting in. But they looked like concentration camps. They were huge complexes housing several thousand people and surrounded by security fences, barbed wire, and lights. Lookout posts stood at the corners and usually a handful of poorly equipped armed guards protected the occupants from attack. These men were under the command of territorial soldiers and our friend Doug was one of those in command. Doug was from that breed of men who had carved a life out of adversity. He was British or so his family tree which went back about eleven generations indicated. His grandfather had come to Rhodesia with the Pioneers and his family had faced the challenge of developing the new land. Doug was born in Rhodesia and grew up on a farm in Matabeleland. When he tried to claim his British heritage he was refused despite the fact that his forefathers were British and served in the South African War and both World Wars.

Doug had a harrowing experience one night while guarding a village. A large contingent of insurgents had moved into the area and had openly flaunted their presence by taunting the guards with shouts of abuse. In the middle of the night they attacked the village despite it housing civilians. Mortars and rockets fell everywhere. Several guards and civilians were killed. Doug's small band of men had small-arms with about two magazines each to repel this substantial attack. They put on a brave front. Rockets exploded around them and mortars landed in their midst. One man had his leg blown off and expired as Doug tried to stem the blood. Another was hit with shrapnel. Rallying his "troops" Doug fought back but he had to constantly warn the guards to conserve their ammo. It was like the Wild West but with no cavalry to rescue them. Eventually the insurgents withdrew but had they known how poor the defences really were they could have overrun the village with relative ease. Meanwhile his wife back home had a premonition about the attack and spent a sleepless night in prayer. She was the granddaughter of a famous Boer General and her family had gone through all the horrors of that war and internment in its concentration camps. Now her family experienced the horrors of this war.

Ambushes and Convoys

The convoy system was an ingenious product of the Rhodesian war effort. As the war intensified vehicles came under attack and civilians ambushed. The army started convoys to provide protection for civilian traffic. Convoys took a predictable pattern. At the front of the column was a small truck with a Browning Machinegun mounted on the open back and manned by a soldier, often an elderly Police Reservist who had fought in the Second World War. There was another truck and machinegun in the middle and another at the rear of the convoy which sometimes stretched to a hundred cars. The convoy was followed by stragglers, usually the cars that could not keep up with the convoy. They came whining along the road going full bore with desperate looking passengers peering ahead to see if the convoy was still there, easy pickings for any ambush. We would sometimes hear the telltale "ping, plop" as bullets whizzed past. Nevertheless, having armed guards on convoys at least allowed someone to shoot back when ambushed. Unfortunately when attacked it was nigh impossible to maintain any semblance of discipline and the soldiers often shot wildly. Bullets rained everywhere and drivers would break rank and take off at high speed in mad panic the faster cars streaking ahead. A kind of free for all got under way. It brought back memories of our wild car races as youngsters. Roadsides became littered with burnt out vehicles, clinics, schools and stores. The "freedom fighters" seemed to take pleasure in destroying anything the colonial government had established even if it was for indigenous people. Abandoned, derelict farms were now a feature in every district. And in town we were serenaded at night to the sound of helicopters coming to discharge their cargo at hospitals, the broken bodies of wounded soldiers.

A year of Death

Dad died suddenly. Dad, who had never been sick in his life, who walked as though he was on a military parade, was gone. He loved Rhodesia and had given his whole life in service to the land of his adoption. When he retired from the Labour Department he went to Fort Victoria (Masvingo) where he enjoyed fishing for Bass at beautiful Lake Kyle (Lake Mutirikwi). But it was not long and the war came to the district with killings and violence and he became tired with it all. He came to live quietly near the shores of Lake McIlwaine (Lake Chivero) near the capital city but stress had taken its toll. One morning he woke and within minutes suffered a coronary and was gone. He seemed to have been a man from a distant era, another age I never knew. It was best he never saw the time that was coming.

In November 1977 and in response to increasing border incursions security forces hit military camps in Mozambique. The quiet little village of Villa Perry where we had feasted on Portuguese cuisine had been renamed Chimoio and in its vicinity were camps that housed up to 11,000 refugees and combatants. From there they sneaked across the border into Rhodesia where they caused havoc with farmers and forest and tea estate workers. It was claimed by the nationalists that these camps had no combatants but only refugees. Army leaders thought differently and justified their attack by claims that there was a huge build up of trained men and women in them. They attacked the camps with air force and 185 troops, the most they could rally for the occasion. The troops parachuted in as fighter planes strafed the camp. The devastating air attack had little effect as complex tunnels protected the inhabitants and the Para-troops were left to face a formidable foe. Many combatants were killed and no doubt many civilians with them and the rest fled into the bush. Within days of this attack the same soldiers were in another pitched battle at Tembue in Mozambique where it was claimed up to 6,000 fighters were based. Many of them were killed. It was terrible slaughter and roundly condemned by the world but these two campaigns gave Rhodesia much needed breathing space. However, terror now stalked the country and it refused to go back in its cage, the terror of death, whether by insurgents or government forces depending on which side one was.

Political Agreement - March 1978

After endless negotiations a political agreement was eventually reached between the Rhodesian government and internal moderate African leaders led by Bishop Muzorewa a Methodist clergyman. He was leader of the African National Congress and had a following within the country as opposed to the two external militant factions who were supported by the OAU (Organisation of African Unity). This agreement paved the way for majority rule or so it was claimed. Things looked hopeful. A "man of God" was going to be in charge and a transitional government would take over power. Unfortunately, the external leaders did not participate in the accord and declared they would continue the struggle through the barrel of the gun and bombs. The war dragged on.

Missionaries Killed

Missionaries were caught between army and nationalist factions. The Catholics had long been in the country and missions were established in most areas and had contributed much to the progress of the people. These missions were targeted by insurgents. Many missions gave assistance to "freedom fighters" for there was little else they could do if they did not want reprisals. Some clergy believed that the conflict was a necessary evil for majority rule to come to the country. Regrettably the help they gave the *"boys in the bush"* did not prevent some of them from suffering at the hands of the same *"boys"*. Eight Roman Catholic missionaries including four nuns were killed. Others also died. These crimes were invariably blamed by the perpetrators on "special forces." However, our friends among the elite units of the army adamantly denied this. I counselled soldiers who experienced dreadful things in the war and some renegade soldiers committed atrocities but the worst crimes I heard of were caused by elements within the communist insurgents. The average man in the street could never understand how the World Council of Churches could justify their support of the "liberation movements" and concluded that they were either deliberately supporting the communist agenda or else were deceived as to the true nature of some "freedom fighters." There were those nationalists who fought for genuine freedom but among them there were others who, trained in methods of terror, used those methods on defenceless civilians.

Missionaries Murdered

In June 1978 we were given a cruel blow when so called "freedom fighters" killed our dearest friends at Eagle School situated in the beautiful Vumba Mountains where I roamed as a kid.

When the Queen Mother came to Rhodesia in 1953 Eagle School was the colony's show piece. She and young Princess Margaret visited the school and all the colonial white children came out and waved little Union Jacks for the Royal Party. However, in the mid 1970s with the escalation of conflict the school sent all pupils to Springvale School near Marondera which was considered to be in safer regions. When they moved out our mission friends moved in and brought all their pupils from the remote north of Inyanga to what they believed were safer premises at Vumba. The missionaries had experienced increasing danger at Inyanga. On several occasions our friend Joan hid under her bed and even out in the bush when insurgents came to the mission and demanded food. They came to "re-educate" the Christians and irrespective of age pupils and teachers were subjected to hours of "brain washing" and political ideological indoctrination. As a result Joan had collapsed with hyper tension and was away on sick leave when tragedy came to Eagle Mission School.

A member of our church was on army duty when early one morning he was plunged into horror. He and fellow soldiers were rushed to the Vumba Mountains. The sight that awaited them was beyond anything they could prepare for. Lying amongst the soft green grass of the playing fields was the evidence of an orgy of carnage, the mutilated bodies of thirteen missionaries. Scattered about like discarded rag dolls were remnants of humanity, heaps of blood-stained clothes and twisted, grotesque bodies. Could these lifeless bits of flesh be our loved ones we wondered? Yes, they were, they had been brutally killed. Most of them had their hands tied behind their backs. All of them had been viciously beaten on the head. Some faces were bludgeoned beyond recognition and they had been bayoneted. One man had his eyes gouged out and was stabbed at least fifteen times. The women were naked from the waist down. The baby's head had been smashed into the ground and bayoneted through. It was the slaughter of the innocents.

So as to remain neutral in the liberation conflict the missionaries had declined an offer by government security forces to guard the mission. The terrorists took advantage of this trust and under cover of darkness sneaked in from nearby Zimunya Tribal Trust Land. They rounded up the missionaries shortly after their evening meal, tied their hands behind their backs, led them onto the soft green grass, raped the women and then bayoneted and bludgeoned to death all of them including the children and baby. During the ordeal the missionaries had attempted to comfort their children by singing hymns. Three men, six women and four children including a new born baby lay dead. One child lay where she had fallen with her little hand reaching out to her mother who lay nearby. Another person died later. A family Labrador had spent all night sitting by the bodies howling and eventually attracted attention to what had happened.

When the horror sank in we went into deep shock and grief. The Security

Forces followed the tracks of the killers which led them to nearby Zimunya Tribal Land where the gang had dispersed to hide. Hot on their trail soldiers found and killed a number of them and captured others before they crossed back into nearby Mozambique. The leader of the gang was later caught and confessed to the deed. It is said that one of the perpetrators who was not caught was so moved by the manner in which the Christians had died that he later became a church minister. Perhaps the way the missionaries had attempted to sing hymns before they were sexually violated and brutally killed had played on his mind. The local people say that on dark nights when the wind sighs through the trees the sound of hymns and wails of fear and pain can be heard drifting across the fields at Eagle School.

The missionaries had come as strangers from foreign shores to give their service to Africa. Joan was the only one to survive and she returned alone to England and we all wept.

Members of my congregation had been killed in the war but now the killing spilled into towns. Early one morning I had a phone call from a member of our congregation, she and her husband had been attacked. I jumped out of bed, pulled on some clothes and drove to their home not far away. The house looked sombre with an air of foreboding. I opened the front door and peered in but could not see or hear anything. I stepped into the hall and walked to the lounge. Lying sprawled on the floor in the middle of the room was a body with blood spattered around and a large pool on the floor. It was our friend we knew so well. He lay where he fell defending his family. He was pale and lifeless and I recoiled. Moans came from within the house. Fearing the worse and not knowing if the killers were still there I carefully stepped over the grisly evidence and made my way down the passage to the bedroom guided by deep sobs. Here I found his wife in a state of shock with her son also in a state of shock, holding onto each other and groaning. The police had not yet arrived. The perpetrators had made their get away. Once again I found myself burying a dear one, trying to give comfort, trying to be strong for those in dire bereavement. Sadly it was people from both sides who suffered not just whites. I knew because I went often into African churches.

Terror in the Sky

Viscount Hunyani was an Air Rhodesia civilian passenger aircraft on a regular flight from Kariba to Salisbury. In September 1978 it was brought down by an air-to-ground missile fired by combatants. My wife and I had flown on it just a few weeks earlier when we had gone for a break to Kariba Lake. It had been a pleasure for us to fly safe above the troubled war zone.

On that dreadful day everything went well as the aircraft lifted out of the Mopani forest that crowded in on the tiny airfield on the shores of the lake and sedately climbed into the clear sky of the Zambezi valley. The passengers settled down to a flight that would take only an hour and avoided the dangers of long convoys on a six hour road journey back to Salisbury. Just as they were getting comfortable and the hostesses were serving chilled drinks a thud impacted the wing. Hunyani was hit. An explosion ripped apart an engine and the aircraft lurched in a sideways dive. Drinks spilled everywhere and passengers screamed. Falling fast the pilot and co-pilot gazed downwards seeking a level place to crash-land. The aircraft ploughed across a field and crashed headlong into a deep furrow. The pilot and co-pilot were amongst thirty eight people killed. Eighteen people survived, several badly injured and all in a state of severe shock. Those who were able administered first aid and got the seriously injured into some shade away from the harsh sun. Five of the survivors who could walk set out to look for help leaving the others behind at the wreckage. Shortly afterwards insurgents arrived and killed all those who had miraculously survived the awful crash, shooting and bayoneting them to death. Three survivors ran in terror of their lives and those who had set out for help heard gunfire from the direction of the wreck and hid. They were later found by security forces hiding in the bush, dehydrated and in severe shock. Forty eight civilians perished, fifteen massacred. Amongst those killed was Cheryl, the daughter of our dearest friends who though not badly injured had stayed to care for the others. Her young teenage brother had been killed a few months earlier when the family came home at night to their small farm on the outskirts of Salisbury. The killers had laid in wait at their security gate and as the youngster opened it a volley of bullets cut him down before the eyes of his parents. Now Cheryl and those with her, having survived a most terrify crash were dead too, brutally killed for no reason. I knew her family; they were loving people who would harm no one. We wept some more and could not stop.

There was no condemnation from the world. At the memorial service for the victims the Dean of Salisbury Anglican Cathedral preached a sermon entitled *"The Deafening Silence"* in which he asked the simple question why there had been no response from the world community to condemn this attack on a civilian airline and survivors. Not a word from the UN, from Britain, from USA, from the Pope, not a word of regret from the perpetrators. What message did this send?

The question some whites asked themselves was, "What has happened to generate so much hatred towards us?" It seemed we had been living in the dark ages and did not realise how strong the feeling against the white government had become. We sank into shock. The next time we flew to Kariba we noticed how the aircraft kept as high as possible until directly above the airfield and then made a rapid spiralling descent over the lake to land quickly. This was to avoid SAM missiles that might be fired at us. It was an eerie feeling as we spiralled down aware that any moment we could be hit out of the sky. The same tactic was used when we took off. The plane climbed rapidly in a cork screw flight and once it attained a safe altitude set out for Salisbury where once again the same method of descent was used at the international airport. Unfortunately it would not prevent a second civilian airliner from being shot down.

Camps Bombed

A new intensity came into the conflict. The government reacted to this horror in a predictable manner, cast off restraint and became even more militant. It was largely in reprisal to the downing of the Viscount and the failure of nations to speak out that Rhodesia attacked camps this time in Zambia from where the perpetrators had come. An insurgent base situated on a farm ten miles outside of Lusaka was the first target. The Air Force destroyed the complex. When I visited the farm some years later people who had been there at the time described the full fury of what happened and I realised the terrible outcome of war. The raids claimed the lives of hundreds of combatants and sadly, many innocent people were killed. It was claimed by the nationalists that the farm was a refugee camp and contained women and youths. That it contained women and children was true but the army considered them to be recruits for war and knew from experience that many combatants were both women and children. Africa is notorious for its child soldiers and whole sections of the liberation army were comprised entirely of women. No doubt many in the camps were refugees but the tragic carnage was the result of Viscount Hunyani and should never have happened.

It did not stop another awful violation of civilian aircraft. In February 1979 the disaster was repeated. This time there were no survivors. Despite the spiralling descent and corkscrew ascent a second Viscount also flying from Kariba was brought down by an air to ground missile. Viscount Umniati was hit straight out of the sky and plummeted to earth. Fifty eight crew and passengers perished. Again there was no world reaction - *just silence.* Would it ever end we wondered? The words of that great hymn were on our hearts and minds, "Abide with me, fast falls the even tide," and once again the nation plunged into shock and sorrow. I will never forget that hymn. To those who have not walked the pits of grief and despair it may mean nothing, to us it expressed our wounded hearts. Almost everyone had lost friends or family. Would the sense of looking over one's shoulder for the sudden ambush on lonely roads, the fear of dark shadows hiding the enemy, the funerals and the sadness ever end? If ever there was a time we felt abandoned it was then. Britain was great because in her darkest hour the colonies rallied to her side. Our fathers and forefathers had stood with her. Now we felt like disowned foster children. It had all gone terribly wrong.

The shooting down of the Viscounts stunned the white community and left everyone in depression and total despair. No one in their right mind, they thought, could excuse the shooting down of civilian planes. When an airliner was later brought down over Lockerbie in Scotland the entire civilised world came out in condemnation. Yet Rhodesia Airways was not afforded such simple decency. This silence puzzled the whites who began to realise just how isolated and expendable the conflict had made them. There was nothing more to be said, just shock, resignation, despair and silence. I think this was a turning point in the war. Retribution was going to be harsh. During the latter years of the war security forces made extensive attacks. With air force and army they lashed out and destroyed camps in Mozambique and Zambia. The army unleashed its military punch on as many of the "enemy" they could find. In war there are no winners, just losers. Shortly after the destruction of the airliners a popular singer brought out a song *"You are no hero when you shoot an airliner from the sky."* It expressed the abandonment and repulsion felt by many. Years later after the shocking events of September 2001 in New York the song was released in USA. It was a fitting tribute for those who lived through the shock and sadness of that awful time. The only memorial for the Viscount victims was a small plaque that hangs in the cloisters of the Anglican Cathedral in Harare with their names engraved on it, if it has not been removed.

Politics in the Church

The church in Rhodesia found itself caught between warring factions. There was disparity among clerics with various stances and the many political leaders who were designated as "Reverends" confused the matter even more. There seemed to be some Reverends who might have been "Terrorists". The church was divided. The World Council of Churches gave support to "freedom fighters" but many local churches either remained neutral or gave allegiance to Rhodesia. We ended up with a situation where Christians were fervently praying against each other, either for the downfall of Rhodesia or for its victory. It was confusing to say the least. The World Council of Churches gave large sums of money to "Liberation Movements". This aid was supposed to have been used only for humanitarian needs. Everyone lived in terror, either in terror of the terrorists or in terror of the security forces. Which ever way one looked at it the country had sunk into a *state of terror* no matter which side one supported.

In our church we had regular prayers for husbands, brothers, sons and uncles in combat, for their protection. We also prayed for "terrorists" and we prayed for politicians that they would come to their senses. We had come to believe we were the last outpost of true Christianity. In all the confusion some extraordinary spiritual experiences were reported. Some people claimed to have seen angels. Rhodesians boasted that their Armed Forces were the finest fighting forces in the world modelled after the British forces. They certainly faced overwhelming odds. I acknowledge without reservation their bravery. Some soldiers fell in combat but some claimed miraculous interventions.

"The End is Nigh"

Towards the end of the war I was stationed in Salisbury the capital city. At that time Salisbury was a picturesque and neat colonial city with broad avenues lined with Jacaranda and Flamboyant trees. In September the Jacarandas flowered with cascades of purple and mauve flowers which covered the pavements in a carpet of fallen blossoms. The Jacaranda Festival was held and culminated in the crowning of the "Jacaranda Queen." Shortly after the Jacarandas the Flamboyant trees came out in flower spewing pavements with a red carpet of petals. It all looked richly luxuriant. At this stage of the war the communal lands in the vicinity of the city were occupied by nationalist insurgents. Just north of the city were huge granite hills that contained a labyrinth of caves and ravines in which fighters hid and from where they made excursions into the city at night. The rattling sound of small arms fire could be heard. The war was no longer a bush war but had come to town and bombs were going off. A large store was bombed and people killed and injured. Then the central fuel depot was blown up and burnt fiercely with black clouds billowing over the city. Fire fighters could not put it out and South African experts flew in to help. It took a week to subdue the flames.

Helicopters evacuated wounded and dying men from battle and brought them to the general hospital. They flew day and night especially when big contacts took place. There were endless reports of casualties and funerals - we could take no more. Another missionary was killed. Some whites began to talk about making a "last stand" just as Alan Wilson had done many years before. They felt they were backed in a corner and had nothing to lose. A scorched earth mentality crept in. People felt the end was nigh.

I was on chaplain duty, it was an unenviable task. Chaplains had to inform people of the death of husbands, fathers, sons, wives, daughters and sisters. The sight of a church minister at the door was foreboding, people knew what it meant. I also visited hospitals. Andrew Fleming Hospital in Salisbury was probably the best equipped hospital in Central Africa and it had lots of war casualties. As soon as injured soldiers recovered enough to travel they were taken to Tsanga Lodge high in the picturesque Inyanga Mountains. This was a rehabilitation centre where they had time to heal. We knew the directors and nurses who gave themselves unstintingly for their recovery.

Was he a Saint?

John Bradbury, who we knew, was an extraordinary man who lived at a leper colony at Mtoko. He was a Catholic lay priest who gave up everything to care for lepers. He had been a highly decorated British regular soldier and although a bit eccentric was well regarded by the people with whom he lived. One day he was murdered and his body left lying in a pool of blood on a road. Everyone in the community knew that it was the work of so-called "freedom fighters." There was no rhyme or reason for his death except that he was British. It was a shock to everyone for many considered him to be a living saint. His funeral was held in the Catholic Cathedral in Salisbury and a large crowd attended. Then a strange phenomenon occurred. In the middle of the service attended by many hundreds of people attention was drawn to the fact that fresh blood dripped out of the casket and formed a pool on the floor. The sight of the blood disturbed people and a tissue was put over it. After the service the casket was opened but no cause could be found for what had happened. However, his Last Will and Testament stipulated that his body should be buried in the habit of his Catholic order and this was discovered not to have been carried out. The habit was placed on his body and the casket sealed. People were stunned by the event and took it as a sign from above.

Referendum - A Bishop Takes Over

In January of 1979 a referendum was held among the white electorate for approval of an agreement between the government and the internal African leadership. Britain had said it would back an internal agreement if it was approved by both Africans and whites. Despite the shooting down of the Viscounts and hardening attitudes the whites approved the new constitution that would effectively see the end of white rule. I think many felt the carnage had gone too far on both sides. Then in April African voters also went to the ballot box. The poll had an overwhelming 64% of the national vote and a substantial majority of these voted for Bishop Muzorewa who represented the internal African National Council. Back in 1972 the ANC rejected a constitutional offer supported by Britain that would have brought about a phased transition to majority rule. One can but wonder how things would have turned out if they had accepted it. Now, seven years later after terrible bloodshed he was voted premier.

A high ranking army officer toured the troops to boost their morale and to inform them what this new government was doing. In a hotel in the small town of Rusape he spoke to local farmers and combat soldiers about the "Internal Agreement" and its implications. He assured farmers that all was going according to plan and there was no need to panic. When it came to question time a young soldier asked the telling question, "Sir, what are we still fighting for?" The chief was frank; they could no longer win the war but were fighting now for the best possible political agreement. What most of those present did not know was that even as he spoke furniture from his nearby farm was being loaded onto removal vans and heading to South Africa. The soldier had been one of those guarding the farm and seen them loading.

Last day of white rule

Rhodesia was dying. On the last day of May 1979 it ceased to exist. In its place was born a hybrid called "Zimbabwe-Rhodesia." It was not to last long for the British government decided not to support it after all. Due to pressure from the OAU they went back on their undertaking to recognise an internal agreement and insisted that the external leaders had to be included in any new government. Bishop Muzorewa had become our new Prime Minister but he was considered by many people to be just a stooge of the white regime. Although he was well versed in Bible verses the Bishop was not versed in ways of intrigue, plotting and double talk and was no match for the seasoned external Nationalist leaders. He was to be out-manoeuvred on every hand and would soon fall from favour. In this final year the war raged on. Unity amongst whites fell apart. The army chiefs squabbled amongst themselves. Accusations were flung about in public. People were accused of being sell-outs and spies. Some people took pay outs and left. Top army officials were accused of using men and equipment for poaching elephant and rhino. Other officials both in army and civil service were accused of being spies. There is no doubt that Rhodesian security had been badly breached. It was discovered that Army HQ was bugged. Confidential information was leaked to forward camps of combatants in the bush. Within a short while they knew what the security forces were planning. Rhodesia was now an embattled country.

In June I conducted the funeral of Steve the son of dear friends. He was killed in action at nineteen years of age. He was a soldier of the crack Rhodesian SAS said to be on a par with the British SAS. Though I had done many funerals this one was particularly difficult. I had known Steve since he was a young child in my church class. He was talented and happy and excelled at sport. Sadly Steve had a premonition of his own death and wrote a few words in haste before he left on his last mission. Within a short time the war would be over and Steve a loving memory. I conducted his funeral with a heavy heart and wept bitterly. Was his supreme sacrifice in vain? Many Rhodesians believed they had been fighting against communism but it seemed in the end to be a battle for survival.

Rhodesians never lost the bush war but they never won it either. They killed "terrorists" and were themselves killed but it all became futile. Behind the statistics the real battle raged in the hearts and minds of the people and the Rhodesians never had a hope of winning. They had forfeited that chance years before when they lost the opportunity at the time of the break up of the Federation of Rhodesia and Nyasaland. Back in the early sixties Sir Edgar Whitehead had offered a deal to Joshua Nkomo, then leader of African nationalism, that would see majority rule within ten years but Nkomo refused and Whitehead was ousted. Any hope of real peace was lost. Britain in turn had not insisted that majority rule should be a step by step process but had sent out word that it would be immediate. Somehow everyone lost their way. Opportunities to improve the lot of Africans, to hear their grievances and act upon them were missed. Nationalist leaders refused to accept delay and insisted on immediate majority rule without safeguards. And the British government gave the wrong signals; to African Nationalists that they could have instant Independence, to whites that they were expendable.

At about this time the army was awarding the last of their medals to their soldiers. Having been in the army for sixteen years I was eligible for a long service medal but my heart was sick and I did not want it. To be honest I only served because it was compulsory just as many others had to. I knew how dad must have felt years before. He had refused to wear his medals and they sat in a drawer as a silent reminder of a forgotten era. The British government had refused attendance of Rhodesian WW11 ex-service men at the Armistice Parade in London. My father and both grandfathers fought for Britain but what does a medal really mean when no one remembers? Africans made up the majority of regular servicemen in the Rhodesian Army and they could not wear their medals either. In fact more African soldiers were killed than white.

Rhodesia once again a British Colony

Having withheld recognition from the Bishop's government Britain called a conference at Lancaster House in London and invited the external leaders to attend. Britain became broker to an agreement in which the Bishop had to step down and new elections under British supervision would be conducted. All the "freedom fighters" were to come in from the bush to special camps for the duration of the elections. On the 12th of December 1979 Lord Soames as Governor arrived in Salisbury to the tune of "God Save Our Gracious Queen" something not heard in Rhodesia since it declared a Republic. English Bobbies flew out from UK to take up posts in the African bush. I never thought I would live to see the day that Bobby helmets gleamed in the African heat. A cease fire was signed on the 21st of December, exactly seven years to the day that the war began in earnest with the attack on Altena Farm.

General elections

By this time the electorate had finally come to realise that the only way to stop the war was to vote the perpetrators of violence into power - in order to stop the violence; a warped way of thinking but nevertheless justified when considering the signals that the International community were sending. Both Britain and America had refused to accept the overwhelming expression of the people's will when they elected Bishop Muzorewa. The flaw had been the lack of participation in that election by external factions who had fought for liberation. The realisation dawned upon us that the white government and moderate internal nationalists were all expendable in the eyes of the world. Nothing would satisfy the world other than the instalment of the external leaders.

The next round of elections was monitored by observers who came from Commonwealth countries. British Bobbies, looking incongruous in their helmets, stood sweating in the African sun. They "guarded" polling booths but combatants systematically worked areas and threatened people. Intimidation now shifted from rural areas into townships and urban people were subjected to the same methods used to subjugate the rest of the country. Old and young alike streamed to the polling stations many of them with only one aim, to vote Robert Mugabe into power so as to stop the violence. It never occurred to them that it might continue and even worsen. Rhodesian officials warned British authorities that wide spread intimidation was rampant but they chose to ignore it. In many areas neither Nkomo's nor Muzorewa's supporters were able to campaign. A United States representative was sent to Rhodesia to witness the election. He claimed that areas under control of Mugabe's party and where his insurgents were operating did not have free or fair elections and he wondered why people were so enthusiastic that utopia was around the corner. He noted that if Mugabe was willing to use ruthless methods to win the election and achieve power why should he be less ruthless in consolidating his position and ensuring its permanence? This observation was ignored and the world now accepted the poll that seemed driven by fear. In a news conference Joshua Nkomo commented about Mugabe's tactics and said that *"the word intimidation is mild. People are being terrorised – it is terror."* If a white person had said this it could have been claimed as an exaggeration but for Nkomo the Father of Nationalism in Zimbabwe to say it one must know how bad it really was.

What signals did the rejection by the international community of the Bishop's overwhelming majority send the people of Zimbabwe? The message seemed clear, only the election of an external leader was acceptable. In a blatant attempt to blackmail Britain Nigeria announced the imminent nationalisation of all assets of British Petroleum thereby depriving Britain of 280,000 barrels of oil a day. At the Commonwealth Conference in Lusaka Britain found itself facing the strange prospect of being expelled from its own Commonwealth. It was all too much. The British Prime Minister went back on her undertaking that elections would be recognised only if they were free of intimidation. The 'Iron Lady' simply buckled like putty and her man in charge, Foreign Secretary Lord Carrington, gave in to the pressure.

Mugabe's ZanuPF party indeed got into power with a large majority. He had become very popular but many people voted just to "stop the war" for they were too terrified to vote any other way.

March 1980 - election results announced

The strange thing was that results of the election were announced before all the ballot boxes had been counted. These boxes were subsequently destroyed by officials without being counted. As the BBC announced results on world news the uncounted ballots were still burning. We knew this as numerous people witnessed it. Scotty was sitting with boxes at Kariba. Neville was sitting with boxes at Matobo. These votes may have given the opposition more seats in parliament. Mugabe's party, however, had an overwhelming victory.

The announcement of ZanuPF triumph caused a shock wave to hit almost every white person and many moderate African people in the country. We could not believe what had happened. Right to the very last we had been assured by our leaders that the moderate Bishop would win the day. I still wonder how they could have been so out of touch with reality. The tension now was tangible. Trucks of chanting bush fighters sped through the cities. Grim faced government troops manned the streets. For a while it looked like a big "punch up" was coming. There was talk of an impending coup by army chiefs who it was rumoured had a plan to kill all the "boys from the bush" and if need be to send the whole country up in smoke in a scorched earth policy. Many Rhodesians felt betrayed, abandoned, cornered and defeated. There was fear and bitterness. The situation was as volatile as any situation could get, anything could happen. We felt like trapped animals. Rhodesians feared all they had worked for would be destroyed before their eyes. It was a time of madness. We held our breath. The nation stood on the brink of anarchy poised for a blood letting. Thousands of undisciplined bush soldiers came in from the bush and let off rifle fire, beat up people, jeered at whites and killed "sell-outs." The Army took up strategic positions. Visions of a repeat of the Congo and Mozambique massacres were in our minds. We had seen too many things in Africa to have any illusions. Would we get out alive was the question on our minds.

A huge crowd of many hundred thousand gathered to meet the new leader when he flew in to a hero's welcome at Salisbury airport. This was his day of triumph and he was the Messiah. We watched appalled at the frenzy of nationalism all around us. If there was any question before we now knew without any doubt that the old order had died and in its place was a wild uncontrolled hysteria. The "freedom fighters" had won. We wondered who were deluded, them or us. The people were incited to extreme euphoria. Mugabe was their Saviour and he had come to town. Joshua Nkomo, who some considered the real "Father of Nationalism", hardly got a look in. The defeat of the Bishop's government isolated moderate middle class, qualified Africans, the kind of people best suited to rise into positions of leadership. Some left the country unwilling to remain. Most quickly came on side.

The miracle many had prayed for, that Mugabe and his companions should be defeated, never materialised. However, perhaps there was a miracle of another kind for the imminent massacre of thousands of people was averted. As already mentioned, plans were afoot to kill as many insurgents as possible. The Army had surrounded important locations and was poised to strike if things got out of hand. The order never came. The "freedom fighters" too were waiting to lash out. They threatened that if they did not "win" the election they would "go back to the bush" with brutal consequences on defenceless people. Instead of violence came restraint. The government troops did not break discipline and remained controlled in the face of provocation. People watched their government fall and stood quietly by and even assisted those who had been enemies. Five days after Mugabe's win the Rhodesian Light Infantry took advantage of the freedom of the city of Salisbury conferred on them some years before and made an impromptu march through the streets. They were the scrawniest soldiers one could ever hope to see, the leanest, meanest bunch one could imagine. They had conducted a ruthless, continuous war for many years and now marched undefeated with live bullets in their guns to the sound of bagpipes and the tune "When the Saints go Marching in". They were hardly saints but they had fought well against a relentless foe. They, and black and white soldiers from other units, were brave soldiers.

A period of adjustment followed, a breather that allowed people to go marching out, or should I say scramble out, mostly whites who could not remain. The Rhodesian Diaspora began long before but this was a big wave of emigration. At one time there were 280,000 whites in Rhodesia, a little community of Britain in its far flung Empire. This number would dwindle to a mere few thousand.

Transition

When it became obvious that the past administration had been "voted" out I decided there was one thing I would do with relish. Most whites had to serve in the army and whether they had done so with consent or not did not really matter as irrespective of political affiliations there came a time when they were obliged to defend themselves and their families. I had a long history with the army having been called up in 1964. I started as a rifleman but soon changed to signals, then to medic and eventually to part time chaplain. This meant I was on call at any time. We had become a war weary people. We had seen too many dead and mutilated bodies. We had buried too many friends and loved ones. We were all desperate for the fighting to end. I was supposed to hand in my uniform but it was with satisfaction and a sense of release that I took my army kit into the back yard, poured petrol over it and set it on fire. I was glad to be done with it. All around the country people were getting rid of evidence, shredding papers, dumping ammo. It was the end of an era and most people were happy it was all over, or so we thought. I had been proud to be Rhodesian, now I faced an uncertain future.

At Independence all military firearms and ammo were required to be handed in. However, many servicemen had accumulated all kinds of stuff so lots of weapons and ammo were dumped in lakes, rivers, wells and mine shafts. Sometimes these were found much later when lake levels sank or rivers ran dry or when a bush fire ignited the ammo. A large amount of ammo, grenades and bombs were thrown down a mine shaft on a farm of a friend and lay forgotten. Over the years creepers grew down the shaft and a bush fire crept down and detonated the cache sounding as if the war had broken out all over again. For years afterwards we found unexploded rockets, mortars and other dangerous explosives lying in the bush. A few years after the war when walking in the hills of Chirundu I looked down aghast to see I was about to step on a rocket. I gingerly lifted my foot away and made a hasty departure. Animals also stumbled onto them and were injured or killed including elephants which became enraged with pain. Landmines killed and maimed unsuspecting people. Some soldiers simply hid their weapons in case they needed them again and "the boys from the bush" did the same. Large caches were established for future use.

"Rhodesiana extinctus"

Many years ago in Northern Rhodesia a Neanderthal skull was found buried deep in a mine. It was called "Rhodesia Man." Its scientific name was "homo rhodesiensis". Perfectly preserved it was extinct. The nation it was named after was now also extinct. Rhodesia and its outdated attitudes was something of the past. But we had been led to believe that we were standing against the tide of communism that was taking over the whole world, we were not just fighting a local conflict but the full brunt of international communism. We were told we were doing our part to keep the world free. That it had degenerated into a tragic mess had not deterred many from "doing their duty". During the war a lonely piper kept vigil on a hill near Penhalonga and played the bagpipes every evening. The music drifted across the hills as testimony to the bravery of thousands of besieged and misled Rhodesians. Now it was over, thank God.

With the end of the war we had time to reflect. We had been deluded. It had been a crazy notion to resist the inevitable march of nationalism no matter what reasons were given. Was it all in vain, the lives lost, the innocent who perished, the mistakes, the triumphs? Now we all needed grace and healing, forgiveness and reconciliation. The words of the barrack songs we sang as young soldiers rang in my heart with mocking tones of self delusion; how we would fight to keep our land free until the "Zambezi ran dry" and how Rhodesians never died. It all seemed so pointless. We had followed our Pied Pipers on a sad march of disaster and it seemed no one had offered an alternative. My mind went back to uniforms and polished boots and the "Great Queen who lived across the sea" whose honour we upheld or so we thought.

The dead of the war including insurgents, security forces and civilians were many thousands. Between 1975 and 1979 some estimate that dead combatants numbered 30,000. The wounded were said to be about 30,000. Refugees and displaced people, internal and external numbered many thousands, a high cost for a small country. Everyone had lost someone. The white regime had been defeated but at awful cost to Africans. What tragedy!

Many white Rhodesians could not stay and went elsewhere. Many mourned the "great Rhodesian dream" they left behind and tried to keep it alive where they went. Most of them left with nothing but a suitcase and a thousand Zimbabwe dollars. That many succeeded in rebuilding their lives was a testimony to their extraordinary tenacity and courage. Ex-Rhodesians generally had a reputation as hard workers. But there were those who did not make it for it had become a nightmare; some had nervous break downs, some just gave up and died. None of them would ever be the same again and there were many who could not leave for one reason or another. Despite rumours that circulated about compensation none was offered to white Rhodesians. No resettlement scheme was planned. For most it was a free for all. Some, although of British stock, were not eligible for British Citizenship. Others were too old or did not have enough qualifications or finances to be accepted in new lands. They were the losers, they were not really wanted in Zimbabwe but had to stay anyway. Some stayed for love of their land. For those who remained it would be a time of massive change. Meanwhile the new government inherited a land that despite the past was free of debt and still had a sound economy and infra-structure. There was still some honey in the pot.

The British government was quite relieved to be rid of the Rhodesian problem. The Union Jack was folded up, the British Empire was closed down and Lord Soames and his Bobbies went home and left us to our fate. Rhodesia had never been very important on the world scene. Its economy was insignificant and it had no oil. Rhodesia was of no consequence. All the ills Zimbabwe now faced were blamed on the previous white regime with no consideration for the historical context or the powerful underlying forces that moulded attitudes and values that pushed the colony down its chosen path. Why had British settlers in Africa chosen such a tragic route? In the end Britain walked away and gave a hundred years of endeavour to those who had fought the whites but also conducted a sometimes brutal campaign on their own people. The Prince of Wales came and the Union Jack which had only flown for a few brief months was pulled down and handed to him to take home, all very proper. It was said "the sun never sets upon the British Empire" but now the sun did indeed set on the last major colony of that very Empire.

Lord Soames commented on the election that brought Mugabe to power by saying that one should remember it was Africa and not little Puddleton-in-the-Marsh and people behaved differently, thought nothing of sticking tent poles up one another's what not and doing filthy, beastly things to one another. It did happen, he was afraid, and it was a very wild thing, an election. [4] And that about sums it up. What needs to be added is the reason why he let the violence go on without attempting to stop it; he believed that Robert Mugabe was going to win anyway. He never tried to stop the violence because he knew it was mostly perpetrated by Mugabe's followers. Did that justify it?

A short time after Margaret Thatcher came to office in Britain she had said that Mugabe's Zanu Patriotic Front were *"Terrorists.* Maybe it was a hasty comment for soon the British government handed us over to that kind of person, through that kind of election, and it was not over yet, this was just the beginning. Was this democracy, we wondered? We felt abandoned all over again.

We were now in the hands of people we had always been told were terrorists. Who was Robert Mugabe? A devout Catholic he had trained as a school teacher but was detained by the Rhodesians for nationalist activities. Something very sad happened during his 11 year detention. His wife and young son were in exile when his son died. Mugabe pleaded with the authorities to be allowed to attend the funeral but was refused. This bereavement profoundly influenced him and strengthened his resolve to fight the white regime. When eventually released he too went into exile. His leadership qualities made him leader of the Zimbabwe African Nationalist Union and now he would soon be our premier.

Book 5

Remember this is Africa – Upside Down Years

African Proverb: "Beware the tree planted upside down."
The Baobab is a grotesque tree for it looks as though it has been planted with its
roots in the sky. There are many myths about it; one is that who ever plucks the
flower will inherit great trouble.

Shortly after election results were announced the Prime Minister designate Robert Mugabe made a speech on National TV. He came over very well, quite civilised and conciliatory. We were surprised. It seemed he had transformed from a revolutionary to a placid, sane statesman. We had thought he was a communist terrorist but it seemed from his words the opposite was true. It seemed as though, like a chameleon, he had suddenly changed his colours. Instead of revolution he now talked reconciliation. It was the same man with a different face. There had been so much confusion and alarm during the war years that his words sounded convincing. He asked whites especially farmers to stay and make Zimbabwe their home and said they had nothing to fear. He even appointed white Ministers of Parliament. Many whites about to leave the country changed their minds and stayed. Maybe at the time he genuinely believed what he said but events conspired against it. In hindsight it seems he simply shelved the revolution for a more appropriate time.

The Baobab is extraordinary. It is a huge tree with massive girth, wrinkled bark and grotesque twisted branches. In some ways it is quite grand. There are many superstitions about it. One is that it is planted upside down. It seemed to symbolise our nation turned upside down. Everything was about to be reversed. Our world became topsy-turvy. The standards that had been our way of life were overturned and the new principles were different. For example the history of the nation was rewritten. Night after night on national TV the "true story" was presented. We had been taught in our official school syllabus that Rhodes and other great Rhodesians were men of high principle. Now we learnt the other view, that Rhodes was a villain and British settlers had stolen the land from the people who really owned it. One official actually described how the settlers came in *Land Rovers* and drove the people off the land which I felt was stretching the truth a bit far. Maybe there was some connection between Land Rovers and land that I had missed. TV documentaries were shown about the war crimes committed by Rhodesians. Liberation fighters were now called "Comrades". Colonial statues including those of Rhodes were removed and street names were changed to honour the new heroes. Salisbury became Harare and other towns had name changes. We certainly got another side to the story we had never heard before. Yet little pockets of the past survived. The Harare Club still had a fine portrait of Rhodes gazing down on its members, a little oasis of colonialism, and the Royal Harare Sports Club still had a beautiful golf course despite a name change.

Now that Zimbabwe was "free" a witch hunt began. Settling old scores became a regular event. Many in the regular Rhodesian Forces hastened to pull out and head for South Africa. Some Africans who had helped the Rhodesian cause were not so fortunate. Some were hunted down. It was pay out time for the winning party cadres and it was retribution time on "sell outs." When Rhodesia became Zimbabwe it put on a new face, or was it a façade? With the change in name and government the country was different yet the Emergency Powers under which Rhodesia had ruled during the war years were retained and used by the new regime to enforce its power. For twenty years and more we were to live under this quasi-Marxist regime. The new regime promised wealth, health and happiness with free health and education for all. The rights of workers were safe guarded. Racism was dismantled. In its place came "affirmative action" a kind of reversed racism where whites were marginalised. In the first years there were considerable achievements and we were all grateful but people became concerned as they realised not all was well. At first the changes looked good and the brutal nature of the regime not disclosed but as the years went by it was impossible to keep them hidden especially when the rule of the "sacred party" was challenged. There is a myth about the Baobab tree. If one has the misfortune to pick or even touch its flowers disaster will result. We were to learn this was no myth. The regime which many felt had been planted upside down through massive irregularities would in time bear terrible fruit.

A New Language - Zimbabwe English

The TV and Radio news bulletins became very interesting in ways other than their propaganda content. Zimbabwe-English became a language of its own. The pronunciation was sometimes quite peculiar. One day the announcer came on air to say that the "Minister of Terrorism" was implementing a programme to get more "terrorists." Our hearts sank for we had thought the war was over. It turned out to mean "Minister of Tourism" getting more tourists. We sighed with relief. Other words were confusing; a "chef" was not a cook or a chief but a chief crook, "no" could very often mean "yes", and "just now" could be from now till the end of the year. This is not to underestimate the intelligence of Zimbabweans many of whom spoke at least two or three languages and could read and write, due mainly to education facilities in Rhodesia.

The new government controlled TV and radio which became propaganda tools for their exclusive use. Every news bulletin was about the President. He became the focus of attention for the whole country. He was liberator and saviour and the main star of the Zimbabwe soap opera. The new National Anthem, "Ishe komberera Africa" (God bless Africa) had a catchy tune and moving words.

Shortly after Independence the denomination I currently worked with called a general meeting for white clergy and about fifty ministers and missionaries attended and each was given an opportunity to share what they were going to do now that the country had achieved independence. At this time a major exodus of whites took place which made things increasingly difficult as congregations shrank. Although we were involved with ministry to both Africans and whites our funds came mostly from white congregations. While the World Council of Churches poured vast amounts of money into "liberation movements" local Christians sacrificed financially to help indigenous churches. For many years churches worked together and we felt we had good harmony. As the country sank further into conflict things changed and the churches were infiltrated by leaders with a political agenda. In services I opened my eyes during prayer to see leaders giving black power salutes and then using the forum to preach politics. It opened my eyes to the tensions that divided the church.

After Independence I spent time contemplating the future and felt the country was heading for disaster. I saw in my mind's eye down-town Harare in violent turmoil as men in military uniforms fought street battles. I felt the country would sink into a state of anarchy that would reach to the heart of the nation. I shared this with church leaders and it was played down as fertile imaginations of an over active mind. So many people so badly wanted stability that anything less was not considered. When it came my turn to speak I said; "I believe the future will be one of more trouble and bloodshed." I was young enough to start in another country and said I was leaving.

After the meeting several colleagues gathered around and began to dispute my decision saying that "It was my duty to stay and tend the Lord's sheep, after all I was their shepherd". I advised them that I would reconsider. I recalled that the new leader had urged us to stay and many people needed help. Now my own colleagues said I should stay. I decided I would become a Zimbabwean. It was a decision of my heart; I loved the land and people. However, those who advised me soon changed their minds and left. Maybe they were the wise ones after all but in some ways I am grateful I stayed.

The Rains Came

After the first hectic year of tension and transition a friend invited me to join him in the bush to get away from everything. He was a ranger with National Parks and was posted at Umfurudzi Game Reserve north of Harare, a grand, majestic wilderness. The park had a diverse ecology of rugged granite hills, woodland and forest. During the war poachers were unable to operate and wild animals multiplied in National Parks. With the end of hostilities poachers moved in and soon another war was in full progress, the "Rhino and Elephant War" that would result in the demise of the Black Rhino and the death of thousands of elephants.

We left for Umfurudzi Game Reserve in the middle of the wet season when it was raining hard. Torrents of water poured from the sky and the rough track into the Park was waterlogged. The Land Rover bravely battled on through sodden mud until it finally bogged down and refused to move another inch. As darkness settled over the drenched bush blanketed by heavy clouds we had no option but to walk to camp. We sloshed on down the squelching track carrying our belongings, wet to the bone. A lion bemoaned the weather by letting off volumes of reverberating roars as it also walked along the track, coming towards us. The low cloud seemed to amplify each roar. Would we meet in the night? What a glorious feeling to have Africa all around us. Everything was thoroughly drenched including us and it was as if we had been baptised into Africa and become part of the hills, trees, and wilderness and washed of the past. At last we made it to the confines of the tent, government-issue and leaking. The lion fell silent and the night closed upon us with nothing but the sound of falling rain. For two long weeks it rained and we sat meditating, drinking tea to keep ourselves warm, talking about everything there was to talk about and when that ran out, grunting to one another before lapsing into silence, each of us lost in our thoughts. It was a time to recuperate after the long years of bloodshed.

As the rain pelted down we listened to the intermittent roars of the lions as they off-loaded their feelings. The low mist and *"guti"* (soft rain) amplified their roars. I have often heard lions in the bush and thought long as to what it is about lions that distinguish them from other big cats. What gives them such an aura all of their own? It is not that they are the largest carnivores for tigers are bigger. They are not the fastest for cheetahs are faster. Neither the most beautiful for none are quite as handsome as the leopard. So what is it? I have concluded it is their roar. No other cat roars like the lion for unlike any other it is unafraid to announce its presence to the world. It is that shattering, reverberating, spine chilling roar that makes the hair on one's neck tingle and forces one to move a little closer to the campfire that is the most defining thing about the lion. No other sound in Africa is to be compared to it. Once heard it can never be forgotten. Once heard one longs to hear it again.

What a time it was, as if the country was being washed of blood and sorrow. There is an African saying, *"Sometimes when it rains bad things are washed away."* Now rivers burst their banks and the bush was dripping with pristine glory all around us. The grass, the trees, the whole of nature burst forth with new life. One could almost see the grass leaping skywards and hear the trees singing. Up on the slopes of the nearby granite hill a family of klipspringers pranced around from boulder to boulder as if releasing all their sprung up energy. At night the lions continued to roar and we saw their massive paws imprinted in the soft mud of the road. When at last the sun came out we swam in the *"spruit"* by the rocks and lay in the sun soaking up the warmth. It was good to be alive, we had been washed and it was now time for healing and a new beginning.

Overseas Visit

After Zimbabwe gained Independence we visited the United Kingdom and looked up family members. They seemed put out that we had arrived and we got a distinct impression that we were considered the "black colonial sheep". However, my uncle was truly glad to see us and brought out the "family tree" meticulously drawn on a long chart that he unravelled and spread on the dining table. I discovered with some amazement that it went back twenty three generations to the thirteen hundreds. So I wasn't just a colonial kid born in Africa, I truly was British after all. My uncle discussed our genealogy with enthusiasm and I asked many questions as it was all new to me. I noticed a member of the family had gone in the late 1800s to Sudan as part of the British administration and had not been heard of since. This was my father's uncle George. My uncle could throw no light on what happened to him. I recalled the Royal Artillery sword that used to hang in our childhood home and began to appreciate in a new way my family's British roots.

Stoned in Jerusalem

We then went on a tour to Jerusalem. Our flight was interrupted half way over the Mediterranean and diverted because of a bomb scare but we eventually arrived safely. During our visit we had a harrowing experience. As we walked through the narrow streets of the old city a group of men for some reason took umbrage at our presence and became hostile towards us. This was disturbing but as we made our way outside the city walls we were suddenly stoned from above. This was exceedingly dangerous for large stones whizzed past our ears narrowly missing our heads. We made a run for it and took shelter within a garden where we felt safe behind tall secluding walls. It was called the Garden Tomb, a site discovered by the famous British General Gordon of Khartoum in Sudan. A couple sat next to us and we introduced ourselves. They came from Zululand.

"Oh," the man said, "we have neighbours by your name."

I gave our address to them and asked if they would give it to their neighbours and in due course a letter arrived. We had found our "lost" family from the 1800s. What a discovery! Dad's uncle George had moved from Sudan to East Africa and eventually settled in Tanganyika. When it gained independence his children who had taken over his family farm were kicked out and they moved to Zululand and started a sugarcane farm. It was a strange coincidence that in this garden discovered by General Gordon of Khartoum we found our lost family from Sudan only days after learning about them. We got to visit our new relatives in Zululand but regrettably they also lost this farm when unrelenting pressure and death threats were brought on them. After surviving a poison attempt they moved away.

The Prime Minister's Cavalcade

A new phenomenon occurred in the country. It was the Prime Minister's cavalcade. We had not seen anything like it before. The Prime Minister of Rhodesia had never travelled in a cavalcade accompanied by hundreds of soldiers and an entourage of hangers on. The new leader did. It was astounding. First the "Out-riders" came, police on motorcycles who took up positions across both lanes of traffic and cleared the road of all civilian vehicles. Then a cavalcade of motorcycles, cars and Land Rovers followed, all full of police and officials, then army trucks full of soldiers and at least one ambulance bringing up the rear. Sandwiched somewhere in the middle was a large black, bullet proof Mercedes Benz in which hunched the Prime Minister. The whole column was accompanied by the wailing of sirens and woe to anyone who did not immediately pull off the road and stop. Even pedestrians were in danger if they did not get out of the way and some cars and people were shot by trigger happy guards with some people seriously wounded and others killed. Elderly people chugging along in slow cars and a bit deaf, unaware of the requirements to get off the road and slow to react to the wailers were victims. Some of the police even wrote themselves off because of the high speeds they travelled. People stood by the roadside in wonder and admiration as their new leader sped by.

The Rhino Holocaust

With the end of the bush war we were able once again to get into wild areas of the country and we visited Mana Pools National Park. The Park is unique and a World Heritage Site. Set on the banks of the Zambezi its wild beauty is stunning. Huge Acacias, Fig Trees and Sausage Trees grow on the flood plain, the river banks and around big pools. There were lush *"vleis"* of grass and stands of Mopani trees and huge Baobabs. The great Zambezi River flowed in superb majesty and the purple escarpment formed a back drop to this stage on which was acted all the drama of the African bush.

Wildlife was abundant. Large numbers of hippos and crocs lived in the pools. Lions were common as were leopards, buffalo and elephant. Sunsets on the river were superb. We would grill fresh fish and watch a crimson sun go down behind the western hills while hippos grunted and yawned with gaping jaws as they prepared to emerge for their nightly foraging trips. Wild geese flew overhead and bats swept over the river catching insects. Reverberating roars of lions punctuated the evening while herds of graceful impala grazed on the lush grass. Few scenes can be so raw with wild scents and sounds. Visitors were permitted to get out of vehicles and walk. We spent many happy days exploring the park. A family of Honey Badgers lived around camp and came at night to raid the dustbins for leftovers. Hyenas skulked around the campfires waiting to pick off morsels of food. One afternoon as we sat in camp having tea a leopard sprang into a nearby tree and lifted its kill, one of the Honey Badgers, from where it had been stored in the branches and dragged it off. One had to be careful walking to the restrooms at night in case one bumped into a buffalo, lion or elephant. One evening a pride of lions cavorted on the sand in front of our tents.

Walking must be done with care, keeping alert and looking out for danger. We had some close encounters. Late one afternoon when we were out walking we came across a family of lions also out walking. With some consternation we realised we had unwittingly joined their hunt and they were all around us but totally intent on their prey, a herd of impala. The nearest lion, a sleek powerful female had a nice fat impala in sight and was no more than twenty meters away. It was disconcerting to be so close to them but no animosity was shown to us.

Another incident was when I was at a pool with a friend watching a herd of elephants. They were ambling towards us and we wanted to photograph them as they crossed a shallow part of the pool. My National Parks friend, decided to help so he sneaked up behind the elephants so as to chivvy them along as if they were sheep. However, the animals got spooked, caught the jitters and stampeded. They came through the water at full speed with spray flying everywhere and then headed straight towards us. To face the largest land animal on earth as it thunders towards one like a mighty steam train at full throttle bellowing and trumpeting is truly awesome and there were five of them. The huge bulk of the animal is beyond description as it looms above one. A big bull came straight for us. We ducked behind a tree and it went past at arm's length in a cloud of spray and dust. Whiffing our scent he gave an ear splitting trumpet and spun around with ears flapping to see where we were. He was already upset and now wanted to locate the source of the problem and began to move towards us only feet away. Fortunately the tree stood on the banks of the pool and we crawled under its roots at the water's edge oblivious to any lurking crocodiles. We crouched there with this huge, majestic animal sniffing us a few feet above, its thick bristled trunk blowing hot air towards us. It was heart stopping stuff. After a while he moved off and we still did not have our photos.

Another exciting incident was when we came across a lioness with three young cubs. This is guaranteed to get the adrenaline pumping especially when one is on foot. The lioness was about sixty meters from us but that was far too close. In a charge a lion can cover that distance in a few seconds and before one can take any evasive action. She snarled savagely and the tip of her long brown tail flicked like an angry snake. We backed off slowly never turning our backs. Africa was always exciting.

Black Rhino were once plentiful at Mana Pools. Zimbabwe had an estimated Black Rhino population of over 1500, some estimated more, the largest number left in Africa. The bush war had served to conserve the Rhino from poachers but when hostilities ended poaching became rampant. A new war started this time on Rhino. It resulted in a holocaust. I knew the Warden and he found himself fighting a war as real as the one that had just ended. This war was against armed poachers who were determined to shoot as many Rhino as possible. National Parks had a two pronged approach. Firstly, they were to track down and shoot all the poachers they could. Secondly, they would capture Rhino and move them to safer places where poachers could not get them. Our warden friend tirelessly campaigned to save the rhino. Not only did he have to fight poachers but he had to battle in a Department that was understaffed, poorly paid and divided with political agendas. He and I would have long discussions about how to save the Rhino. I said the only way Rhino could be saved was to capture and dehorn every single one of them before releasing them into protected areas, private farms or zoos. Sadly, this was not official policy at that time and he believed they could win the war against poaching despite the failure of every other African country to do so.

National Parks staff began to move Rhino to safe areas but it did not take long to see that despite all their efforts Rhino were slaughtered at a terrible rate. Carcasses were found lying in the bush minus their horns. Our friend constantly wore a worried frown. Then rumours leaked out that top Zimbabwe officials were involved with Rhino poaching and smuggling horns through diplomatic bags. The route was traced through various embassies to the Far East. An alternative route went through Zambia. Although Parks staff fought bravely to protect their animals they were poorly financed with little back up. White wardens were arrested on trumped up charges and languished for days in jail; our friend was falsely charged with murder and detained in jail from where he was unable to stop the poaching.

Rhino continued to be slaughtered and so were elephant. The Zimbabwe government said that the elephant population was too large. I attended the International Cites Convention held in Harare during 1990. World conservationists had successfully imposed a ban on all ivory trade but Zimbabwe argued against this saying because they were so good at protecting elephants and had to cull them to keep numbers down Zimbabwe should have the right to sell ivory in order to raise funds. They requested the ban on ivory to be lifted. Figures in excess of sixty thousand elephants were quoted as living in Zimbabwe yet when I spoke to people who worked in Parks they invariably told me they had not seen those numbers. Neither did funds from ivory sales always go to National Parks budget for conservation but went to central government. The Parks were inadequately funded with poor equipment and abysmal wages.

People of Courage

The early years after Independence were a time of respite. It was a time when people tried to remake their shattered lives. Life slowly began to return to a semblance of normality. The aftermath of war began to sink in. There were injured people both African and white, in wheelchairs, on crutches or with artificial limbs. There were others who had mental and emotional wounds. Nationalist fighters came back to a land they themselves had devastated. There were burnt out farms, clinics, schools, homes and missions. It was time to rebuild the country. We tried to help where possible. I visited different areas and held services in district clubs as well as on farms with both farmers and staff. We went to communal lands and held meetings. There was a spirit of reconciliation among the people. I had opportunity to minister into different denominations throughout the land. People were helping each other in positive ways. There was new hope and the future looked bright.

Every morning my wife caught a bus to work and sat next to a woman who had one arm and one eye and walked with a severe limp. Her name was Mim and she was a casualty of the war. It had not been Rhodesian policy to target civilians but regrettably security forces had sometimes done things that were not right. There were a few renegade soldiers who had no regard for official policy and deliberately took advantage of their power. As things deteriorated abuses were committed but war makes people do horrific things and often civilians suffer the consequences.

Mim had suffered such a deed. The roads into rural villages were often booby-trapped by insurgents so as to kill security forces and often the local people knew where mines were placed. Soldiers were tired of being blown up and Mim and her husband were made to sit on the bonnet of an army vehicle as surety that there were no land mines planted on the track leading into their village. The vehicle hit a mine which killed her husband and severely injured her. We grew to love Mim. She was a beautiful person who bore no malice and even though badly disabled was working hard to bring up her children.

Another person who became our friend was Stella the divorcee of a cabinet minister in the new government. She had remained faithful to him all through the long bush war when he was in exile but on his return at Independence he had dismissed her for a younger woman. Now she was struggling to bring up her family. She was part of our church and was a tonic of inspiration and courage. One day I had to go to the office of her ex-husband and do some business. A massive man over weight with the good life he sat in the plush surroundings of government and was very amicable but I felt I should not push him too far by mentioning our friendship with his ex-wife.

So life continued with a façade of normality but not all was well. Six foreign tourists were kidnapped on the main road to Victoria Falls. They were never seen again. A massive manhunt was conducted but only years later were their remains found. They had been bludgeoned to death. An insidious evil stalked the land.

Rumblings of more conflict

In the early 1980's a veneer of peace rested upon the country but underneath it simmered. In Matabeleland white farmers once again came under attack from what were now called *"dissidents"*. Farmers were killed and cattle stolen. The Zimbabwe army moved in. There was much ill feeling between internal factions in the new Zimbabwe army which was comprised of three different hostile forces; the remnants of the Rhodesian Forces, and opposing Zanu and Zapu nationalist forces. Inter-faction fighting resulted and the South African white regime took advantage of it by creating mayhem to destabilise Zimbabwe. It is said they set up "Super Zapu" using disgruntled ex-fighters in Matabeleland. In December of 1981 all was peaceful in busy Manica Road in down town Harare. Traffic and pedestrians moved along the street. Suddenly a massive explosion blasted the area shattering windows and shaking buildings. Office workers in nearby buildings picked themselves up from the floor where they had half fallen and half flung themselves and peered through the window onto a scene of carnage. The bomb had gone off in ZanuPF offices. Seven people were killed and 124 injured. Bodies lay where they were flung. Shattered glass littered the ground. The scene was one of carnage and outrage. People poured onto the street to help the injured. It was a scene they would never forget. They moved among the dead and bleeding giving what assistance they could. It was blamed on inter-faction rivalry.

Anglican Church Occupied

It did not take long for the ruling party to begin a campaign to establish a one party state. Some people felt it imperative to block this by voting for anyone apart from a candidate of the ruling party but there were not a lot to choose from. One of the opposition parties was led by a man called Tekere, an ex-combatant and one of the "Fathers of Nationalism." I saw him one day in the bank. I was close up, in fact right next to him. Around him were his body guards bristling with weapons, men you did not want to meet on a dark night and he leaned over the counter with eyes as dead as door nails. Tekere was a law unto himself. His men invaded the Anglican Church in Mutare where our friend was priest. At that time Tekere was the political strong man of the town and he decided he would teach Christians a lesson. He and his storm troopers stormed the church, desecrated the sanctuary and occupied it for weeks. They lived in it, slept in it and defecated in it. All were powerless to stop him until he and his men grew tired of their games and left. As perhaps one may imagine the church needed more than a sweep to clean it afterwards. Tekere went further than that. Shortly after Independence he was charged with the gunning down of a white farmer. He had a personal vendetta against the farmer and one day he and his body guards invaded the farm, cornered the farmer and shot him dead. When the case came to court he escaped the consequences through political machinations of government.

Tekere, however, left the ruling party and challenged Mugabe's intention to establish a one party state. When parliamentary elections came I decided to vote for him as did other people. I voted only twice in Africa, once for a Bishop and once for a killer. To vote for such a man seems absurd, ludicrous, nonsensical and irrational - what words can one use for such folly? But such was the calibre of our leaders, few of them had clean hands and if Tekere could stop a one party state then he was the man to vote for. Opposing political factions, however, held grudges and killings took place. Some people were killed in the most unlikely ways. One of them was found dead in his swimming pool. Another was thrown off an upstairs balcony. Some just disappeared. A favourite way to dispatch an enemy, it was said, was to arrange a "car accident" often with a reinforced army truck or other heavy vehicle and several notable people ended up dead.

The CIO (Central Intelligence Organisation) was the secret police of the new regime. They inherited it from the Rhodesians and turned it into an organisation that became greatly feared. The CIO conducted investigations into private lives, opposition parties and suspect organisations. They tapped telephones, opened mail and did everything else to protect the regime. They had eyes like a chameleon that could look everywhere and anywhere.

Army Barracks Blown up

The weather was idyllic that afternoon of August 1981 as we sipped tea in the lovely suburban garden of our Harare home. Sunlight filtered through evergreen trees, the roses were coming into bloom and birds flitted through the undergrowth. Hueglin Robins had begun to sing their afternoon song. Suddenly the peace was shattered. Thirty miles northwest of the city was a large army barracks. On this quiet afternoon and without warning it began to self-destruct. Massive explosions shook the city as bombs, rockets, mortars and thousands of rounds of bullets ignited in a deadly cocktail of explosions. Fire and brimstone rained down on the surrounding area and soldiers fled panic stricken into the neighbouring countryside. They emerged hours later and miles away in a dazed state of shock some of them in torn and shredded clothes. "Someone" had decided to blow the barracks sky high. We poured ourselves some more tea and listened to the reverberating thud of massive explosions that shook houses and shattered windows. The attack was very professional and very "destabilising".

Air Force blown up

Another attack followed this time on the Zimbabwe Air Force. Thornhill Air Force base was just outside the sleepy town of Gweru. In the early hours of a morning in July 1982 it was attacked by unknown saboteurs. "They" blew up seven Hunters, a new British Hawk Mk60 and a Lynx aircraft as well as damaging three other Hawks and a Hunter. Who ever "they" were flew in under cover of darkness, breached the security of the base, moved through the hangers at will, placed explosives and detonated them and got out of the country without being caught. The aftermath of this was far reaching. The Zimbabwe Government was embarrassed and angry. An immediate witch-hunt was conducted in traditional manner which meant that suspects were arrested, tortured, forced to confess and then declared guilty. Six top-ranking white officers were detained and subjected to medieval methods of torture in order to get confessions. They were held illegally for months under appalling conditions, suffered torture including electric shocks, were deprived of sleep, isolated in solitary confinement and barely fed. For most of this period their whereabouts were kept secret and lawyers prohibited visits. All six men "confessed" to a crime they never committed. Many cynical comments passed around at the time. When they were eventually brought out to the public a reporter asked them "When they said they were going to charge you did you realise they meant with electricity?"

The High Court ordered the release of the men but they were promptly re-arrested on the direct orders of the Minister of Defence. Western governments were impotent to intervene but eventually after many months they were brought to trial and acquitted. The State had no case but they were immediately re-arrested and detained on the direct instructions of the Minister of Home Affairs, a particularly obnoxious individual who vowed they would "rot in prison". After more threats and even more tears all of them were fortunate enough to eventually be deported. The Minister who was responsible for their illegal detention soon died, of Aids it was rumoured, and Britain and Western nations continued to pour financial aid into Zimbabwe.

The witch hunt

Shortly after the bombing of Thornhill the CIO took control of the Air Force. All white personnel were scrutinised and many were detained and questioned. Our air force friend from the old days was caught in the witch hunt and detained for interrogation. The CIO was desperate for convictions. As far as they were concerned every white officer was guilty of sabotage. The traditional way of conducting a witch-hunt was to give all the suspects poison and those who survived were declared innocent. They came for him early one morning. The first session was fairly civilised but then they came again and again. He was newly wed and his wife became suspicious when he spent so much time away from home. He kept on making excuses to her not wanting to alarm her but she knew something was wrong. Not only was he dodging her questions but each session with the CIO became more difficult for him. Instead of having pleasurable evenings at home he was stripped stark naked and interrogated for hours. It seemed to his young wife as though her husband was falling apart before her eyes and she did not know why. He knew he had to do something and next session he took the initiative.

"Gentlemen" he said looking around at the half dozen heavies surrounding him, "I ask you all to stand together in a circle and hold hands with me."

The request took them by surprise and perhaps thinking he was about to make a confession they meekly obeyed. He then prayed as he had not done before, out aloud, asking God to show the truth, to help the men to do their jobs and to intervene in his situation. His prayer seemed to convince them that he was innocent and after that the pressure on him relaxed. In the meanwhile his young wife had found out the truth, sold the house and next time he came home whisked him out of the country.

Bulawayo Uprising

It was not long after Independence that rebellion erupted. Large amounts of armour and weaponry were still kept in Zambia and some at Gwaai River. Because of mistrust between Shona and Matabele factions clashes had become more frequent and the Matabele faction decided to make Matabeleland an independent state. About 5000 Russian trained guerrillas with artillery and motorised transport rolled down the highway from Gwaai towards Bulawayo. The Zimbabwe army were called in to stop them. The African Rifles commanded by ex-Rhodesian officers faced the brunt of the attack. What a reversal, ex-Rhodesians now fought to keep in power the very people they had fought to keep out. The African Rifles was a crack regiment with a proud history. They had fought in East Africa in the First World War and in Burma during the Second World War. This was to be their final action and shortly after this the unit was dissolved, the end of a fine regiment loyal to Britain. Their last battle crushed the Matabele army and entrenched Mugabe in power something they must have surely loathed. Ninety years before in 1893 the first Rhodesian forces crushed the Matabele warriors of Lobengula and now Bulawayo was again to live up to its name as *"Place of Slaughter"*.

The "Battle for Bulawayo" commenced. Armoured cars fought duels in the streets and the city rocked to the sound of intermittent bombs and small arms fire. Army fought army and street battles raged in the townships. It lasted a couple of days but the Matabele were no match for the African Rifles. Many Matabele fighters were killed and others rounded up but some escaped to the bush. This was to have tragic consequences. The war came to Matabeleland all over again this time in the form of renegade freedom fighters or "dissidents" who were supposed to have support from the South African Apartheid regime. Mugabe would never forgive the Matabele and he branded their leader Joshua Nkomo a "cobra" that had to be eliminated. His answer to these events was to let loose his North Korean trained 5th Brigade comprised of loyal ex-guerrillas who reported directly to him.

"Gukurahundi"
Gukurahundi means – "The storm that washes away rubbish."

In 1982 Mugabe raised his notorious 5th Brigade trained by North Korea and comprised of ex-liberation fighters. At his announcement of the formation of this unit he referred to a Shona proverb, the "Gukurahundi" which was a term used for the destructive power of a storm. Mugabe unleashed his *dogs of war* upon the defenceless Matabele nation. They wore distinctive red berets and were dreadfully feared.

Between January 1983 and 1987 they were to conduct a war of terror. Indoctrinated in the ways of communist propaganda and terror techniques they ravaged the Matabele people. This was to be a repugnant and horrible campaign that totally violated all human rights. Matabeleland was closed to all reporters whether local or international and all news was censored.

The Fifth Brigade started their campaign by conducting *"pungwes"* a term given for all-night indoctrination meetings during which party songs were sung and "sell outs" or traitors were weeded out and punished. Everyone in the community had to attend even little children. Subjection to days without sleep was in itself a means of torture and subjugation. After "sell outs" had been identified they were beaten in front of the people. Witnessing such brutality and hearing the screams of victims had a devastating effect upon the people. The entire Matabele people slumped into despair. *"Pungwes"* were no different than the barbaric "sniffing out" ceremonies conducted by witchdoctors in medieval Africa. People were killed in public executions. The largest number was at Lupane where 62 men and women were publicly shot. One Fifth Brigade leader was a man called "Comrade Jesus." He had a speech that he gave when he came to a community. This is some of what he would say: ***I have gallons of blood in my car. The blood comes from people. My life is to drink human blood. I want more blood because my supply is running low and so I have come to this place to kill and get more blood.***"[5] Can one imagine what this did to his captive audience?

The Land of "no Tears"

People were taken away and never seen again. Torture camps were set up the most notorious being "Bhalagwe" where thousands of people were held, and many tortured and killed. It was said that methods of torture were brutal; beatings and floggings, held underwater until nearly drowned, having a cloth stuffed down ones throat and then having water poured into it, electrical shock treatment, arms tied tightly to restrict flow of blood, gang rapes, the list is diabolical. Spikes were pushed into genitals, some had their genitals beaten. Some mothers were made to witness the murder of their children. Some infants were buried alive. Limbs were broken. Some corpses were not allowed burial but left to rot. Any bereaved people caught shedding tears were beaten. No one dared to cry. There were accounts of trucks loaded with bodies moving through the streets of Bulawayo under cover of darkness. Corpses were hurled down deserted mineshafts, some into Antelope Mine near my childhood haunts. Rhodesians had also dumped corpses of combatants into mine shafts and it was claimed they used torture during interrogation of captives which they will deny, but they did not do so on this scale. There were horrific accounts of widespread torture. What sort of things happened? A woman and her husband were killed in front of their family and friends. They were accused of being "sell outs" and she was strung up by her ankles and a fire lit under her head and roasted until she was dead. Then they killed her husband too.[6] Other horrendous events were reported. A close friend of ours was witness to a murder. While in the employment of the Zimbabwe Roads department he had to travel with a 5th Brigade escort to inspect a bridge under repair. On the way back he noticed the soldiers had detained a man on the back of the truck. On a quiet stretch of road the truck stopped, the soldiers marched the man into the bush and a shot rang out. They returned with only the handcuffs. Our friend went into shock.

Eventually Joshua Nkomo leader of the opposition in parliament and considered by many as the true leader of African Nationalism fled the country. It is estimated that at least 20,000 civilians were killed by 5th Brigade. Others say this is a very conservative number. Many more must have died from sickness and starvation for no food was permitted to enter the Matabele homelands and any found there was destroyed. Thousands of people resorted to digging roots and eating grass. Many elderly and weak people must have died including infants and children. In fact, an entire people were subjected to State induced hunger. It was a bitter harvest. Brave journalists risked their lives to expose it but the world did nothing. Now that Zimbabwe was "free" the attention given by world media lapsed as the new regime got down to the serious and murderous business of staying in power. The western press blinded by its support of Mugabe and his fight against the white regime turned a blind eye to what now took place. It seemed no one cared what happened to innocent defenceless people. It was another dreadful "Deafening Silence" from the world. We all kept silent. Ghastly stories filtered out but no one dared say a word. We could do nothing. This was not democracy that we now witnessed, it was more like genocide. Mugabe continued to wine and dine as an honoured guest to foreign governments. He inspected guards of honour and walked down red carpets. It was something to behold as he was feted with lavish banquets but back home his *"dogs of war"* trampled underfoot the blood of thousands. Did he not know? He must have. The Catholic Commission for Peace in Zimbabwe recorded these atrocities in a written report *(Breaking the Silence Building True Peace)* which was given to Mugabe who conveniently lost it. Fortunately copies of the report were made public. Catholic priests could verify its contents for they had first hand encounters with 5th Brigade. Its contents are barbarous. Yet, the British Government knew all along and said and did nothing. What signal did this send Mugabe and his regime?

Adventures at Kariba

From time to time we were able to go into wild areas and especially enjoyed going to Lake Kariba. It was a water wilderness that abounded with fish, birds and wild animals, including big game. One could see elephant and antelope along the shoreline near Fothergill Island with herds of up to a thousand buffalo.

On one of our visits we were told that lions had been feeding on a dead hippo near the Banana Farm so we strolled down to have a look. Sure enough we found the dead hippo but there was no sign of the lions. Cautiously, for the lions could well have been lurking nearby, we walked closer until we were at the carcass. It was a massive beast and how the lions overcame it was astounding if in fact they had. As we stood looking at it I glanced down at my feet and nearly fell over with shock for there curled in the grass was a tiny lion cub. I reached down and picked it up whereupon it let out a deep throated, rasping meow. Cold shivers ran down my spine as I realised that if mother was within earshot we were as good as dead. I cuddled the little kitten to my chest. My mind worked overtime as I wondered what to do. It appeared to have been abandoned and was dehydrated and weak. To leave it meant it would perish. On the other hand we had to get out as fast as possible otherwise we all might perish at the savage fury of its mother. We turned and ran for our lives. After several hundreds of yards through the bush we came to a halt panting wildly still clutching the cub. We were lucky for if the mother had seen us she would have killed us. He was a cute little feline and our friends at the Banana Farm took him and nursed him. Why he had been left behind we could not tell. Perhaps his mother was coming back for him but I will never forget the day I held the mighty King of Beasts in my arms even though he was such a tiny mite.

The lions at Kariba were a fairly respectable bunch but they behaved badly when they decided to eat a young safari guide. He had come from England, was trained in Zimbabwe and worked for a safari company operating in Matusadona National Park on the shores of the lake. One night he was left in charge of a tented complex with a group of foreign visitors. After supper he zipped them all safely into their tents and then decided he would sit up and listen to the lions roar. Unfortunately it was hot and he left the flaps of his tent open and the lions caught him and ate him within ear shot of the visitors who were understandably upset. When they got up in the morning there was very little of him left. It was not the sort of news that promoted tourism and it gave lions a bad name. It brings to mind a pride of lions in the 1930s that became man eaters and ate dozens of workers when the road to Chirundu Bridge on the Zambezi was cut out of wilderness.

Fothergill Island was named after Rupert Fothergill who rescued stranded wild animals when Kariba was formed in the late 1950s. Rob, our friend, developed a safari camp on the island which became world famous. He started with a small tent when there was nothing but wilderness. He had many close encounters with wild animals. One incident nearly ended his career when he took a party of tourists on a bush walk and they came across a herd of elephants. Rob had instructed his party that in the event of meeting elephant no one should move or run. However, one tourist lost his nerve, turned and bolted, fell over a root and twisted his ankle in the process. The matriarch of the herd sensed things were not right and charged. Rob moved forward to divert the animal away from his party of tourists and not willing to shoot the elephant attempted to shoo the creature away as if she was a big duck. Sometimes this tactic worked but she would have none of it and came for Rob intent on doing him serious bodily harm. Rob dodged around a tree trunk. She followed him, her long trunk reaching after him. She caught him, threw him to the ground and then attempted to pin him down and gore him. He found himself looking into the beady eye of the massive beast and decided it was time to get out of there. On hands and knees he scampered between her front feet, under her belly and out between her back feet. The elephant swung around wondering how he had vanished so quickly for he was now hiding behind a bush. A German tourist filmed most of it on video and thought it was all part of the show. He got a shock when he realised it was not, dropped the video and bolted. The elephant picked up Rob's scent and came for him again. Rob ducked around another tree. When the elephant came around the left side he dodged around the right. When it came around the right side he dodged to the left. They played hide and seek until the elephant nearly succeeded in grabbing him, suddenly tired of it, and hurried off after her clan who had by this time dashed away squealing and trumpeting. A shaky Rob gathered up his tourists like a mother hen would gather her chicks, bandaged the ankle of the one and carefully led them home. It had all been very exciting.

Daisy became a main tourist attraction at Fothergill Island. She was an Egyptian Goose. She was given to us as a tiny abandoned chick rescued on the Zambezi. We named her Daisy and she grew up as one of the family. She bathed in a basin we left by the back door and would walk through our house dropping poos. When she was fully grown we gave her to Rob who took her to Fothergill Island. Daisy became a favourite with the tourists. They came to see lions and elephants but were captivated by the charm this little goose exuded wherever she went. When tourists arrived at the jetty she welcomed them as if they were long lost friends and waddled with them to the camp. If they went too fast she flapped her wings and ran along side sometimes taking off and honking as only Egyptian Geese can honk. She swam in the swimming pool and wandered around the open dining area getting crunchy salads off the tables. Eventually she spent more and more time at the harbour where she teamed up with a wild suitor and they went off and made a home around the corner of the bay. She still honked at the people but when she hatched a family of her own she went thoroughly back to the wild. Visitors could see her proudly waddling along followed by a crowd of goslings. She was a true success story of an animal returning to the wild. We sometimes think about her and how she is doing in the wilds of Africa.

On one of our visits to Fothergill Island Rob took us on a boat to view wild life in the bay. A regal Fish Eagle sitting on a dead tree caught his attention and with all eyes of the tourists fixed on it Rob throttled gently forward. We noticed a short distance away some hippos bobbing and snorting and drew Rob's attention to their presence.

"Don't worry about them" he assured everyone "they are not dangerous because they are used to us" and we continued our advance.

With no warning a huge hippo surged from the murky depths below and with mouth agape hit the boat with an almighty crash tearing a huge gash with its giant tusks and narrowly missing my arm by inches. The boat rocked precariously and the impact threw a passenger in front of me onto the deck and one woman began to shriek hysterically. The foreign clients went into shock and Rob turned a ghostly white despite his sun-tanned skin. Kariba was certainly exciting!

One day while staying on the island I went for a walk with one of the professional guides, a real old timer with many years of bush experience. His name was Uro and he was getting on in age and was deaf and short sighted. He originally came from Russia and was a real gentleman. He loved the bush and carried his rifle over his shoulder with the air of familiarity that comes from years of experience. We waddled along behind him like goslings following their mother and felt as safe as safe can be. There were plenty of elephants on the shores of the island and fortunately most of them were also real gentlemen. It was not long before we noticed a big bull feeding just off the path. We had all seen him but our guide could not hear or see too well and had not seen him and was leading us closer and closer to the enormous animal. I tapped Uro on the shoulder and pointed it out to him and he was quite pleased to see it. If one gets too close to the big bulls they usually give a warning with a short mock charge shaking their heads and flapping their ears in a grand display of strength before moving slowly off with an exaggerated air of hurt pride. If one does not know about these tactics one can have several heart attacks in quick succession for the sheer bulk of the animal is awesome. The problem is few people can tell if it is a real charge or a mock charge until it is all over. True to form this big elephant reacted predictably by giving us a bit of a rev so as to show his agitation at us being on his turf. He put his head up and looked down his long nose and then came straight towards us. Everyone's heart leapt into their mouths and we waited for our guide to respond accordingly. With the experience of a lifetime he swung his gun off his shoulder and into the firing position, flipped off the safety catch and we all held our breath. Lucky for the elephant it turned away and lived another day and we all went back to camp to tell our story especially the foreign clients who believed they had come within a hair's breath of being flattened. What most of the group did not know was that the old man had not loaded his gun and it was all a big bluff on both sides. The old timer refused to shoot anything. From Kariba he moved to Chikwenya safari camp on the lower Zambezi and died there not long afterwards when one night as he walked back to his tent after relieving himself in the bush he was killed by an elephant. This time the elephant did not bluff and put a tusk right through him killing him instantly. It was probably the way Uro had wanted to go, not lingering in an old age home.

Because of poaching elephant numbers decreased. Some were killed and others fled to the hills. Friends and I went to the Mavuradona Mountains, a spectacular rugged range that formed part of the Zambezi Escarpment. With cliffs rising nearly a thousand feet, deep ravines, well wooded slopes and a unique bamboo belt a bit like that found in tropical West Africa the hills were a natural treasure of scenic beauty. We walked through thickets and bamboo glades to the boulder strewn Mzarabani River that gushed through deep gorges and where big evergreen trees shaded the banks. Heaps of dung and broken branches were signs that elephant were there and we wondered how they could negotiate the steep inclines but negotiate them they did for we came upon a herd quietly browsing on the slopes. It is remarkable how agile elephants can be. For centuries they had migrated through these hills from the central plateau down to the sultry Zambezi valley and they knew the paths as if recalled from some ancient primeval mind. We did not disturb them for they had climbed into the hills to get away from people and we did not think it fair to unsettle them. So we watched them from a distance, these huge gentle giants of Africa hounded in their ancient terrain.

Foot steps on our bed

During the days of the colony there was a government programme to spray mosquito breeding places and Malaria had been eliminated in many areas and greatly reduced elsewhere. However, after Independence this programme fell away and Malaria began to spread again and become worse than ever. After a visit to Kariba my wife went down with malaria. She was very ill. Malaria causes a pounding headache with high fever often producing delirious hallucinations. It kills more people in Africa than anything else, except now days for Aids. She suffering badly and after several days was in a poor way. One night when she was very ill I awoke to find "someone" walking softly on the bed. Slowly I rolled over and opened my eyes to see what was happening. In the twilight of the room, with moonlight beaming through the window, I could see nothing on the bed not even our Siamese cat. Yet the footsteps continued gently down one side, along the base and up the other side. It was weird but my heart was full of peace. I went back to sleep. In the morning my wife had made an extraordinary recovery but I said nothing to her. Several days later she mentioned that she had felt footsteps on our bed at the time she was so ill. I confirmed that indeed there had been footsteps and that she had not imagined them in her delirium. Who was it? Was it an angel sent in her time of need or maybe a departed family member come to strengthen her? It was very strange!

Jack the Demolisher

We suffered a plague of rats at our home. Hundreds of them moved onto our premises and we could hear them scampering in the ceiling and squealing around the garden. We also had numerous Giant Gambian Rats which are the largest in Africa weighing 3kgs and eighty centimetres in length. One night I was rudely awakened by a large rat that sprang through my bedside window right on top of me. I woke with a start and leapt out of bed. The commotion woke my wife who decided to go to the bathroom. If anything is guaranteed to get a Jack Russell going it's the sight and smell of a rat. Soon I had turned the bedroom upside down hunting for the guilty culprit. As I moved furniture the rat ran from place to place with Jack in hot pursuit barking his head off. It then ran into the next room and the same process was repeated. As my wife came from the bathroom the rat ran straight towards her. With a scream she placed one hand on the dining room table and sprang into the air. The table was unable to take her weight, broke at the legs and crashed to the floor with plates, jars and cutlery that had been laid out for breakfast tumbling upon her. She sat on the floor dazed as the dog, barking in hot pursuit, leapt over her and careered after the rat this time into the lounge. Coffee tables tumbled, the carpet was upturned and the room turned chaotic as it dashed around in a desperate attempt to find a way out with Jack close behind. Eventually it retraced its tracks, jumped onto the bed and leapt through the window. The entire house was in a state of chaos. It looked as though a team of professional hit men had given our home the once over. The table was dismembered, crockery and cutlery lay scattered and the wardrobe lay on its side, coffee tables were upturned, the carpet pulled up and the whole place in upheaval. After that we called our dog "Jack the Demolisher" but I am sure he would have also chased off any burglar.

Police and Thieves

At times we found ourselves praying for protection from the police, an absurd prayer when one thinks about it but very real for us. It would take on more significance in the days ahead. During the Liberation War if one lived in the towns the evenings were punctuated with the sound of helicopters bringing in the wounded. Towards the end of the war when conflict spilled into the suburbs one often heard gun fire. After Independence the pattern continued. Gun shots were regular occurrences at night and we heard running gun battles when fleeing men ran through the grounds of our home. One night I stirred in my sleep and in a semi conscious state saw an intruder half way through the bedroom window. Even half asleep I knew that if he got into the house we were in trouble for usually burglars were armed and easily overcame their victims, tying them up and even killing them. Without thinking and with a loud scream I sprang out of bed towards him knocking him off balance so that he tumbled backwards and fell out whereupon fortunately he was gone in an instant.

Theft became a major problem in the land. In the old days one could go out and leave one's home unlocked and crime was mostly petty offences because most people had basic commodities. There was employment and the cost of living fairly reasonable. However, after Independence "guerrillas" were no longer running around the bush and needed something else to do and what better than for some to turn to a life of crime. Some of them had no jobs and no benefits. The Zimbabwe government signed off veterans with a handshake of only Z$600. Unemployment grew. The government continued to promise wealth, health and happiness and received vast amounts of Western aid to fulfil their promises. Conferences were held with international delegates flying in to discuss some new topic and flying out leaving promises. The government came up with regular five year plans. They promised health for all by the year 2000 as well as wage reviews and housing schemes. A few brave officials tried to implement some of these promises and the country held together but one cannot help but ask how? In my opinion, having been there and seen it all, it was the commitment of everyday working people that held it together in spite of what the government did or did not do. Farmers, businessmen, tradesmen and factory workers continued to work for a better future. Government slapped tax levies on almost everything they could find. Aid money did not seem to help except to provide posh vehicles. Crime escalated to new levels, car hijackings became regular events as well as murder and rape.

Bandits mixed a special concoction that was blown into windows of homes while people were sleeping. It seemed to paralyse the occupants who could see in a kind of dream-like trance but were powerless to respond. Thieves then moved through the house at will. We lived on a large four acre plot owned by friends who lived in the main house and we stayed in a cottage. To protect ourselves we set up gadgets to warn us of trespassers. A length of thin twine was strung between two points. At night this could not be seen and any intruder would unwittingly trigger a falling weight which discharged a blank cartridge. Several times we were awakened by the report and heard the intruder fleeing for his life thinking he had been shot. The real thing was not far behind him for under my pillow was my revolver loaded with real ammo. We had a large powerful Rotweiler that was strong and loyal and could have torn to shreds anyone she thought an enemy. We had our Jack Russell and Stafford Terriers that slept by our beds and we also shared another massive dog that belonged to the main house. Trespassers were lucky not to be mauled.

Travelling on the roads sometimes caused difficulties when we came to Police blocks for although some police were pleasant there were those who looked for an excuse to use their authority. It always helped to crack a joke or compliment them on the great work they were doing. The important thing was to never argue with them but I got away with it, once. One day a policewoman stopped me and wanted to charge me for having a dirty engine. I was taken aback. "Under what law are you going to charge me?" I asked. She evaded the question and repeated she would charge me. I resisted and said, "In all my years I have never heard of a law that said it was illegal to have a dirty engine." After some sharp exchanges she relented and stalked off flinging back a parting shot that I must not be caught again. In retrospect she clearly wanted a handout and nothing else.

Another occasion proved quite different. I pulled up at a police block and the officer bent down and peered in. He asked the same old questions.
"Who are you? Where are you going?"

"I am a minister" I answered to his first question.

He got a shock and I could see his mind working overtime as he leapt to attention and waved me through thinking I was a Minister of Parliament. I chuckled as I looked in the rear view mirror and saw his colleagues remonstrating with him for they knew there was no way I could be a Member of Parliament.

On yet another occasion I was careful to give a totally different answer. The Zimbabwe police had arrested a group of American "missionaries" who had flown in with rifles and ammunition in their possession. The missionaries said that these were part of their hunting equipment for not only had they come to evangelise but also to do some part time hunting something many Americans liked to do in Africa. They were promptly thrown in jail and police put on national alert for it was claimed an immanent attempt to assassinate the President was about to take place. It was feared that other members of the "armed gang" were on the loose. We were stopped at a police road block and the officer leant down and asked the same old questions. I knew this time that if I let on I was a missionary I would be detained as a potential assassin for the police seemed unable to differentiate between missionaries and mercenaries. I was careful to evade the question by saying I was a safari guide. This was true for I had my own little enterprise taking groups of people canoeing on the Zambezi. Meanwhile the Americans languished in jail for months in appalling conditions and subject to the same old methods of interrogation before they were eventually released and deported.

It wasn't just police we had to look out for on the roads. One early morning when it was still dark we left for Kariba and were travelling on the highway when we saw in the headlights something lying in the middle of the road. Fortunately we had time to screech to a halt within feet of a body. We got out and found the body of a man. He looked dead but on closer examination we discovered he was totally blotto. We dragged him into tall grass where he was safe from traffic and hoped he would recover sufficiently to find his way home. It was a close shave for him because if we had hit him he most certainly would have been dead.

The Police and the Ladies

The authorities decided there were too many ladies on the streets at night and this reflected poorly for tourism. The regime failed to understand or acknowledge that the problem came from the failing economy and that more and more ladies needed a way to make a living. Harare had become a centre for conferences but visitors indulged in the night attractions and the ladies had an international cliental, a sort of sex tourism. The government responded in the way they knew best. Anti-prostitute drives took place and police swooped on the "ladies of the night". Indiscriminately they rounded up hundreds of women irrespective of whether they were prostitutes or not and took them off to police stations and jails. Inevitably innocent women were also caught even some wives of Members of

Parliament were arrested. After several days of screening those considered "innocent" were released. The rest were trucked into camps in the bush where they were interred for re-education. If that was not bad enough some of them never came back or so it was said.

The regime also came out strongly against gay people. Harsh words were uttered against them by the President with threats that they should go back to Britain as if it were all a racial issue, all gays were white. There was no regard for human rights or any respect for gay people. One afternoon my wife went to tea with the President's wife and found her to be a pleasant lady. Mugabe's first wife, Sally, was from Ghana and eventually died from kidney failure. She cared for orphans and was in many ways a gracious person. Sally seemed to have a calming and restraining influence on her husband and her death seemed to mark a turn for the worst for he seemed to throw off restraint and tolerated more and more wrong doing in a climate where eventually all manner of crimes could be committed without consequences.

The case of the missing mental patients

It was reported in the paper that twenty mental patients were missing. They had been travelling to a hospital in Bulawayo on a special bus when the bus driver stopped at a *shebeen* (brothel). He left his passengers in the bus for a short while but when he returned they were all missing. Now he was in trouble but had a clever idea. He went down to the local bus station and announced free travel to Bulawayo and quickly gained another twenty willing passengers. On arrival he immediately took them to the mental hospital where they were signed in under strict control and with much protesting. Some had to be restrained. It took three days for doctors to realise the error. The original patients were never found. It could only happen in Zimbabwe!

Under the Effluent

Alan was an electrician and worked on a project at Chinhoyi to upgrade the sewerage farm. New pumps were installed to cope with the increased effluent that passed through the works. He installed a massive new pump that was placed at the base of a shallow well and which had large flexible tubes leading in and out. A friend with him was responsible for the installation of these large pipes that carried effluent. All was complete and a celebration held to mark the switching on of the pump to which the Mayor and other influential dignitaries came clad in their official regalia. Speeches were made and then came the moment to switch on. The affluent looking group gathered around the top of the well peering down at the gleaming pump. Alan moved over and flipped the switch. The pump sprang into action with a loud whooshing sound which grew in volume as it sucked up hundreds of litres of liquid sewerage. Everyone peered more intently down the well. Alan's friend also gazed down concerned that all was going according to plan but his eyes grew large when he saw the flexible pipe had bulged to unnatural proportions. He caught Alan's arm and hastily pulled him back. The whooshing sound reached a crescendo and without warning the flexible pipe burst and emitted sewerage like an artesian well. It all happened so quickly that a powerful spout of stinking brown liquid surged upwards and drenched the dignitaries who fled slipping and sliding in all directions.

Once out of the pump house they stood on the lawn and demanded the local janitor to hose them off. They looked a sorry sight and smelt even worse. It was what is known as "being under the effluent". What a palaver!

Shiloh Mission
In the mid-eighties we joined a mission in Enterprise Valley. This district was prime agriculture land and farms supplied Harare with fresh produce. Farmers had worked very hard in developing a sound agricultural economic base to the nation. This had been achieved in the face of great difficulties. The country had been famous for its dairy products, beef, tea, food crops and fruit and this enterprise had continued after Independence through the dedication of commercial farmers. Shiloh was a small Christian mission on a farm owned by friends. It was founded to serve local people. The leader was an ex-captain in the British army and had fought in the Far East. He was also a dairy farmer and loved his Jersey *"mombies"*. We enjoyed fresh farm produce. Local and international visitors came to the mission. However, the sweet aroma of prayer ascended in the midst of a strong odour of pig stench for we were right next to a pig farm and the smell was at times quite overpowering. I went off pork for good.

One night we were deep in sleep on the farm when we awoke to a tremendous earth-shattering explosion. We sat bolt upright in bed. It felt as though the whole earth had exploded and everything was shaking. I wondered whether the war had started all over again and if we had been hit by a rocket. A brilliant light lit the room and the entire landscape and then gradually faded. It went quiet like the ominous silence of disaster. It turned out to be a large meteorite that exploded right above us as it entered the atmosphere. Somehow it was the prelude to the next act.

Abducted - May 1987
In May of 1987 Renamo rebels in Mozambique abducted members of our mission Phil and Vicky together with their infant daughter. They had been serving at Maforga Mission in Mozambique. Rebels fighting against Frelimo Government warned the mission that they must close down which they had refused to do. One night a band of rebels closed the mission for them. Our friends heard the approaching sound of gun fire. There was nothing they could do but gather together and hide in the toilet. Phil, Vicky, their infant daughter and several others all squeezed like sardines into a tin can. It was a frightening experience. They could hear the men moving through the mission trashing buildings, burning vehicles and destroying equipment. When the rebels got to their house they burst

in and moved from room to room. The toilet door was flung open and the missionaries looked down the mussels of AK automatic guns and what seemed to be certain death. Rough hands grabbed them and hauled them out and marched them into the African night to the sound of the burning mission and exploding fuel tanks of vehicles. It was the start of a gruelling experience. It became apparent that the rebels would not harm them as long as they did what they were told. They were marched right across Mozambique through hundreds of miles of bush and dense jungle, crossing rivers and climbing mountains, walking at night and hiding by day in an epic journey which they barely survived. They lived off bush food such as caterpillars and rats and the little they could get from poverty stricken people along the way. There was no word about them for months and we did not know whether they were dead or alive. Eventually a message got through that they had arrived in Malawi and released into the care of the American Embassy. How they survived the rigors of the bush is amazing especially with a young infant. After such an arduous experience one would think it would cure anyone of mission work but soon they were back on the job but eventually Phil took his family and left the dangers of Africa.

Massacre of our friends - November 1987

Not long afterwards another mission with which we were closely linked was also attacked, this time in Zimbabwe and this time the result was horrible. Persecution of the Matabele people still dragged on and their leader Joshua Nkomo held talks with the regime but in April these talks finally broke down. However, Mugabe was determined to get his one party state and would stop at nothing. It came to a head in the early hours of the 26th November when sixteen missionaries at the mission just south of Bulawayo were crudely hacked to death. They included our dearest friends. The "Community of Reconciliation" had an aim much like ours, to reach local people in a spirit of reconciliation. The mission comprised two small adjoining farms, one called New Adams and the other Olive Tree, beautifully situated as they nestled between majestic granite boulders in the foothills of Matobo hills.

Hazel, our childhood friend, was a member of the mission. She had an adventurous spirit and with her family had spent eight years on the Atlantic high seas. She had sailed all around the Caribbean and other places but came back to serve the people she loved. One glorious day I was privileged to baptise her out in the open at Tony's farm. All our friends were there, the sun shone brightly and we sang songs of praise. She had a tender heart for the people of Zimbabwe and dedicated herself to them. The community lived in sacrificial ways giving aid, education and other essentials to help local people. Community life is never easy and they had to overcome many issues but a depth of commitment grew with the indigenous farmers in the vicinity.

After some years, however, they were confronted by people who did not appreciate their presence despite their sincere intentions. Even though the farms had been legally purchased squatters moved on to the land and claimed that through the spirits of their ancestors the farms were rightfully theirs. A gang of dissidents threatened the occupants with dire consequences if they did not immediately abandon the farms. The missionaries tried to talk but things grew worse. They held a meeting to decide what to do and felt they should remain on the land and try and negotiate. They had a sincere spirit of service towards the local people who they loved. However, their presence would not be tolerated.

That very night a gang of about twenty "pseudo squatters" came undercover of darkness and forced a woman employee at the mission to lead them to the homesteads. They entered the first home and killed the occupants with axes. Then they moved to the next house and repeated their ghastly act. They tied the hands of the men, women and children behind their backs and then one by one axed them to death. A young six-year old lad managed to wriggle from their grasp and scramble out of a window and run for his life into the wild dark bush. His baby brother just six weeks old had his head bashed in against the kitchen sink. Hazel was axed but her young daughter also managed to escape into the darkness. One by one our friends were killed including another baby. Only the two children survived who fled into the Matobo hills where they spent the rest of the night in utter terror. When the authorities came in the morning they found the gruesome, grizzly evidence. One homestead had been totally gutted by fire leaving only unrecognisable charred human remains but in the other home bits of flesh and hair, congealed blood and beheaded corpses remained. Thirteen Zimbabweans, two Americans and a Briton had given their lives to bring reconciliation in a beautiful land. The perpetrators left behind a sinister letter telling all people of *"Western and capitalist orientation"* to leave the land.

Yet something very strange happened that night. The woman who was forced to show the way spoke of it afterwards. As the awful deed was committed she was outside and witnessed a very strange thing. She saw what appeared to be a large glowing star descend from a cloud and land in front of the house. It lit the lawn and garden with an aura of light and lingered for a while. She was adamant about what she saw. What did it mean? Was it another exploding meteorite? But there was no noise. Was it a shinning messenger?

We drove to Bulawayo to attend the funeral of our friends. It certainly was the *"Place of Slaughter"*. The service was held in the city hall. Our missionary friends were well respected and a large crowd had gathered and people spilled onto the streets. An air of solemnity rested upon the proceedings and conveyed the awful price of martyrdom. The sombre atmosphere expressed the depths of horror the people of Matabeleland felt at this latest atrocity and somehow we knew that there was more to this than met the eye. Many people believed that so called "dissident activity" had been perpetrated by elements within the regime so as to crush the Matabele people. The Community of Reconciliation was now wiped out. They had given their lives to bring reconciliation to Zimbabwe and in a way represented the sacrificial attitude of many Africans and whites. They had perished and our hearts were broken. Why had it happened? No one seemed to know.

The leader of the mission and only survivor was overseas at the time but returned to a community that was annihilated. He was utterly devastated. He met with local administrators, district governors, local MPs and even went to the Vice-President to get help to resolve the problem of the squatters. No one helped him. Having exhausting all human agencies he spent much time in prayer. From it he gained a distinct impression that things would reach a climax in *"ten years"*. He shared this with many church leaders but his words were discounted and I became concerned by the apparent lack of understanding. In hindsight he obviously realised something most people did not. He could see the way things were going. President Mugabe appeared on national TV to say that the perpetrators of the crime would be brought to justice. He described the act as one of unbridled savagery. Of the missionaries he said *"their tragic death in defenceless circumstances must move the heart of every peace-loving Zimbabwean."* It did not take long to catch them for the murders had been carried out by known thugs. They were arrested and brought to trial, found guilty and in keeping with Zimbabwe law sentenced to death.

As mentioned the 5th Brigade had subjected the Matabele people to heinous crimes to force them to join the ruling party. The aim was to establish a one party state. In fact shortly after this massacre the ruling party comprised mostly of Shona people and the opposition party comprised mostly of Matabele resolved their differences on paper at least. On December the 22nd Nkomo signed what was called the "Unity Accord" which joined the two parties. A big thing was made of Mugabe's and Nkomo's "reconciliation" but Nkomo now became a non-entity in Zimbabwe. The accord was probably considered by Nkomo as the only way to stop the persecution of his people. The massacre of the farmers may have been the final straw. The Matabele were a proud and dignified people and although they endured great persecution the injustice and horror of the massacres seemed to break their resolution. With Nkomo's capitulation Zimbabwe became a "de facto" one party state. In his book "The Story of My Life" Nkomo, considered by many to be the Father of Nationalism in Zimbabwe, wrote how he wept when he saw what the country had become and denounced it as being totally undemocratic. However, Mugabe said he wanted to be Life-President and everyone rejoiced, outwardly anyway. He also passed an amnesty that pardoned people who had committed crimes. It was his grand show of reconciliation. Political detainees were released and the barbaric murderers of the missionaries were among them and they returned to the scene of their crime. The significance of this was not missed by people for it seemed that to kill whites for land was quite acceptable. Was this justice, we wondered? It seemed our world had turned upside down, good was punished and evil triumphed. Over the years political thugs received Presidential amnesty. ***Exactly ten years to the day*** into the future the appalling consequences of this policy bore fruit when Mugabe unleashed upon defenceless white farmers and their African staff his paramilitary "war veterans" who killed and brutalised many who were on farms.

In the meanwhile the Ethiopian leader, Col. Mengistu Haile Mariam, had fled to Zimbabwe. Wanted by his country for mass murder he not only found sanctuary but was afforded State protection at a luxury home in an upmarket Harare suburb. I used to visit an Ethiopian family that lived directly behind his house and they expressed outrage at his presence. Armed guards patrolled his residence and escorted him wherever he went. He was sentenced to death in Ethiopia for his crimes and an attempt by Ethiopian secret agents to apprehend him failed and he continued to live in luxury in Zimbabwe.

A War Veteran who served his Land

Second World War veteran Des was a member of our congregation. He was known as "Ginger" in the famous "Great Escape" of Allied Prisoners of War from a Nazi POW camp during the Second World War. Des was a British bomber pilot shot down over Europe and incarcerated. He was one of the leaders who planned the daring tunnel escape and was in fact number thirteen out of the tunnel. No one else wanted to take number thirteen so Des claimed it. Seventy-six men got out but seventy-three were recaptured of whom Hitler ordered fifty to be executed. Des was number nine on the execution list but was not executed as he was the last prisoner to be recaptured and was subsequently held by Gestapo for questioning. He was on the run in Nazi controlled Europe for over two weeks and held for many months by Gestapo and survived incredible odds. After the war he embarked on a career as an air survey pilot in the Far East. He travelled extensively, was involved with mapping the border between Pakistan and India and eventually after many adventures came to Rhodesia.

He was a great inspiration. His near death experiences gave him a zest for life and his enthusiasm was contagious for he lived every minute to its fullest potential. During the bush war in Mozambique he conducted an air photographic survey of the land. One day anti-aircraft flak exploded around his plane and next thing ground to air missiles were shot at him but he managed to dodge them and flew out unharmed. It conjured up memories of his war time flights over Europe. Des kept bees and buzzed around on his scooter in his overalls, gloves and veil as he visited numerous hives. He would strap a hive to the passenger seat of his scooter and career off followed by a tail of angry bees in hot pursuit. African bees are very aggressive and dangerous. Des was kind and loved to take in the homeless, often drunks who needed a bed and time to dry out. One man who stayed with him ended up dead. He fell unconscious on the bed after drinking. The bottle of booze he had sneaked into the house slipped from his hand and the contents spilled over his body and bed. The smell of alcohol enraged an angry mass of bees that covered him and stung him to death. African bees are not to be taken lightly. We saw what they could do in just a few moments when they stung our chickens and ducks to death. They would have killed us too and our dogs had we not barricaded ourselves in our house. Our house was on a regular bee route and one day we came home to find two of our beautiful Brazilian Parrots hanging upside down in their aviary stung to death. I grew to dislike bees for I often dashed amongst swarms to rescue my parrots.

1992 - The year of the Great Drought

Mother passed away after morning coffee. They found her the next day when no response came to their frantic knocking and they broke open the door to her apartment. She grew up during a difficult time, had trained at Bulawayo Teachers' College and as a young woman set out on a lifetime of teaching. I visited her one last time and sat on her bed where she lay still and cold and I wept. She had given her life in service to others. Many others yielded lives that year of 1992 the year of the great drought the worst in living memory. Thousands of animals died and people also died, the young and under nourished and the old and infirm.

Shortly after the great drought we visited Gona-re-zhou National Park in the lowveld, a vast and lonely place situated in the south-east of the country. This area was hit by drought but the lions had grown fat and we found a couple of big males feeding on a dead giraffe. It seems in times of trouble the fat cats always prosper. We pitched our tent under massive branches of an ancient Umgusi tree (Teak) growing on the banks of the Lundi River one of the truly great rivers of Africa. There were glades of magnificent Teak, Jackalberry, Sausage and Mahogany trees. I walked along the river banks and counted where the buffalo had died. They had come for water only to collapse at the last few stagnant pools that had turned bad. Bleached skeletons lay at every turn. The drought had now broken and as I walked quietly along the tangled, boulder-strewn river bank a pair of graceful Klipspringer stood like statues on a boulder gazing intently into the undergrowth. I knew that Klipspringer, like other antelope, will not run away when they see danger. These stood statue-still peering intently at something they could see and I could not. I followed their gaze searching the tangle bush but saw nothing. I looked back at the Klipspringers and they had not moved. I searched again trying to see what they could see. Then it moved, lithely slipping through an opening in the grass and gracefully gliding towards me like sprung steel waiting to unleash pent-up power, a magnificent leopard. The Klipspringers sprung away, the big cat melted into the bush and the scene returned to peace. I was left alone and yet all around me was my motherland.

Mother died that year. Despite everything her life had been triumphant. She had laboured for years as a schoolteacher sacrificing luxury in her commitment to educate underprivileged children. She had travelled widely and lived in isolated places. When Rhodesia declared independence she decided she would seek new pastures. She did not support white supremacy but at the same time frowned upon people who had "glib pronouncements of sanctimonious rubbish", as she put it, about solutions for Rhodesia especially outsiders who had never lived in the country or those who gave advice from afar. She had no time for hollow words from those who had never experienced the daily challenge of the country and were unwilling to get their hands dirty. Yet she had served well in difficult times and gave her life to educate under privileged children and often volunteered for remote posts not wanted by others. She taught in Zambia and also Swaziland. She eventually moved to UK but her hankering to travel got the better of her and she left for Australia. She travelled overland from UK through Europe to the Middle East and on through Turkey, Syria, Jordan, Iraq, Iran and Afghanistan, then by small aircraft to India and on to Thailand, Hong Kong and Japan. From there she caught a boat across the Pacific to New Guinea and eventually Australia. She ended up in the Northern Territory where she taught Aborigine children. When Zimbabwe attained Independence she returned to a post in Harare. After several years she finally retired but was diagnosed terminally ill and given six months to live. She did not tell a soul. She just carried on, for another four years. One day she made herself a cup of coffee, lay down in the morning and died. She was a brave woman but as I sat bedside her I knew we had never bonded. I could not reproach her. In our broken home we had never bonded right from my childhood.

South Africa's Independence

The 1980s and 90s were strange years for us. We had ringside seats on developments in South Africa and watched as the country spiralled into urban violence and became ungovernable. Finally the white government released Nelson Mandela and things moved towards the first South African democratic election. At this time the civil war in Mozambique dragged to an end. Not only had people died but animals. Wildlife in the Gorongoza Game Reserve at one time one of the prime areas in Africa was reduced to seventeen spooked zebra, a mere handful of terrified elephant and two nomadic lions that somehow survived the carnage unleashed by automatic weapons. Thousands of hippos were dead as was almost everything else.

In 1994 South Africa held elections and a miracle came about. South Africa attained majority rule. We sat enthralled at events but we noticed something disturbing. Our own President's stance towards whites became openly aggressive. With the threat from the white regime in South Africa removed his mask began to slip. Whites could do nothing right. They were the cause of all the problems in Africa and were the "enemies of the State" he would rant and rage. Perhaps he felt he had been eclipsed by South African statesman Nelson Mandela and was determined to make a come back even if it was a bad one. Where Mandela offered reconciliation Mugabe offered war. He had been centre stage ever since

Zimbabwe Independence and travelled the world, even dined with the Queen of Britain but his long act was becoming tiresome. Back home his people were not happy. He had lost popularity and his answer was to blame the whites.

We swam the Zambezi River

To fulfil my youthful dream of canoeing Kariba Gorge I conducted canoeing tours with small groups on the Zambezi through the gorge to Mana Pools National Park. The river was full of massive crocs. They sunbathed on rocks in the gorge and seldom even moved as we slipped by. The current was fast and there were whirlpools which made canoeing dangerous. The Kariba Gorge is a beautiful bit of African real estate. The setting is majestic. Steep cliffs rise in weathered rocks that reach down to the water's edge and one can see rock layers with twisted folds of extraordinary geological formations covered in tangled vegetation. Bird songs echo across the gorge and are amplified by the narrow cliffs.

There was a hippo that lived on the lower stretch of river and was notorious for his bad behaviour. "Bad tempered Harry" was his title and he often charged unsuspecting canoeists. Harry took umbrage when canoes trespassed on his section of river and one of our canoes had a close encounter with him. When Alan and Shane came drifting nonchalantly along Harry lurched out of the water and came at them with his mouth open and a wicked leer on his face. Alan and Shane soon realised that they could not out pace him and took the only other reasonable course open to them, they abandoned ship, dived into the water and swam to the bank fortunately quite close. The momentum of diving off the canoe propelled it backwards towards Harry but fortunately the current swept the canoe away from his awful jaws. We recovered the canoe and Alan and Shane survived unharmed. Many people have been killed by these powerful creatures. They can bite a dugout in half and can do the same to a person. They have twelve huge ivory tusks that are the most lethal in the world.

Crocs were also dangerous! Years ago a man came into the museum where I worked. Rankin was his name and he was minus an arm and a leg and a whole lot of fingers too. He had fallen asleep on the banks of the Zambezi and a croc had grabbed him and dragged him in. He yelled to his faithful camp guard who jumped in after him and somehow beat the croc off and hauled him out, an act of great courage that saved his life. Martin Olds, a white Zimbabwean did the same and was awarded the highest civilian award for bravery when he too jumped into the Zambezi and pulled a man from the jaws of a huge crocodile. The medal was pinned on his chest by none other than President Mugabe.

During our river trips we often got close to crocs. It was always a worry as to how they might react. They are cunning and take advantage of an easy kill. They have occasionally taken people right out of canoes. A terrible incident occurred on the Zambezi when a young woman was snatched from a canoe and never recovered. On one trip on the Zambezi we took a narrow side channel only to find a hippo had died there and its bloated body floated in the centre. As we approached we were alarmed to see that the channel was full of crocs that had gathered in a feeding frenzy tearing at the great beast. It seemed we were floating straight into the jaws of death. As we got nearer they sank beneath the surface but it was an eerie feeling as we floated just a few inches above so many huge monsters. We could have easily been attacked and if capsized would have been instantly torn to shreds and it was with relief that we made it through. Another time I was quietly drifting beneath the steep sides of Kariba Gorge when a sound like an avalanche erupted above me. It was a most unusual sound as if a large sack of boulders was being dragged down the cliff. As rocks fell around me I thought it was a landslide but all of a sudden a massive crocodile flung itself from above me and arched in a graceful dive plunged into the river just a few meters away. It was a stunning sight and a near miss for if it had landed on me I would still be in the river.

In 1994 my long time friend Phil and I canoed the Zambezi. Phil's grown son Steve and his friend accompanied us and we set off from Chirundu Bridge in two canoes. On this stretch of river there were hundreds of hippos and due to there being people living on the Zambian bank most of them gathered during the day on the Zimbabwe side of the river. The result was that we found ourselves increasingly in danger of colliding with hippo and were gradually pushed into the main stream of the current to get away from them. We continued for several miles to a place where the river takes a turn and is very wide. It was here that a strong wind suddenly caused choppy waves to rise and quickly flood our canoes. The result was catastrophic. Within a short time the canoes capsized and were swept down stream. We found ourselves treading water in the middle of the river with the bank about five hundred metres away. Knowing Phil was not a good swimmer I asked him whether he thought he could make it. His reply was truthful but frightening, "no chance" he said. I knew there was little chance for me either. Scenes from Tarzan films flashed before my eyes where Tarzan out-swam the crocodiles and the realisation of just how impossible that was chilled me with fear. The river has some of the biggest monsters in Africa. As we swam the Zambezi I knew we could not make it without a miracle. We were looking at almost certain death either by drowning or by crocs. Although the two youngsters were swimming strongly Phil was not and neither was I. There was one desperate thought going through my mind apart from the nagging terror of being snatched by a crocodile and that was that I did not want to survive if Phil or the others perished. I had recently heard of the dreadful snatching of a safari operator by a crocodile near that very place. He was guiding a canoe safari and had waded in knee deep to secure a drifting canoe. They never found his body.

The river was full from bank to bank and the current powerful. However, the river is not as deep as it used to be for it is gradually silting up. It made me think of those words sung by Rhodesians during the war years that they would fight "until the Zambezi ran dry" and I kind of wished it would right then. They were stirring words but misguided. Phil began to flounder, bobbing along gulping for breath and I was getting tired. We needed a miracle otherwise we were finished. Then it happened. Unexpectedly Steve, a tall man, found a spot where he was able to stand on the river bed. He called to us and with some effort we pulled and pushed each other to where he stood braced against the strong current. Catching our breath with our chins just above water we stood for a while in the middle of the river. Then we walked in the Zambezi as Steve led us along the top of an underwater sand bank until it came out on a small muddy island where there were fresh tracks left by a basking crocodile. I sank in shock and collapsed. Baptism in the waters of Africa was one thing but this was a bit much. I had just about swallowed the whole river.

After a while we recovered and as we looked around grasped the seriousness of our situation. It was getting late with the sun sinking in the west. The river was rising and the thought of spending a night on the mud with nothing to defend ourselves was a frightening prospect. "What should we do?" we wondered. Phil was a clergyman and prayed "Lord send us a speedboat". I was not impressed and thought to myself he should pray realistically as boats are prohibited on that section of the river. Far away on the Zambian side we saw a solitary figure in a dugout who was attempting to paddle to us and I put my faith in him but after a long time he had made little headway against the current. Then we heard the unmistakable drone of engines and around a bend in the river came not one but two boats at full speed. This was unexpected to say the least. As they got near to us they throttled back and chugged to our island. We could hardly contain our joy. "What made them come?" A few miles down stream on the Zambian side was a safari camp and the staff had seen some of our gear float past and alerted the manager. She in turn drove along a track on the bank of the river to find out what had happened and saw us through her binoculars marooned on the muddy island. She radioed to another camp some miles up stream to send the boats even though it violated the law. We felt it was a miracle. It was croc feeding season and I think the only reason we were not taken is that none of them saw us capsize. Only a few months before a similar incident had ended in tragedy with the tour leader savaged by a croc and the rest of the group fending off another massive croc that attacked them when they too had been marooned in the middle of the river.

We jumped aboard one of the boats while the other went off to recover our equipment. The boat took us to the Zambian bank where our benefactor met us with a string of suitable but unprintable vocabulary expressing her pleasure at our rescue and we sat down at a table laid out with white cloth and refreshments. It was like a banquet. The events and setting all seemed surreal. One moment we were struggling for our lives, next we were sitting down to wine and dine. The doves cooed in the background. From a watery grave and crocodile food we were treated as VIPs. Such are the contrasts of Africa.

Open season on farmers

As the one hundredth anniversary of the 1896 rebellion or *"chimurenga"* as it was called drew nearer there was a noticeable increase in government rhetoric about the dreadful things white settlers had done when they occupied the land. A professor from Zimbabwe University expounded about them on TV and local magazines contained articles about them. Spokesmen for the war veterans became vocal in expressing their dissatisfaction at the lack of progress government had made towards giving land to the "landless peasants" and they threatened to go back to war and start yet another *"chimurenga"*. Politicians gave speeches and it became fairly obvious to us that pay back time was coming. Whites began to once more feel on edge.

We had numerous farming friends. One farm was where Tim and Di lived north of Harare. Tim had worked hard all his life. He started as an apprentice, worked up to farm manager and shortly after Independence had purchased a medium size farm. He lived in an old homestead and worked even harder. He established a thriving business and after many years eventually built his family a new home. It was their pride and joy. He constructed a dam, sank boreholes and constructed new houses for his workers. He was a proficient farmer who grew food crops but refused to grow tobacco. We often went there on weekends and he proudly took us around the farm. A conservationist at heart he protected the soil and woodland from erosion and fires. He was one of numerous commercial farmers in the district who funded a local orphanage that also had a hospital to care for abandoned babies with HIV. They established a non-denominational church, a school and a clinic and every year sent tractors to plough the fields of neighbouring African farmers.

We liked to go to the farm and walk through his lands and admire the rainbows glistening in the spray from irrigation sprinklers. To see the beautiful stands of maize with long tassels and huge cobs gave one a sense of well being. This was food for the nation. The soft rhythmic sound of sprinklers, doves cooing and guinea fowl scratching on the fringes of the fields made it all so peaceful. The peace was not to last. The commercial farmlands became a war zone. Tim and Di like many others lost everything.

As economic conditions worsened more people departed, professionals and younger people. Whites left the country and those who remained were often old and tired people confused as to what was happening. They could not understand when visitors said "How cheap everything was." They barely lived on dwindling pensions eroded by galloping inflation. Local people could not even afford to buy sufficient food. Intimidation and violence occurred with beatings and house breakings, car thefts, hijackings, rape and murders. Sometimes people were followed home and attacked at their gates. Gangs arrived at homes posing as police officers or meter readers and demanded access to the houses which they then ransacked.

Some officials sent out a message that whites were vermin and deserved any abuse that came their way. There were numerous incidents. A couple we knew rented a small cottage on a plot near town. In the middle of the night the wife awoke to the sounds of a scuffle. She arose and went into the sitting room where she found her husband in a life and death struggle with an intruder who was entirely naked and had oiled his body so that it was impossible for anyone to hold him. The intruder was squeezing the life out of her husband and he was down on his knees unable to breath. With the strength of desperation she grabbed something and hit him across the head loosening his grip. Her husband began to gulp for air and she continued to hit the man with all the fury she could muster and he made a run for it. She saved her husband's life. A newly widowed friend of ours with two sons, one about fifteen and the other about twelve, were attacked by two club wielding intruders. The three of them also miraculously managed to beat them off. The last I heard involved an elderly couple who were attacked by a gang of five men. The gang stole valuables, viciously beat and tied up the couple and then gang raped the woman. I became more vigilant about our home security.

Rampaging mobs of protestors became fairly regular and we became adept at avoiding them whenever we saw them. They often comprised government supporters, warvets or youth groups, and they moved through the streets shouting and singing war songs and carrying weapons of various kinds; chains, clubs, sticks, even knives and hatchets. People caught in their path were whipped, beaten, clubbed. Peaceful marches by anti-government demonstrators, university students, NGOs or unions turned violent because of the appearance of violent counter demonstrators. As soon as we saw a crowd we swung down an alley or side road to escape. We did the same when we saw a police road block for they were best avoided if possible. It was nerve racking and frightening.

Murdered while in Prayer

A colleague of mine who was minister in a local church resorted often to a quiet spot at Cleveland Dam a few miles out of Harare where I too used to go. The setting was conducive for quiet meditation among beautiful picturesque woodland with birds calling in the trees and ducks on the lake. It was an idyllic place for reflection. One morning my colleague went out to the lake and while quietly sitting under some trees praying two men jumped him from behind, stabbed him several times and went off with his wallet and car. He died on the spot. After that I never went back to the place for it had lost its appeal.

Meanwhile pensions dwindled to a pittance due to the collapse of the Zimbabwe dollar on world exchange rates and rampant inflation. The pensions of thousands of elderly whites were rendered totally useless. Their savings had been lost by the Zimbabwe regime. With no one to help them some ended their lives out of utter desperation. One couple died after they had spent all their money, sold all their possessions and had no food left. They were found dead on their last possession, a mattress. Others died because they could not afford medicine they needed.

Lost Hope

I spent time counselling people including some who tried to end their lives as well as those in hospital, sick or injured, the elderly, the distraught and others in trouble. I was on call twenty four hours a day and the phone rang at any time. Many people lost hope. It was a repeat of the old war days but worse. A mutual friend and I were called out in the dead of night to hospital to help a woman we knew after she tried to end her life with an overdose of drugs. Her stomach was pumped and we did what we could to care for her afterwards. On another occasion I spent a long time in the early hours of a morning persuading a lady not to end it all. There were others. International Aid and Diplomatic Missions gave financial support for political agendas yet needy Africans and whites were left struggling. The SPCA was stretched to breaking point yet received no help and the numbers of orphaned kids because of Aids multiplied.

Our Orphanage Turned Down by Government

In 1994 friends of ours returned to Zimbabwe from UK to start an orphanage. Years before when they were members in my congregation they sold their farm and entered mission work. It was in the middle of the war. Nevertheless, they ministered in farming areas in disregard of their own safety. After years on the front line they moved to Scotland but returned to Zimbabwe after assurances were given by government officials that they were welcome. Our friends had a plan to build an orphanage for the increasing numbers of Aids orphans and asked me to help set up the mission. At the time the Zimbabwe government had appealed for international help to cope with growing numbers of orphans. In some communities, especially on main trucking routes, it was said over 90% of pregnant women were HIV positive. Large numbers of orphans lived on the streets or in the bush. Our friend had financial backing in UK as well as millions of dollars worth of his own equipment. The major contribution, however, was his remarkable skills for he was a master builder and experienced farmer. He obtained support from local churches and the Mudzi council allocated land next to a beautiful dam. The orphanage would include a school, a clinic and home for the aged, all part of a training farm where young people could learn trades such as building, carpentry, livestock and crop farming. Not only was there great need to care for orphans but also a pressing need to train farmers. An exhaustive process of negotiations ensued as we waded through all the red tape required. Endless interviews were held, forms filled in and fees paid. Government certainly did not make it easy.

Eventually after many months government turned down the application. Another application was submitted and we waited. It was turned down. A third was put in and the reply came back again, a flat "no". He had an interview with the authorities to enquire why. The answer he got? "We do not have to tell you why we do not want you." One wonders why his application was refused. Was it because they could not control the money coming in? Did they want a bribe? There is still no orphanage at Mudzi despite the local MP promising government would build one.

National disasters

Buses in Zimbabwe were known as "Travelling Coffins" or "National Disasters" for they were involved in serious accidents resulting in the deaths of hundreds of people. Not only were drivers reckless and even drunk but vehicles were poorly maintained and overloaded. The speed limit was ignored and tyres, brakes and steering on most buses not maintained. There were major accidents, often as buses approached a curve or steep incline at a bridge. The speeding vehicle would career off the bridge spilling people, chickens, wardrobes, grain and everything on it for they were invariably loaded with furniture, bicycles, animals, suitcases, sacks and everything else imaginable. Sometimes a really bad "National Disaster" involved two buses in a head on collision. This could result in the deaths of up to a hundred people at one time. It required great ineptitude and gross negligence to cause such accidents. These accidents were proclaimed "National Disasters" and occurred on a regular basis with the State promising to pay large sums of money to victims and families. I listened to a speech from the Minister of Transport who promised to stop the carnage on the roads and thought to myself "Who are you fooling?" It would require administration and discipline beyond the capabilities of the nation. The only answer was to keep a sharp eye open for approaching buses either coming towards one or speeding up behind one. They would crab along the road at reckless speed and if one did not get off the road one could be pushed off with a sideways swipe.

Extraterrestrials

ETs were also a sight to behold. In Zimbabwe ETs were not extraterrestrials. They were "Emergency Taxis" and believe me it had to be an emergency for anyone to travel in them. They were often ancient Peugeots or minibuses and were held together with bits of wire and always packed tight with numerous bodies and loaded high with *"katunda"* (luggage) on the roof. They contributed towards keeping the population down for when they hit something the kill rate was very high. The highest death toll that I heard of in an ET accident was twenty two people. In the latter years of the nineties there was a visit from real extraterrestrials or so it was claimed. A small private school in the county side at Ruwa catered mostly for children of white farmers. One morning almost the entire school looked out of their classroom windows and saw a bright "space ship" hovering near the playing fields. It landed in a patch of tall grass in an overgrown field. Children on tea break and some adults approached closer to try and see it better. After a while it silently flew off. We travelled to the school and spoke to both teachers and administrators and viewed drawings many of the children had made of it. The incident was reported in newspapers. What had they seen? They had definitely seen something? Was it an elaborate hoax, or mass hallucination, or was it yet another omen of some kind?

A Funeral

My friend Kebu was an extraordinary man. A sincere Christian he withstood great adversity and persecution. Back in the 1980s he lost his house when political thugs went on the rampage and destroyed it. That was shortly after Independence when the country was experiencing a political purging and people were killed. They came for him one night and hauled him away for interrogation. He was a local Church minister and considered a "sell out." After beating him and verbally abusing him they took him outside and told him to sit on the ground with his legs straight in front. They surrounded him and wanted to execute him by chopping his feet off but as he sat there like a lamb about to be slaughtered no one could strike the first blow.

Kebu did extraordinary things. On one occasion he went to Mozambique to preach. Unlike western evangelists who flew in with all their modern conveniences he walked many miles to reach people in need. He went into some of the most isolated and poverty stricken areas of the nation. Mozambique was ravaged by civil war as well as severe drought and the people were starving. On a bush track he found two women. One seemed dead, the other sat beside her companion weeping. The older one had collapsed of exhaustion and hunger and seemingly had expired on the side of the road. Kebu prayed for her. Shortly after this the "dead" woman stirred and opened her eyes. "Well," people may say, "she wasn't dead after all." According to Kebu she certainly looked dead. He went to the village and told the people to go back and help the women. They found both women alive and walking on the path. The younger woman told the amazing account of how the older woman had revived and the impact of it opened the way for Kebu to minister widely in Mozambique and without any support or aid from abroad he helped numerous people. He had a simple faith and as far as he was concerned if it was in the Bible it was true. Many times he prayed for sick or dying people and saw them recover, people who had no doctors, hospitals or medicine.

I attended the funeral of Kebu's grown up child. The results of the great drought were long and severe and there had been many funerals. The 1990s were difficult for most people. He phoned me to tell me his daughter had suddenly died. She was rushed to hospital in the morning with a headache and was dead in the afternoon. Even his prayers had not helped. They were going to bury her, would I come to the funeral? "Yes, of course," I replied. I was the only white person among hundreds of Africans. From early morning people steadily arrived, on buses, bicycles and cars, old and young from far and wide. It was like a carnival as brothers and sisters, uncles and aunts met after long separation. Their greetings were mixed with sadness yet they rejoiced in victory, the victory that simple faith has in the midst of sorrow. Speaker after speaker rose to testify about her life. Her mother's name, Faith, symbolised the faith of her parents. We wept and laughed and wept again. At last it seemed all that could be said was said and the afternoon was almost through. It was time to go. Then unexpectedly, from the very back arose an aged man who began to softly speak as he slowly made his way through the crowd, stepping over people spread-eagled on the floor. He was withered and grey. How many seasons had he seen, I wondered? He himself could not remember he said, but he could remember the day he first believed in God's grace. He called his wife forward and she came and stood by his side. I looked at them and concluded they were in reality Abraham and Sarah. They stood as giants among these pilgrims. His words did not come from eloquence learnt in classrooms or university but from years of experience, adversity and trial. He told of his conversion and how he had been ostracised by the community and how the *"ngangas"* had put spells on him all to no avail. His life was nearly over he said, soon he and his wife would join their granddaughter but even in the midst of death he exhorted his family to choose a life of faith. That day I heard the voice of an African patriarch. This was no mere Sunday sermon preached to tickle the ears of those who came for an hour or so. This was the valedictory message of a man and a woman who had followed their chosen path no matter what obstacles or difficulties stood in their way. I will never forget it. People who have not worked with African Christians can not imagine what many have endured.

Omens and Signs

We had strange things happen as we approached the new millennium and the country slid towards disaster. I tried to cautiously warn about world developments and local trends and hired hotel conference halls for public meetings. On one occasion I spoke in a well known Harare hotel. During a session it was claimed by people present that a glowing light became visible as I spoke. It had no apparent source and remained behind me throughout the entire evening. A similar event was repeated in another gathering. During one talk suddenly and without warning an alarm sounded over the microphone. After a while it stopped but it certainly caught the attention of everyone present. At another place this time in the northern farming area where I was speaking the local minister opened in prayer. As he spoke over the public address system a voice interrupted him. It happened so unexpectedly that the words were hard to capture but I and others heard the message. *"Get ready, a great explosion is coming,"* said a strange unearthly voice. The church technicians examined the electronic system but there was no explanation of how it happened. One person commented that it was like "a time warp and came straight out of the air." Electronic voice messages are known phenomena and have been heard by people. How it happened I cannot say but everybody in the congregation heard it! It was significant that soon after this incident State sponsored violence plunged the whole area into chaos. Farms were invaded, homes trashed and farmers and their workers fled for their lives. I felt like a lone voice trying to warn of impending disaster while some church ministers urged farmers to stay on their farms, with disastrous consequences.

At about this time we had another strange omen. We were sitting at home one evening when a foul, pungent smell permeated the room. It was the smell of smoke, mixed with sweat, unwashed clothes, and dirty flesh. It was the unmistakable smell that accompanies people who have not washed for weeks. Cautiously I checked our home to see if there was an intruder. However, despite the odour there was no one. After a while the smell departed but the strange incident unsettled us. What would happen next?

An Accident and threat of jail

I had an accident. A schoolchild ran across the road straight in front of my vehicle. My brakes and reflexes were good and that together with her suitcase which absorbed the blow saved her from serious injury. I had to report to the local police station to make a statement and give my details. The police had run out of forms so a young constable took everything down in longhand on a sheet of scrap paper. I thought nothing of it until three months later when an official letter came in the post saying that because I had not reported the accident I was going to be charged and must report that very day at the main Police station or else my absence would be an admission of guilt. It came as a shock. Immediately I went back to my local police station and asked to speak to the member in charge. He was not in and so I waited. Eventually late in the afternoon he strolled in and I asked to see him straight away and explained about my accident and that I had reported it on such and such a date. He thought for a moment and recalled there were no forms at that time and was not surprised the report went missing. Then he said in a serious tone that he knew the police woman in charge of prosecutions at the main station and that she was a real hardliner and law unto herself. However he said he would write me a letter but I had to get it to her that very afternoon. This was when there were still reasonably professional policemen and he was most helpful. He scrawled out some sentences on an official letterhead and wished me luck and I raced to the main police station arriving there a few minutes before the closing of the traffic section and ran up the stairs in time to meet a stern, officious looking police woman step outside her office and lock the door. My heart sank. I stammered out that I was reporting as requested but she looked at me with absolute contempt and declared that as I was not on time she was going to send me to jail. My heart sank some more. I pleaded with her that I had a letter from the member in charge explaining that I had reported the accident. The mention of "member in charge" must have caught her attention and she hesitated. I held out the letter and she looked at it with disdain. I could see she was now fed up with the unexpected delay. With reluctance she took the letter and then let out a tirade of threats that she would nevertheless see me in jail because I was no doubt guilty anyway. She turned away and I slunk off while I was still free. Fortunately I never heard from her again and missed being charged by a second or two. At this time people were thrown in jail on trumped up charges. It was all part of state machinations to intimidate people, whites in particular. A white woman we knew was put in jail for a minor offence. Others were too. They tasted prison cuisine and accommodation and then paid heavy fines to get out and most of them had no wish to remain in the country. Believe me the Zimbabwe prisons were not an enjoyable experience in over crowded, dirty, smelly cells with no running water or toilet facilities, very little food and no bunks, blankets or clean clothes.

Lest We Forget

We went on a visit to the Eastern Districts. There is an old church at Penhalonga called St Andrews in the Field with a neglected, overgrown, forgotten pioneer graveyard and memorial to First World War dead. It was strange to think that from this unknown village in the heart of Africa people had given their lives for Britain. I read the roll call and walked among the forgotten graves in the pioneer cemetery and paused to read the epitaphs on weathered stones. These faded, corroded words gave testimony to men and women who built a nation out of wilderness. I found myself wondering about them. They had escaped the disappointment of later disillusionment, the collapse of Rhodesia and the mess of Zimbabwe. I lived in Zimbabwe for twenty two years after Independence and never heard a single word of thanks from the regime for what the British administration had done. Instead there was denigration and accusations.

We travelled from Penhalonga down a twisting gravel road and gazed at rural huts and fields. After twenty years of independence the people were poorer than ever. Villages were scattered haphazardly between great granite outcrops. Every now and then we saw a hut balancing a radio aerial - a nice lightning conductor. Then we saw a posh Mercedes parked outside a cluster of four huts - wealth, in decline, the people poorer than before and the rich richer. The *chefs* drove expensive cars but there was no medicine in the clinics. A bus approached in a cloud of dust and flying stones, another "national disaster" in the making and we hastened to pull aside.

HIV - AIDS

HIV was first evident in Zimbabwe in the early eighties. No one realised to what proportions it would grow but people began to die. After a while surveys were done and conferences held with endless discussions and recommendations. People continued to die. Slowly the truth became evident, large numbers of Zimbabweans were HIV positive. We noticed that young Europeans came to Africa and some were sleeping with locals. It seemed to be a sort of sex tourism and we knew that many of them were going back home with HIV. The plague ran rampant through the population. Some communities had large infections. The army was said to be 75% positive. Hospital visitation became a pitiful event. Young and old lay dying, without hope. The most pitiful were the young. One teenage girl will always haunt my mind as she lay weak, thin and ravaged by the killer virus, her sunken eyes filled with resignation as she approached death.

My wife was in the habit of getting up early in the mornings and going for walks. One morning she did not return and I became worried. This was Africa, what had happened? Eventually she returned but was supporting a woman at her side. She had found her lying on the side of the road dying. She was a young woman in her early twenties but was thin and weak. We got her warmed up with hot tea and food. Leah, our wonderful house keeper, came and prayed for the woman and she seemed to gain strength. We got her into our car and took her to hospital. I will never forget the dignity of this young woman when she reached hospital. She summoned all her resolve, took a deep breath, and walked unaided through the doors of what had once been the finest hospital in Central Africa. Hospitals in Zimbabwe had by this time collapsed. They had no drugs, equipment was broken, linen was stolen and patients had to provide their own food. Professional care was dismal even though some doctors and nurses were dedicated. At some hospitals people died in the queue waiting for attention; so much for "free health for all" promised by government. Average life expectancy had dropped from over sixty years in Rhodesian times to about thirty five. It made me weep to see her walk into an institution that could offer her nothing. She never came out and died a few days later. At least she had a place to die and not in a roadside ditch but it probably was not much better. Thousands of others like her were dying. It was a tragedy. A bit later her old mother found us and expressed her gratitude that we had cared for her daughter. We wept all over again.

My wife stopped going for walks when she was accosted by a young man who threatened to rape her. She was alone but fortunately he ran off when some people appeared near by. *"Ngangas"* advocated that men with HIV only needed to have sex with a white woman to be cured. Better still if she was a virgin the cure was certain. Rape became a means to be healed. Such are the ways of Africa.

I was called by one of my staff to a road accident. A pedestrian had been knocked down by a bus which had not stopped and he was left lying on the road for over an hour as police and ambulance had failed to respond. The police station was only a few hundred yards away! Fortunately for him he was in a semi-conscious state of "blotto" and felt no pain. His leg was buckled in a position that not even an India-rubber man would achieve and bone protruded. We carefully lifted him into the back of my truck and took him to casualty. On arrival I walked past a long line of people in various stages of misery and went in to speak to the sister in charge to tell her about the man who needed urgent attention.

"He will get the same attention as everyone else" she said with an air of exasperation.

I looked around at the treatment others were getting and felt sick myself. I was shocked to see how badly things had deteriorated. The hospital was filthy, beds were broken and patients lay in the corridors. People were dying through lack of medicines and others were dying of ineptitude. The funeral operators were swamped and could not cope. Unclaimed bodies were left in the morgue because families could not afford to claim them. They were taken away and buried in mass graves. Yet the government got huge amounts of overseas aid. Where was it going was the question? Heaven help you if you got sick in Zimbabwe, no one else will.

Talk of War

Car hijacking became a real threat. My wife's daughter had bought a vehicle. Unfortunately it was a model that others also wanted. One night she was on her way home along a main road in Harare when a taxi pulled in front of her and hemmed her in. Two men jumped out and attacked her from both sides. One forced open the driver's door and tried to grab the keys and haul her from her seat. She wedged her knee against the keys and fought with all her strength. She managed to push him away and then wrenched the door from his hands and slammed it against him eventually causing him to let go whereupon she put her foot on the accelerator and miraculously got away. Examining the door when she got home she found it covered in blood and was shocked at her desperate reserves of strength that repelled the attack.

Leah was a wonderful woman in every way. She was our housekeeper but more important she was our friend. She shared with us her fears for the future and we had long talks. She, like so many others, was afraid yet brave. She told us about the mood of the people and of the national revulsion growing against Mugabe and his cohorts. Opposition was building against him but the Generals who controlled the regime and had won the Liberation War were not going to give up power. She told us of the awful repression by the police and of terrible oppression in the townships by the army and of house raids, beatings and torture. The talk was that war was coming, a war between the people and Mugabe the man hailed as saviour at the end of the Liberation War in 1980. In my observation the war had never fully stopped.

The city of Harare had an annual agriculture show which I attended and during the show the President visited and I was able to observe him close up. He was small of stature and seemed to move with a swagger. He had a small moustache that reminded me of Hitler. I wondered whether it was a deliberate attempt to emulate that man. His body guards, however, were clearly not to be messed with. They were muscular and looked deadly even in their smart grey suits.

Set up in a Drug Deal

One day in Harare I was approached by a smart looking man dressed in a grey suit. He greeted me like a long lost friend. Because of many years in missions I was known to many people. I greeted him and tried to establish whether or not I knew him. He insisted that he knew me, his name was Edward and we had met before or so he said. He asked for a lift to a private hospital called Montague Clinic. Always ready to help I agreed and as we drove along he told me he was working for the Customs Department and supplied drugs for a Doctor at the clinic. Private hospitals in Zimbabwe struggled to obtain adequate drugs due to foreign currency shortages. I stopped outside the clinic and he dashed in and reappeared in a minute to say the doctor would be right out, which I thought a little strange. The doctor soon appeared and after greeting me lifted a bulging bag into the front of the vehicle and unzipped it to expose a huge amount of money all carefully tied in bundles. My eyes widened. A quick estimate indicated that there was at least a million dollars in the bag, when a million was still worth something.

The doctor engaged Edward in conversation.

"Here is the money as you can see," he said, "but I need the rest of the consignment of drugs."

"Give me half the money" said Edward "and then I'll get the rest for you."
"No" said the doctor, "I can only pay you when I get all the drugs."
"Ok" replied Edward, "we'll go and get the rest."

The doctor zipped up the bag, politely said goodbye and departed. Edward turned to me and requested I take him a few blocks down town to where the rest of the consignment was stored. By this time I was feeling apprehensive but reluctantly agreed. Edward expressed his thanks and assured me he would make it "worth my while".

"I'll pay you ten thousand dollars" he said, "We need to help each other in Zimbabwe." I certainly needed a few extra bucks but became even more apprehensive.

"There by that big tree" he pointed and I pulled over thinking he would get out and I could leave him to his mischief. However, two large men immediately approached the car. The spokesman leaned into the cab and Edward introduced me, "This is my friend who is a church minister," he said.

The man registered no surprise as if he already knew all about me and politely greeted me. He then engaged Edward in conversation. "Where is the money?" he asked. Edward explained that payment was only possible if he could have the remaining drugs. The large man turned to me and said "If I give you the drugs you must give me your passport." He obviously implied that I was involved in the deal.

I was taken aback and explained I had nothing to do with their "business" as I did not know Edward and was only giving him a lift. The big man looked incredulous.

"I still need your passport" he said.

I realised I was caught in a transaction of black market drugs and could not get away. A heated argument followed and I became more concerned. I studied the face of the man, a large strongly built man with heavy cheeks and the tell tale touch of the "good life" in layers of fat. I concluded that these men were either gangsters or plain clothed police, or maybe both. Coldness gripped my heart at the thought that I had been set up. This man Edward, who seemed to know so much about me, was he CIO? The man leaning into my cab and speaking so confidently, was he police? The other powerfully built man standing by my window, was he a drug dealer? Either way I was in big trouble. If they were gangsters they could pull a gun on me, highjack the vehicle and abduct me. If they were police they could arrest me. If they were CIO then I was in even bigger trouble. People in Zimbabwe had been imprisoned for things they had never done. Others went missing, kidnapped and killed. I was now implicated in a crime from which I would not be able to extract myself. I had to do something and took charge of the situation.

"Look," I said to the big man, "the only way we can sort this out is for you to come with us to the hospital. When we get near you can get out and watch so that after Edward has the money you can straight away get it from him. In this way you will be very close but not be seen by anyone."

He was not very happy but conceded to my suggestion and they climbed in. Now I had three gangsters, police or CIO, in my car and I was their chauffeur. It did not look good and I had visions of spending the next five years in Chikurubi Prison, the overcrowded jail just outside Harare. Silently I prayed "Please get me out of this." We approached the clinic and I pulled over.

"Here's where you get out" I said politely. The men reluctantly disembarked. I drove to the clinic's entrance and stopped.

"Edward," I said with as firm a voice as I could muster, "this is where you get out. I cannot help you any more and I am late for my appointment. Get out."

With a look of concern he said, "But I need your help" he remonstrated, "I'll give you ten percent". Visions of tens of thousands of dollars flashed through my mind. I did not budge.

"Get out" I commanded.

Looking in the rear view mirror I saw the two men rapidly approaching. I leaned over, opened the door and with a great heave shoved Edward out and sped away as fast as I could without looking back. With a sigh of relief I promised myself never again to help any "long lost friend" in Africa.

Bobby the legless parrot

I journeyed to Zambia to visit a friend who had a farm just outside the little town of Chingola. Zambia is a well-wooded land that seems to go on endlessly. Distances are vast and as one drives along the countryside unfolds before one and closes behind with mile upon mile of sparsely populated woodland and forest. Regrettably at that time much of the wildlife had been depleted. Along the roads of Zambia are "informal butcheries" where hunters sold their wares, crudely dismembered haunches of "bush meat" in various stages of putrefaction. Anything that was edible including monkeys, antelope, rats, birds and insects hung in grotesque, macabre stances. There seemed no regard for the treasures of African nature among people who held their custody. Africa is a continent under siege by its own people. Further to the south the Kafue River flows through the Kafue National Park and there are still herds of Lechwe, Buffalo and Zebra as well as in Luangwa National Park. Remote areas still retain wildlife. The "informal sector" in Zambia is everywhere. There were "informal garages" on the side of the road that siphoned fuel out of long distance haulage trucks and sold it to motorists at reduced rates. Police road blocks almost within sight of the illegal trade did not seem to stop it. There was "informal" trade in other items, baskets, carvings, counterfeit gems, diamonds and sadly, live animals. Anything that could be sold was sold. A dozen little mole-rats hung by their feet at the side of the road. They were barely alive in the midday heat.

Bobby came from the road side. He was a Parrot. He had no feet for they were ripped off when he was caught in sticky glue smeared on a branch. When he alighted he stuck fast. His captor pulled his feet off and then Bobby went on sale in a tin cage hanging in the sun by the side of the road. My friend rescued him and I took him back to Zimbabwe as his stumps were sceptic and he needed nursing to survive. I had to smuggle him through the border. Anyone who has lived in Central Africa will be used to smuggling, not drugs but personal things. Some officials were so unreasonable that even the most innocent imports might be taxed or require a bribe. Most people had a pittance of foreign funds obtained at exorbitant rates and no extra money to pay unwarranted duty.

One had to be very careful at border posts for thieves lurked there. They knew that travellers had money on them and if one was not vigilant money and possessions were stolen from right under one's nose. A friend and I experienced this one day when thousands of dollars were stolen from us by a man who was as clever as a magician. One moment the money was there in our hand next it was gone. It disappeared before our very eyes and we did not even see him do it. When we realised it was gone we ran after him but he too was gone lost among the milling crowd, disappeared before our eyes. We once watched a man at Beit Bridge Border Post hand his papers across the counter with a bribe hidden amongst them. Quite calmly the official slipped the money into his pocket, stamped the papers and waved the man through.

One envies the birds that migrate without having the hassles of border controls. However, a stork fell foul of the authorities in Africa. It was fitted with a satellite device in South Africa so as to allow scientists to follow its migration flight north. It was caught by a tribesman in Burundi who took it to the local authorities who saw its electronic fittings and promptly "arrested" it as a spy. When news of this came to the ears of South African ornithologists they arranged for representatives to see the relevant authorities and diplomatic negotiations took a while for them to let the poor bird go.

I put little Bobby in an open basket by the front seat in the cab of the car. I also put some trash in the basket and he was covered with the rubbish of a long journey, empty tins, soiled tissues, some dirty socks, orange peel and some smelly rags. It looked convincing. We approached the border gate and the customs official stopped us and asked some questions. I made the mistake of contradicting something he said and he indicated we should pull over and get out. Rule number one, never contradict an official. He proceeded to search the car looking in every likely place, the cubby-hole, the ash tray, under the dash board, behind the seats. As he did so his face passed Bobby's open basket by inches. Bobby began to growl, the loud unmistakable grating sound of an angry parrot. I began to speak to the official, quite loudly, asking him what he was looking for, how I could help him, would he like to look in the back of the truck. The more Bobby growled the more I spoke. The official knew something was up but could not pin point what. He glanced in the basket and Bobby growled louder. I do not know why he did not hear the bird, maybe he was deaf. I had visions of being charged with illegal animal trafficking. He was determined to find something wrong and asked for my wallet. It contained a little more cash than allowed and he confiscated it and waved us through. Money always seemed to work. Bobby's stumps eventually healed and we could take him out of his cage and he would hobble across our soft carpet. He never really tamed which is not surprising after what humans had done to him. Little Jack would sneak up and sniff him and Bobby would growl and lunge with his beak but Jack never harmed him. Other injured parrots were let out in the evenings, our family of waifs; a rare Cape Parrot that was blind, a Senegal Parrot that had a gammy wing and little Poo the Lovebird who had a vicious bite.

One-Armed Bandits

Bobby with his little stumps makes me recall the awful consequences of landmines placed in the bush during the war. For years people and animals suffered when they stumbled on them. Elephants detonated mines and died slow deaths with mangled legs. People lost limbs when they stepped on them or unwittingly picked up unstable explosives. In some places the bush was full of landmines. When walking at Chirundu near the Zambezi I looked down just in time to prevent myself stumbling on a live rocket. I went cold and gingerly stepped away. While on the topic of disabled animals one could often see baboons at Kariba with missing limbs. Their disfigurement was caused by the huge power lines that carried electricity from the power plant to the rest of the country. The baboons would climb up the girders to the cables and thousands of volts would short circuit through them. This often killed them but some survived, minus a limb or two. One particular baboon was missing both an arm and a leg but still managed to make a living. These baboons were called "one armed bandits" after the local casino slot machines. There were other robbers in Kariba. Leopards would come into town and take domestic dogs, elephants used to raid the pawpaw trees and of course there were local thieves from whom one could never get away. One had to lock everything and even then it was not safe. One group of tourists canoed the Zambezi River. At sunset they pulled their canoes on to the bank and made camp. They retired to sleep and woke in the morning to find everything they had was gone except their sleeping bags in which they were sleeping. A band of robbers from Zambia had seen them and under cover of night paddled across the river and carried everything away. It was the ultimate international robbery.

Zambia was an impoverished country as we discovered when we travelled to remote areas. The people were hospitable yet one had to constantly be on the look out for thieves. One also had to have gifts as handouts to officials. We journeyed to the northern shores of Lake Kariba where the Tonga people live along the banks of the lake. Traditionally they are a fishing people and also keep a few indigenous livestock. Their primitive villages are scattered throughout the hot Mopani scrub lands and rocky hills of the Zambezi Valley. We met the old chief of this huge district. He sat on a rickety chair and we sat on stools a little lower than his as is the custom for the chief must always be higher than his subjects. It is also the custom to come into the presence of a chief with gifts and the first thing he asked for was Coca Cola. We did not have any but we did have some oranges and his aids immediately peeled several and he gulped them down. I looked at his feet with poor circulation and his almost blind eyes and came to the conclusion that he was very ill. He was unable to get the medication necessary for his ailment. In the entire area there was only one small hospital. It was built and administered by a lady missionary from UK. The land was as poor as the dark ages. We camped on the beautiful shores of the lake. Everyday the women and children set out in small bands and spent the day gathering whatever was edible. We watched them return in the evenings carrying on their heads what they had found, from bark to tortoises, berries, wild fruit, insects, lizards and bird eggs, all going into the pot. This kind of pressure damaged the ecology of the region which was already greatly suffering. The men would laze about at the lake and catch fish which formed their main diet. It was a primitive community.

The Elephants of Mana Pools National Park

During winter months at Mana Pools elephants would gather to feed on the lush flood plain of the Zambezi River. These elephants were normally quite well behaved. Tourists, however, made the mistake of thinking they were "tame" and would throw them oranges and other food. Some elephants acquired a taste for sweet things, especially oranges. This caused problems. One old bull had an addiction for oranges and everything sweet and periodically raided the tourist camp like a naughty prankster looking for sweets in a cookie jar. He pushed a car right through the bush to get at the contents, some oranges hidden under the seat. He could smell them from afar.

One night he came into our camp. He appeared out of the darkness standing on the edge of the camp light. One moment he was not there, next moment he was. We had not heard a sound. He confidently strode up to my truck where he placed his great ivory on the windscreen. There was a loaf of bread on the dash board and I could literally see him contemplating his next move which was to smash the glass. I walked quietly towards him stopping at about fifteen paces and spoke softly to him. I asked him to move along and not damage the vehicle and I was very polite. He stood statue-still as if not even breathing and listened attentively. For a moment he paused then quietly and deliberately strolled off moving methodically through the campsite to every tent and vehicle and raided the fruit, bread, biscuits, cool drinks and oranges. The campers reacted with loud shouts, banging pots and pans, and sounding hooters but it had no effect upon him and he ended up right back where he started just a few meters away from us. At this camp he uprooted the tent, squeezed the plastic cool-drink bottles and drank their contents and plucked the biscuits up after carefully peeling off the cellophane. He did not hurt anyone. A young honeymoon couple in a small one man tent right next to the elephant were either so engrossed in their own company or so terrified that they did not even peek through the flaps to see what was going on. The big bull did not harm them. Eventually a camp guard arrived with a shotgun and gave him a load of buckshot up his backside and he ambled off.

In the morning the National Parks laid an ambush for him and shot him a dozen times or more. Squealing in pain and fear he rushed around in frenzy but they got him in the end. Elephants can communicate by inaudible low frequency sounds that travel for miles but the whole park could hear his panic-stricken trumpeting as bullet after bullet plugged into him. A mile away a herd of female elephants with calves heard the commotion and became upset. The matriarch of the herd laid back her ears and charged a party of tourists who were quietly following their professional guide like chicks follow a chicken. The guide lifted his rifle and put a well placed bullet into her forehead and she dropped at his feet. What an unnecessary tragedy that two magnificent animals lay dead for no cause. After the handsome bull elephant had been cut up and his beautiful ivory tusks extracted we went to look at his remains, a heap of meat and bones and our hearts bled with his. Having been associated with National Parks in the time of Rhodesia I thought they had made some real blunders but the ineptitude of the Zimbabwe Parks was sometimes as bad. The Rangers were dedicated to their job but were so badly paid, equipped and funded that they were often unable to do their jobs. Their lack of expertise was exasperated by a department controlled by political appointees. The well-kept accommodation and equipment in National Parks and more important the safety and conservation of wild animals deteriorated and despite the dedication of rangers poaching increased. The army also shot elephants for rations. Zimbabwe boasted large numbers of elephants but some of them had migrated across the Botswana border and were not resident in the country. I remember the days when one could see herds of buffalo, elephant, sable, kudu and much more in the hills at Kariba. On my last visit I was lucky to see a few Impala.

The last time I went to Mana Pools it was wild with plenty of game and magnificent lions. I hope it still is. I accompanied the Warden to make replicas of dinosaur footprints in the rocks of a river in the Chewore Game Reserve. There were several fossilised footprints imprinted in rock. We took impressions of the tracks and spent several days camped in the bush. One night the lions came to see us. We had no tents, just stretchers placed under the stars of Africa with a little fire to cheer us. The lions started roaring early that evening and came nearer with each roar, that exhilarating, soul-tingling, awesome sound of Africa. We retired to our stretchers and lay listening until they seemed to be just beyond the flickering light of the fire. We shouted at them and told them to shove off and leave us alone and they grunted and fell silent, a sound even more awesome than their roaring. We lay in bed hardly daring to breathe. Then a nightjar sang and eased our fears.

Speaking to Animals

It is said that Francis of Assisi spoke to animals. There is a language of signs and signals with tone and action that convey meaning and are understood by animals. Threatening body language speaks volumes and conveys aggression. One's voice can carry calm or alarm. An animal picks up one's spirit. I think we all have an aura of energy that animals of all kinds can pick up. I have often spoken to animals and seen them respond. When I was a child I spoke with animals just as Mowgli had done when growing up in the jungle. I felt if he could I could too. I spoke to a hyena once when I walked along the banks of the Lundi River. Huge evergreen trees formed a canopy above me and thick tangled bush grew below. As I stepped around a clump of thickets the hyena was there just a few feet in front of me. It was badly wounded with deep gashes around face and neck and a torn foot. This sudden meeting could have been extremely dangerous as a wounded animal is unpredictable. Our eyes met and for a moment I looked within its very soul. Something passed between us and transferred from one to the other, a moment of intense empathy rarely experienced in life. There was no fear or upset from either of us, just mutual respect and almost a sense of bonding as my heart went out to the animal. Here was an animal much maligned and yet hyenas cause less suffering than other carnivores for they live mostly off animals already dead. It is true that they look ungainly and because of their diet are often dirty. Yet, this animal was a world apart from the kind of carnage we had seen perpetrated on innocent, defenceless people by men of violence. Who were the real hyenas? I spoke to it with soft tones and it listened as if it understood and then turned and dragged itself into the undergrowth. I felt it had heard at least one kind word from the human race.

Talking about hyenas reminds me of a friend who raised two that had the run of his house. He was my pal from school days and the two hyenas came to him as helpless pups. Being a sucker for small animals he and his family took them in and nursed them and they grew strong. They were cute but the bigger they got the more discipline they needed and he had to take on the role of pack leader. No one dared to come near the house and they only obeyed him and even the staff couldn't go near them. Once the hyenas got big things became serious. Not only were they chewing everything they could get their teeth into from shoes to furniture their exuberant play was too much for the children. One day he came home to find his children had taken refuge on top of the wardrobe. Then he decided to get rid of the hyenas but no one wanted them. In the end he moved them outside and they went wild and roamed the farm putting fear into all the locals.

It seemed that no matter how much care the hyenas were given they quickly reverted to their wild instincts!

Book 6

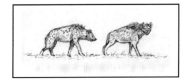

The Rage of Africa – Rape of a Nation

In Africa hyenas are viewed with superstition. It is believed that wizards ride upon them and travel through the land. Men turned mad with killer instincts now rampaged through our land of tears.

"Champupuri" - Reaping the Whirlwind

I was in Zambia flying from Chingola to Lusaka in a small six-passenger plane. On the western horizon a massive mauve wall of thunder clouds darkened the sky as a huge storm swept in from Angola. The summer rains were about to unleash all their fury and the little plane was tossed about like a balloon in the sky. We barely missed the storm and landed in Lusaka as the first gusts of rain swept in. From Lusaka I returned to Zimbabwe which was about to be lashed by a terrible storm. We drove north of Harare to visit friends and as we travelled saw in the sky a daunting omen. It was one of those incredibly turbulent African skies with swirling clouds and powerful winds twirling about with great force. In astonishment we watched a tornado whipping about like a mad snake out of control. Fortunately the tail did not touch down and after a while it vanished but something even more powerful was about to be unleashed upon us.

In Shona a whirlwind is called *"champupuri"* and is the name given to what we call "dust devils" that whisk about in dry months. They are like mini tornadoes and sweep across the ground gathering dust and leaves in whirling clouds but they are not dangerous. However, we were soon to have a real tornado hit us, a ruthless monster in all its fury, the ultimate madness, land designation, just another way of saying legalised land robbery by the warlords of destruction. Over the years we had become complacent in a third-world African de facto one party State. Like many others we had learnt how to stay out of trouble, to ignore mismanagement and to dodge people who were dangerous. Perhaps we had forgotten our painful origins as a nation born in violence; an "upside-down tree".

November 1997 – "Black Friday"

A forewarning of aggression towards farmers had been given back in 1987 when sixteen missionaries were killed and their farms taken over by squatters. However, few people had understood the significance of that event or the warning it contained. On 25th November 1997, ***exactly ten years to the day***, President Mugabe made an announcement that he was to award large amounts of money to his ex-guerrillas or so-called "warvets" in order to reward them for services in the bush war of the 1970s. This would require exorbitant expenditure which the government did not have. He also announced his plans to "appropriate" 4 million hectares of white owned farm land. This was about half the country's commercial farm land. On November 28th his government printed a list of 1503 farms amounting to 45% of Zimbabwe's prime production land that would be confiscated. This was only the start. These announcements sent shock waves into the community and undermined investor confidence but were in fact the logical outworking of what had happened exactly ten years earlier when white farmers on New Adams and Olive Tree Farms were murdered and the farms taken over by squatters.

In the early hours of the morning shortly after the President's announcement we were unable to sleep. An awesome electrical storm exploded above us. Africa is renowned for its frightening storms but this was unlike anything we had ever witnessed. Massive lightning bolts of pent up power crashed around us without let or pause. Our dogs hid under the bed and the whole planet seemed to shake. It continued without interruption for several hours as if heaven itself was at war and all the angels in conflict as two worlds clashed. The night was dark; there were no rainbows, only violent flashes of lightning. It was impossible to sleep and somehow we felt that a massive violent squabble had been unleashed within the nation. Our minds went back to the Community of Reconciliation and the words of our friend, ***"Wait ten years."*** We calculated the interval between that event and the present time and found it to be exact to the day. Was this just a coincidence? We felt something momentous was taking place. The next day the national power grid failed and the nation plunged into darkness, the Zimbabwe stock market crashed and the Zimbabwe dollar plummeted on international exchange rates. It became known as "Black Friday." The destruction of the Community of Reconciliation seemed to have been a precursor to national disaster. Any chance for national reconciliation now died not because Africans and whites did not desire it but because Mugabe slammed the doors on it. He had given in to his hardliners and chosen a path the consequences of which would be worked out to their bitter end. For years Zimbabweans had prayed for intervention in the land. It had come but not in the way we wished. Things began to move towards the outworking of years of corruption, lies, murders and genocide, all coming to fruition. The nation was ripe and the grim harvest would be bleak.

Events moved fast. We had noticed in recent years a change in the behaviour of the Zimbabwe leader had taken place. From the mid-nineties it seemed he had become outspoken and blatantly prejudiced in his speeches. He blamed all the problems in the country on Britain and the whites. This was not new, he and his officials had spoken badly of Britain before but their speeches now became sinister. Mugabe would appear on TV and his eyes would flash and his face distort in what can only be described as demonic rage. The way he changed character reminded one of a chameleon. One moment he was calm and rational, next he was raving. It was evident that he was mentally deranged, or so people said. It seemed that whites, in his thinking, were the problem for everything. He blamed *all the ills* of Africa on them. There was not a word of gratitude for what had been achieved as a British colony, the schools, the hospitals, the clinics or for the massive amount of aid money poured in after Independence. If we had not noticed before we were now to witness the strange way democracy worked in Zimbabwe; *"One man one vote, as long as it was for him."* People everywhere were tired of his ranting but because he had lulled everyone into a sense of false security the realisation that he would cling to power with such vicious tenacity caught everyone off guard. People had hoped that he would retire gracefully but he clamped down harshly on every perceived threat to his regime especially whites, black opposition, the private media and every other threat. He charged opposition parties with being white stooges as if they had no mind of their own. His ranting created more and more of a climate in which people were attacked with impunity and in the next years things deteriorated further.

An elderly couple lived on a farm in the Midlands. As a youth I had visited their home and felt their warm hospitality. They came from a well known farming family and their farm had become a beacon for the whole district. One evening the man, now old and infirm, stepped outside and walked to the gate to lock up for the night. The evening air was pleasantly cool after the heat of the day. Suddenly screams came from the house. He ran back as fast as he could and found an intruder had slipped in and was bludgeoning his wife with a metal bar. She had collapsed under the heavy blows and was attempting to shield herself and simultaneously pray for the man who beat her. He attempted to intervene but was set upon. He sustained broken bones and a terrible smashing. She died of her injuries. He ended up in hospital but recovered, if ever one can recover from such an experience. Afterwards he expressed forgiveness. Bandaged and bruised and barely able to cope he spoke at his wife's funeral and testified of her amazing faith. Such is the calibre of true saints.

2000 - The New Millennium

On New Years day 2000 there was a celebration service for residents in the Nyanga district who gathered on a hill near a place called "World's View." This was a spectacular spot for it overlooked a panoramic view with mountains on every surround and the valley stretched below for many miles. It seemed as if one could see forever. The gathering was nondenominational and people came from every faith. A rough cross was fashioned by placing a beam in the branches of a tree that grew on the edge of the precipice. Before this living cross people gathered, seated on granite rocks or folding chairs and behind the cross a great expanse revealed the "view of the world". The service started and as our song lifted unhindered to heaven it was as if our spirits expanded into limitless sky. These were the hills I loved and knew so well. Never before had I spoken in such a grand cathedral my theme being the eternal qualities of Faith, Hope and Love. Everyone was encouraged. During the service there was a strange phenomenon. A translucent light radiated beams upon the tree-cross which shimmered in sparkling rays. Was it another sign?

National Referendum - 2000

Soon after this a referendum was held for a new constitution which contained two crucial elements; land appropriation and the extension of the President's term of office. The President wanted to legitimise his land grab from white farmers and also to stay on as President indefinitely and he wanted to change the constitution to allow him to do so. The electorate expressed their dissatisfaction with a resounding *no* vote against the President. The massive rejection of the proposed constitution brought a ray of hope for change in the country. People were smiling again, talking of the future and planning for it. But it had caught the President off guard and it was not what he had wanted. He went on TV and sounded conciliatory like he sounded when he first took power. He said the people had expressed their wish and it would be adhered to. It sounded good. It reminded me of his speech in 1980 when he asked whites to stay and we all had high hopes for democracy. Had we forgotten how quickly a chameleon can change its colour? Had we forgotten how a cobra can play dead and suddenly deliver a fatal bite?

The euphoria lasted barely a few weeks. Within a short time not only had he ignored the referendum but plunged the country into an abyss of despair and bloodshed. He unleashed his secret weapon on us. In the 1980s he had crushed the Matabele with his 5th Brigade, now he would do the same to the opposition party and whites this time with his war veterans. These were so-called ex-combatants from the liberation war twenty years previous. However, to have fought in that war would require them to be at least thirty years old but many of them were just youngsters. They were led by older disgruntled men kept for this day and hour. Many genuine veterans had no part in this. The President harped on about whites being the problem. The old excuse that colonialism was the cause of all Africa's woes had become tiresome. Now it was the turn of white Zimbabwean's to be bashed. All of a sudden they had been withholding land from the majority, or so it was said. The President went on TV in one of his rages, breathing out vengeance on all his enemies; whites, the opposition party who he claimed were white puppets, and the British in that order took the brunt of his tongue lashing. Would the chameleon lash out more than just a tongue?

At Independence white Zimbabweans were asked by the President to stay and many had subsequently purchased farms which had "No Interest" certificates. This meant that the regime had officially declined first option on the farms despite millions of pounds provided by Britain for resettlement. Now the regime accused white farmers of not growing food. Some of them had diversified into flowers because food crops were no longer viable due to government controlled prices. However, flowers, beef, tobacco and other crops earned foreign currency desperately needed by the regime and therefore encouraged by it. Commercial farmers also grew the entire wheat crop and much of the maize required for the national population. Zimbabwe was one of the few African nations that had surplus food. This was entirely due to commercial farmers who had established dams and boreholes and were able to irrigate even during drought years. That they were white was not their fault, they were Zimbabwe citizens. They gainfully employed the largest segment of the national labour force. Government had instructed farmers to upgrade staff accommodation to acceptable standards. Farm wages and work conditions were legislated by law all in the name of caring for farm labourers. Many white farmers went beyond the legislation and not only helped their own workers but assisted neighbouring African farmers. They helped them with seeds and tractors to plough lands. Most farmers were not against change but wanted an open, transparent and legal way for land redistribution in a manner that would not destroy the agriculture industry established over a hundred years. Now they were about to see how the regime would do it.

April Fools Day

It was April the first. A peaceful demonstration was planned by the National Constitution Assembly, an independent body formed to advise government. A multiracial crowd of peaceful demonstrators marched through central Harare. A large contingent of riot police armed with firearms and tear gas stood nearby. All went well until an unruly rabble of so-called warvets armed with clubs, chains and other weapons appeared suddenly and letting off blood curling shrieks surged towards the demonstrators and lashed out at all and sundry. People including elderly bystanders were injured as police stood by and did nothing. When at last they took action they fired tear gas straight into the milling crowd of civilians causing even more harm. Some of our friends were beaten. It was April Fools Day and this was just the beginning.

Happy Easter - 2000

Our Easter present for the new millennium was not an Easter pageant but the real thing; the cruel beating and slaughter of farmers, the trashing and burning of their homes and farms and the beating and dispersal of tens of thousands of farm workers. These were the farms I used to visit as a minister. On April 15th a farmer and his staff were attacked by militant squatters. He farmed near Marondera in the rural parish I knew so well. Warvets burnt his barns and staff homes and he and his African manager were abducted. Five other white farmers fled to the local Police Station for protection but were forcibly removed by warvets without intervention by the police. The farmer was beaten and shot at point blank range and his manager also killed. The war cry of the seventies, "one farmer one bullet" had not been forgotten. One of the farmers was severely assaulted but his life spared through the pleas of a woman who persuaded the warvets not to kill him. Two other farmers were taken into the bush and were badly assaulted and left for dead. They lay in the bush all night until the early hours of the morning when they regained consciousness and staggered to an abandoned farm where they were able to get help. The remaining two farmers were assaulted but escaped to the hills where they were found cowering late the following day. They were lucky not to have all been killed. Images on international TV showed people so badly beaten that they could not walk or talk. The white farmer left a widow and four children. He had done much to improve the lot of his workers and community as had the other farmers. What was their crime? They were members of the opposition party. Any pretence of reconciliation was now over, the revolution was upon us. The generals behind Mugabe were not about to let anyone else into power

The Wild West

Early on the morning of 18th April, Zimbabwe Independence Day and Easter weekend, a large number of men armed with AK military rifles and amour piercing bullets surrounded the farm home of Martin Olds a farmer in Matabeleland. A two hour gun battle ensued.

Martin had won the highest civilian award for bravery in Zimbabwe, the Bronze Cross, and in an ironic coincident it had been pinned on his chest by the President himself *exactly ten years earlier* to the day. Martin was given the award in recognition of his bravery when he rescued a man from the jaws of a crocodile in the Zambezi. He was a farmer who had started a school for farm workers, supported Zimbabwe war veterans and went out of his way to help African farmers. He was highly regarded and perhaps because of this was singled out by the marauding killers. This was their way, to select the most respectable and likable person of the area and to kill him as an example to everyone else. A convoy of thirteen vehicles each loaded with armed men arrived at his farm early in the morning. The gun battle was fierce. Martin had sent his family into Bulawayo and was alone. He was wounded in both legs and while under fire managed to make a splint for his one leg which had sustained a shattered bone. He continued to fight, all the time calling for help on his mobile phone. Neighbours rallied and rushed to assist him but police threw a road block across the farm road and prohibited anyone from getting in. An ambulance came to help but was prevented from going further. His mother from a nearby farm attempted to get to him but her friends physically prevented her from going further and facing certain death. All they could do was stand by and listen to the sounds of battle until the last bullet was fired and a morbid silence settled.

What had happened? Martin had defended himself with his hunting rifle, moving from window to window. The house was set on fire with petrol and began to burn fiercely but although wounded he kept firing. At least two of his assailants were wounded but rumours were that he killed several. When he ran out of ammo he discarded his weapons and retreated to the bathroom where he attempted to keep cool by running the taps and splashing water onto the roof and ceiling hoping that help would arrive. Eventually the heat was too much and Martin crawled through the back window where he was set upon and bludgeoned to death. The killers spent hours picking up every empty ammunition case and cleaning all evidence from the site and then departed with no attempt by police to apprehend them.

A well known former liberation fighter and Zimbabwe Minister of Education who now worked for the United Nations in New York said of him when she heard of his brutal slaying that he had gone out of his way to help schools and also helped ex-combatants to establish themselves as farmers on neighbouring farms giving generously of his time and experience. It was with a sense of shock that she had heard that he had been murdered on his farm in a racist attack by purporting ex-combatants. She placed on record that this murder of one of the strongest supporters of ex-combatants should be condemned without reservation. No condemnation came from leaders either in or out of the country including the President.

His widow, a polio victim with young children fled to the UK to stay with friends. Unable to return she applied for refugee status. Her application was dismissed by British authorities. If it had not been for loyal friends who took up her cause she would have been expelled. However, her case was reviewed and eventually she was granted permission to stay. When asked by a reporter why she had been refused a government official said it was a "clerical error." Some error!

Next it was the turn of the Virginia farming district. Farmers were subjected to such battering that they could not stay on their land and moved off with the few things they could load onto trucks. Convoys of vehicles moved across the land like funeral corteges carrying pitiful belongings of fleeing families. It was as if a whole district was dying. Mines and businesses were invaded and brought to a standstill as management were held to ransom. On the 7th of May another white farmer was bludgeoned to death on his farm south of Harare as his family looked on helplessly. He was a well respected man who had done much to help the community. All over the country warvets attacked farm workers. Near Marondera thugs rampaged through farm compounds beating and killing people. The screams of their victims could be heard a mile away. We had gone right back to the days of the bush war. For years white settlers had been portrayed as rich millionaires living off the fat of land they had stolen from Africans. This was far from the truth and a very simplistic notion. Although there were some wealthy farmers most were just ordinary people trying to make a living. Many of them had purchased their farms subsequent to Independence and had to pay them off and some of them had done much to assist farm workers and neighbouring African farmers.

Following the Lancaster House Agreement in 1980 Britain provided millions of pounds for the regime to obtain farms but only the elite got them. When new Labour came to power Britain withheld further funds. By doing so Britain pulled the plug on the safety of whites in Zimbabwe for now it was made into a racist issue. Mugabe was incensed with what he saw as British double standards and he used the land issue to create a state of anarchy to serve his own purposes. It also caused hundreds of thousands of Africans to lose everything they had, their homes, livelihood and heritage.

The Third *"Chimurenga"* had begun

In the next few months over a thousand farms were invaded and pegged by squatters. Unofficial road blocks were set up in country districts and manned by so-called warvets. Violence came to our home district in Enterprise Valley, a well established farming area developed over four generations. Warvets invaded one of the most productive farms of the valley. Smoke billowed as homes were torched. The next farm, one of the most fruitful market gardens in the area was also invaded. Dogs were beaten to death, workers brutalised and homes torched. The area became a war zone. People fled in panic, some in cars, some on foot into the bush and hills. Our friends on the farm with teenage children fled for their lives. TV images of dogs being beaten to death shocked the world but what was not shown was the beating of farm workers. Another family who were our close friends and had little children barely escaped.

In towns peaceful demonstrations by Churches and opposition groups turned into violent street clashes as warvets indiscriminately attacked people. Running street battles took place as police stood by or shot tear gas into peaceful marchers. A friend of ours was so badly beaten that he had deep welts and open wounds. Others were caught and subjected to harsh lashings. Some tourists were raped. Police in riot gear took on crowds of protestors and peaceful citizens were caught in the middle. My vision in 1980 of street fighting in Harare constantly appeared before me. Things I had visualised mentally were now enacted before my eyes. Over the years we had become accustomed to dodging violence and when we saw a stamping, screaming mass of people we would slip down a side road. Shortages of bread, fuel, petrol, diesel and paraffin caused long queues. During that year there was a huge increase in the cost of living and the foreign currency black market spiralled out of control. Inflation was to go into millions of percent as the local currency completely collapsed.

The country now sank into a pit of despair. From an air of optimism only a few weeks before it changed to one of abject despondency. When it seemed that democracy could at last bring about a change in the nation the awful truth about the regime's methods hit home - nothing had changed. It was not democracy but demon-crazy. People wept openly.

The Victoria Falls Conference

Regional leaders of southern African nations met at Victoria Falls. Their agenda was the land grab and violence on farms. We sat glued to our TV and watched as they emerged from their deliberations. President Mugabe strutted around like the ruling party icon, a cockerel, and looked very pleased. Leaders of South Africa and Mozambique smiled submissively. Then we were subjected to a torrent of threats from a delegate who declared that whites should be happy that they were not all arrested as war criminals. It left us flummoxed. I knew that at the turn of the 19th century Herero people in Namibia were almost annihilated by the colonial government and that the Belgium royal regime had decimated millions of Congo people in a terrible holocaust. I knew that thousands had died on both sides during the liberation struggle, many of them combatants but I thought back on my own life to recall if I had ever beaten, tortured or murdered anyone and could not recall a single incident although I had seen ghastly things perpetrated by supporters of Mugabe. I tried to remember if I had ever seen my parents commit such crimes and definitely had not. It was after this that we lost hope that there was a place for us in Zimbabwe. If this consensus of opinion was the common mindset of regional leaders then our future was sealed. That day the flicker of hope in our future finally went out.

The Darkness Deepens

The leader of the warvets, a man called "Hitler", went on State TV to say that he was going to take away all land from whites despite what they may say or do. He said he was not afraid of the High Court and that the judges must resign for their days were numbered. He said he was telling what he and his "comrades" wanted and not what the law said. He publicly advocated the subjection of whites by every possible means. He walked around with a crazy grin on his face and a constant laugh and castigated the British, the whites, the judiciary and the parliamentary opposition, threatening dire reprisals for all those people who did not step in line with his warvets. Hitler had a dubious qualification as a doctor and had a surgery in Harare where it was said his followers took unfortunate victims and tortured them. It all seemed like a grotesque nightmare. The hyenas had come out of hiding and were laughing with fiendish madness.

Richard, my top employee, was a placid, quiet spoken man who never discussed politics. I asked him once "whether things would come right?" "Yes," he said optimistically, "they (the ruling regime) will have to listen to the people." One night political thugs caught him without a ruling party membership card and beat him so severely he staggered home with blood coming out of his ears and mouth and he died in the arms of his young wife. He left a child and tiny baby of whom he was so proud. He was an expert in his profession. Not only had I lost my top man but a wife became a widow and children lost their father. Tourism collapsed except for a few back-packers. A thriving tourist industry that had taken years to establish came to a standstill. Hotels stood empty. The Ministry of

Tourism seemed to have become a Ministry of Terrorism after all. No one wanted to come to Zimbabwe and who could blame them? My small business catered mostly for foreign tourists and I closed it.

In June 2000 we sold up and prepared to leave. We had lost our livelihood, could not afford to keep our home and most of our friends had left for distant destinations. We were severely traumatised. Daily we were bombarded with insults and threats from state controlled news media. It seemed whites were perceived as "the enemies of the state". In the turmoil it was difficult to keep a balanced perspective. One day I found three baby shrews in my storeroom. I heard their soft cries for help. Our packing had unsettled their mother and now they were abandoned, a bit like how we felt. I gathered them and nursed them using a tiny syringe with a length of bicycle valve tube on the end. Two of them were badly dehydrated and died but the third grew stronger. Once it had learnt where its new source of milk came from it would grab onto the rubber valve and suck the syringe dry in no time. Almost totally blind, shrews have a rapid metabolism and eat their own weight of insects every day. I set up a box for its home with grass and sand and hollow logs and then set out daily to catch grasshoppers and crickets which it devoured with relish. It was a fierce little hunter and once a grasshopper was thrown into its box the little mite would listen carefully and sense its location with its long whiskers. With a lightning strike it seized the insect and thrashed it around until it was senseless much like a terrier shakes a rat. I learnt a lot from keeping the little fellow and grew to respect the tiny creature with so much pluck. All animals universally have 23 chromosomes whereas shrews are unique in that they have anything from 7 to 25. Sometimes it is only by keeping an animal that one can see it through new eyes. Shrews have a short lifespan and this one grew rapidly. After several weeks it was big enough to release so one night I took it to the rockery and let it go. It scurried off into the big world and we went back to our packing. Worlds within worlds, I thought to myself.

Within the grounds of our cottage we held a sale of household goods. The setting was superb. Our cottage was a converted farm shed that had been built many years before. It was not posh but the surroundings were outstanding. Huge Mahogany trees gave cool shade during hot months. White Faced Owls, Paradise Flycatchers, Turtle Doves and Bulbuls nested in the branches. Purple Crested Louries called loudly from the trees and the beautiful song of African Robins rang in the evenings. It was a bit like paradise. Everything we owned went on sale at ridiculously low prices. People flocked to get the bargains. Despite the low prices a gang of thieves moved among our stuff and proceeded to steal what they could.

The Stolen Elections - 2000

In June 2000 parliamentary elections were held. Mugabe had disregarded the results of the February referendum but people still hoped that these elections might bring a new government. It was a forlorn hope as the country plunged into chaotic conditions. The opposition party made a brave stand and many Zimbabweans courageously withstood the verbal battering from government leaders and the physical battering from their thugs; warvets and youth militia. People were murdered, thousands assaulted and many lost their homes and livelihood. Fear ruled as malicious gangs turned on defenceless civilians and inflicted severe punishment on all who dared to defy Mugabe. We saw heart-rending images on TV of hundreds of farm workers frog-marched to indoctrination meetings and forced to sing revolution songs. The look of fear on their faces was distressing to see. They were herded together for all-night *"pungwes"* and forced to sing the old *"chimurenga"* songs in praise of the regime. Old people and even little children were not spared. Hundreds bravely endured this humiliation. The calibre of government candidates was reflected in their names; Stalin, Mau Mau, Hitler.

When results of the election were announced people were shocked when Mugabe declared victory. No one believed the results and they realised he would stop at nothing to stay in power. Most people thought that the opposition should have won a landslide victory. Mugabe held a trump card that allowed him to appoint 30 seats by decree. His followers had beaten and pounded the people into submission and he now declared himself the winner.

We had already euthanized our two big dogs and now flew our smaller ones out of Zimbabwe unwilling to leave them in a country that had no resemblance of stability and where their future would be endangered. We could not leave them for fear they would be attacked and killed or left abandoned as hundreds of others were. We had originally got our dogs from the SPCA and as members we knew all too well what was happening to abandoned pets. I gave away over one hundred rare birds; parrots, lovebirds and others. Unfortunately I could not get them out of the country and instead gave them to local breeders in the hope they would ultimately survive. I would have wished to air lift numerous people from the country as well, those who were aged, infirm, beaten and traumatised, people who could not get out on their own, had no finances and were left to face the brunt of economic collapse and state orchestrated terror.

In December a farmer was gunned down on his farm near Kwe Kwe. His son sustained nine bullet wounds and was critically injured and left for dead by the perpetrators who used AK automatic military weapons. Many courageous farmers tried to carry on regardless but crops were destroyed, implements damaged, irrigation sabotaged, vehicle burnt. As mentioned, tourism crashed, no one wanted to come to a place where they would be in danger. Tourist agents in Europe took Zimbabwe off their destinations it being considered too dangerous to visit. Hotels and holiday resorts lay idle. Meanwhile the President continued his world travels as if nothing was amiss. Every few weeks, as was his custom for twenty years, he was off to a conference where he was received with great acclaim.

Famine Looms

The nation sank into an eerie silence. The people had been beaten into silence. The situation deteriorated into a massive witch-hunt. Journalists were arrested, farmers were chased off their property and workers were beaten. The rhino holocaust continued in private parks. It was said that over eighty percent of wildlife in sanctuaries was slaughtered. In order to force farmers off their land pets were maimed or killed in horrific ways. Some dogs were crucified by being impaled on hooks and hung on fences and left to die. Some ponies had a hoof severed, horses driven through grids broke their legs and sheep were slaughtered. Livestock were hamstrung and some burnt alive as fields were set alight. SPCA ran out of drugs for euthanasia and could not cope with the numbers of abandoned animals that needed to be put town. Some farmers were given half an hour to get off their farms and were unable to take their animals with them. One farmer shot all ten of his horses to save them from mutilation. The harvest of 2000 failed. The rains were poor and the few pitiful crops planted by squatters withered in the heat. The Minister of Agriculture's policy had led to total ruin. Some people called him the "Minister of Famine." Millions of people faced famine while food from international donors was withheld for party members only.

Back in the 1960s the Liberation Movement, led by the Generals still in power, made a broadcast from Zambia to the people of Rhodesia. The gist of it was that farms that were occupied by Europeans should be surrounded and the occupants driven away. Buildings and crops on farms should be burnt and factories should not continue to function and must be closed. If they could be burnt then they should be. As for the cattle, they should be taken, if they were unable to be taken they should be killed. Burning down farms and factories and killing livestock was barbaric but the same people who advocated it then were doing so thirty years later. The demise of the nation had not happened secretly but in full view of the world. Madness had crept in like a rabid dog and pounced on the gentle people. The country I knew was gone. It had been crucified.

Scramble out of Africa

Within one year thousands of whites left the country. It reminded me of the epic run by Trooper White when he ran for his life. The name of his farm "White's run" was now appropriate for the whole country. The agriculture sector was reduced to shambles and there were hundreds of thousands of internal refugees who had no where to go, people robbed of their homes and jobs and displaced within the country of their birth. They became the "forgotten people". Groups of traumatised nomads could be seen wandering around carrying a few belongings. When asked where they were going their reply was "no where". Their lives had been reduced to nothing; they had no homes, no food and no rights. Land seizures were co-ordinated by high officials and the number of displaced farm workers was appalling, a million people faced disaster. When squatters moved onto farms the workers ended up homeless, camping in the bush or living in shanty towns. Thousands of livestock were rustled. This, plus the foot-and-mouth outbreak in 2001, effectively devastated the national herd that was the pride of the country. Our friend Dave was badly beaten and kicked off his farm. He could not stop crying for weeks. African nations said nothing. The United Nations did nothing. The diabolical thing was that Mugabe seemed to have convinced the world that it was a popular uprising and he could not stop it.

African people fled Zimbabwe into neighbouring countries. Every week thousands of them crossed the Limpopo River and climbed through the border fence to escape the harsh conditions. Others crossed at Beit Bridge border not in the normal manner but under the girders of the bridge spanning the Limpopo River where the elephant in Kipling's "Just So Stories" had its trunk pulled by a crocodile. Crocs can still be seen lurking in the water beneath the bridge and a South African TV report about this unofficial crossing mentioned that several climbers had slipped and fallen into the pool where imagination must take over as to what happened. Those who made it across were rounded up and sent back.

In case we had not grasped the message of April 2000 Mugabe's informal troops made sure there would be no further misunderstanding. In the next year his fast-track land acquisition claimed over 90% of white commercial farms and farmers were forced off their land, some badly beaten, some permanently injured, some killed. No compensation was paid to them by the Zimbabwe regime. The so called "spontaneous" peoples' uprising was carefully orchestrated and progressed in a predictable manner.

Old Mrs. Olds, Martin's mother and a widow, had farmed in the Nyamandhlovu area most of her life. When they killed Martin she bravely remained on her farm. One day, early in the morning gunmen came for Mrs. Olds and shot her a dozen times or more as she opened the security gate to the farm house. They shot her two dogs too. When her surviving son drove to the farm later that morning he found her body lying on the drive with the dogs dead beside her. Her long grey hair was matted with congealed blood. He sat a lonely vigil by her body not allowing anyone to approach. After many hours his priest persuaded him to release her body and he eventually agreed.

In Chipinge farmers were held captive for days and subjected to excessive levels of intimidation. The price of fuel increased 1000%, the first of many hikes, and the cost of living, in more ways than one, shot up overnight. In some cases the cost of living was whether one had a ZanuPF party card or not. The regime passed new legislation on citizenship or the lack of it. A bill was passed which required people to renounce all possible claims to alternative citizenship. The situation was absurd. Whites and even some Africans had to get official certificates to confirm they had renounced citizenship of other nations even if they did not currently hold that citizenship. More laws were passed enforcing every person to carry identification documents and imposed penalties for those caught without. It seemed we had gone full circle back to the days of the *"situpa"*. Warvets stole documents of opposition party members which effectively prevented them from being able to vote.

Statements became even more outlandish and racist – *"whites are not human beings"* said none other than the Vice-President. Maybe that explained why we had no human rights. During the Bindura by-election the ruling party established centres to "re-educate" people on how they should vote. People called them "torture centres". Court rulings were ignored by the regime and the Judiciary was neutralised when judges were threatened with their lives and forced to resign and replaced with party cadres. Britain now took the brunt of acrimony from the Zimbabwe regime.

Towns were not exempt from violence and intimidation. Groups of warvets invaded businesses and demanded exorbitant amounts of money from managers and directors on trumped up fictitious grievances. Some executives were kidnapped and not released until payment was made, sometimes of millions of dollars. As a result companies that had endured adverse economic conditions for years closed with hundreds of staff losing jobs. A couple we knew were abducted from their safari farm outside Harare, taken to ZanuPF headquarters and subjected to abuse for hours on end. The woman was cuffed, the man beaten about. Towards the end of the day they were released but while there saw Asians with broken limbs and badly abused Africans.

A friend, Jill and her teenage son were attacked in their home by several men. One powerful intruder grabbed Jill around her neck and attempted to strangler her. The others ransacked the house and generally ran amuck. Her teenage son ran to the bedroom and managed to load a shotgun Jill kept there. When he appeared with the weapon and saw his mum fighting with the man he screamed for him to let her go. The man then attacked him so he shot him in the chest and he fell on the carpet and expired, blood everywhere. The others fled. Jill called the police and as it was a shooting in self defence and they were not on a farm the police brought no charges. However, shortly after this Jill received threatening phone calls and they moved and slept with friends. A friendly cop phoned Jill and warned her to get her son out of the country or he would be killed. He flew to UK where he remained for his own safety.

June - 2001

In June of 2001 the boastful statements of Hitler came to a sudden end. Hitler's rise to stardom was violent and his career as the warvet's spokesman was brief and then he suddenly died, officially of malaria, unofficially of Aids. When he first started he looked healthy even though devoid of his senses. He had a perpetual mad grin on his face and laughed constantly at his own outrageous statements. Then in June he rapidly declined and became even madder, next thing he was dead. Just weeks before this the Minister of Defence and another man, a ZanuPF governor, both of whom orchestrated much of the violence died in separate car crashes. I was still in Zimbabwe although my wife had now left. In June a Solar Eclipse occurred and I went to our friends' farm to view it. They had been barricaded by mobs of squatters who thumped their drums all night, sang war songs and shouted abuse. My hosts had endured it and now enjoyed some respite from the thugs who had left to intimidate others. The scene looked deceptively calm. Tables were spread with food and people relaxed from the harsh sun in shade from garden trees. It all seemed so peaceful and normal, nothing seemed awry. When the time approached we walked into a nearby field and as the eclipse started a shadow fell across the land and an eerie other world feeling fell upon us as we watched the sun go out. The birds began to roost and the cattle started lowing. It seemed to illustrate what was happening in our nation. A shadow of madness had fallen on us; it was "the shadow of death".

August - 2001

In August farmers were arrested at Chinhoyi on a trumped up charge of causing a riot. Their friends and family heard about the arrests and came to the Police Station to see if their loved ones were alright and another fourteen men were arrested and also thrown inside. Amongst them was the local church minister who had come to see his flock. The police kept them in jail illegally for weeks, shaved their heads to humiliate them and generally treated them badly. The nights were bitterly cold and the men had nothing but flimsy prison tunics to keep them warm. When it was discovered that a sympathetic policeman had rationed them a few smelly blankets these were taken away, the policeman was disciplined by his superior officers and the incident was brought up in Parliament as an example of racial preference towards whites. At this time civilians in Chinhoyi were attacked, women were beaten and cars smashed. Over fifty farms were gutted. Houses and barns were burnt, animals killed, property stolen. We were shocked by the savagery of it all. Farmers fled their homes but ran the gauntlet of road blocks set up by armed squatters and were forced to spend the night huddled on the open veld. This sort of thing was repeated all over the country. Mobs were trashing farm houses. They stole doors, window frames, toilets, sinks, roofs and everything else they wanted in the way of furniture, linen and clothes and then burnt or destroyed the owners' belongings; books, photos, personal documents, computers and all else. Another farmer was killed. His hands were tied with wire and then he was axed, the favourite method of dispatching someone. The Commissioner of Police meanwhile acquired a white owned farm, no doubt a reward for a job well done. It was Mugabe's land grab and it brought ruin to the country. I recalled the foreboding voice that had warned of violence to come. Some months before this the Mayor of Chinhoyi was arrested for having a human head in the boot of his car. Strange luggage to say the least! The explanation he gave was that he had found it on the side of the road, a victim of a hit and run accident, he said. I never heard the outcome of it but he was never brought to book. It reminded me of early days after Independence when a young policeman manning a road block was given instructions to search cars, including the "boots". The young officer followed his orders precisely insisting that the car occupants remove their shoes so that he could check inside them. Why should the Mayor have a human head in his boot? It sounded like witchcraft.

None of this should have happened. A once thriving country was reduced to chaos, lawlessness and abject poverty. Farms that had been developed over years of hard work were reduced to desolate, abandoned, non-productive ruins. The policy of the regime was that because whites had "stolen" the land in the 1890s Africans were justified in taking it back now. The land invasions were declared the third *"chimurenga"*. Actually it was really a war against the electorate. Loyal Zimbabweans were robbed of homes and possessions simply because they had the wrong colour or supported the wrong party or worked for the wrong people. All opposition to Mugabe was perceived as British instigated as if Africans could do nothing for themselves. No assistance was given to the homeless.

Persecution of Clergy

Our missionary friends had established churches on farms. These were targeted when thousands of farm workers were driven off the land and African clergy threatened and some badly beaten. Remember, these people had no recourse to hospitals or drugs when injured. They could not call on the police to protect them. They had no means to defend themselves. A CIO exercise dubbed "Operation Zion" targeted missionaries and clergy. CIO had dockets on missionaries and harassed some of them from time to time. They would arrive unannounced usually in the middle of the night and search for evidence of opposition towards the government. Clergy were arrested for holding "illegal meetings" when they gathered in small groups to say prayers. A group of thugs invaded a retirement home in Harare. They barged through the gates past security guards and thumped on the door of our dear old friend, a doctor who was residing there. When he opened the door they assaulted him, thumping him around the chest and face. It does not take much to hurt a 77 year old man and he was badly bruised with broken ribs. They falsely accused him and whisked him off to Central Police Station and further badgered him. As a child he survived holocaust death camps and later come to serve the people of Africa. This was his reward.

I accompanied a friend to the tax office to get a tax rebate. We were shocked to see the entire department in total disarray. Files lay on the floor with no semblance of order, staff sat around in small groups and talked in subdued tones. Eventually we were shown into the office of a high ranking lady who explained that the entire tax department was in confusion as 70% of top staff had been either dismissed or transferred to rural areas. She was unable to comprehend why this had happened and sat dazed, wondering whether she would be next. It seemed to be a way the regime marginalised the middle class in Zimbabwe and made them increasingly ineffective. She apologised profusely to us and we left without having had our business attended to.

Going, Going, Gone......

The auction houses were full of remnants of fragmented lives; furniture, farm implements, clothes, discarded shoes, saddles, photos, pictures, broken ornaments, treasured knick knacks, the ragged relics of a hundred years in Africa. They were thrown in heaps on auction floors to fall for a pittance beneath the hammer blow; going, going, gone - all that was left of the lives of thousands of men and women, like flotsam tossed upon the shores of a nation, shipwrecked treasure washed up from the broken homes of once happy families.

For twenty years we had watched the Zimbabwe soap-opera unfold with nightly bulletins from state-run TV. The leading star was the President, supported by his cast of cronies. When he fought the Liberation War he had claimed to be fighting for democracy. He said he would establish a Democratic State when he came to power. The first few years seemed good especially for people in the ruling party. However, after the first decade this began to change. Zimbabwe was the *"Jewel in Africa"* but the jewel was tarnished, broken and stolen, the wealth of the country destroyed. For over twenty years we followed this serial of calamity. Before our eyes we witnessed a harvest of duplicity and violence. We were subjected daily to the speeches of leaders with the mentality of the dark ages. A de facto state of emergency existed, free press was curtailed, instigators of violence were never brought to court and the opposition party were declared "terrorists." Yet they had no guns, no weapons and no army. By the end of 2001 high court judges had been replaced and the Supreme Court of Zimbabwe had declared land invasions legal. Some spirit mediums supported the regime's land policy and were linked to the highest echelons in power. What was more disturbing was that it seemed the hierarchy in some churches also supported the land invasions instead of standing against the abuse of human rights. Top Catholic Church leaders considered Mugabe their favourite progeny and some leaders in other churches supported him. The nation had become divided. The regime announced a solution for unemployed youth; "youths" up to thirty years of age had to attend a three-month course in "patriotism and entrepreneurship." They were issued semi-military uniforms and attended parades at camps. When applying for employment whether in the private sector or government, not that there were many jobs, they would need a certificate to say they had attended the course. They were aptly called "Green Bombers". Some of these young men committed atrocious crimes with impunity. Warvets controlled entire districts and became the new warlords. The chief warlord seemed to be the President himself and the powerful generals behind him. Having been in the country and seen all this I have no hesitation in saying that most of the violence was carried out by Mugabe's lackeys. Many defenceless people were severely abused.

Threatened

One day I went to central Harare and parked my car near Parliament Buildings. Lost in thought I strolled briskly through the car park between Samora Machel Avenue and the Houses of Parliament. A few soldiers loitered about. One of them stood to attention and said politely as if warning me "excuse me, you cannot go this way." His words came too late as a grim, sullen soldier dressed in fatigues barred my way with a loaded AK gun menacingly stuck in my belly.

"Who are you, what are you doing here?" he demanded, "This area is prohibited."

I tried to answer each question shot at me as his crooked finger grasped the trigger of his AK which he prodded deeper in my stomach. He was gloating over his capture. It is marvellous what affect a loaded AK can have on one's tummy; a fluttering sensation came from my bowels. This man was not the type of individual one would choose to have an argument with and his malevolent face could not mask a sadistic killer. I looked into his dead pan eyes. They revealed a man who had killed before and would do so again without even blinking. These were days when people were apprehended by the army and sometimes never heard of again. I apologised for my indiscretion and attempted to explain that I was just passing through, but I had strolled right into an area of army control around the top offices of power. He looked at my ID and gloated some more and gave me some mouthfuls of Zimbabwe vocabulary reserved especially for people like me as he prodded his gun deeper in my guts as if tempting me to do something to which he could react. Flash backs to childhood when I was threatened with death by the strangler gave me resolve to stand my ground and look the killer straight in his evil eyes. I had seen those eyes before. They were just like those of the strangler; dead, dull, glazed in an expression of smouldering hatred. I held my breath and time stood still. I was in his hands and there was nothing I could do. He told me to stand in a certain spot and left me to contemplate my fate no doubt hoping I would make a break for it and he could be justified in taking further action. After a while he released me with further threats of what would happen if ever he saw me again.

The Drums of Hunger

Every night the Zimbabwe TV announced the latest government propaganda with its signature tune of loud drumbeats. With fewer crops in the ground the country was facing starvation but it was announced on TV and in the state sponsored newspaper that because people had taken back the land Zimbabwe was now going to have "bumper crops three times the normal yield". However, an independent report said Zimbabwe needed to import hundreds of thousands of tons of maize to avert a massive shortfall. The leader of the Commercial Farmers Union broke down and wept openly when giving his report on the food situation. The regime denied there were shortages yet there were no fields of crops. The land lay fallow in what used to be prime farming area. In a country that had fed its people for years and always had a surplus people were dying of starvation, others were searching the bush for edible roots, leaves and grass. A kg of rats suddenly shot up in price and the Zimbabwe dollar collapsed. Inflation continued to spiral. A money factory was opened in Bulawayo and government minted tons of coins. Some older Africans who could remember said quietly *"It was better in the days of Ian Smith."* This must surely be the final indictment on a regime that destroyed the Jewel of Africa. The average life span fell from the sixties to the mid thirties.

There is a saying, *"Whom the gods destroy they first drive crazy".*

The Zimbabwe debacle was bigger than most people realised. If people had thought they were oppressed in the colonial days they were about to find out what oppression meant under independence. Some settlers in Africa had done dreadful things but many of them were decent people who worked to correct wrongs. Zimbabwe had everything possible done for it. It had huge amounts of aid poured in and received expertise and generous assistance much of it from Britain and the West. And for years Zimbabwe cried foul whenever anything went wrong. Its leaders blamed everyone else except themselves for the problems. Corruption and mismanagement weakened the economy but this was blamed on the West. A popular local singer brought out a song, *"this beautiful country Mugabe has turned into hell".*

The Slave Trade

In August 2001 a conference was held to debate the slave trade. It called for reparation from the West for the suffering caused through slavery. However, no mention was made of merchants from the East who traded slaves for many centuries. Arab raiding parties had subjected whole communities to death and slavery. In fact millions of slaves were exported through East Coast slave markets. Westerners played a horrendous part in the slave trade but they did not send raiding parties into villages to capture slaves but bought them at ports. From whom did they buy them? They bought them from the middlemen of the trade, Africans and Arabs who traded slaves for centuries. Westerners boosted the trade but it could never have existed without these middle men. Unfortunately history is not very palatable for either East or West but it was eventually through Western concern that slave trade was halted. The American Civil War was fought to stop slavery and devout men campaigned to bring a stop to it in Africa. When Livingstone saw the extent of slavery, both commercial as well as domestic slavery, he gave his life to eradicate this "open wound" and many others gave their lives in service to Africa.

Great Zimbabwe's Secret

The hue and cry about the slave trade brought to mind a secret that had been kept hidden about Great Zimbabwe. Having worked in Museums I was interested in this ruin for it was the icon of the nation. Much research has been done on how it grew through trade with the East and Middle East. Merchants came to trade for goods such as gold, iron, copper and ivory and also *slaves*. Everyone knew that slaves were traded at Zimbabwe but perhaps not the full extent of it. Great Zimbabwe was a major Slave Market. Such a concept is politically unacceptable and academics refuse to be dragged into debating it. One researcher having made a careful study of the layout of Great Zimbabwe dared to broach this topic.[7] He noticed significant features others had ignored and came to a startling conclusion, it was a slave market. He endorsed this by a persuasive explanation of the overall design of the whole complex especially the "Great Enclosure" for it has obvious features of a prison. The walls are the standard height for prisons worldwide with only three small entrances that were originally so small as to allow entry for only one person at a time and easily guarded. The narrow passages are similar to those found in prisons the world over and are designed to control movement of people from one section to another. There were pens for different classes of slaves such as women, children and men and the small gateways had bars to secure prisoners. There were platforms where slaves were paraded and the conical towers situated in key places were control points that overlooked the entire area. All prisons have similar lookout towers. A chain of ruins, each a day's march apart, linked Great Zimbabwe to the East Coast where slaves were exported. Other features are significant and all point to one thing, it was a Slave Market. It is the most logical explanation for the structure. This was not politically palatable and many people discounted this researcher. Some claim that his dates are wrong.

However, if this was not enough then a world renown Guardian of African History confirms it was a slave centre.[8] He wrote with great reluctance of a place called *"Zima-Mbje"* because it was a story of such shame that he felt it should never be repeated. He described it as a guilty place, an ugly and forbidden structure and its name should always be mentioned with a curse and the evil practised there should never be allowed to recur. He wrote that *Zima-Mbje* was a story that must be remembered and yet at the same time forgotten and referred to the ruler as a great bandit filled with pride and cruel vanity. This renowned African author explained that there was "The Eye" from where one could see all around and described how this great structure became a lair of the feared "Arabi" slave traders who found refuge there and he declared it was a blot on the African people. This statement from a leading guardian of African tradition explained the folklore and psyche that the structure established in the minds of the people. It is now generally believed that slaves were traded at Great Zimbabwe. The nation of Zimbabwe was named after these ruins and sadly under Mugabe's regime the majority of people became political and economical slaves. The truth was that one man brought the nation into political slavery and financial poverty. *"The old man has gone mad"* was the statement heard on the lips of Zimbabweans when referring to the President. It seemed at times he was irrational, ranting on about whites, African puppets, the British and the West. Was he really mad or was he feigning? The frightening thing was how many people believed his story. He had driven the whites off the land but at awful cost to the nation.

The Land Was Burning

It was September when I drove on the long road from Beit Bridge border. I looked at the landscape all around me. Zimbabwe was burning. A thick smoke blanketed the land. Fires raged and billows of dense smoke mushroomed into the sky darkening the air and shedding a dusky light over the landscape. Millions of hectares of grazing and bush were going up in smoke. Sixty percent of the country was burning including the World Heritage Site of Matobo and other National Parks. No one can estimate the amount of destruction uncontrolled burning causes to flora and fauna; from tiny field mice with their spring litters to buck, birds and their nestlings. The horror was too much for my mind to take in. I used to love September for it is Africa's spring with Msasa leaves shooting out in pinks and reds and other trees in full flower with birds nesting and buck dropping their fawns. Instead the trees were burning. I was particularly upset because the local news media blamed the fires on whites burning their farms when everyone knew it was caused through rampant destruction by squatters.

A huge bush fire raged nearby. As I watched the flames I noticed that thousands of grasshoppers frantically fled and a troop of hungry monkeys were jumping into the air and catching them, stuffing them into their mouths. The monkeys were so hungry they risked their lives to catch grasshoppers. During fifty years in Africa I had never seen anything like it. Here these little insects had sufficient intelligence to take appropriate action. When faced with the fire they knew they had to get away despite the danger the monkeys posed. Some of them might be eaten on the journey but most were getting away from the fire. Even the monkeys were in danger, their cheeks were bulging and yet they still grabbed more. I felt it was a visual lesson of what I should do.

Baboons and monkeys have a destructive habit when raiding crops. They will run into a field of maize and break off cobs and stuff their mouths and cheeks with as much as possible. If disturbed they will then grab as many cobs as possible, one in their mouth and one in each hand and as many as they can under their arms. However, no matter how many they grab they invariably end up with the same amount as they are unable to run holding them all. The result was a field destroyed with cobs scattered everywhere. This same mindless principle was what we were witnessing with the squatters. What they could not steal they destroyed. The old hunter's story of how to catch a monkey played on my mind. A calabash was filled with food, the monkey put in its hand and grasped it and the monkey was caught. Yet all the monkey had to do to escape was to let go and withdraw its hand. As hard as it might be it was time to let go and leave land and home and friends and all we held dear, all we had worked a life time to achieve. There was a fire burning right through Zimbabwe, it was called "land acquisition" but was really nothing less than ethnic cleansing and state theft. A revolution had started, a revolution that had as its war cry "land for the landless" and "kick the whites out". We were like monkeys in danger of getting burnt in the flames.

In December 2001 an International Aid group sent representatives to Zimbabwe to investigate conditions. Their official statement made clear that widespread human rights abuses, torture, kidnapping and murder were not the result of a popular uprising but were carefully co-ordinated by the regime. At last someone confirmed what we had known all along. George Orwell wrote in Animal Farm "No one is more equal than others" but Zimbabwe sounded like his story gone wrong. The Zimbabwe Parliament passed laws to ban criticism of the President, and police were given sweeping powers to detain people who did so. Yet the President criticised and threatened his opponents with impunity. No longer were police supposed to stop crime but had become a military wing of the ruling party. Mugabe declared *"all out war"* on all those who opposed him. The President had engineered his own coup to stay in power. It was certainly different!

Pursued by two Men

I felt insecure as I walked to the bank to draw funds. Always conscious of the presence of thieves and hijackers perhaps that day I was more alert than normal and a little nervous. I kept glancing around. Two men loitered in the arcade. One seemed familiar, those heavy cheekbones I had seen before. Having drawn funds I came out of the bank and looked for them again. They had gone, melted into the crowd, but I felt their presence. As I walked to the Post Office I walked past a street beggar. Beggars had now become a feature of Zimbabwe towns. With a little enamel bowl containing a few coins she gazed through her sightless eyes and sang her mournful lament, the well known hymn "Abide with Me." It left me feeling hollow inside. I cleared my post box and walked to the car. Were those men following me? Yes, I glimpsed them over my shoulder. Pushing back panic I walked faster, ducked round a corner, crossed the road, mingled with people, doubled back and jumped into the driving seat of my car. From the security of the interior I searched the crowd. They were not visible but I knew they were close behind me and quickly pulled away.

Last Impressions

I recall the afternoon we had enjoyed soon after Independence in 1980 with Guy Clutton-Brock and his wife. Guy was the only white to have had the "honour" of being buried in "Heroes' Acre." They were sincere people, the salt of the earth, committed, sacrificial in life. They had campaigned tirelessly for majority rule. They had a hope for the future that rubbed off on us. "Things will come right" they said, "just give it time." That hope withered within us. We had faced State Terror too long; threats, violence and racial tension whittled our resolve away. Years of living under an authoritarian regime robbed us of strength and hope, years of running from thugs and several near death escapes left us emotionally exhausted. In over twenty years I had not heard one single word of thanks from leaders in Zimbabwe for anything that Britain had achieved.

What Rhodesians had in their own way attempted to stop the Zimbabweans had tried to remove with the ballot box. Both had failed. I asked myself "What was the Liberation War for?" People on both sides fought for what they perceived to be right and sacrificed their lives to achieve their goal. It achieved nothing but a State of Terror. Terror is defined as: *"the systematic use of intimidation and violence against civilians to create a state of terror".* The Rhodesian regime fell into the trap of blocking African advancement under the delusion that this would prevent the spread of communism. The Mugabe regime fell into a quagmire of violence and terror against its own people.

The Rhodesians were considered racists and given no assistance from Western nations. What made them embark upon such a disastrous route? They were men and women who in WW11 had fought in North Africa, Europe and the East, who had faced great odds and had worked hard. Regrettably some of them also had instilled within them the old colonial attitudes of supremacy and Empire. They were naive to try and stand against the tide of African Nationalism that had reached high water mark and which nothing could stop. It was foolish for Rhodesia to think it could turn time back. World trends were not going to change just because a small tribe of whites wanted to cling to power. However, if Mugabe was ever the shining angel so many thought him at first to be he became more like a fallen one. It could be argued that if Rhodesia had agreed to quick majority rule these events would never have occurred. Perhaps, but does a leopard change its spots? Would capitulation have stopped such a ruthless leader from rising to power? For Rhodesians the gamble was too great for they felt from the dismal track record of some African nations that the odds were stacked against them. When the years saw no progress in a political agreement the opportunity for peace was lost. Under Smith the nation was polarized into black and white. The awful results should have been predictable to everyone. When Rhodesia became Zimbabwe it is said that whites refused to serve the new order and still felt they were rulers instead of guests but many stayed with a genuine commitment to make up for past wrongs. Farmers and businessmen worked hard to keep agriculture, commerce and industry going. They made a fatal mistake; they thought democracy could work and when given an opportunity many voted for the opposition party. Even though Mugabe had permitted them to stay on their farms and in business many whites did not support him because of the awful killings that continued after Independence. When they voted against him it was perceived by the "old guard" as arrogant rejection of the reconciliation offered to them at Independence. It was considered rebellion and treason. However, it was not just whites that wanted change, many Africans did too. Moderate Africans perceived the real enemy was nationalism hijacked by leaders who had no intention of serving the people but only to empower themselves.

In hindsight one wonders whether a better solution could have been reached. For white settlers it would have meant conceding to majority rule, for Nationalists it would have meant accepting a phased transition, for Britain it would have meant standing against extremist pressure. Caught between the unyielding attitudes of hard line settlers, African Nationalists determined to overthrow them and a British government that had the confidence of none of them, the people went to war. When Bishop Muzorewa finally met the conditions required by Britain for recognition of an African government it was Britain that reneged and refused to accept the poll. The Bishop won with an overwhelming vote and the British Foreign Minister Lord Carrington said in June 1979 that the election had been "free and fair". The British Prime Minister indicated that Britain would honour the election but pressure from Africa and the world made the "Iron Lady" buckle. When the world forum ignored the wishes of that poll it was a signal to the Zimbabwe people that only the election of external factions would be accepted against whom the Bishop did not stand a chance.

Historians say that Great Britain became great because of her colonies. They enriched her and served her well. Now many British descendants in Zimbabwe were denied British citizenship due to legislation that prevented it being given beyond a second generation or through the maternal line. British offspring were trapped in a land where they were not wanted. No compensation was offered to any of them. It was a scramble to leave. Most left with very little and many who stayed lost everything. Zimbabwe could not even pay pensions. No nation came forward to offer refuge to elderly and destitute whites with no means to leave. Disowned and abandoned they became the casualties of history. The sad thing is that African Zimbabweans became worse casualties. The *Jewel of Africa"* was plundered. There was no honey in the pot for anyone and certainly no treasure at the rainbow's end. The intransigence of bigoted, stubborn leaders both black and white had driven the nation to destruction. In an interview in February 2002 Mugabe claimed to be Africa's "hero". One can but ask if it is heroic to promote violent beatings, to pardon political thugs, to ignore property rights, to enact oppressive legislation, to rob people of their livelihood and homes, to condone the lies of State Media. The *"Jewel of Africa"* had degenerated into a *"State of Terror"* led by what seemed to be an embittered old man. Was he mad or just another malingering despot kept in power by his hardliner generals? Still clinging to power after nearly three decades they dragged the entire country into an abyss. For many of his own countrymen he lingered too long. Yet to others he remains Africa's Hero.

The Price of Silence

In a BBC TV programme aired on 16th March 2002 entitled *"The Price of Silence"* it became evident that the British Government had known all along about the genocide conducted on the Matabele by the Fifth Brigade during the bitter years of the 1980s. The British Home Secretary of that time confessed to having known. The British High Commissioner in Harare also said he had known. The British Officer in charge of the British Military Team in Zimbabwe likewise admitted he knew. According to this documentary the British government knew that thousands of people were being killed yet said and did nothing to stop it. Britain was party to covering up the deaths of thousands of people. Why did they say or do nothing? One explanation given was that Britain did not want to unsettle the delicate situation in South Africa which at that time was moving towards majority rule. If South Africans had known that the Zimbabwe regime was behaving in such barbaric manner that knowledge may have hindered the move towards transferring power to a majority government. Instead, Britain kept silent and laid out the red carpet and wined and dined those who trampled upon the blood of thousands of people. Perhaps the red carpet had new significance. Britain's silence certainly gave Mugabe the idea he could get away with anything and must have contributed to his subsequent use of violence.

Farewell Zimbabwe - 2002

I drove to Golden Valley to visit friends being forced off their farm by squatters. This was where I had stayed as a child not far from my childhood home. I arrived in time to help them finish packing. As they moved out squatters began to demolish the house. We could hear them tearing off the roof and knocking out the doors. They were stealing the whole house, dismantling it bit by bit to use in the construction of their own make-shift shacks. We dared not stay a moment longer. My friends and I wept as we embraced and bade farewell. On I drove through a life time of memories. The district looked derelict, the farms abandoned. We had enjoyed the good times, now the land was weeping. Here was the bush where I had ridden my horse as a child, where I had swum in the rivers and where I had walked the farms. Now the farms were abandoned, the fields overgrown with weeds. These tough, resilient farmers had lost everything, blown away by the whirlwind. Can a hundred years ever be recovered, I wondered? I did not think so. One last call to dad's simple headstone and mother's little plaque, forgotten citizens of the Empire. These were soon to be ripped up by thieves, the plaque to be melted down and sold and the tombstone to be broken. I stooped and lifted a handful of dust and let it fall through my fingers. It was the dust of our lives, the dust of Africa blown away by "The Winds of Change". Even though dad had so many sad memories of England during the depression I knew that in his heart he still cherished his land of birth.

I recall our last trip to the Eastern Highlands, those glorious hills that I knew so well. What a lovely few days we enjoyed in their beauty. All around were special memories of happy days. This is where I grew up, climbed the rugged peaks and enjoyed the medieval grandeur of Leopard Rock Hotel deep in the heart of Africa. The hotel was like a fairy castle with turrets and towers and huge trees covered with moss and ferns. The Queen Mother and Princess Margaret had stayed there. It stands in the shadow of the mountain sheered in half by some ancient cataclysm and I recall the legend. Once upon a time a village nestled beneath the mountain but angry tribal spirits destroyed the inhabitants because the villagers were inhospitable to strangers and generally disrespectful. Half the mountain fell upon them. The legend says that on some misty nights ghostly voices can still be heard drifting through the forests and across the hills.

As I hiked across mountain trails and forest paths every cranny and nook held a memory. Standing on the peak that towers above Leopard Rock Hotel we could see the land to full advantage. A vast panorama spread around on every hand. This had been my home range. The air was filled with an orchestra of birdsongs. I knew them all, they were my childhood friends. They floated up from the forest below. Was that ghostly voices I heard mingled with the call of forest birds or was it moans from butchered missionaries, our dear friends? Everywhere I walked I could hear whispers from the past. I had been at one with this place of grandeur. The bark of monkeys echoed to me and the soft, melodious, sad announcement of an Emerald Spotted Wood-Dove caught my ears and I joined its plaintiff refrain as if singing a hymn, *"My mother is dead, my father is dead, all my relatives are dead, oh, oh, oh, oh, oh, oh."* It was true. The wind whistled in the air and a Red Wing Starling gave a forlorn cry echoing in the vastness of the panorama and the emptiness of my soul.

Passing by Mutare cemetery I pulled in. There were dearest friends here and I quietly walked among the graves reading the tombstones. Special memories of each came back; Peter who led the missionaries, Albert who loved everything even snakes, Frank my childhood buddy. There were other tombstones too, dating back to early settlers of the 1800s. A large metallic gun-grey Cobra lay sunning itself in the warm afternoon rays but as I approached it slithered down a hole into grave number eighty-four. "Albert would like that," I thought. The caretaker's cordial greeting rang out. With sweat dripping from his face he cut logs for the next cremation which would take place in the old incinerator that stood in a dilapidated shack in the middle of the graveyard. A pile of cut wood was stacked against a crumbling red brick wall. It seemed I was transported back to a forgotten era.

Leaving the cemetery I went on to the museum where Charles, the curator, showed me around. The displays had not changed in nearly forty years. He was very pleased to have a member of the original staff visit and showed me with great pride the zoological collections with so many of the old records in my name. I had forgotten that I had collected so many specimens; insects, reptiles, skulls, shells, a Palm Civet, and others. I felt sad at what now seemed to have been a pointless exercise. He showed me the Antiquity Department full of memorabilia of early Rhodesia, the forgotten treasures of a forgotten people; books, letters, uniforms, photos, spectacles, hats and knick knacks, flags and more. It reminded me of the Holocaust.

I visited my old school. It was neglected, dirty, decaying, nothing like I remembered it. I drove out to Fern Valley and walked to the rocks where Stretch and I sat as youngsters and sorted out the problems of the world. Dangary's weathered face was unchanged but the leopards had gone, retired to more remote places. I had come home but it was like coming to an aged worn out loved one who was very sick.

As we drove from the Vumba hills down to Mutare to hold a Sunday morning service at the local church an elderly African man stood on the side of the road. In the rising heat of the morning sun he stood erect and dignified, dressed in a dark suit with tie. He waved for a lift. We pulled up and he jumped into the back, beads of sweat bursting from his brow. We wound down the twisting incline. I glanced in the rear view mirror and noticed that he had pulled out a small packet and carefully took out a row of gleaming medals that he clipped on his suit. Arriving at Mutare we saw a band of African people marching in the high street. Assuming that he had come to take part in this march we stopped to let him off. I enquired whether he was part of the group. He looked with disdain at the disorderly mass and with a voice of contempt said *"No, not these Zimbabweans."*

He was going to the Legion Club to celebrate with other veterans of the British Empire. I had forgotten it was Armistice Sunday but he had not forgotten. Now pinned to his chest were his war medals; World War 11, Burma, the Rhodesia medal and others. It would have been too dangerous to wear them before arriving at his destination. He and many like him had served Britain but now were forgotten. We gladly took him to the function where he joined other men and women, wrinkled, weathered, from another era. We watched them as they came marching in, old and frail, leaning upon one another, in uniforms, blue and white and khaki, representing the many who had given of themselves. They were the ones who had grown old and weary but had not forgotten. It was a moving scene. We could not stay as we were already late for church and I was the speaker but we could not forget what we saw for it represented the passing of time, the union between the living and the dead, and the link for us all, our parents before us and those before them all gone to their destiny.

Near Mutare there is a cenotaph at an abandoned cemetery where many of the early people lie buried. On the WW1 memorial engraved in stone are the words *"Lest we forget"*. All that is left of the settlers of that time are broken grave yards like the refuse of another era. Brave entrepreneurs still carry on, tired and bewildered old timers struggle to live and disenfranchised Africans are rendered poverty stricken. Throughout the closing years of the Rhodesian war a lone piper kept a lonely vigil every evening on a hill outside the town. The emotive sound of his pipes sent out a message such as only the pipes can do. The piper has long since gone and is forgotten. Silence now rings across the hills but whenever I hear the pipes I cannot help but think of Grandfather who left Aberdeen for the great savannahs and vast blue skies of Africa and now lies in his resting-place in the land he gave his life to.

We went to our morning service held in an old converted town hall with the paint peeling from the ceiling and worn chairs having seated a thousand worshipers. We were late and as we entered I breathed in the lingering smell of booze and fags and memories of New Year parties when at the stroke of midnight we all held hands and sang "Auld Lang Syne", "when old acquaintance be remembered" and the pipes played and images danced in my eyes of people, names, friends.

More Elections – March 2002

In March of 2002 a white farmer we knew was attacked by a mob of thugs on his farm at Norton near where I went to school and where the first settlers were killed more than a hundred years earlier. Besieged in his home through the night he called the police but when it was clear they would not help he made a desperate attempt to escape at dawn. He did not make it. Warvets rammed him with a truck. Captured and beaten senseless by a mob of squatters he was tied to a tree and shot through the head. When neighbours found him his little seventeen year old Jack Russell terrier "Squeak" was curled at his side. The traumatised dog had escaped the marauding vermin and lay next to his master. Photographs of faithful Squeak curled up beside the corpse were sent throughout the world. Images of the first *"chimurenga"* a hundred years before and the lonely prospector killed in the bush near Mazoe with his little dog flashed through my mind. "Nothing has changed" I said to myself, "A hundred years in Africa, and it's no different." There was no excuse or justification for the barbaric conduct of Mugabe's supporters. We were all supposed to be getting more enlightened; this kind of scene came from the dark ages. During this time SPCA euthanized hundreds of abandoned animals.[9]

Just days before presidential elections of March 2002 Mugabe awarded himself a substantial salary increase. News reports said he was one of the wealthiest of African leaders. During the chaotic elections international reporters were banned but thousands of human rights abuses were recorded and observers declared them not free or fair. The result convinced people it had been rigged. One must ask what the War of Liberation was about if not to allow people to freely vote. It was a betrayal of what true "Freedom Fighters" had fought for. Brutal tactics were used to maintain power. In fact in 1998 Mugabe had boasted that he had many "degrees in violence". This was not democracy but a sham. He and his closest aides and generals perceived themselves as the only legitimate leaders and refused to allow any other expression of African aspirations.

A whole generation was brought up on the propaganda of the regime. Although brave men and women spoke out against the abuse very few church leaders could do so. In some churches ruling party cadres were in positions of leadership. The Mayor of Harare had even said that Robert Mugabe was "God's other Son" and people should thank the Almighty for him. When the Zimbabwe regime made a mockery of democracy, violated human rights and persecuted thousands of people no African nations said anything. Few dared to criticise Mugabe. Was it because they perceived him as the *"other Son of God"* who could do no wrong and must never be criticised?

My wife's daughter was trapped in Zimbabwe due to repressive legislation passed by the regime which deprived her of her citizenship and rendered her stateless without travel documents and unable to leave the country. Numerous people who wanted to leave were unable to travel. I too lost my Zimbabwean citizenship. I stood in line with thousands of others at the Passport Office in Harare all of us trying to make sense of the nonsensical legislation that deprived us of our birthright. The scene at the office was one of confusion. Born in Zimbabwe I was nevertheless required to renounce all alternative citizenship otherwise lose my Zimbabwe citizenship. The organisation for the process was abysmal but after a long, hot wait I came within a few feet of the desk only to be told I was standing in the wrong queue. It was too late to change queues and meet the deadline. It was at that moment that I lost my birthright to the land in which I was born and to which I had given my entire life in service. Not only was I no longer a citizen but I no longer had the right of abode. I was stunned at the speed and finality of it.

I was fortunate enough to have British Citizenship and requested assistance from the British Embassy to get our daughter out. Her Zimbabwe citizenship had been terminated on the grounds she was born in Zambia but that country did not even recognise her as a citizen. The comment I got from the British Embassy was "Britain will only help British citizens." I explained the serious circumstances she was in and how she was denied her passport and as a British citizen I asked for help to save her from possible danger. Back came the reply, "Only British citizens will get assistance." I pointed out she had been born in a British Colony, Northern Rhodesia, born of British parents, was in violation of her human rights, had been rendered stateless and was in a country where she was not wanted and unable to get out. Back came the parrot, "Only British citizens." Despite her obvious British ties she was not wanted by them. Britain has always been hospitable and welcomes thousands of ethnic groups from all around the world yet they would not help her.

After all these years in Africa I had to accept I was not wanted and probably never had been but to realise that my own countrymen could not help us in our hour of need truly was a sad revelation. It would take many months for her to find a way to get out of Zimbabwe during which time she lost her job through "affirmative action" and had her life threatened. Eventually she got out but no thanks to the authorities. Churchill's words in 1940 rang hollow in my mind; "Let us therefore brace ourselves that, if the British Empire and its commonwealth should last a thousand years, men will say 'This was their finest hour'". Churchill's 'thousand years' seemed as short as Ian Smith's and just as empty. The authorities had been unable to help one woman in her hour of need. It truly was the end of the Empire.

Our family had come full circle. Having lived in Rhodesia and Zimbabwe we had seen both sides of the face of Africa. I spoke with Rick a young man I knew well. The one side of his face was horrendously disfigured through a hideous event of which he could not speak; blinded in one eye, his arm missing and his face horribly distorted, but if one looked at his good side he was very handsome.

"What are you hoping for in the future?" I asked.

"I have no future unless things change. I need help to survive," he bravely replied. He was scraping a living on odd jobs, handouts and scraps. He needed food, training, plastic surgery and opportunities, all non existent in Zimbabwe. He was like Africa, one side truly beautiful the other ruined and sad.

I stand witness to those days of madness and slaughter, when the blood of the innocents flowed to the tune of *"chimurenga"* songs - *"Long live the revolution"*. Yet despite such outrageous events the majority of Zimbabweans faced the abuse with resilience and dignity. The National Referendum of February 2000 clearly expressed the majority decision that Mugabe and his regime were no longer wanted. That decision was swept aside. The Parliamentary Elections in June 2000 despite savage intimidation by the ruling party resulted in the election of a substantial opposition. Many believed that if those elections had been truly free and fair the opposition would have had a landslide victory. In the following years the people were beaten into submission as political thugs roamed the country. Thousands of homes were bulldozed and nearly a million people made homeless. The 2008 elections were horrendous and the full extent of violence against opposition parties can never be fully documented. With the army in charge many believed it was rigged. Previous elections had been questionable. The 1985 election in the midst of genocide was fraught with irregularities. In the late 1980s students held rallies at Harare University but the regime used emergency powers to crush them. The students issued a statement describing government actions as *"state terrorism"* and compared it to Apartheid. In the 1990s ZanuPF held the country to ransom by threatening to *"go back to war"* if they did not win.

I stand witness to the murder of my friends, loved ones, colleagues, employees and fellow countrymen. So much for democracy! Mugabe threatened white farmers, ***"We will cut off your tails. We will bring you down to size."*** It seemed we were all monkeys and needed our tails cut off.

Epilogue – Thanks for the Memories

What of all my dear African brothers and sisters with whom I sang, laughed and cried? My final service in the church I knew so well was heart rendering. Fear was etched on the faces of teenagers and a look of confusion and weary sadness on the faces of thin, gaunt old people. Undernourished babies cried. These people had a bond forged in adversity. Will they endure the days of tribulation?

Sometimes I get lonely for Africa, for the aroma of the bush. To see the heat haze rising off the sun-baked earth, to hear the cry of the Go-away bird telling one to shove off and the crystal, monotonous call of the Bush Shrike, chiming in rhythm as the bush shimmers under an auburn sky. To see the great banks of dark clouds gather with huge reservoirs of water ready to dump on the parched earth drenching man and beast in torrents and to smell again the smell of rain on dust. Oh, to climb the great granite hills and explore the rocky crags. To see the broad backs of an elephant herd push through tangled grass and see their steaming dung piles or to hear the mighty roar of lions and the wild song of the jackals. All these impressions are part of me and cannot soon be forgotten, they are captured within, grafted into the fabric of my being, indelibly imprinted on the corridors of my mind deep within the strongholds of my soul, there etched upon my spirit. I think I miss the monkeys most. Their dark, wizened little faces and quizzing eyes seem to hold both mischief and wisdom not seen in other animals. Yes, Africa has made monkeys of us all and blind, deaf and dumb we had been like the three little monkeys.

At Independence we, like others, had stayed for love of the land and her people. What had we gained? Years of labour to build a land and make something of it all wiped out. Now, like others, tired of being scapegoats we opted to become "escape-goats." We were taking "White's run". We had our reward, memories of Africa, four generations of endeavour, but we were no longer welcome. The good that may have been achieved was lost. We were the last colonials. Were we also the last patriots? I hope not. "We came to loot" they said "to live like kings". If only they knew! White settlers may have embarked on the biggest land grab of that time but in their wake came many people who gave their lives to build something of value for everyone. Now we were looted, robbed of our homes, our citizenship and our heritage. Our business in shreds, our finances failed, our lives threatened, we had no choice but to leave. All around us were the remnants of a once thriving nation with a vibrant economy and a people who could have achieved so much. Now the empty, broken homes and farms, the run down clinics, the pot-holed roads and empty stores gave testimony of the decline and ruin of a once flourishing land. Perhaps someone might say "you are white and deserve to lose it all" but I was lucky. I feel sad for the great majority of gentle, kind, hospitable people who had their lives destroyed by a regime of leaders who clung to the mentality of *"pambere chimurenga"* – "on with the struggle." Most people had moved away from that attitude long ago and yearned for change.

I am glad I grew up in Africa. We lost everything but no one can take away our love for one another or our memories. I am a part of Africa and the people of Africa enriched me with their generosity, hospitality, courage and dignity and I profoundly thank them. With our Zimbabwe citizenship denied us we left with nothing but our integrity. Thousands of others did the same. To those who cannot leave, old and young and even children I lift my glass in honour; "to the valiant people of Zimbabwe" who carry on in appalling circumstances.

So, dearly beloved, this is my sorry tale of woe, my true "Just So Story". Brave men and women still endure but for us it is over, a hundred years in Africa. We saw miracles but we wept tears of grief as we buried loved ones. We survived street riots, the bush war, the State of Terror but we lost homes, friends and possessions. Somehow we got through the long nights, survived armed terrorists sent to kill us and thieves, car hijackers and state militia. We survived the dangers of a wild land with its wild creatures. Bitten by snakes, stung by bees, jumped by a leopard, charged by hippos and elephant, I walked with lions and swam with crocodiles. We rubbed shoulders with great men and women. More than this we were blessed. We saw people transformed. We sang with angels, saw lights in the sky and felt footsteps on our bed.

A Warning from a Friend

My old friend Kebu phoned and asked to see me. We arranged a time and meeting place. It was good to see him but he was burdened. Now living on a pitiful income he looked haggard and aged. After greetings were exchanged he came straight to the point, unlike the usual convention of discussing the weather, one's health and every other topic.

"You must leave," he said.

"I am planning to do so within a little while," I replied. I was still trying to tie things up.

"No, you must leave soon" his voice hushed with a rasp of urgency. I sat shocked.

"Why?" I asked, concerned that my dear African friend wanted me to go.

"CIO has dockets on all missionaries and clergy and they are checking everyone. Its best you leave." I had never seen him so sad and distraught.

I remembered the two men following me at the bank and wondered whether they were sent to get me. I tried to recall their faces. Then it hit me with a sensation of shock. Were they the same men who had set me up with the drugs deal? Could they trump up a case against me? At times I had spoken against the regime. I concentrated on trying to recall their features and remembered the main man, tall, powerfully built his full strong face with the tell-tale layer of blubber that indicated a good life. I went cold and decided to move my departure closer.

Farewell – 2002

As I walked into Harare's new airport built to cater for large numbers of anticipated tourists I cautiously looked around. There were no tourists in sight. A few men in civvies lounged at either end of the building. CIO, I wondered? I approached the immigration counter and handed over my Zimbabwe passport, still in my possession but about to become defunct. "How will they react?" I thought, for it had no visa for South Africa, my first stop over.

The official peered at my passport. He apologised that he was unable to let me travel on my Zimbabwe passport as I was required by South African law to have a visa to enter that country.

He lent nearer and whispered "You must have another passport, what have you got and do you have it on you?" I was surprised, was it a trap?

"Yes" I replied, "I have a British Passport."

"That's alright then" he said, "I will let you go out on your Zimbabwe passport but you must promise to go in on your British."

I sighed with relief and thanked him for his gracious consideration. He smiled and I sensed the enduring rapport of goodwill between African and white.

Next was the customs counter. I approached it with some consternation for hidden in my underwear was all the wealth I had in more ways than one. Converted into foreign currency at an exorbitant rate on the black market and swelling my pants was all the money I was able to redeem from a collapsed business and the mediocre sale price of our home. To carry this was very illegal but "Why should I let them take everything?" I reasoned to myself. The little I had after a lifetime in Africa was going with me or I was not going at all for, if caught, I might face time in jail in appalling conditions. "Why should they steal it?" besides, I would need every cent to start again. Like so many before me I was leaving with nothing but a suitcase of clothes and what I could carry. Tales from the past of people fleeing India, Congo, Mozambique and other places flitted through my mind. I walked through the electric gates and diverted the attention of the customs officials by declaring a small pair of scissors. Ever willing to please they kindly wrapped and labelled them for me and I continued through to the boarding lounge to wait the call.

As I sat contemplating my life I knew this was the end of Africa for me. I was about to join thousands of others who had left and my heart felt at breaking point. Many who left had developed farms from virgin bush and struggled against insurmountable obstacles. Others had worked all their lives in commerce and industry. Most were patriotic and loved the land and nation with a passion. They would have done almost anything for their nation. Intensely proud of their roots they had suffered under a brutal regime. Perhaps Joshua Nkomo, the man some consider to be the true "Father of Zimbabwe", summed it up when he said of the Mugabe regime *"The hardest lesson of my life has come to me late. It is that a nation can win freedom without its people becoming free."*

When the call came I walked across the concrete apron to board the sleek silver bird. Before climbing the stairs I turned one last time to gaze back and wave goodbye. My heart was heavy and a lump sat in my throat. I had been saying goodbye to people for thirty years, now it was my turn. I was leaving land of birth and happy childhood, this land of tears and shattered dreams and "place of slaughter". Strapped in my seat the heavenly bird lifted off and sped to the clouds. What will the future hold I wondered? Will I be able to sleep without my faithful revolver tucked under my pillow? Will I ever again hear the fearless roar of a wild lion across the endless bush? Time will tell. What a testimony, we had survived the painful years. There will be new adventures and I will be free of the savage side of Africa. As we ascended through soft rain it was as if the clouds were shedding tears at my departure.

I turned to the man dressed in a conservative dark suit sitting next to me and introduced myself to him and we exchanged niceties. I already knew who he was for I recognised him from newspaper photographs and had in fact met him years before with the Clutton-Brocks when he was Speaker of the Zimbabwe Parliament. He now held the post of Spokesman for Foreign Affairs, Security, and Land Redistribution one of the very highest positions in the regime. A couple of stout looking gentlemen in grey suits sat in adjoining seats. "Bodyguards" I thought to myself, "perhaps I'd better be careful, I'm not yet completely free".

Here I was, having lost home, friends, country and citizenship and with the measly savings I could rescue hidden in my underwear, sitting next to one of the men who had caused it to happen. I wanted a flame of indignation to rise within me. He smiled amicably and said he remembered the occasion when we met although I wondered whether he was not just being polite. I asked him how he was and he replied "Still working for the party." I wanted to boil but nothing even simmered. I was shocked at my own lack of acrimony as if I was devoid of feelings on the issues of life and death. My insides felt dead and I was doing a lot of crying. This was my golden opportunity for he was literally sitting "in my lap." I wanted to tell him how much suffering his policies had caused for all people both Africans and whites, so many dear folks I knew and loved. I thought "what can I say." Nothing came. I studied him as he sipped his drink and read the government propaganda paper. To him and many loyal followers Mugabe was still the infallible "son of God" even if he destroyed the entire country. I wondered what could be said that had not already been said. I seemed to hear a quiet voice within me say "Don't bother saying anything to him; he has heard it all already." I realised I had nothing to say, others will judge him and time will tell.

Shortly after this in August 2002 this man who I sat next to on my flight when asked by a BBC correspondent on the extent of political manipulation of food aid replied that Zimbabwe had true friends like China, Libya and the Arab world and the rest should stay away and keep their money and aid. A few weeks later he added these chilling words, *"We would be better off with only six million people* (that is half the people), *with our own people who support the liberation struggle."* In the years to follow millions of people fled Zimbabwe as political and financial refugees. They were driven out by conditions the regime seemed to have itself created. Those who remained faced starvation and persecution and it will never be known how many young, infirm and aged died. In July of 2002 the UN declared Zimbabwe *"a pseudo democracy that had reverted to the authoritative ways of its predecessors."* So the wheel had come full circle. People who gained Independence in a once prosperous nation were now impoverished and enslaved. Unfortunately when elections are rigged and people reduced to starvation and outgunned by police, army and thugs it is almost impossible for them to help themselves. Democracy is a fragile concept. The people of Zimbabwe did not deserve such tyrannical treatment. In December Mugabe made another outburst against whites when he warned of revenge against them and said *"We saw the British monster. We will not rest until the serpent is dead. We must cut off its head. We must send them into the sea and see them drown."* Not only must whites have their tails cut off but their heads too and then drown. It was ironic that the regime should spew such hatred against people who had given so much in the way of aid and help. With hate speech like that is it any wonder we left the country?

As the aircraft rose through the rain it entered thick clouds. Darkness lurked as if two kingdoms clashed while their citizens wept. I felt the sadness all around me. Then we broke into sun light. It was African Magic. Sprays of cheerful jewelled raindrops formed rainbows and I was weeping tears of joy and sadness.

Mother was right after all, life is a **"Monkey's Wedding"**.

Through all my mixed emotions, the hurts, grief and sense of injustice I felt strangely free. The loss of home, family and friends, employment, pension, finance and homeland gave me a sense of freedom I had not known since I walked the hills as a kid. The theme song from the film about Elsa the lioness lifted in my heart; to be born free, as free as the wind blows and as free as the grass grows, to be free to follow my heart. All people seek freedom. Even animals yearn to be free and not be caged. I yearned to be free. Free from the past. Free from trying to help. Free from Africa. Free to be who I am and not have to apologise for it.

I turned my mind to the future. I was looking forward to seeing Stretch my childhood buddy who left the country years before. Even as I wondered how and where to make a new home I knew I would never forget the people with whom we had forged a sacred bond when together we looked into the face of terror. Africa had been kind to me, most of her people gentle, forgiving, hospitable. There had been good times and I was grateful to be alive. I leant over to gaze through gaps in the clouds at the earth below. The sprawling city of Harare was soon gone and there were little villages, hills, tracks and kopjes. From a distance it looked so peaceful but it was a nation in pain. I was not sure how many left behind would survive. Then I lifted my eyes to the heavens and breathed a prayer for them all, "Be strong beloved - till better times."

It was 2002, exactly a hundred years from when Grandfather first arrived.

Things in Zimbabwe went badly. In 2008 Mugabe lost the elections but refused to step down. Violence was once more unleashed on the people and the country was bludgeoned into submission and he remained as President. The people had tried every way possible to remove him from power yet he and his regime refused to step down. Inflation spiralled to millions of percent. There were no medicines in the hospitals, no food in the shops, no crops in the ground. Power was intermittent, water purification and sewerage systems were broken. Malaria was prevalent. Thousands died of disease, starvation and Aids. In 2009 cholera broke out and killed thousands. Zimbabwe was a dying nation held captive by a reactionary regime entrenched in power. When I was young I remember Zimbabwe as a happy land. Even the poor people laughed. Now it was a Land of Sorrow, a Place of Slaughter. Will there ever be a solution for her broken people?

This is the story that must be remembered and yet forgotten at the same time. It is the pitiful story of oppression and abuse of thousands of Zimbabweans. It is also a tribute to their courage and forbearance.

For me it is too painful to remember but I can never forget it.

Benediction

"There is a land, dearly beloved, of beautiful dawns and peace-filled sunsets and in between these glorious events laughter rings like waterfalls and birds wing in flight to peaceful fields of pure delight where sunlight sparkles through huge evergreen trees beside pure, deep streams and where everyone is a friend, a brother or sister. This is the land we call home, the land we knew long ago and for which we look with hope and joy. Be brave and at peace."

254

Notes
* Foreword – Indaba My Children – Vusamazulu Credo Mutwa, Blue Crane Books – Johannesburg, SA, 1964

1. - W.A. Elliot, "Gold from the Quartz", Ms, London, 1910
2. - John Ruskin's inaugural address at Oxford University in 1870
3. - In Search of Lost Civilizations, A.Landsburg, Corgi Books
4. - Cry Zimbabwe, Peter Stiff, Galago Publishing (Pty) Ltd, Alberton, SA
5. - Breaking the Silence Building True Peace
    A report on the Disturbances in Matabeleland and the Midlands 1980 to 1988 - The Catholic Commission for Justice and Peace in Zimbabwe, The Legal Resources Foundation, Zimbabwe
6. - The Battle for Zimbabwe, The Final Countdown, Geoff Hill, Zebra
7. - The History of Great Zimbabwe – Willfrid Mallows – Robert Hale Ltd., Clerkenwell Clerkenwell House, Clerkenwell Green, London - 1985
8. - Indaba My Children – Vusamazulu Credo Mutwa, Blue Crane Books – Johannesburg SA, 1964
9. - Innocent Victims – Catherine Buckle, Merlin Unwin Books, UK

- Take good care, Goodbye – R Pletts

Printed in Great Britain
by Amazon.co.uk, Ltd.,
Marston Gate.